# Business Vocabulary Builder

'ING CENTRE

Macmillan Education
Between Towns Road, Oxford OX4 3PP
A division of Macmillan Publishers Limited
Companies and representatives throughout the world

ISBN 978–0–230–71682–7

First published 2009

Designed by Carolyn Gibson
Illustrated by Peter Harper and Julian Mosedale
Cover design by Katie Stephens

Author's acknowledgements
The author would like to thank Anna Cowper for commissioning the book, Karen Spiller for her usual outstanding contribution on content editing, and Karen White for her thorough proof reading and seeing everything through to publication. Thanks again to Marna Warner for transcribing the original interviews on which the listening scripts are based. Once again there were many students at International House, London who gave up their time to be interviewed for the listening material, and I would like to thank Adina Săvuţ, Celine Perez, Claudio Sella, Emilhano Lima, Fabrizio Farinelli, Francesca Merella, Frank Kaiser, Israel Moosery, Julian Cowan and Massimo Lucchini.

The author and publishers would like to thank the following for permission to reproduce their photographs:
Cartoonbank.com/Charles Barsotti p23, Cartoonbank.com/Leo Cullum p57, Cartoonbank.com/Marisa Acocella Marchetto p7, Cartoonbank.com/Barbara Smaller p35, Cartoonbank.com/James Stevenson p15, Cartoonbank. com/P.C. Vey p33.

Printed in Thailand

2015  2014  2013  2012
10  9  8  7  6  5  4  3

Paul Emmerson

# Business Vocabulary Builder

## Intermediate to Upper-intermediate

*The words & phrases you need to succeed*

MACMILLAN

# Contents

**BUSINESS TOPICS**

**The business world**

1   The economy                                          6
2   The business cycle                                   8
3   International trade                                  10
4   Setting up and growing a business                   12
5   Company types and corporate governance              14
6   Global issues for the 21st century                  16

**Management**

7   Management styles and qualities                     18
8   Organizing time and work                            20
9   Planning and setting objectives                     22
10  Leading and motivating                              24
11  Insurance and risk management                       26

**Production and operations**

12  Manufacturing and engineering                       28
13  Inside a factory                                    30
14  Procurement and purchasing                          32
15  Supply chain management and logistics               34
16  Lean production                                     36
17  Quality                                             38

**Sales and marketing**

18  Sales                                               40
19  Customer service                                    42
20  Markets and marketing                               44
21  Product                                             46
22  Distribution (place)                                48
23  Promotion                                           50
24  Price                                               52
25  Marketing management                                54

**Company finance**

26  Income statement                                    56
27  Balance sheet                                       58
28  Cash flow statement                                 60
29  Managing cash flow                                  62
30  Profitability                                       64

**Financial markets**

31  Financial markets                                   66
32  Investing in stocks                                 68

**Human resources**

33  Recruitment                                         70
34  Pay and benefits                                    72
35  Issues in the workplace                             74

**EFFECTIVE COMMUNICATION**

**You and your job**

36  Your background and career                          76
37  Your company                                        78
38  Your job                                            80

**Telephoning**

39  Telephoning – making and taking calls               82
40  Telephoning – messages                              84
41  Telephoning – checking, clarifying, active
    listening                                           86
42  Telephoning – arranging a meeting                   88
43  Telephoning – complaints                            90
44  Telephoning – review                                92

**Emails**

45  Emails – basics                                     94
46  Emails – internal communication                     96
47  Emails – commercial                                 98
48  Emails – customer issues                           100
49  Emails – arranging a visit                         102
50  Emails – review                                    104

**Presentations**

51  Presentations – opening                            106
52  Presentations – main body                          108
53  Presentations – closing and questions              110
54  Presentations – trends I                           112
55  Presentations – trends II                          114
56  Presentations – review                             116

**Meetings**

| | | |
|---|---|---|
| 57 | **Meetings – opinions** | 118 |
| 58 | **Meetings – making things clear** | 120 |
| 59 | **Meetings – problem-solving** | 122 |
| 60 | **Meetings – leading a meeting** | 124 |
| 61 | **Meetings – negotiating I** | 126 |
| 62 | **Meetings – negotiating II** | 128 |
| 63 | **Meetings – diplomatic language** | 130 |
| 64 | **Meetings – review** | 132 |

**Business reports and proposals**

| | | |
|---|---|---|
| 65 | **Business reports and proposals – reports I** | 134 |
| 66 | **Business reports and proposals – reports II** | 136 |
| 67 | **Business reports and proposals – proposals I** | 138 |
| 68 | **Business reports and proposals – proposals II** | 140 |
| 69 | **Business reports and proposals – linking words** | 142 |
| 70 | **Business reports and proposals – review** | 144 |

**SPEAKING PRACTICE**

| | |
|---|---|
| **Discussion topics** | 146 |

**WRITING PRACTICE**

| | |
|---|---|
| **Writing tasks** | 151 |

**LISTENING PRACTICE**

**Interviews with business people: exercises**

| | | |
|---|---|---|
| 1 | Interview with a private equity investor | 153 |
| 2 | Interview with an entrepreneur | 153 |
| 3 | Interview with a management trainee | 153 |
| 4 | Interview with a supply chain manager | 153 |
| 5 | Interview with a sales manager | 154 |
| 6 | Interview with a marketing director | 154 |
| 7 | Interview with a finance director | 154 |
| 8 | Interview with a human resources director | 155 |

**LISTENING SCRIPTS**

| | |
|---|---|
| **Listen and repeat exercises** | 156 |
| **Interviews with business people** | 157 |

| | |
|---|---|
| **ANSWER KEY** | 164 |

# 1 The economy

What drives the world economy? The simplest answer to this question is 'consumer spending'. And what drives consumer spending? Some combination of the factors below is generally considered to provide a reasonable answer.

## GDP growth for different countries

Gross domestic product (GDP) measures the size of a country's economy. It represents the total value of all goods and services produced over a specific time period. Growth in GDP is one of the primary indicators used to gauge (= measure) the health of a country's economy. Usually, GDP is expressed as a comparison to the previous quarter or year.

## Government trade policy

The two poles of government policy are liberalization and protectionism.

- 'Liberalization' is associated with free markets, open borders, deregulation and the free movement of capital around the world.
- 'Protectionism' is associated with government intervention, subsidies, quotas and tariffs, and restrictions on the movement of capital.

National governments do have some genuine choices here, even if they are constrained by the policy of their regional trading bloc (eg the EU, NAFTA, ASEAN). In the end most countries have a mixed economy which is somewhere between the two extremes.

Generally speaking, free markets promote growth in the world economy, and protected markets slow down the process (although they may have a beneficial effect on particular industries inside a country).

## Consumer confidence

If consumers are confident about tomorrow, they will spend more. The main factors affecting consumer confidence are the level of unemployment – if people's jobs are at risk, or they don't have a job, they will spend less – and house prices – if people's houses are worth more than they paid for them, they feel rich and will spend more freely.

## Interest rates

Interest rates are set by Central Banks. When interest rates are low, consumers and businesses can borrow money cheaply and there is a stimulus to the economy. But the cheap credit also causes inflation and too much liquidity in the system. This liquidity leads to bubbles in stock markets, housing markets, etc. When the Central Bank sees the need to control inflation and cool growth a little, it raises interest rates.

## Exchange rates

Currencies fluctuate against each other: the euro against the dollar, the yen against the yuan. This is due to many complex factors such as the underlying strength of the economy, interest rate differentials and speculation. Having a strong currency makes imports cheap for domestic consumers, but hurts exporters (whose products become more expensive overseas).

## The business cycle

Economies go through cycles of growth and contraction (= slowdown). This is covered in unit 2.

---

## *Effects of globalization*

| *Economic* | *Financial* | *Political* | *Informational* | *Cultural* | *Ecological* |
|---|---|---|---|---|---|
| Worldwide supply chains, markets and products | Worldwide financial markets; easier access to external financing | Closer relationships between governments | Rapid flow of information across the globe | Cross-cultural contacts; travel and tourism; immigration; access to foreign products and ideas | Global environmental challenges needing international co-operation |

✔ *Arguments in favour of globalization*

- General prosperity: lower prices, more employment, higher standard of living.
- Increased opportunity and social / personal mobility.
- Improvements for poor countries: life expectancy, infant mortality, literacy, participation of women in society.

✖ *Arguments against globalization*

- Inequality of wealth within nations – not much 'trickle down effect' (when financial benefits are passed down from big business to consumers and ordinary people).
- Human costs: injustice due to increased power of local elites, erosion of traditional cultures.
- Environmental damage.

# Exercises

**1.1 Find a word in the text opposite that matches each definition below. The words appear in order.**

1 makes something work; provides the power for something
_____

2 removing the rules and laws that control business activity
_____

3 money that the government pays to support industries or reduce the cost of products _____

4 official limits on the amount of something
_____

5 taxes on goods coming into a country _____

6 limited, restricted _____

7 the amount of money in circulation _____

8 periods of time when people pay more than the real value of something; balls of air in a liquid _____

9 with an important effect, but one that isn't easy to notice
_____

10 (*formal*) the degree of difference between things
_____

**Now do the same for the words in 'Effects of globalization' opposite.**

11 when people have money and everything they need for a good life _____

12 the ability to read and write _____

**1.2 Make phrases by matching an item from each column.**

1 consumer            movement of capital
2 free                and contraction
3 growth              borders
4 life                spending
5 open                of living
6 standard            expectancy

7 environmental       rates
8 goods               strength
9 interest            and services
10 cheap              mobility
11 social             damage
12 underlying         credit

**1.3 Use phrases from 1.2 to complete the sentences below. The phrases are not in order.**

1 The economy will grow if _consumer spending_ is rising.

2 Consumers and businesses can take on too much debt if there is easy access to _____ .

3 Economic growth brings material comforts, but also higher prices for the basic necessities of life. In other words, your _____ goes up, but so does your cost of living.

4 Economies go through cycles of _____ (= boom and bust).

5 The main tool available to a Central Bank is its ability to set _____ .

6 Over the long term, exchange rates depend on the _____ of the economy.

**1.4 Read the article about the US economy, then answer the questions below. Check any unknown words in a dictionary.**

> **M**anufacturing in the US slowed more than forecast in October as factories received fewer orders and production contracted, an industry report showed today. Manufacturing is on the verge of stalling as the deepening housing slump weakens demand for construction equipment, furniture and appliances. But, on a more positive note, the weaker dollar is boosting exports and helping companies that do much of their business overseas.
>
> These figures make it clear why the Fed cut interest rates by a quarter point last week. In their statement, Fed policy makers said that, 'the outlook for the economy is uncertain, even after solid growth last quarter.' They added that, 'upside risks to inflation roughly balance the downside risks to growth.'

**Find a word in the text that means:**

1 (*five words*) nearly stopping in its progress
_____

2 period when something is much less successful than before
_____

3 helping something to increase _____

4 (*short form*) Central Bank of the USA _____

5 approximately _____

**See page 146 for some discussion topics.**

*"This isn't for me—it's for the economy."*

MARISA ACOCELLA

History shows that there is a business cycle that repeats again and again, although of course the details vary each time. Look at the diagram below. The outer circle is the cycle of economic expansion and contraction. The next circle inside shows some sectors of the economy that tend to do well at particular times during this cycle. The circle inside that shows interest rates and inflation. Finally, the inner circle shows the stock market cycle.

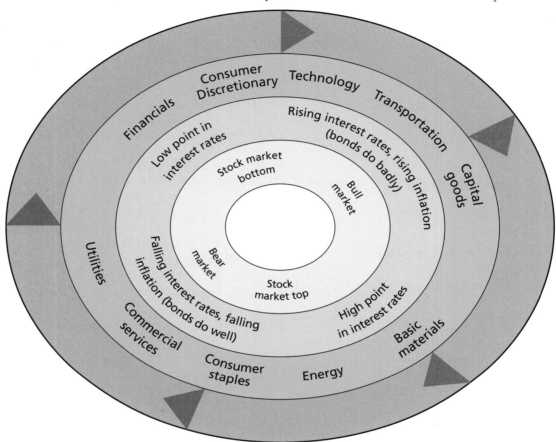

## Growth

Let's go round the diagram, starting at twelve o'clock. This point marks the end of weakness in the economy and the early signs of growth. What has caused these green shoots? The clue is interest rates, which bottomed out around eleven o'clock. Low interest rates mean cheap borrowing for individuals and companies. Amongst the quickest sectors to respond are consumer discretionary (eg restaurants, leisure, travel) and technology.

Once there are early signs of growth, transportation picks up (more goods are being shipped), and industry spends more on capital goods (eg machinery). During this period, inflation starts to rise, and so bonds suffer. Bonds pay a fixed rate of interest to their bondholders, and the value of this interest is eroded over time as inflation goes up.

## The peak of the cycle

All good things must come to an end. It's six o'clock on the diagram. By now inflation has become a problem, and Central Banks have raised interest rates to deal with it. That means that credit is tight, and borrowing is expensive. The stock market recognizes that the end is coming, and peaks just before the final peak in the economy. Investors now switch to more defensive stocks like consumer staples (eg food, household products) and utilities.

## Contraction

Now it's seven o'clock and we've entered the period of contraction. Stock markets are falling. But Central Banks see the danger and are lowering interest rates, to encourage spending and avoid a recession. Bonds respond positively to the drop in rates, and they also benefit from a 'flight to safety' effect as investors become cautious about stocks.

## The bottom of the cycle

Eventually, financials start to recover as they anticipate more borrowing, and then the general stock market finds a bottom about six to nine months in advance of an upturn in the real economy. Just like at the top of the cycle, the market seems to know that a turn in the real economy is coming. Now the economy is starting to show signs of strength and the whole cycle repeats again.

# Exercises

## 2.1 Put the words in italics in order 1–4.

a The economy, starting at twelve o'clock on the diagram, shows …

☐ *contraction*  ☐ *a downturn*
☐ *expansion*  ☐ *an upturn*

b The stock market, starting at eleven o'clock on the diagram, …

☐ *bottoms*  ☐ *peaks*
☐ *recovers*  ☐ *turns down*

## 2.2 Match each sector of the economy 1–10 with an industry group a–j.

1 Basic materials ☐  6 Energy ☐
2 Capital goods ☐  7 Financials ☐
3 Commercial services ☐  8 Technology ☐
4 Consumer discretionary ☐  9 Transportation ☐
5 Consumer staples ☐  10 Utilities ☐

a hotels, restaurants
b steel, chemicals
c employment agencies, auditing
d machinery, equipment
e household goods, food retailing
f banking, insurance
g software, communications equipment
h oil production, gas production
i electricity, water
j airlines, logistics

## 2.3 Underline the correct words in italics. Check any unknown words in a dictionary. Some ideas below are also covered in unit 1.

1 The consumer discretionary sector of the economy starts to recover when interest rates are *high / low*, and just before the general economy *picks up / turns down*.

2 Investors favour the consumer staples sector at the *beginning / end* of the growth cycle, just as the markets are *picking up / turning down*.

3 If a government or company wants to borrow money, it can issue *a bond / an obligation*. Investors receive a *fixed / variable* rate of interest over a fixed period of time, and then get their original investment back at the end.

4 A rise in interest rates makes borrowing *cheaper / more expensive*. This *cools / stimulates* the economy.

5 Central Banks lower interest rates if they think the economy is likely to *grow / contract*, and will act aggressively if they think there is a danger of a *boom / recession*.

6 Stock markets tend to *anticipate / move in line with / react to* changes in the real economy.

7 Interest rates tend to bottom out *before / after* both the stock markets and the real economy.

8 A rising market is called a *bear / bull* market. People who think that a particular market is going to rise in the future are described as being *bullish / bull-like* on that market.

## 2.4 Complete the text about dealing with the business cycle with the phrases in the box.

government debt   labour market   new borrowing
policy makers   side-effects   tax cuts

What can central bankers and government
1 _____ do? Can they prevent a contraction from turning into a recession? What tools are available to them? The following three are the most important:

**Interest rate adjustments**

The strongest and fastest tool in a weakening economy is the Central Banks' ability to cut interest rates. For companies and individuals with existing bank loans, repayments are reduced; for others,
2 _____ becomes less expensive. Most Central Banks drop rates by quarter-points or, at crucial times, half-points. Lowering rates still takes two or three quarters to benefit an economy, and it does also have unfortunate 3 _____ .
The negative consequences are that it weakens a nation's currency, and that any growth it causes may be inflationary.

**Economic stimulus**

A national government can choose to spend money – usually money it must borrow – on all sorts of projects in order to stimulate the economy. This puts money back into people's pockets so that they can buy goods and services to boost the economy. 4 _____ are another way of achieving the same effect. The problem arises when these measures lead to high levels of
5 _____ . Eventually that debt will have to be repaid.

**Regulatory reforms**

A country can implement reforms to the law in order to stimulate growth. These include measures to enhance competition, to liberalize the
6 _____ , to make it easier to start a new business, etc.

See page 146 for some discussion topics.

# 3 International trade

## Deciding to export

Why export? The two most important reasons are likely to be:

1 To increase sales and revenue. Exporting will allow you to take advantage of any under-used capacity, increase production, reduce unit costs through economies of scale and increase profits if things go well.

2 To diversify. Relying on just your own domestic market is risky. Selling to other countries allows you to spread the risk.

But before deciding to export there is a lot of research to be done on the foreign market:

- Background: economic situation, political stability, currency risk.
- Market size and likely product demand.
- Competition: similar products already in the market.
- Distribution channels: agents (who act on your behalf and receive a commission, but don't buy goods on their own account), or distributors (who actually purchase goods from you for resale, like a wholesaler).
- Promotional material: sales and support material needed in the local language.
- Customer service: procedures for enquiries, complaints, warranty claims, servicing, etc.
- Legal requirements: technical, safety and environmental standards.

The first step in exporting is likely to involve an intermediary (eg local agent, distributor). They will have local knowledge and contacts in the unfamiliar market. If things go well, the exporter may then decide to establish its own presence in the foreign market such as setting up a sales office and warehouse. This allows direct contact with customers, faster delivery and more control of the local market.

Two key issues for an exporter are a) the method of payment – see the table below – and b) who pays for transportation. This latter issue is covered in the contract by specifying the relevant Incoterm (International Commercial Term) for that particular consignment (= quantity of goods shipped at the same time).

## Other options

Exporting is one way to sell your goods into a foreign market, but there are other options available to larger companies:

- Joint venture: two companies (a foreign company and a local partner) work together but keep their own legal identity.
- Foreign Direct Investment (FDI): a business sets up operations in a foreign country, or acquires (= buys) a local company.
- Licensing: a company sells the right to use a patented manufacturing process, or some commercial expertise, or a trademark, in exchange for a fee or a royalty. One particular case of this is franchising.

## FINANCING INTERNATIONAL TRADE

### Cash-in-advance (Pre-payment)

The importer pays the invoice in advance, before shipment. Where they only pay a part in advance, it's called a 'down payment'.

### Letter of credit (L/C)

One bank guarantees payment to another bank. The importer pays when the exporter presents certain listed documents to their bank. Typical documents needed are: transportation documents (eg bill of lading), insurance documents, commercial documents (eg invoice).

### Documentary collection

A cheaper variation of an L/C. The two banks make no guarantees, but simply handle the exchange of documents.

### Open account

The supplier ships the goods, and the importer pays later, according to the terms of the contract. This is more risky, and is only used if the importer has established a good credit history.

### Consignment purchase

The importer receives the goods and holds them in stock, but only pays for them after they have been sold to the end users.

# Exercises

**3.1 Find a word in the text opposite that matches each definition below. The words appear in order.**

1 *(three words)* spreading costs over a larger number of units, and therefore producing things more cheaply

   _____

2 *(three words)* instead of you, or as a representative of you

   _____

3 written promise that a company will repair something if it breaks; guarantee _____

4 big building where large amounts of goods are stored

   _____

5 special skills or knowledge _____

6 name or design on a product that shows it's made by a particular company _____

7 money paid for professional services, or a one-time amount

   _____

8 money paid to someone whose ideas or inventions you're using _____

**Now do the same for the words in 'Financing international trade' opposite.**

9 document requesting payment (also called a 'bill')

   _____

10 *(three words)* list giving details of goods that a ship, etc is carrying, also acts as a contract to transport those goods

   _____

**3.2 Make phrases by matching an item from each column.**

1 take advantage        just your domestic market
2 rely on               on somebody's behalf
3 spread                of any under-used capacity
4 act                   the risk
5 establish a presence  to the terms of the contract
6 keep your own          of documents
7 handle the exchange    legal identity
8 pay according          in a foreign market

**3.3 Study the methods of payment shown in the box opposite. Then complete the diagram by writing the five methods on the horizontal axis.**

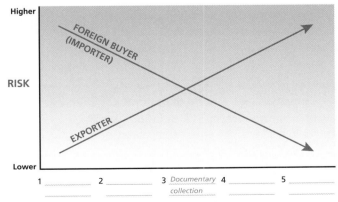

Higher

RISK

Lower

FOREIGN BUYER (IMPORTER)

EXPORTER

1 _____ 2 _____ 3 *Documentary collection* 4 _____ 5 _____

**TYPES OF FINANCING**

**3.4 Complete the text about Incoterms with the words in the box. Notice the glossary at the bottom.**

| clearance | customs | documentation | freight |
| handling | loading | premises | terminal | transit | truck |

### What are Incoterms?

Incoterms state the responsibilities of buyer and seller in relation to marine transportation – not just the shipping costs, but all other associated costs such as insurance, [1] _____ duties, and ground [2] _____ .

### The buyer pays for the sea crossing

A price quoted EXW is where the seller makes the goods available at their own [3] _____ , and the buyer collects them there. The buyer has responsibility for all the other transport costs and risks from that point onwards.

If the price is FAS, then the seller also covers the cost of inland transport (by [4] _____ or rail) to the port of shipment, and of unloading the containers onto the dock. The buyer pays for [5] _____ onto the ship plus all the costs from that point.

FOB is almost the same, except here the seller pays for loading onto the ship, not the buyer.

### The seller pays for the sea crossing

Now the goods are on the ship. If the price has been set so that the seller also pays the [6] _____ (= goods and the system of moving these goods) costs, then there are further Incoterms to be used.

With CFR the seller pays the freight costs and handles the export [7] _____ (= paperwork), but does not pay the insurance while the goods are in [8] _____ at sea. With CIF the seller pays insurance as well. But in both cases their responsibility ends at the port of destination, while the goods are still on board. The buyer has responsibility for unloading fees, local storage at a [9] _____ , the import licence, duties and taxes, the custom broker's fees and onward delivery to the buyer's own premises.

In the final case, DDP, it's the seller who pays for everything, and who also has to handle any customs [10] _____ problems. The buyer has no additional costs or risks at all – but of course the price quoted in the contract will reflect this!

| Glossary | |
| EXW: Ex works | CFR: Cost & Freight |
| FAS: Free Alongside Ship | CIF: Cost, Insurance & Freight |
| FOB: Free On Board | DDP: Delivered Duty Paid |

See page 146 for some discussion topics.

# 4  Setting up and growing a business

## Initial idea

Someone has an idea for a new business (a 'start-up'). Maybe they spot a gap in the market, or maybe they have an idea that is similar to existing offers, but with a competitive edge. Potential sources of finance for this new business include self-funding, backers such as friends and family members, a bank loan, and a venture capital firm.

A bank will want some sort of security in case the loan is not repaid, and sometimes the person's house is offered as collateral. The fourth option, venture capital (VC), is attractive for businesses with a high profit potential in the medium term, but high start-up costs. A VC company will offer funds and take on the risk of the business failing, but in exchange will want a large number of shares. They aim to sell these later, when the business goes public.

When financing is in place, the business is registered as a legal entity: sole trader, partnership, limited company, etc. See unit 5.

## Early months and growth phase

Now the business can start trading. The risk of failure in the first two years is very high. Often the problem isn't sales, but cash flow: the company has to wait for its invoices to be paid, and meanwhile the debts are piling up. The bank will only extend its line of credit up to a point.

But hopefully the business achieves a critical mass of customers, and establishes itself in the marketplace. It enters a growth phase. This early growth tends to be organic – turnover increases, the company employs more staff, it develops a supply network, etc. The majority of small companies just continue in this way – growing or shrinking year by year depending on their managerial skills and general market conditions.

## Selling the business

However, there are other possibilities. The founder of the business may decide to sell the business as a going concern. They might sell to a competitor, or to a company wanting to expand into that market. The buyers here are looking to grow through a strategy of acquisitions (= takeovers), an alternative to the strategy of organic growth.

## IPO

Another possibility is that the founders may decide to go public (= float/list on the stock exchange). Here, they sell their original privately-held shares at an IPO (initial public offering). This brings in a huge amount of money, some going directly to the owners as reward for their hard work, the rest going back into the business as reinvestment.

## TEN REASONS WHY A NEW BUSINESS CAN FAIL

### 1 Poor initial market research

**Cause:** Starting a business with a good idea, some money and a lot of enthusiasm – but no serious research

**Solution:** Take time to research the market thoroughly before you start trading

### 2 Cash flow problems

**Cause:** buying too much stock, customers paying late or not at all, suppliers needing to be paid on time

**Solution:** produce realistic cash flow forecasts and pay strict attention to budgets

### 3 Failure to listen to customers

**Cause:** Sticking with your own original ideas for too long

**Solution:** Actively seek the views of customers, and act on what they say

### 4 Bad business location

**Cause:** false economy – a cheap lease in the wrong neighbourhood

**Solution:** remember that accessibility for customers is crucial

### 5 Ineffective marketing

**Cause:** thinking that a good product will sell itself

**Solution:** be creative, constantly review the marketing plan

### 6 Overexpansion

**Cause:** being too ambitious

**Solution:** be realistic

### 7 Overspending

**Cause:** spending your seed money too soon

**Solution:** planning, keeping some cash in reserve

### 8 Poor customer service

**Cause:** behaviour of some employees

**Solution:** training, monitoring, company culture

### 9 Underestimating the competition

**Cause:** assuming that you have customer loyalty

**Solution:** watch competitors closely

### 10 Failure to change

**Cause:** complacency after initial success, lack of innovation

**Solution:** be flexible, recognize opportunities, adapt

# Exercises

**4.1 Find a word in the text opposite that matches each definition below. The words appear in order.**

1 small advantage _____
2 people who support a plan, especially by providing money

_____

3 property or money that you promise to give someone if you cannot repay a debt _____
4 *(formal; two words)* business that is a single unit from a legal or accounting point of view _____
5 documents giving details of products that someone has bought, and requesting payment for them

_____

6 *(phrasal verb)* increasing in a way that is difficult to manage

_____

7 income, revenue _____
8 *(three words)* a successful business _____
9 companies that have been bought by other companies

_____

**Now do the same for the words in 'Ten reasons why a new business can fail' opposite.**

10 carefully and completely _____
11 *(informal; phrasal verb)* continuing to do something without changing it _____
12 *(two words)* something that is cheap but could have bad results _____
13 small area of a town _____
14 *(two words)* money that is used to start a new business

_____

15 being faithful to a product / brand / company, etc

_____

16 being too satisfied and confident, so that you stop trying to improve _____

**4.2 Make phrases by matching an item from each column.**

| 1 | achieve | a gap in the market |
| 2 | wait | more staff |
| 3 | grow | for invoices to be paid |
| 4 | employ | a critical mass |
| 5 | spot | the risk of the business failing |
| 6 | take on | or shrink year by year |
| | | |
| 7 | bring in | of credit |
| 8 | enter | the business as a going concern |
| 9 | extend a line | public |
| 10 | go | a huge amount of money |
| 11 | grow | a growth phase |
| 12 | sell | organically or by acquisitions |

**4.3 Fill in each gap with one word from each box, written together.**

| *over    under* |
| --- |

| *charge    cut    estimate    ~~expand~~    perform* |
| *ride    spend    take* |

1 If you grow a business too quickly and take on too much risk, you ___*overexpand*___ .
2 If you sell goods at a lower price than your competitors, you _____ your competitors.
3 If you don't make as much money as expected, or you're less successful in your job than expected, you

_____ .

4 If your company goes past another in terms of sales, profits, market share, etc, then you _____ it.
5 If you use too much money, or more than you planned, you

_____ .

6 If you ask a client for too little money (usually by mistake), you _____ them.
7 If you use your authority to reject somebody's decision, you _____ them.
8 If you think that something is smaller or less important than it really is, you _____ it.

**4.4 Read the text about franchising, then answer the questions below.**

Would you like to start a new business, perhaps running a small retail outlet? Franchising is an obvious option. How does it work? The parent company (the 'franchisor') offers you (the 'franchisee') its trademark, products and business methods. You pay them an initial fee to use the name, and then pay a percentage of the turnover as well.

You will need to fulfill certain corporate identity standards such as those relating to furniture or staff uniforms. It's hard work, but the advantages are many: you're buying a well-known brand and the risk is minimized.

From the franchisor's point of view the benefits are clear. They can leave the day-to-day running of the business to you, while getting a share of your turnover.

**Find a word from the text that means:**

1 any place where a product is sold _____
2 money you pay to do something (or to a professional person for their work) _____
3 do something promised; reach _____
4 levels of quality or achievement _____
5 operating and managing _____

**See page 146 for some discussion topics.**

# Company types and corporate governance

## Company types

In law, there are various types of business entity. For each one there are different legal arrangements to register the company, different requirements for presenting accounts, etc. The main business types are:

### Sole trader (UK) / Sole proprietorship (US)

A single person owns and operates a business. Legally, the business has no separate existence from its owner (proprietor). This means that all the debts of the business are the debts of the owner.

### Partnership (UK and US)

Two or more people work together and share the risks and profits. Just like a sole proprietor, the partners are fully liable for (= responsible for) any debts the business has. This is referred to in law as 'unlimited liability'.

### Company (US and UK) / Corporation (US)

The business is a legal entity that is separate from its owners – the shareholders. The owners are not fully liable for the debts of the business. Instead, their liability (= potential risk) is restricted to their share capital. This is the amount of cash that they have contributed to the company. This is referred to in law as 'limited liability'.

There are two main types of companies:

- Private company: the shares (AmE stocks) are private in the sense that they cannot be bought by members of the public. The vast majority of companies fall into this category. They're often smaller companies, with shares held by a few business associates or family members.
- Public company: the shares are openly traded on a public stock exchange. These are the large, often well-known businesses. The word 'public' should not be confused with 'state-owned'. A 'state-owned enterprise' (SOE) is owned by the government.

## The Board

Public companies are controlled by a board of directors ('the Board'), elected by the shareholders. Not all Boards are fully independent, but in general their role is to:

- Set long-term strategy.
- Appoint a Chief Executive Officer (CEO) and other members of the senior management team to run the company day-to-day.
- Ask questions about any short- or medium-term strategy developed by the CEO, and then support it once they have agreed.
- Oversee the preparation of the financial statements.
- Appoint and ensure the independence of the company's auditors.
- Oversee and manage risk.
- Set an annual dividend.

Who chooses the Board? In theory, it's the shareholders. At the Annual General Meeting (AmE Annual Meeting of Stockholders) the shareholders can question Board members, vote to accept or reject the dividend, vote on replacements for retiring Board members, etc. But, in practice, the situation may be different. In particular, most shares are held by large institutions, and these may simply sell their stake if they aren't happy, instead of trying to change the Board. In reality many Board members are chosen by the CEO and the shareholders simply approve these members.

## Corporate governance

This whole issue of the role of the Board, how senior managers are responsible to shareholders, and how the company is run, is referred to as 'corporate governance'. Traditionally, different regions of the world have had different models of corporate governance.

**Anglo-American model:** separation of ownership (ie shareholders) and control (ie managers); priority given to the interests of shareholder.

**European / Japanese model:** similar to the Anglo-American model, but a greater recognition of the interests of other stakeholders such as employees, suppliers, customers, lenders (eg banks), and the community.

**East Asian / Latin model:** family-owned companies with no independent Board or outside shareholders.

Nowadays this traditional pattern is breaking down, and the situation is more mixed. However, the following basic principles of corporate governance are widely accepted:

- Respect for the rights of shareholders.
- A clear definition of the roles and responsibilities of Board members.
- Integrity and ethical behaviour.
- Disclosure (= giving full information) and transparency.

# Exercises

**5.1 Underline the correct words in italics.**

1 Money that a person or company owes is *debt / liability*. The word *debts / liabilities*, when used in the plural and in a formal context, has the same meaning – but it can also have a wider meaning of 'legal responsibilities'.

2 The word *owner / proprietor* means that you legally have something – anything. The word *owner / proprietor* means that you have a business (and is more formal).

3 If you and your business partners all have the same risks at the same time, then you *divide / share* the risks. If you separate the risks into smaller parts or different categories, then you *divide / share* them (= split them).

4 A *shareholder / stakeholder / stockholder* is someone who owns part of a business, in British English. A *shareholder / stakeholder / stockholder* is the same, in American English. A *shareholder / stakeholder / stockholder* is anyone who has an interest in the success of a plan, system or organization.

5 If you're a shareholder in a company, then every year you receive *an income / a profit / a dividend* paid out of the company's *income / profits / dividends*.

**5.2 Read the definition below and find the word in the text. (It appears twice.)**

*(formal)* 'a general term for any institution, company, partnership, government agency, or any other organization which exists in law as a separate and complete unit.'

_____

**5.3 Fill in the missing letters.**

1 If you're completely liable for something, then you're f_ _ _y liable.

2 If you're liable for something in law, then you're le_ _lly liable.

3 If you as an individual are liable for something, then you're per_ _ _ally liable.

4 If you may be liable for something, then you're pot_ _ially liable.

5 If you keep shares for a long time, then you h_ _ _ them.

6 If you buy and sell shares, then you tr_ _ _ them.

**5.4 Find a word in 'The Board' section opposite that matches each definition below.**

1 watch the progress of something to make sure it's done correctly; supervise _____

2 external firms that officially examine the financial records of a company to see that they're true and correct

_____

3 an amount of the profits that the company pays to shareholders _____

4 money invested in a business _____

**Now do the same for the 'Corporate governance' section.**

5 the quality of being honest and having high moral standards

_____

6 doing things in a way that allows other people to know exactly what you're doing _____

**5.5 Make word partnerships by matching one item from each box. Then use the word partnerships to complete the text below.**

| detailed | legal | limited | non-profit |

| entity | legislation | liability | organization |

The letters that follow a company name can tell you about its status in law.

In the UK, a private company has 'Ltd' after its name (because of the [1] _____ of its owners) and a public company has PLC (standing for Public Limited Company).

In the US, 'LLC' (Limited Liability Company) and 'Corp' are approximate equivalents to 'Ltd' and 'PLC', although the [2] _____ governing company formation is different in the two countries.

The letters 'Inc' (meaning 'incorporated') are also used in the US, and they cover a very broad range of organizations. They can refer to any [3] _____ that is separate from its owners such as a private company, a public company, a [4] _____ , or a sports club.

**5.6 Cover everything on these two pages with a piece of paper. Write down the full form of these abbreviations: *CEO, AGM, PLC, LLC.***

See page 146 for some discussion topics.

*"All in favor of a cap on our liability?"*

# 6 Global issues for the 21st century

## Geopolitics and the world economy

What big-picture issues are likely to dominate geopolitics and the world economy in the coming decades? Here are some suggestions:

### 1 The growth of the BRICs

The big story of the 21st century is the growth of Brazil, Russia, India and China (plus the Middle East). This is certain to translate into increased geopolitical influence for these countries.

### 2 The decline of the dollar

One impact of the previous trend is that the dollar will lose its status as the world's reserve currency. Central banks will hold fewer dollars, and oil will be priced in a range of currencies. But what else will happen in the currency area? Will a common Asian or Latin American currency emerge? And what about the internal conflict over the euro – should it be strong to fight inflation or weak to help exporters?

### 3 Climate change

Global warming is happening. However, any solution that holds back the progress of developing countries is likely to be resisted. Developing countries can accuse the developed nations of hypocrisy – western countries have already been through their industrial phase and now have the luxury of thinking about sustainable growth. Developing nations don't have this luxury.

### 4 Peak oil

Global oil production is going to peak very soon – there's just not enough left in the ground. So supply is shrinking. Also, developing nations are hungry for oil – for transport, industry, etc. So demand is rising. Put together falling supply and rising demand and you get one thing: much higher prices for the foreseeable future.

### 5 Energy security and alternative energy

Some countries have a lot of energy resources, others don't. And if you don't, you have a major geopolitical problem. It's called dependency. Put this issue together with peak oil, and it points in one direction: alternative energy. But some green activists are unrealistic about this – solar, wind, tidal, etc can only meet a fraction of the world's energy needs. The one technology that might make a difference is nuclear. And that, of course, is controversial.

### 6 Shortages of other resources and commodities

The bad news continues. As well as a shortage of energy, we're also short of water (in China, Southern Europe and the Middle East). And as living standards rise, we'll find that many agricultural commodities (eg wheat, corn, meat) are in short supply as well.

## Management and business

Managers were asked, 'What do you think will be the key business issues of the 21st century?' Read their replies below.

> For me, **branding and design** are the key issues. Customers can easily find good quality and value-for-money – all our competitors offer this. To survive, you need more than this, you need branding. Without a strong brand, you have no customer loyalty and no pricing power. And linked to branding is design – customers will pay for design. These are the major battlefields in modern business, not cost or quality.

> In our organization, **finding and developing talent** is going to be a major issue. There's a declining birthrate, and the increased mobility of labour means that workers can choose where they work and for whom. So talent is going to be in short supply. And that's particularly true for knowledge workers and creatives. We will need to find ways to motivate them and retain them inside our organization.

> In the modern workplace, **managing diversity** is going to become increasingly complex. We've got issues of gender, ethnicity and age. We try to make equal opportunities work, but we haven't done as well as we'd like. And now we have new problems of multicultural management across national borders. Imagine the problems when team members from different cultural backgrounds hold virtual meetings on the web without the chance to get to know each other in person.

> The issue that we talk about more and more these days is CSR – **corporate social responsibility.** I'm talking about fair trade, the environmental impact of business, the effect on local communities, sustainable development, labour practices and stuff like that. Campaigns by activists can affect your profits and destroy your brand.

> In many industries a major issue is **the threat caused by the Internet.** Basically, if it can be digitized, it can be pirated. The music and software industries have already been hit badly by this, the film industry is next and publishing will follow.

> Generally speaking, globalization has been good for business. But now there is a **backlash against globalization** amongst the public. This is creating political pressures for protectionism and for local sourcing to protect jobs. For us that means reduced access to world markets and higher costs.

# Exercises

**6.1 Make phrases by matching an item from each column.**

| | |
|---|---|
| 1 geopolitical | warming |
| 2 climate | influence |
| 3 global | growth |
| 4 sustainable | change |
| | |
| 5 peak | activists |
| 6 green | standards |
| 7 major | oil |
| 8 living | battlefield |
| | |
| 9 pricing | worker |
| 10 declining | power |
| 11 knowledge | impact |
| 12 environmental | birthrate |

**6.2 Complete the beginning of each phrase with its correct ending.**

| | |
|---|---|
| 1 be short | supply |
| 2 be hungry | future |
| 3 be in short | decades |
| 4 have a common Asian | of resources |
| 5 price oil in | for resources |
| 6 accuse someone | of hypocrisy |
| 7 in the coming | to world markets |
| 8 for the foreseeable | a virtual meeting |
| 9 hold | currency |
| 10 have access | dollars |

**6.3 Find a word from the section 'Management and business' opposite that matches the definitions below. The words appear in order.**

1 good quality (or quantity) in relation to the price
_____

2 being faithful; always giving support _____

3 people who use their imagination or skills to make things
_____

4 (human resources) keep someone _____

5 the fact of being either male or female _____

6 capable of continuing for a long time at the same level
_____

7 a strong, negative reaction to something that was previously popular _____

8 getting a product or component from somewhere
_____

**6.4 Fill in the gaps with a different form of the word in brackets. The new form may be a noun (singular or plural), verb or adjective. Some words are not in the text.**

1 Global _____*warming*_____ (warm) and the _____ (destroy) of the environment are _____ (threat) the planet.

2 Green _____ (active) and other pressure groups are becoming increasingly _____ (influence) in determining the _____ (environment) policies of large companies.

3 Genetic _____ (engineer) is very _____ (controversy), but many developing nations see it as the only way to ensure continuing _____ (grow) in agricultural _____ (produce).

4 Their government's _____ (economy) strategy is one of rapid _____ (industrialize). This has both _____ (strong) and _____ (weak).

**6.5 Complete the text about fair trade with the words in the box.**

| | | | | |
|---|---|---|---|---|
| access | gender | overproduction | poverty | premium |
| | principles | standards | subsidy | |

Fair trade is an organized social movement which promotes
¹ _____ for labour, social policy, environmentalism and sustainable development.
Key ² _____ of fair trade are:

● Creating opportunities for economically disadvantaged producers by paying a fair price. It is a strategy for reducing ³ _____ .

● Developing producers' independence by opening ⁴ _____ to new markets and building management skills.

● Safe and healthy working conditions.

● ⁵ _____ equality.

● Good environmental practices and responsible methods of production.

But fair trade has its critics. People say that too much of the ⁶ _____ price paid by consumers goes to the retailers. And over the long term fair trade operates as a hidden ⁷ _____ . It puts a price floor under a commodity and therefore encourages ⁸ _____ .
This can eventually lead to lower prices for growers everywhere.

See page 146 for some discussion topics.

# 7 Management styles and qualities

## Management styles

Every manager will be different, but over the years management theory has established three broad categories of management style:

### 1 The authoritarian manager

This person is strict, demanding, controlling and probably too rigid in their views. They take a top-down approach. But some staff like this – they know where they stand and what their responsibilities are. Their jobs are clearly defined.

### 2 The consensual manager

This person believes in consultation, and in coaching and mentoring their staff to help them develop. Subordinates usually like this type of manager, but the manager may lack vision and fail to show leadership.

### 3 The hands-off manager

This person delegates everything, or just leaves problems in the hope that they go away. They will justify their style as empowerment (ie giving control over decisions to other people), but subordinates will feel a lack of guidance and support. Liaison between colleagues (co-workers) will be uncoordinated.

An important point is that management style might reflect the company culture as much as the personality of the individual. So a hierarchical company with a bureaucratic decision-making process will suit one type of manager. On the other hand, a decentralized company where low-level managers can take the initiative will suit another.

We also have to remember that different business situations will require different management qualities:

- Consider the manager who is methodical, systematic and organized. Is that always a good thing? Maybe there are situations where it's better to be intuitive and flexible, or to take decisions quickly without knowing all the facts.
- Consider the manager who is a good team player, co-operative and supportive. Is that always a good thing? Maybe there are situations where it's better to work on your own, being self-motivated and proactive.

## Qualities or skills?

Here is something interesting to think about: notice that in the text above there is reference to styles and qualities, not to skills. This distinction is important. Qualities are a part of your character and personality – they were present at birth or formed early in your life and you will find it hard to change these things. Skills, however, are things you can learn – like how to speak another language, or give a good presentation. Skills can be developed and improved through practice and experience, qualities much less so. That raises many issues for training, personal development and career choice.

## Person specification

When looking for candidates for a particular job, many companies produce both a job specification and a person specification. This helps recruitment agencies and/or the human resource department to find suitable people. The person specification will include the skills needed, experience needed and personal qualities of the ideal candidate. The example below shows the final section, personal qualities.

## PERSON SPECIFICATION

### Skills and abilities

The ideal candidate will be able to demonstrate the following skills:

- An ability to …

### Personal qualities

**Business knowledge**

The ideal candidate will:

- have a good understanding of the market
- keep up to date with developments in the field

**Strategic ability**

The ideal candidate will:

- be able to translate company strategy into individual business unit objectives
- be able to balance conflicting business interests within the organization

**Organizational ability**

The ideal candidate will:

- be a good administrator
- be a good time-manager
- be conscientious and thorough
- be a good team-builder

**Relation to subordinates**

The ideal candidate will:

- have an ability to motivate
- know when to delegate and when to refer upwards
- keep good lines of communication
- have an 'open door' policy
- be a good listener
- have an ability to control and give feedback in an appropriate way

**Character**

The ideal candidate will:

- like challenges
- be prepared to take risks
- be honest and transparent
- be single-minded and determined
- be able to recover quickly after a setback
- stay calm under pressure

# Exercises

**7.1 Find a word in the text opposite that matches each definition below. The words appear in order.**

1 expecting other people to obey rules completely

_____

2 needing a lot of your time and energy _____

3 involving the agreement of most people in a group; democratic _____

4 giving training or advice for a specific job or task

_____

5 advising and helping someone more generally over a longer time period _____

6 exchange of information between people so that they work well together _____

7 where people and jobs are divided into many levels of importance _____

8 taking action before it's needed, rather than waiting until problems develop _____

**Now do the same for the words in 'Person specification' opposite.**

9 showing a lot of care and attention _____

10 including every possible detail and avoiding mistakes

_____

11 wanting to do something very much so that you will not let anything stop you _____

12 a problem that delays or stops progress

_____

**7.2 Change each adjective into an opposite meaning by filling in the letters. If there is a prefix, it may be de-, dis-, in- or un-.**

| | |
|---|---|
| 1 simple | bureau _ _ _ _ c |
| 2 centralized | _ _centralized |
| 3 co-operative | _ _co-operative / _ _helpful |
| 4 coordinated | _ _coordinated |
| 5 direct | _ _direct |
| 6 flexible | _ _flexible / ri _ _d |
| 7 hands-off | hands- _ _ |
| 8 honest | _ _ _honest |
| 9 intuitive | rat _ _ _al |
| 10 methodical | carel _ _ _ |
| 11 organized | _ _ _organized / me _ _y |
| 12 stressed | re _ _ _ed / c _ _m |
| 13 supportive | _ _supportive |
| 14 top-down | b _ _ _ _ _- _ _ |
| 15 transparent | _ _clear |

**7.3 Choose the best adjective from those in 7.2 (both columns) to describe these managers.**

1 He's under a lot of pressure and looks worried all the time. He's really _____ .

2 Once she's made a plan, she doesn't like changing it. She's a bit _____ .

3 He likes to get involved and do things, rather than just talking about them or making other people do them. He's very _____ .

4 Her desk is so untidy – papers everywhere! It's really

_____ .

5 He produces complicated rules for everything. His approach is very _____ .

6 She's honest and open and doesn't try to hide anything. She's very _____ .

**7.4 Make phrases by matching an item from each column.**

| | |
|---|---|
| 1 lack | on your own and be self-motivated |
| 2 know | the initiative |
| 3 work | vision and fail to show leadership |
| 4 take | where you stand |
| 5 keep | quickly after a setback |
| 6 give | general strategy into specific objectives |
| 7 recover | up to date with developments in the field |
| 8 translate | feedback in an appropriate way |

**7.5 Complete the text about teams with the words in the box.**

| | | | |
|---|---|---|---|
| breathing | carry out | feedback | guiding |
| issuing | progress | report back | running |

The ability to lead teams is a key skill in the modern business world. The team leader has to move between a variety of approaches: [1]_____ instructions and supervising closely at times, [2]_____ and encouraging and offering advice at other times.

The team leader is of course responsible for monitoring overall [3]_____, but once the team is up and [4]_____, and the objectives and team roles are clearly defined, then he or she may be able to take a back seat for short periods of time.

Team members like to feel that they can [5]_____ their roles without the leader [6]_____ down their neck all the time. However, they do need to [7]_____ regularly, and the team leader is expected to give them constructive [8]_____ on their performance.

See page 146 for some discussion topics.

# 8 | Organizing time and work

At the planning stage of a project the amount of work required can look frightening. To make it manageable, you need to develop an overall time frame (timescale) for the project and a schedule (timetable) to show the dates or times when individual things should happen. Hopefully, through good time management, you will be ahead of schedule. Anyway, as long as you're on schedule, there's no problem. What you definitely don't want is to be behind schedule. That means you'll be under a lot of stress, and when you're totally stressed out, your work will suffer. You might have to work long hours to catch up. And if you're a manager, you probably won't get paid overtime – it's just expected of you.

Of course, it's not always your fault. There can be delays for all sorts of reasons. Things can take longer than planned because of circumstances beyond your control. In that case … well, deadlines might become guidelines.

What can you do to improve your time management? Here are some tips:

## Time management tips

✔ Use a diary (AmE calendar) to plan your time. Software packages such as Outlook include this function, but many people prefer a wall chart with stickers and colour-coding to show different activities.

✔ Make a realistic plan and then prioritize the tasks. Do the 'A' tasks first – the important, unpleasant, or time-consuming ones. Then you'll turn to the less important ones with a clear mind. Don't get distracted by doing the small, easy tasks first.

✔ Use checklists.

✔ Know and use the filing system on your computer properly. A lot of the workflow in business involves electronic paperwork, and you need to know how to access documents, modify them, share them and archive them.

✔ Delegate.

✔ Don't try to be a perfectionist in everything. It takes time to get things absolutely right, and time is money. Short cuts can be acceptable; a 'quick and dirty' solution may be OK. Try to balance quality, cost and time.

But of course you know all that, and you have already implemented these suggestions. You use careful time management to plan your workload. You never put off unpleasant tasks or lose concentration. Because of this, your work is stimulating and rewarding. You do everything with calm and focus. At the end of each day you go home with a sense of achievement. You say to yourself, 'The world is a better place today because of what I did in my job.' Right?

# What do managers manage?

## Operations
Planning
Setting and achieving targets
Improving productivity
Controlling, delegating and giving feedback
Decision-making
Satisfying customer needs
Managing quality
Managing change

## People
Planning staffing needs, and recruiting and selecting new staff
Developing the team, supporting and guiding individuals
Delegating and monitoring
Motivating
Managing conflict
Carrying out performance reviews
Rewarding achievement

## Finance
Preparing and negotiating budgets
Monitoring the budget
Controlling costs
Making investment decisions

## Information
Chairing and/or participating in meetings
Replying to emails
Telephoning
Accessing information on the company IT network
Reading and writing reports and proposals
Keeping files up to date
Speaking in public, giving presentations

## Career development
Managing your boss
Developing your skills and competencies
Attending conferences and seminars
Reading about recent ideas and developments in your field
Minimizing stress

# Exercises

**8.1 Fill in the missing letters.**

1

66 The project is going very well. In fact, we're _ _ _ _ d of schedule. The workf_ _w is organized efficiently, and we have a big wall ch_ _ _ with sti_ _ _rs showing the different stages of the project and what everyone should be doing. I like our team leader – she has established the general gu_ _ _lines for our work, but she leaves it up to us to pr_ _ _tize our tasks on a day-to-day basis. Of course, there are always cha_ _ _nges to fa_e, but so far we've been able to m_ _t those challenges. It's a great experience. I find the work sti_ _ _ating and rew_ _ _ing. It's given me a real s_ _ _e of ach_ _ _ _ment. 99

2

66 The work_ _ _d in this project is far bigger than anyone expected. There's a lot of unexpected pa_ _ _work that is very time-con_ _ _ing to complete. Things are not going well. In fact, we're _ _ _ _ _d schedule. We might even miss the dea_ _ _ _ _ _. Everyone is totally st_ _ _ _ed _ _ _. People are taking sh_ _ _-c_ _ _s and quality is suffering. It's just so frustrating, and it's not even our fault – it's entirely due to circu_ _ _ _ _ces b_ _ _ _d our control. The only way we're going to finish this work within the given time fr_ _ _ is by finding some kind of qu_ _ _ and di_ _ _ solution. I know it isn't ideal, but what else can we do? 99

**8.2 Complete the sentences with the verbs in the box. They are all used with time expressions.**

| | | | |
|---|---|---|---|
| allow | find | make up | put in |
| run out of | save | spend | waste |

1  How much time do you _____ on reading books about management?
2  I know you're busy, but I wonder if you could _____ some time tomorrow to check my report?
3  That's it. We have to finish now. We've _____ time.

4  Please _____ ten working days for delivery.
5  Last week I _____ six hours overtime. They're going to pay me time-and-a-half.
6  This really isn't important – we'll _____ too much time if we do it. Let's just leave it.
7  That's an excellent idea – we could _____ around two weeks on our planned schedule by doing it.
8  I got distracted this afternoon. I'll have to _____ time by staying late at the office tonight.

**8.3 Look at 'What do managers manage?' opposite.**

1  Find a word that is used in two ways:
a) a plan of how to spend money, and b) the money itself
_____

2  Find a formal word that is used in the field of human resources to mean: 'specific knowledge and skills'. In other words, knowledge and skills that are used for a particular task in a particular job _____

**8.4 Read the text about delegating, then answer the questions below.**

All managers have constraints on their time – so many tasks seem urgent and vital, and yet no one person can tackle them all. Delegation is the answer.

Once you've appointed the person responsible for the particular task, you need to brief them thoroughly. How much autonomy are you going to allow them? How often should they report back to you with progress updates, and in what detail? And who else needs to be in the loop? After all, it's not just you who needs to know what's happening.

Control will be a key issue. What happens if they hit an unexpected snag? You can't take all the responsibility away from them – figuring out solutions to problems will be a challenge and a motivation for them. However, you do need to make sure that tasks are completed successfully.

**Find a word from the text that means:**

1  limits _____
2  deal with _____
3  give necessary information _____
4  (four words) be part of a group of people that has information about something _____
5  (informal) problem _____
6  (phrasal verb) being able to understand; solving
_____

**8.5 Read the following sentence and decide if it's grammatically correct.**

*Once you've appointed the responsible for the particular task, you need to brief them thoroughly.*

**Compare with the third sentence in the text above.**

See page 146 for some discussion topics.

HH LEARNING CENTRE
HARROW COLLEGE

# 9 Planning and setting objectives

## What is a plan?

An organization's vision (typically 5–10 years) shapes its strategy (2–5 years), which in turn shapes its plans (1 year). A plan:

- has objectives which can be measured.
- answers questions that stakeholders (eg shareholders, banks, employees) will ask.
- builds in options.
- identifies and quantifies risks.
- shows how to minimize those risks (and perhaps includes a contingency plan for what happens if things go wrong).
- allows progress to be measured.

Other points to note are:

- That there is a cost to planning in terms of management, time and research.
- That all plans make assumptions, although these are often not stated explicitly.
- That there are some very specific types of business planning (eg project management is a distinct business function in its own right).

## Elements of a plan

A comprehensive business plan for a large company might involve the following:

- Internal analysis: this covers the strengths and weaknesses of the organization, historical performance, trends in the business activity and current resources.
- External analysis: this covers markets, customers, the competition, tax, legislation, the general business environment, etc.
- Gap analysis: this starts with the key issues raised in the first two points above, and highlights those areas where there is a gap between where you are now and where you want to be.
- Action plan: what needs to be done to close the gaps? Do products need to be improved? Does technology need to be upgraded? Do staff need to be retrained?
- Resource assessment: what the action plan needs in terms of human resources, material resources (eg plant, space inside buildings, equipment), IT resources and financial resources.
- Targets: specific targets for financial returns, costs, market share, sales, growth, customer satisfaction, quality, etc.
- Financial issues: cash flow forecasts, projected profit and loss (P&L).

Look at the Contents page of the business plan on the right. It is the kind of plan that a small or medium-sized business might produce to define its strategy going forward. The plan might also be needed to show to a bank if new funding is required.

## Business Plan: Contents

1 **Summary and main conclusions**

2 **Introduction**
- 2.1 Current situation
- 2.2 Need for change

3 **Internal analysis**
- 3.1 Internal strengths
- 3.2 Internal weaknesses

4 **Market analysis**
- 4.1 External opportunities
- 4.2 External threats

5 **Marketing plan**
- 5.1 New product ideas
- 5.2 Pricing issues
- 5.3 Sales targets and market share targets
- 5.4 Geographical diversification
- 5.5 Improvements to distribution channel
- 5.6 Advertising campaigns

6 **Operational plan**
- 6.1 New plant and equipment
- 6.2 Efficiency of production process
- 6.3 Productivity issues
- 6.4 Ideas for saving costs
- 6.5 Outsourcing proposals
- 6.6 Quality issues

7 **Financials**
- 7.1 Cash flow forecast
- 7.2 Profit and loss forecast

8 **Resource requirements**
- 8.1 Human resources
- 8.2 Capital investment
- 8.3 IT

9 **Appendices**

# Exercises

**9.1 Find a word in the text opposite that matches each definition below. The words appear in order.**

1  all those people who have an interest in the success of a plan, system or organization _____

2  (two words) a course of action that you will take if something bad happens in the future _____

3  beliefs that are used as the basis for an idea, but which may not be correct _____

4  gradual changes or developments, tendencies

 _____

5  (formal) laws _____

6  makes people notice something and think about it

 _____

7  a factory or building where an industrial process takes place, and all its heavy machinery _____

8  things that you try to achieve _____

9  (two words) phrase often used in a business context to mean 'in the future' _____

**Now do the same for the 'Contents' page opposite.**

10  prediction _____

**9.2 One verb from each group does not go with the noun at the end. Cross it out.**
**Check any unknown words in a dictionary.**

1  cut, estimate, implement, recover   costs

2  access, achieve, get hold of, withhold   information

3  consider, keep open, meet, suggest   options

4  be based on, carry out, do, make   research

5  identify, minimize, quantify, reach   risks

6  boost, forecast, generate, set up   sales

**9.3 Match a group of verbs 1–3 and a group of adjectives a–c to the nouns below.**
**Check any unknown words in a dictionary.**

1  achieve, exceed, fall short of, meet, reach

2  clarify, deal with, discuss, explore, focus on, raise, tackle

3  come up with, go ahead with, implement, keep to, put forward, shelve

a  ambitious, contingency, detailed, five-point, long-term, realistic, strategic, three-year

b  ambitious, annual, high, initial, realistic, sales

c  basic, central, complex, crucial, main, side, unresolved, vital

[1] [b] target   [ ] [ ] plan   [ ] [ ] issue

**9.4 Rewrite the sentences using a verb + an adjective from exercise 9.3. Keep the same meaning.**

1  We will go above the target we had at the beginning.
 We will ____exceed____ our ____initial____ target.

2  We will go below our yearly target.
 We will _____ our _____ target.

3  We decided to start the plan for the next three years.
 We decided to _____ the _____ plan.

4  We will have to stop our plans for the future (although we might continue with them later).
 We will have to _____ our _____ plans.

5  The issue that they wanted us to consider is very complicated.
 The issue that they _____ is very _____ .

**9.5 Match a group of verbs 1–3 and a group of adjectives a–c to the nouns below.**

1  arrange, follow, go according to, revise, stick to

2  achieve, fail in, fulfil, meet, reach, set

3  approve, cut, increase, plan, reduce, stick to, submit

a  clear, key, limited, long-term, major, overall, primary, specific

b  annual, draft, fixed, limited, low, tight, marketing

c  ambitious, busy, strict, tight, weekly

[ ] [ ] objective   [ ] [ ] schedule   [ ] [ ] budget

**9.6 Rewrite the sentences using a verb + an adjective from exercise 9.5. Keep the same meaning.**

1  At this point we just need to decide our general objectives.
 At this point we just need to _____ our _____ objectives.

2  We must keep to the schedule – there's only just enough time.
 We must _____ the schedule – it's very _____ .

3  I have to give a provisional budget so that they can make a decision. (It can be changed later.)
 I have to _____ a _____ budget.

**See page 147 for some discussion topics.**

"Damn, I think I ate Plan B."

## What is leadership in business?

Clearly, an entrepreneur shows leadership. They start their own business, and then build it up from scratch. But the head of a team, department or large organization can also show leadership. What do these people have in common? A good way to answer this is to look at the difference between leadership and management. To simplify greatly:

- Leaders look at the big picture, welcome change, are good at motivating and influencing, and work well alone (or at the head of teams).
- Managers look at the details, welcome stability, are good at supervising, and work well as team members.

In addition, managers tend to get their authority from their role (a boss with subordinates), while leaders get their authority from their personality. People just turn to leaders for guidance, regardless of their position. They have a quality of personal impact.

## Eight characteristics of a good leader

1 Vision: this means generating ideas about the way ahead, and then getting buy-in (= commitment to a shared goal) from other people.

2 Motivation: as well as obvious things like salary, this includes praise, appreciation and recognition.

3 Emotional intelligence: this used to be called empathy or intuition. It means 'reading people' – knowing what they want or need.

4 Empowering others: tell people what you expect from them, give them the tools they need to succeed, and then get out of their way. Learn to listen; nothing is more empowering than being heard.

5 Being trustworthy: your behaviour should be consistent with your beliefs, otherwise people won't trust you. Actions speak louder than words.

6 Taking risks and managing change: leaders need to be change agents – in a fast-moving world, any organization that stands still will fail. But change brings resistance. Leaders have to explain why change is necessary, establish a process, involve everyone, provide support, communicate the outcomes and share the benefits.

7 Focus and follow-through: this involves setting priorities and doing what you say you will do. Unfortunately, many leaders are poor finishers.

8 A sense of humour: the ability to laugh at yourself is a good way to bring others along with you. It demonstrates a degree of self-knowledge.

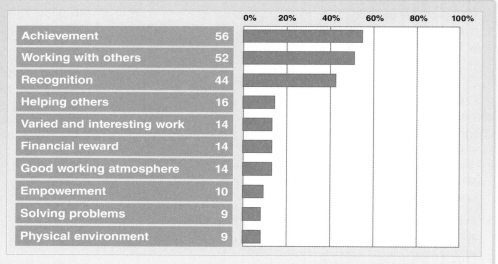

# Motivation

**A survey by Kaisen Consulting asked people in a wide range of industry sectors what made them feel good at work. Here are the results:**

| | | 0% | 20% | 40% | 60% | 80% | 100% |
|---|---|---|---|---|---|---|---|
| Achievement | 56 | | | | | | |
| Working with others | 52 | | | | | | |
| Recognition | 44 | | | | | | |
| Helping others | 16 | | | | | | |
| Varied and interesting work | 14 | | | | | | |
| Financial reward | 14 | | | | | | |
| Good working atmosphere | 14 | | | | | | |
| Empowerment | 10 | | | | | | |
| Solving problems | 9 | | | | | | |
| Physical environment | 9 | | | | | | |

### Notice the dominance of the top three categories:

A sense of achievement, and having that achievement recognized, appear to be strong motivators. Positive working relationships are also important. Notice also that 'financial reward' was only ranked sixth. This is quite surprising.

The researchers then asked people what made them feel bad at work. Here, the most common response by far was 'a negative experience with colleagues'. A range of other factors were also mentioned: lack of recognition, company politics, stress, boring work, etc. Items that were mentioned less often included: lack of support, having a bad boss, lack of direction and unsatisfactory levels of pay. These did not seem to be important demotivators.

### The researchers drew the following conclusions about motivation:

- In a task-oriented business world, it's important to remember that relationships and the 'emotional' dimension to work are very important.
- Recognition and positive feedback are the oxygen of motivation.
- Employees ask, 'What's in it for me?' Business success and customer satisfaction did not appear as motivational factors.
- Motivation and demotivation are not equal and exact opposites. For example, while 'achievement' was the strongest motivator, 'failure' was rarely mentioned as a demotivator.

# Exercises

**10.1 Find a word in the first two sections of the text opposite that matches each definition below. The words appear in order.**

1 *(two words)* from the beginning _____
2 *(three words)* the whole situation, not just one part of it

_____

3 the way in which someone is involved in an activity; position

_____

4 understanding how other people feel _____
5 knowledge that is based on feelings rather than facts

_____

6 giving someone more control over their life and work

_____

7 able to be trusted _____
8 results _____

**10.2 The text mentions 'praise, appreciation and recognition' as being a part of motivation. Which one of these is the strongest motivator?**

_____

**10.3 Learners of English often use the word 'sympathetic' when talking about someone such as a good leader. Put a tick (✓) by the definition which matches how a native-speaker uses this word.**

1 friendly, nice ☐
2 willing to understand someone's problems and help them ☐

**10.4 Make phrases from the 'Motivation' section of the text by matching an item from each column.**

1 positive          achievement (motivator)
2 negative          feedback from your boss (motivator)
3 sense of          recognition (demotivator)
4 lack of           experiences with colleagues (demotivator)
5 company           oriented business world
6 physical          politics
7 task-             reward
8 financial         environment

**10.5 Complete each sentence with the correct form of the word in italics. Sometimes you will need to use a negative form (de-, un-).**

1 *lead*
   a It's the _____ company in the field.
   b It's the market _____ .
   c She showed excellent _____ ability.

2 *motivate*
   a Sense of achievement is probably the number one _____ factor.
   b I left my job because it offered no new challenges. I was bored and _____ .

3 *manage*
   a _____ change in a fast-moving world isn't easy.
   b This situation is out of control. It's completely _____ .

4 *satisfy*
   a A job well done gives me a great feeling of _____ .
   b My working conditions are terrible. They're just totally _____ .

5 *analyze*
   a She's good at separating a complex problem into its parts – she's very _____ .
   b On the whole, I agree with your _____ .

**10.6 Read the text about influencing, then answer the questions below.**

Leaders are good at influencing people. It's a hidden skill – very important, but often ignored. Influencing may take the form of persuading people to adopt their ideas, inspiring people to achieve certain goals, or creating relationships.

Influencing requires a mix of interpersonal, communication, presentation and assertiveness skills. And most importantly, you need to be able to adapt and modify your personal style when you see the effect it's having on others. You can't force your ideas on other people – they have to feel acknowledged, understood and appreciated.

There's a kind of buzz around a good influencer. They don't moan, blame and complain. They see what needs doing and then start talking to others to try to get agreement and action.

**Find a word from the text that means:**

1 reach, succeed in getting _____
2 ability to express your ideas firmly and confidently

_____

3 heard and accepted _____
4 *(informal)* feeling of pleasure or excitement

_____

5 *(informal)* complain in an annoying way _____

**See page 147 for some discussion topics.**

# 11 Insurance and risk management

Every business faces risks, and many of these are insurable. Insurance may be obligatory, or optional, but it is certainly a part of prudent risk management. There are two basic types of business insurance: liability insurance and property insurance.

## Liability insurance

Liability insurance covers damage caused to other people. An employee might suffer a work-related accident, or a visitor might slip on a polished floor and break an arm. In either case, they can sue you and will try to prove negligence (= failure to take enough care). There is also product liability insurance (in case someone sues you after using a product), and professional indemnity insurance (AmE malpractice insurance) in case a client sues you for making a costly mistake while advising them.

## Property insurance

Property insurance covers damage to the insured's own property. Damage might be caused by fire, vandalism, etc. The company might also need automobile insurance.

Some policies include the services of a lawyer (AmE attorney) in the event that you're sued, while others don't. And it's important to remember that your protection is limited to the maximum on the policy. If a court awards damages that exceed this figure, then you're liable for the difference.

## Policies

When you take out an insurance policy (ie contract), you make a regular payment called a 'premium' to an insurer. The policy states how much will be paid and under which circumstances. Read it carefully, check the small print, and in particular check any exclusion clauses. After a year, before the contract expires, you will be sent a renewal notice.

Insurance is available through several channels: agents (who work directly for one insurance company), independent brokers (who search for the best policy amongst many alternatives) and direct selling (often over the Internet). Agents and brokers work on commission.

## Claims

If you need to make a claim, you fill out a form and wait for it to be processed. If the insurance company suspects that you're underinsured, or claiming too much money, they can appoint a loss adjuster (AmE claims adjuster) to examine the situation. Eventually, they pay out and you receive your compensation.

If an insurer feels that they have taken on too much risk, then they can go to a reinsurance company to provide cover for themselves.

## But you can't insure against ...

| Strategic risks | Integration problems arising from a merger or acquisition. |
| | Changes in the market such as a new competitor or changes in demand. |
| | New technologies that threaten your business model. |
| | Political / Economic instability in an export market. |
| **Operational risks** | Breakdown of key equipment. |
| | Supply chain problems: late delivery, quality issues, etc. |
| | IT failure: loss of data, damage due to viruses or hackers. |
| | Poor accounting that fails to show the real financial situation. |
| | Employee issues: recruitment difficulties, lack of people with the right skillset, etc. |
| **Financial risks** | Cash flow (ie liquidity) problems. |
| | Bad debt. |
| | Increased bank charges on a loan (more expensive credit). |
| | Changes in foreign exchange rates. |
| | Embezzlement (= when someone steals money from their own company). |
| **Failure of compliance (with new laws)** | New employment legislation. |
| | New health and safety legislation. |

# Exercises

**11.1 Find a word in the text opposite that matches each definition below. The words appear in order.**

1 sensible and careful _____

2 legal responsibility for something _____

3 start a legal process to get money from someone _____

4 formal protection against loss or damage _____

5 deliberately damaging things _____

6 *(two words)* makes a decision to give someone compensation _____

7 *(two words)* sections of a contract that say what isn't covered by the contract _____

8 *(two words)* written reminder that a contract is going to end soon and you must pay if you want it to continue _____

9 *(phrasal verb)* give money as the result of an insurance claim _____

10 money that someone receives because of damage they have suffered _____

**Now do the same for words in 'But you can't insure against' opposite.**

11 *(two words)* money that will never be collected from customers _____

12 *(formal)* the practice of obeying a law _____

**11.2 Make phrases by matching an item from each column.**

| | |
|---|---|
| 1 be legally | for the difference |
| 2 try to prove | damages |
| 3 award | obliged to do something |
| 4 be liable | negligence |
| | |
| 5 take out | a renewal notice |
| 6 take on | an insurance policy |
| 7 be sent | the small print |
| 8 check | too much risk |

**11.3 Cross out the item which has a <u>different</u> meaning to the others.**

1 to *dispute, file, put in, submit* a claim

2 to *meet, pay, reject, settle* a claim

3 *considerable, high, potential, serious, significant* risk

4 to *avoid, face, run, take* a risk

5 to *assess, measure, minimize, weigh up* the risks

**11.4 Underline the correct words in italics.**

1 How much is the insurance *to / on* your car?

2 Do you have insurance *for / to* anyone to drive the car?

3 You have to *take out / take up* building and contents insurance as a condition of the mortgage.

4 This policy provides insurance *against / in favour of* loss or damage *by / up to* €5,000.

5 We've insured all our IT equipment *for / with* over a million euros.

6 Can you claim the damage *by / on* your insurance?

7 They *did / made* a claim *for / of* damages.

8 There is a risk *to / of* consumers *by / from* these products. We will have to withdraw them from the market.

9 We are *at / with* risk *to be / of being* sued.

10 You should go to *court / the judge* – you have a *right / rightful* claim.

**11.5 Complete this text about risk management with the words in the box. Check any unknown words in a dictionary.**

| | | |
|---|---|---|
| contingency plan | damage limitation | escalation procedure |
| exposure to risk | remedial action | risk assessments |

Some companies have a risk-taking culture, while others want less [1] _____ . But in any case, the senior managers of large companies are likely to prepare regular [2] _____ . A typical tool here is a risk map. This has probability on the horizontal axis and impact on the vertical axis. Key risks are brainstormed and then plotted on the map. The plotting process helps to clarify the risks, and then leads on to a discussion about risk management.

Some risks can be reduced or eliminated, others will have to be accepted. For those in the latter category, the company needs to have a [3] _____ (= back-up plan) for when things go wrong. This could involve some initial measures as the situation deteriorates, and then an [4] _____ (where more senior managers take responsibility) if it turns into a crisis.

And crises do happen – managers have to respond to fast-moving events and take [5] _____ (intended to improve the situation) on the spot. In a worst case scenario, the whole thing just becomes a [6] _____ exercise.

**See page 147 for some discussion topics.**

## Manufacturing

Manufacturing is the transformation of raw materials into finished products. It happens in factories, plants (= large factories) and mills (used for specific industries, eg steel and textiles).

The word 'manufacturing' is often associated with industries like autos, chemicals, iron and steel. These industries, based on mass production, were once major employers in areas like America's 'Rust Belt' (Illinois, Indiana, Michigan, Ohio) and England's 'West Midlands' – regions associated with readily available coal, labour and inland waterways (= canals). In the period after the Second World War these industries provided jobs for large numbers of blue-collar workers, working in secure, well-paid jobs and protected by unions. During the 1970s and 80s these industries became unprofitable in America and Europe. Production methods were increasingly outdated, and this type of heavy industry switched to other countries, particularly Japan.

In Japan a new approach to manufacturing emerged. It had many labels, but Toyota Production System was the most common. Key elements of this approach were elimination of waste, reducing inventory levels, and increasing efficiency through the simplification and standardization of processes and procedures. Many of the core concepts still in use today are Japanese words such as 'kaizen' (continuous improvement) and 'kanban' (checking inventory levels with simple visual signals).

This new approach led to a renaissance in manufacturing all over the world, and evolved into modern-day philosophies such as Lean Manufacturing and Just-In-Time (JIT). These areas are explored in unit 16.

Nowadays the term 'manufacturing' has a much wider scope. It includes aerospace, automotive, biotech, chemicals, clothing and footwear, electronics, food and beverages, paper and printing, pharmaceuticals, plastics and polymers, shipbuilding, steel and textiles.

## Engineering

If a company makes mass-produced products, it's generally referred to as a 'manufacturing company'. If it's responsible for complex projects with a high degree of customization, it's generally referred to as an 'engineering company'.

Engineering as a professional activity involves designing, building and testing things. Engineers are fascinated by how and why things work.

A simplified breakdown of the many branches of engineering is shown below.

### TYPES OF ENGINEERING

**CIVIL ENGINEERING**
commercial and residential buildings, bridges, roads (AmE highways), dams

**MECHANICAL ENGINEERING**
automobiles, aircraft, heating and cooling systems, industrial equipment and machinery, medical devices

**CHEMICAL ENGINEERING**
plastics, paints, pharmaceuticals, agricultural chemicals, food processing

**ELECTRICAL ENGINEERING**
power production and distribution, electronics, control systems, telecommunications

**ENVIRONMENTAL ENGINEERING**
land management, water and sewage systems, pollution, waste disposal, recycling

**INDUSTRIAL ENGINEERING**
making industrial processes more efficient, making products easier to manufacture and more consistent in quality, increasing productivity

**SOFTWARE ENGINEERING**
databases and operating systems, computer graphics, embedded computers in everyday products, monitoring and controlling industrial processes

# Exercises

**12.1 Find a word in the text opposite that matches each definition below. The words appear in order.**

1 *(two words)* natural substances, before being made into something _____
2 red substance that forms on metal when it gets old or wet _____
3 working class _____
4 organizations that represent the workers in a particular industry _____
5 not modern enough to be useful _____
6 all the items in one particular place; stock _____
7 all the things that a particular subject deals with; range _____
8 information that has been separated into different groups _____

**Now do the same for the words in 'Types of engineering' opposite.**

9 walls built across a river to create a lake _____
10 machines or tools that do a special job (NOT 'equipment') _____
11 the process of getting rid of something _____
12 fixed firmly and deeply in something else _____

**12.2 Make phrases by matching an item from each column.**

| | |
|---|---|
| 1 mass | job (protected by unions) |
| 2 well-paid | industry (eg steel) |
| 3 heavy | concepts (of a philosophy) |
| 4 core | production (methods in industry) |
| 5 continuous | quality (of industrial products) |
| 6 wide | improvement (= 'kaizen') |
| 7 residential | scope (of a subject or activity) |
| 8 consistent | buildings (in civil engineering) |

**12.3 Underline the correct words in italics.**

1 Machines, especially large ones, are called *equipment / machinery*; all the tools, machines and clothes, etc that you need for a particular job are called *equipment / machinery*.
2 A series of actions that have a particular result is a *process / procedure*; a way of doing something, especially the correct or usual way, is a *process / procedure*.
3 Useless materials and parts that are left after a process is finished are called *pollution / waste*; damage caused to the environment by harmful chemicals is called *pollution / waste*.

**12.4 Match three verbs (one from each column) with a similar meaning. They are all typical activities of an engineer.**

| | | |
|---|---|---|
| analyze | establish | keep an eye on |
| construct | put into operation | find out |
| determine | examine | carry out |
| implement | supervise | go over |
| monitor | assemble | put together |
| | | |
| eliminate | replicate | get rid of |
| evaluate | fix | be in charge of |
| manage | remove | model |
| repair | assess | weigh up |
| simulate | run | put back into working order |

**In general, are the verbs in the third column more formal or more informal?**

**12.5 Complete the text with the words in the box.**

economies of scale    mould    reliability    risk
sum    upgrade    up and running    workforce

A forge is a place where metal is heated and then poured into a [1] _____ – it's the first step in the supply chain for many car parts. And the biggest forge in the world is Bharat Forge, in Pune, India.

The company was founded in 1961, and in the early decades gained a reputation for quality and [2] _____ . Then, in 1988, it spent a huge [3] _____ of money on building a high-tech German-engineered plant. Along with this investment in technology came an [4] _____ of manpower. Traditionally, Bharat Forge had employed a poorly educated [5] _____, but now it started replacing them with white-collar college graduates.

When the outsourcing wave hit the auto parts industry in the 1990s, Bharat's new plant was [6] _____ and ready to compete.

More recently, it has begun a strategy of acquisitions in Europe and China. Most of its production is still in India, with its [7] _____ and low labour costs, but the addition of small plants nearer to the customer reduces supply chain [8] _____ .

See page 147 for some discussion topics.

# 13 Inside a factory

Study the diagram of an automobile plant and the notes that explain what is happening in the different areas. It is based loosely on the Volvo Trucks plant in Gothenburg, Sweden, and some of the vocabulary below is specific to the automobile industry. (Check in a dictionary if necessary.) The assembly line starts on the left and moves to the right, and various assembly stations along the line are shown by small squares.

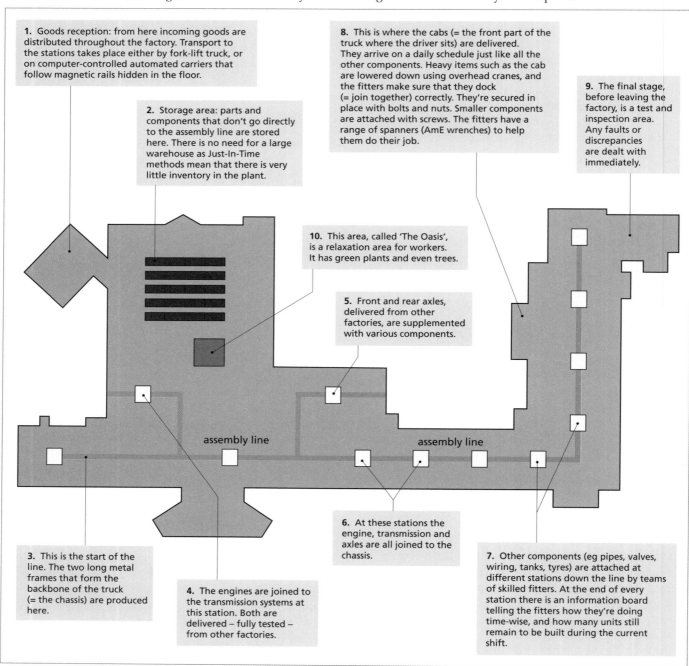

**1.** Goods reception: from here incoming goods are distributed throughout the factory. Transport to the stations takes place either by fork-lift truck, or on computer-controlled automated carriers that follow magnetic rails hidden in the floor.

**2.** Storage area: parts and components that don't go directly to the assembly line are stored here. There is no need for a large warehouse as Just-In-Time methods mean that there is very little inventory in the plant.

**8.** This is where the cabs (= the front part of the truck where the driver sits) are delivered. They arrive on a daily schedule just like all the other components. Heavy items such as the cab are lowered down using overhead cranes, and the fitters make sure that they dock (= join together) correctly. They're secured in place with bolts and nuts. Smaller components are attached with screws. The fitters have a range of spanners (AmE wrenches) to help them do their job.

**9.** The final stage, before leaving the factory, is a test and inspection area. Any faults or discrepancies are dealt with immediately.

**10.** This area, called 'The Oasis', is a relaxation area for workers. It has green plants and even trees.

**5.** Front and rear axles, delivered from other factories, are supplemented with various components.

assembly line

assembly line

**3.** This is the start of the line. The two long metal frames that form the backbone of the truck (= the chassis) are produced here.

**4.** The engines are joined to the transmission systems at this station. Both are delivered – fully tested – from other factories.

**6.** At these stations the engine, transmission and axles are all joined to the chassis.

**7.** Other components (eg pipes, valves, wiring, tanks, tyres) are attached at different stations down the line by teams of skilled fitters. At the end of every station there is an information board telling the fitters how they're doing time-wise, and how many units still remain to be built during the current shift.

This particular factory is a very modern facility and the finished trucks are tailored to specific customer orders. If there are no problems the plant can achieve very high levels of throughput – perhaps 200 trucks rolling off the line every day.

However, sometimes the line has to stop and the machinery is idle. Of course the machinery is designed for heavy use,

but there will always be some wear and tear. A simple mechanical fault may be easy to fix, but if a key piece of equipment is out of order, then it's a very serious problem. Delays are very expensive, particularly when there is a full order book and the plant is working at maximum capacity. The system relies on regular maintenance so that downtime is reduced.

# Exercises

**13.1 Find a word in the text opposite that matches each definition below. The words appear in order.**

1 large factory where an industrial process happens

_____

2 people who put together or repair machines or equipment

_____

3 *(informal)* a suffix (= letters at the end of a word) used with many nouns and adjectives to mean 'speaking of' or 'referring to' _____

4 period of work time in a place where some people work during the day and some work at night

_____

5 differences between things that should be the same

_____

6 a building used for a particular purpose

_____

7 made specially for someone's particular need

_____

8 the amount of work that is done in a particular period of time _____

9 *(phrasal verb)* moving steadily off _____

10 not being used (machines or factories) _____

11 *(three words)* damage which happens when something is used a lot _____

12 the period of time when a machine isn't working

_____

**13.2 Study the language box below. It shows language for describing objects in a factory. Check any unknown words in a dictionary.**

| Measurements |
| --- |
| *Its length / width / height / depth / thickness is 30 cm.* |
| *It's 30 cm long / wide / high / deep / thick.* |
| *It's 2 m long by 1.5 m wide by 1.2 m high.* |
| *The pipe is 75 cm in diameter.* |
| *The area of the cross-section is 4 square metres.* |
| *The volume (capacity) is 8 cubic metres.* |
| *It weighs 20 kg – rounded up to the nearest kilogram.* |
| *Its weight is 20 kg.* |

| Shapes |
| --- |
| *It's flat, curved, square, circular (round), rectangular, cylindrical, L-shaped, shaped like the letter L.* |

**Cover the language box above with a piece of paper. Now look at the diagram at the top of the next column and fill in the missing letters in the dialogue below.**

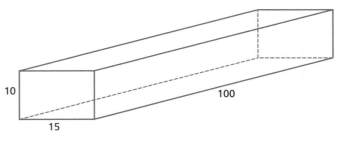

A: How big is the steel bar?
B: It's 100 centimetres ¹l _ _ by 15 centimetres ²w _ _ by 10 centimetres ³h _ _ _ .
A: I'm sorry, the noise in the factory is very loud! Did you say that the ⁴l _ _ _ _ is 100 centimetres?
B: Yes, and the ⁵w _ _ _ _ is 15 and the ⁶h _ _ _ _ _ is 10.
A: OK, that means that the area of the ⁷cr _ _ _-sec _ _ _ _ is 150 ⁸s _ _ _ e centimetres.
B: That's right.
A: And how heavy is it?
B: It ⁹w _ _ _ s 82 kg, ¹⁰r _ _ _ _ed up to the nearest kilogram.

**13.3 Study the language box below. It shows language for describing problems and adjustments in a factory. Check any unknown words in a dictionary.**

| Problems |
| --- |
| *The gears have seized up.* |
| *A bolt has worked loose.* |
| *A blade has snapped off.* |
| *The screws have come loose.* |
| *The seal has burst.* |
| *The lever has jammed.* |
| *A valve is faulty.* |
| *The parts have run out.* |

| Adjustments |
| --- |
| *We need to dismantle the unit.* |
| *Can we lengthen / shorten / widen / tighten / loosen it?* |
| *Can we speed it up? Can we slow it down?* |
| *It's working OK, but now we need to reset the machines.* |

**Now match these verbs with the definitions below:** *burst, be jammed, run out, seize up, snap off, work loose.*

1 not have any more left _____
2 break off with a short loud noise _____
3 break open suddenly _____
4 become not firmly fixed _____
5 no longer work because something is stopping the parts from moving _____
6 suddenly stop working _____

See page 147 for some discussion topics.

## Procurement or purchasing?

The word 'procurement' means 'finding and purchasing supplies or equipment, especially things that are difficult to get'. The word 'purchasing' inside that definition is a formal word for 'buying'. The job title 'purchasing manager' is still used, although these days this person might be called a 'supply chain manager' and have broader responsibilities for sourcing, logistics, etc.

## Procurement

Procurement is a crucial function in business – it's probably the area where cost savings can be made most easily. It involves:

1 Finding suppliers: you may make direct contact with potential suppliers, or you may use public advertising in the form of a Request for Information (RFI), a Request for Quotation (RFQ), or a Request for Proposal (RFP).

2 Background research: once a number of possible suppliers have been found, you need to discover more information about their product quality and also their track record for installation, maintenance and warranties. You may examine product samples and perhaps carry out some trials.

3 Negotiation: you negotiate price, availability, customization possibilities, delivery schedules, etc. A contract is drawn up.

4 Fulfilment: the supplier prepares, ships and delivers the product. Any installation and training is carried out.

We often think of procurement in a manufacturing context, involving all the items that go to make up the finished product (ie raw materials, components and parts). But it happens in every business, and includes the purchase of a wide variety of goods and services – from low value items like office supplies to complex and costly items like consulting services.

Procurement is the area of business most open to corruption: either a backhander from a supplier to a manager as a thank-you for being chosen, or collusion between the two to falsify prices, quality levels, etc. The EU has a very strict system of competitive tendering (= bidding) to avoid these problems, and many companies also operate a three-way check of paperwork. This involves all invoices and deliveries being verified by a purchasing manager, the accounts payable department and the plant manager.

## Global sourcing

The related term 'sourcing' means 'finding and evaluating suppliers'. 'Outsourcing' is subcontracting work to external companies. If these external companies are in another country, then it's 'global sourcing' (or 'offshoring').

Global sourcing is controversial because of its impact on jobs – a large number of production and back-office jobs are lost onshore. However, if the company becomes more successful as a result of its lower costs, then new jobs (eg in sales, marketing, consulting, project management) can be created onshore. And certain jobs are nearly always better done by onshore staff – those requiring creativity and flexible thinking. Offshore counterparts tend to rigorously follow instructions.

Two recent trends in global sourcing have been:

1 The movement offshore of IT-driven service sectors like banking, telecommunications and media (ie not just manufacturing).

2 Nearshoring rather than offshoring, for reasons of political pressure, high fuel costs, logistics and management control.

## Global sourcing

|  Benefits |  Drawbacks |
|---|---|
| Big reduction in labour costs | Complexity of communications between people of different cultures dispersed around the world |
| Superior service levels (eg 24-hour support) | |
| Ability to undertake smaller (previously unprofitable) pieces of work | Extra transportation costs (oil prices affect shipping costs) |
| Improved access to skills | Extra costs (eg travel and living expenses) for offshore workers visiting the onshore offices |
| Synergy from working with a partner (eg a transformation of business processes arising from new ideas and new ways of working) | Issues of security of data and privacy when other companies get involved |

# Exercises

**14.1 Find a word in the text opposite that matches each definition below. The words appear in order.**

1 a written statement of exactly how much money something will cost _____

2 *(two words)* an organization's successes and failures over time _____

3 extended periods of testing _____

4 supplying the things that have been ordered _____

5 money that you pay illegally and secretly to get something done; bribe _____

6 secret activities of people who work together to do something dishonest _____

7 *(formal)* process of inviting suppliers to bid for a contract _____

8 documents for goods or work done _____

9 the internal operations of an organization that are not accessible or visible to the general public _____

**Now do the same for the words in 'Global sourcing' opposite.**

10 start to do a piece of work _____

11 extra effects when people or businesses combine and work together _____

12 disadvantages _____

**14.2 Complete the sentences with the most appropriate word from the box.**

| *estimate*   *proposal*   *quotation/quote*   *tender* |
| --- |

1 If you tell someone how much a job will cost, and you limit yourself to that amount, then you give them a / an _____

2 If you tell someone how much a job will cost, but you reserve the right to change the amount (eg if circumstances change or the work takes longer than expected), then you give them a / an _____

3 If you produce a formal plan for a more complex project, telling the customer how you will carry it out and how much it will cost, then you make a / an _____

4 If you do the same as in #3, but in response to a public invitation to bid for the job, and in competition with other similar companies, then you put in a / an _____

**14.3 Complete the simplified explanation below with these words: *sourcing, procurement, purchasing.***

_____ = _____ + _____

**14.4 Complete the words by adding a preposition at the beginning (as a prefix).**

In a business context, we can use the word $^1$_ _ _shore to mean 'in / from <u>another</u> country', the word $^2$_ _shore to mean 'in / from <u>your own</u> country', and the word $^3$_ _ _ _shore to refer to a country that is <u>geographically close</u> to your own, or to a region of your own country.

**14.5 Study the words in lists A–E. Check any unknown words in a dictionary. Then answer the questions below.**

| A to | give (somebody), ask for, get, prepare, provide (somebody with), submit, accept | a quotation |
| --- | --- | --- |
| B to | draw up, make, accept, consider, put forward, outline, reject, submit | a proposal |
| C to | invite, bid for, put something out to, announce, submit, put in, award, win | (a) tender |
| D a / an | key, external, large, foreign, leading, major, outside, overseas, principal, offshore | supplier |
| E a / an | lengthy, unsuccessful, protracted, fruitless, prolonged, unproductive | negotiation |

1 Divide the words in list A, based on whether the supplier or customer does it.
   1st group: _____
   2nd group: _____

2 Divide the words in list B, based on whether the supplier or customer does it.
   1st group: _____
   2nd group: _____

3 Divide the words in list C, based on whether the supplier or customer does it.
   1st group: _____
   2nd group: _____

4 Divide the words in list D, based on the meaning.
   1st group: _____
   2nd group: _____

5 Divide the words in list E, based on the meaning.
   1st group: _____
   2nd group: _____

See page 147 for some discussion topics.

## What is the supply chain?

The supply chain is the flow of parts and raw materials from their point of origin to the factory gates, then through the factory as work-in-process, and finally out of the factory as finished goods to be delivered to the final customer.

A modern manufacturing operation might have hundreds of suppliers providing different parts and components, and each of these suppliers will in turn have their own suppliers providing simpler parts, raw materials, etc. This is the upstream end of the supply chain. Similarly, the downstream end of the chain might consist of distributors, multiple customers, etc, and will involve batches of goods being shipped at different times to different places.

## Supply chain management

During the whole process, from beginning to end, inventory (ie parts and goods) needs to be stored in warehouses and distribution centres and then transported as needed. All of this involves a huge amount of computerized information about the location of inventory, its expected arrival time at the next point, etc. This information has to be shared across many different companies and IT networks: suppliers, customers, third party logistics providers and the manufacturer itself. The management of this information is critical to the success of the business.

So, supply chain management (SCM) makes sure that the right items are in the right place at the right time and in the right quantities. There are of course wider strategic issues:

● How many suppliers should there be? And where?
● Where should the production facilities, distribution centres and warehouses be located?
● What distribution channels should be used?
● Which logistics companies should be used, both upstream and downstream?
● How can IT be used to integrate all the processes, make them more efficient, flag up potential bottlenecks, give clear signals of demand downstream, etc?
● How is cash flow and payment to all the parties involved in the supply chain going to be managed?

The aim of SCM is to collaborate with all the supply chain partners to improve the visibility and velocity of inventory.

## Logistics

The word 'logistics' refers to the practical issues surrounding transportation, warehousing and inventory management. Where there is an external focus it's more or less a synonym for SCM, but it can also have an internal focus, getting materials from site A to site B inside a company at different stages of the business process. The term 'logistics' is also used in smaller companies where 'supply chain management' seems too grand.

## *The complexity of logistics*

✳ It involves both inbound and outbound goods.

✳ It includes reverse logistics (ie, when goods are returned to the manufacturer, either because of customer returns, or overstocked inventory at the retailers, or outdated merchandise that can no longer sell).

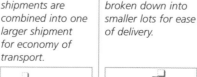

✳ It involves unloading items from one means of transport and loading onto another. This can be at a distribution centre or a warehouse. There are three possibilities:

| Hub and spoke | Consolidation | Deconsolidation |
|---|---|---|
| *Materials are brought in to one central location and then sorted for delivery to a variety of destinations.* | *A variety of smaller shipments are combined into one larger shipment for economy of transport.* | *Large shipments are broken down into smaller lots for ease of delivery.* |
|  |  | 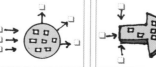 |

✳ It involves materials handling inside the factory: goods are placed on pallets and moved around on fork-lift trucks.

✳ It involves inventory management at every stage using IT. This includes the ability to track items in transit.

✳ It involves co-ordination with related business functions such as purchasing and plant management.

✳ It involves a choice of means of transport: air (using special cargo airlines); sea (with containers stacked up on top of each other); road (vans, or trucks with trailers); rail (using wagons / freight cars).

✳ It involves a decision whether or not to use a third-party logistics provider (3PL). These companies provide integrated pick-and-pack, warehousing and distribution. They can also act as forwarding agents to handle shipping arrangements.

# Exercises

**15.1 Find a word in the text opposite that matches each definition below. The words appear in order.**

1 at an earlier stage in a process _____

2 at a later stage in a process _____

3 groups of things that are made (or dealt with) together _____

4 large buildings for storing goods _____

5 *(two words)* buildings used for the storage of goods which will later be shipped to retail outlets _____

6 *(four words)* external firms that provide specialist services such as transportation and warehousing _____

7 *(phrasal verb)* draw attention to something _____

8 delays in one stage of a process that make the whole process take longer _____

**Now do the same for the words in 'The complexity of logistics' opposite.**

9 coming towards or arriving at (eg a factory or airport) _____

10 *(formal)* goods for sale _____

11 taking goods off a vehicle _____

12 *(three words)* the design of the inner part of a wheel, with a central part and lines coming out of it _____

13 flat wooden structures used for moving or storing heavy goods _____

14 *(two words)* vehicles with special equipment at the front for lifting and moving heavy objects _____

15 follow the progress of _____

16 *(phrasal verb)* arranged into a neat pile _____

17 back sections of trucks that can be separated, and are used for carrying heavy objects _____

18 process of starting with a large quantity of goods, sorting them according to different destinations, and then re-packaging them with new shipping labels _____

**15.2 Read the definitions and complete the examples with one of these words: *cargo, freight*.**

1 goods carried by ship or aircraft [+ *of*]
   Example: *a ship carrying a* _____ *of oil*

2 goods carried by ship, train or aircraft; the system of moving these goods
   Example: _____ *services*

**15.3 Make phrases by matching an item from each column.**

1 supply            provider
2 finished          customer
3 final             chain
4 logistics         agent
5 distribution      goods
6 forwarding        channel

**15.4 Complete the text about logistics using the words in the box.**

| balancing ensuring forecasting handling |
| linking negotiating selecting warehousing |

'Logistics' is a term that is used in many different ways. Using a broad definition it can include all of the following:

**Customer service**
1 _____ the right product is at the right place at the right time.

**Demand** 2 _____ **and planning**
Determining the quantity of goods that need to be ordered in the future.

**Inventory management and materials** 3 _____
Keeping the supply chain flowing, with no bottlenecks, by 4 _____ the quantity of items at different locations and different stages in the process.

**Communication technology**
5 _____ the organization to its suppliers with IT, for example to provide information about demand patterns to facilitate Just-In-Time delivery.

**Transportation**
6 _____ the best means of transportation (ie air, rail, ship, truck).

**Purchasing**
7 _____ with suppliers about price, availability, quality, etc.
8 _____
Locating and designing facilities that allow efficient storage and distribution.

All the above activities must be coordinated properly. Inevitably there will be trade-offs – less of one thing and more of something else – in order to achieve the best outcome overall.

**See page 147 for some discussion topics.**

*"I hope you kept the box it came in."*

B. Smaller

## The Toyota Production System (TPS)

TPS is the basis of modern manufacturing. It was developed at Toyota at the end of the 70s and during the 80s, but is now used right across industry. TPS focuses on two things: adding value and eliminating waste. Value is defined as any item or feature for which a customer is willing to pay. Anything else is waste and has to be removed. TPS identifies seven categories of waste:

1 Overproduction: producing too much, or too soon, or too quickly. Overproduction is minimized by using a 'pull' system; this means that work isn't performed unless the part is required downstream – so in the end products are made only as a direct result of customer activity.

2 Materials handling: inside and outside the plant.

3 Movement: performing tasks manually that could be automated.

4 Waiting: idle time between work stations along the production line.

5 Over processing: doing more than the customer required or is willing to pay for.

6 Inventory: exceeding one-piece flow. One-piece flow (also known as 'continuous flow') is when items are processed one at a time and then moved directly to the next process.

7 Defects: rework, repair, or waste in its simplest form. Defects are rigorously analyzed to make sure that they don't happen again (ie 'error-proofing' the system).

## Just-In-Time (JIT)

JIT is a closely related concept. Here, parts and components are delivered only as they're needed: at the right time, in the right amounts and in the right sequence. Delivery to the factory gate should be JIT, as should delivery to individual work stations on the assembly line. The aims of JIT are: minimizing inventory, producing items at a rate set by the customer, eliminating any unnecessary lead time, and generally optimizing the flow of materials from suppliers through production and up to the point of sale of the finished product.

All of these ideas are recycled in the modern concept of 'lean production' (lean = with little fat). A lean manufacturer is constantly trying to reduce manpower, materials, money, machines, time, space, mistakes and effort.

## Kaizen

Behind all the techniques described above lies the idea of 'kaizen'. This is Japanese for 'continuous improvement' – making changes in small, incremental steps. This is seen as being done through teamwork, personal discipline and involving workers directly in the process of improving quality. A practical implementation of kaizen is 'the five S' approach to workplace organization. See below. This is derived from five Japanese words beginning with 'S', and English translations have tried to find five 'S' words.

### The five Ss

**S1: Sort**
Review everything in the work area, separating what is needed from what is not. Remove anything unnecessary.

**S2: Set In Order**
Arrange everything in a neat, tidy and easy-to-use manner.

**S3: Shine**
Once the work area has been sorted and set in order, clean it up so that everything shines! Clean the area itself, as well as equipment and tools.

**S4: Standardize**
Create clear, simple and visual standards for S1–S3.
**Example 1:** shadows on work surfaces and inside storage boxes show which tools should be where.
**Example 2:** a re-order card (called a 'kanban') is attached to an item and placed somewhere after the item is used. This gives a visual signal when a new item is needed.

**S5: Sustain**
Continue to operate and improve S1–S4.

**Principle:** a place for everything, and everything in its place

**Key ideas:** discipline, simplicity, pride, standardization and repeatability

# Exercises

**16.1 Find a word in the text opposite that matches each definition below. The words appear in order.**

1 *(two words)* time when a machine isn't working or being used _____

2 the continuous movement of something _____

3 faults in the way something is made _____

4 making something again _____

5 trying to avoid (or protect against) future mistakes _____

6 taken to a place (eg house, office, factory) and given to someone _____

7 *(two words)* time that must be allowed for completion of an operation or process _____

8 all the workers that are needed to do a particular kind of job _____

9 increasing gradually _____

**Now do the same for the words in 'The five Ss' opposite.**

10 have a bright, attractive appearance; produce (or reflect) light _____

11 things that you hold in your hand and use to do a particular job _____

12 *(two words)* containers where things are kept until they're needed _____

**16.2 Make phrases by matching an item from each column.**

1 add — waste (from a process)
2 be willing — a task (manually)
3 deliver — value (to a product)
4 eliminate — parts (to the factory gate)
5 make sure — to pay for something
6 perform — something doesn't happen again

7 attach — inventory (using JIT)
8 clean up — the flow of materials (using JIT)
9 error-proof — materials (inside a plant)
10 handle — the equipment so that it shines
11 minimize — a system (by rigorous analysis)
12 optimize — a kanban card to an item

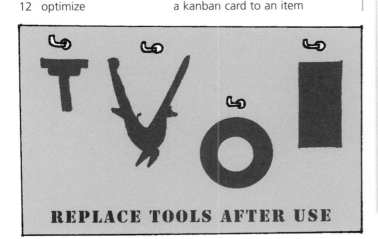

**REPLACE TOOLS AFTER USE**

**16.3 Fill in the gaps with a different form of the word in brackets. The new form may be a noun (singular or plural), verb or adjective.**

1 TPS has had a big impact on ____*industrial*____ (industry) processes in many sectors of the _____ (economic). Generally, it has made manufacturing much more _____ (produce).

2 It is important to make a detailed _____ (analyze) of which items and features add value, and which don't. There is no point making _____ (improve) if the customer isn't willing to pay for them.

3 In a badly run factory, many processes are _____ (waste) and levels of inventory are _____ (exceed).

4 With JIT, _____ (deliver) to the factory gate or the _____ (assemble) line is made only when it's needed.

**16.4 Complete the text about the 'Theory of constraints' with the words in the box.**

> bottleneck   branch   customized   shape   straight
> sub-assemblies   synchronization

The 'Theory of constraints' (TOC) is another approach to maintaining flow in production. A 'constraint' is a
[1] _____ in a system – something that limits further progress. TOC has identified four possible plant layouts, where the production lines inside the plant are arranged in the [2] _____ of different letters of the alphabet (I, A, V and T).

An I-plant is the simplest. Here, the work is done in a
[3] _____ line. The constraint is simply the slowest operation.

Next is an A-plant. Many [4] _____ converge for a final assembly. Here, the problem is
[5] _____ , with converging lines arriving at the final point.

With a V-plant, one raw material is made into many final products. Here the problems occur immediately after the divergence point – any operation along one
[6] _____ of the V can rob (= steal) material meant for the other branch.

Finally, we have a T-plant. A number of basic units are produced on a line and then [7] _____ at the end. There is a wide variety of final products. This type of plant combines the problems of most of the others!

**See page 147 for some discussion topics.**

## What is quality?

The word 'quality' has an everyday meaning that has to do with features, reliability, performance, durability, aesthetics, value for money and conformance to requirements. It has more specific meanings, particularly those in the next few sections.

## Quality control and quality assurance

Quality control is about detecting defects after they happen. It involves random sampling, spot checks, inspection and testing.

Quality assurance is about prevention rather than detection. If a failure happens, then it's isolated, the causes are analyzed, and there is a redesign of the process or of the parts to make sure it doesn't happen again. The aim is zero defects, to get things right first time.

## Quality management

Total quality management (TQM) is a philosophy that was very popular in the 1980s and 90s. It aims to put an awareness of quality at the heart of all organizational processes (eg customer service) and not just production. It puts an emphasis on a continual increase in customer satisfaction combined with lowering costs by eliminating waste. It is similar in many ways to the ideas discussed in units 15–16: SCM, Toyota Production System, Lean Manufacturing, kaizen, etc.

## European Foundation for Quality Management

This organization has taken the ideas of quality management and is trying to apply them to all organizations, including those in the service sector and public sector. It has a framework for assessing and improving organizations that is based on eight concepts of excellence: results orientation, customer focus, leadership and constancy of purpose (ie being faithful to aims and objectives), management by processes and facts, people development and involvement, continuous improvement and innovation, partnership development, and corporate social responsibility.

## A variety of approaches

As can be seen, quality is a topic that occurs under the umbrella of many different philosophies. This is good news for the army of consultants called in to explain and implement the latest management fad. But certain things are common to all the approaches: measuring and systematizing processes; reducing variation, defects and cycle times; and employee involvement and teamwork.

The differences between the approaches (and others not mentioned above, like Six Sigma) are related to which tools, checklists, measurements and training they use.

### QUALITY COSTS

Quality isn't free – it comes with a cost. But if there are no quality procedures, then the cost is much higher: continuing problems with the product, a loss of confidence in the brand, and fewer sales as a result. Here are just some of the ways that companies have to spend money and time to ensure quality:

#### Prevention costs (quality assurance)

Engineers have to spend time with marketers during the development of new products to facilitate design-for-manufacture. There have to be supplier capability surveys to make sure that suppliers can achieve the quality levels that they claim. There have to be regular meetings, education and training about quality improvement.

#### Evaluation costs (quality control)

The company has to inspect and test incoming material, material that is being processed, and the finished product. There is also the cost of buying and servicing any equipment used for measuring and testing.

#### Failure costs before delivery

There may be scrap, rework, re-inspection, re-testing, etc. If these continue at a high level, then perhaps there will be a fundamental review of suppliers and materials.

#### Failure costs after delivery

Time is needed to process customer complaints, to process customer returns, to deal with warranty claims and to handle product recalls.

# Exercises

**17.1 Find a word in the text opposite that matches each definition below. The words appear in order.**

1 things that a customer is particularly interested in; selling points _____

2 lasting a long time _____

3 *(three words)* being similar to what customers expect

_____

4 taking occasional small quantities for testing

_____

5 *(two words)* examining a process suddenly, without warning _____

6 materials that are left after a process and have no use

_____

7 set of ideas or rules on which decisions are based

_____

8 *(two words)* an emphasis on achievements, especially sales and profits _____

9 something that is popular or fashionable for a short time only _____

10 *(two words)* how long various activities take to complete (eg one production run) _____

**Now do the same for the words in 'Quality costs' opposite.**

11 looking at how easy it is to make a new product, not just the features _____

12 *(three words)* asking questions to find out if your suppliers are able to meet quality standards

_____

13 materials or small parts that are no longer useful

_____

14 *(two words)* the return of products, for example because they're faulty or dangerous _____

**17.2 Fill in the missing letters. Most of the answers are not in the text.**

1 If quality is really good, then it's outst_ _ _ing quality.

2 If quality is usually good, but not always, then it's vari_ _ _e quality.

3 If quality isn't as good as other similar products, then it's inf_ _ _ _r quality.

4 If quality is bad, then instead of saying 'bad' we often say p_ _r quality.

5 If you make certain that something has quality, then you ens_ _e the quality.

6 If you improve the quality of a product, then you enh_ _ce the quality.

7 If you state the quality that you want in an exact and detailed way, then you spe_ _fy the quality.

8 If you regularly watch or check the quality of something to find out what is happening, then you mon_ _or the quality.

**17.3 Make phrases by matching an item from each column.**

1 random       checks
2 spot         first time
3 zero         orientation
4 right        sampling
5 results     defects

6 continuous    time
7 employee      improvement
8 cycle         recalls
9 warranty      involvement
10 product       claims

**17.4 Complete each definition below with a pair of words (and phrases) in the box. Each term in bold is commonly used when discussing quality.**

> compliance / certified    parameter / vary from the norm
> methodology / eliminating defects    ~~performance / best in class~~
> mark / spoils the appearance    warranty claims / improve quality
> measures / throughout business    predict / fewer mistakes

1 **Benchmarking** is measuring your __*performance*__ against other companies that are '__*best in class*__', and then using the information to improve.

2 **Tolerance** is the amount by which a _____ (eg size) can _____ before the piece becomes a defect.

3 **ISO 9000** is a set of international standards of quality. Companies can be audited for _____ with one of the standards, and then publicly state that they're 'ISO 9000-_____'.

4 **Nonconformance** is when a requirement has not been met. It does not need to be a serious defect, it could be a simple _____ on the surface that _____ .

5 **Six sigma** is the name of a well-known quality _____ . It takes a highly disciplined approach to _____ in manufacturing. The term 'six sigma' originally comes from statistics.

6 **Key performance indicators (KPIs)** are statistical _____ of how well an organization is doing in particular areas. The term is particularly common in production and operations, but is used _____ .

7 **Leading indicators** are those that _____ a future outcome. For example, levels of staff satisfaction are often a leading indicator of quality. A more motivated workforce will make _____ .

8 **Lagging indicators** are those that show a result. For example, _____ are a lagging indicator of quality. Fewer claims mean that earlier actions to _____ are now working. (A 'lag' is a delay between two events).

**See page 148 for some discussion topics.**

## What sales thinks about marketing!

Sales consultants will quickly tell you how their job is different to marketing. They're the ones who have direct contact with the customers, they're the ones who really know what is going on in the market, and of course they're the ones who live with the insecurity of sales targets and commissions. The marketing guys just sit in their offices on fixed salaries, dreaming up fancy promotions, or thinking of new products that later research will tell them no-one wants. If only the marketing guys spoke to the sales guys more often, the business would do so much better.

## What qualities does a salesperson need?

A salesperson needs to be:

- Knowledgeable (of the customer and their needs, of the products being sold, and of the industry and technical area).
- Visibly well prepared, organized and well-presented to inspire confidence in the other person.
- Reliable (eg they phone back when they say they will).
- Flexible (eg they're able to respond to changing customer needs and offer tailor-made solutions).

It is an old-fashioned cliché to think of a modern sales consultant as behaving like someone who sells second-hand cars. These days an aggressive hard sell very rarely works. Customers want to be helped to make their own decisions, not to be pushed before they're ready. The box below gives some ideas for modern sales techniques.

There are a variety of methods to close the deal: a direct request, a command, a reference to an immediate gain, fear, presenting alternatives, a summary, and finally simply an assumption that the customer is going to buy (ie behaving as if it's true even though the customer hasn't actually said yes).

 ## Sales techniques

### General points

Try to identify the different roles inside a company. Who is the decision maker? Whose advice will they listen to? Who will actually be using the product?

Take time to socialize and build rapport in the first few moments. In particular, show interest in the customer.

### Discovering customer needs

Have 'big ears and a small mouth'. Ask lots of questions. Listen actively: focus your attention on the other person and take notes. Knowledge of customer needs is a major competitive advantage – just as important as the product features or the price.

Check needs by restating them.

Refer to the information you have collected throughout the rest of the meeting.

### Presenting the best case

Build a case slowly, based on the individual customer's needs, rather than working from a script.

Be clear and precise, judge the level of detail required, and avoid jargon.

Emphasize benefits (ie what a product does – how it will make life better for the customer) and not just features (ie what it is).

Use the cumulative effect of a number of benefits.

Sell the price by demonstrating value for money. (Being cheap is rarely a virtue.)

Differentiate from the competition, without openly knocking them.

Show how your case is tailored.

Be credible: show confidence, display your knowledge, and give attention to detail.

Make your case believable by referring to some form of proof: a demonstration of the product, a mention of other satisfied customers, giving the results of tests and research, using the power of numbers (eg 100,000 sold; 20 years in the market).

Refer to an ongoing relationship with the customer.

### Handling objections

View objections as an opportunity – they're a sign of interest and are inevitable. First, acknowledge the point. Then, either remove the objection, or minimize its significance, or turn it into a positive.

### Closing

Look out for buying signals that show the customer is nearly ready to make a decision:

★ The customer makes a reference to the product in use, perhaps with an assumption in their way of talking that they're the users.

★ The customer asks about what results they can hope to achieve after they have been using the product for some time.

★ The customer asks after-sales questions, ie, questions about installation.

# Exercises

**18.1 Find a word in the text opposite that matches each definition below. The words appear in order.**

1 expensive and complicated _____

2 customized; personalized _____

**Now do the same for the words in 'Sales techniques' opposite.**

3 a relationship in which people like, understand and respect each other _____

4 *(two words)* something that helps your company do better than another _____

5 written words, like the ones that actors use

_____

6 words used by people in the same profession that are difficult for other people to understand _____

7 criticizing _____

8 accept that something exists _____

**18.2 Match the techniques 1–8 to the sales consultant's comments a–h.**

1 Responding to the customer's needs [a]

2 Selling the price by showing how it can be divided into smaller parts [ ]

3 Showing how a feature has more than one benefit [ ]

4 Selling the price by showing how money can be saved [ ]

5 Selling the price by offering something extra [ ]

6 Saying something when you're unable to give a tailor-made solution [ ]

7 Acknowledging an objection [ ]

8 Checking understanding [ ]

a 'Because you said that timing was important, let me take that point next.' / 'You said earlier this had to be cost-effective, so …'

b 'Is that clear?' / 'Would it be useful to give you more detail?'

c 'This has multiple advantages.' / 'This will also improve your existing …'

d 'You know it would cost a lot of money to do it that way, and you would lose the exceptional value for money that you're getting here.'

e 'You get this plus this.'

f 'You can spread the costs over …' / 'The use can be shared by different departments.'

g 'It will help you to reduce costs.' / 'This will eliminate the need for …'

h 'Yes, that's certainly something we need to review.' / 'Yes, that's a fair point. Let me give you some background to explain why we do it that way.'

**18.3 Techniques 1–7 are all ways of closing a deal. Match the techniques with the sales consultant's comments a–g.**

1 Direct request [ ]

2 Command [c]

3 Immediate gain [ ]

4 Fear [ ]

5 Alternatives [ ]

6 Summary [ ]

7 Assumption [ ]

a 'If you give me the go-ahead now, then I can have it up and running within a week.' / 'We have a special offer this month.'

b 'We have them in stock for immediate delivery, but you know they're selling very fast.' / 'If you can't give me the go-ahead today, the delivery time you need is going to be difficult.'

c 'Right, let's get this organized.' / 'Let me have written confirmation as soon as you can and I'll start the ball rolling.'

d 'Shall we go ahead?' / 'How much would you like?' / 'When shall we start?'

e 'Are you more interested in the regular model or the executive model?' / 'Do you want to schedule this for this month or next month?'

f 'Yes, I can see that this is going to work really well for you.' / 'OK, if you have no more questions, I'll just get the paperwork from my bag.'

g 'So, this solution gives you something that works well with your existing equipment, is easy to install, and gives you significant cost savings. Can we go ahead?'

**18.4 Underline the correct (or most likely) words in italics.**

1 So, it looks like this solution works well for you. Shall we *go in front* / *go ahead*?

2 We can have it *up and running* / *up and going* within a week.

3 I don't want to *knock* / *critic* the competition, but this is a much better product.

4 This is the *actual* / *latest* model.

5 You're lucky – it's *for sale* / *on sale* this month. We're running a special promotion.

6 Yes, the one in the shop window is *for sale* / *on sale* – you can buy it.

7 In the week before Christmas we usually see very high sales *volumes* / *quantities*.

8 North America *counts for* / *accounts for* 40% of our worldwide sales.

**See page 148 for some discussion topics.**

The phrase 'customer service' can refer to pre-sales (eg enquiries, quotations), sales (unit 18) and post-sales (eg order processing, returns, complaints, warranty claims). The phrase 'customer support' is usually limited just to post-sales.

Customer service is a key business function that is often overlooked. In an age when many competing goods and services are very similar, the quality of customer service can make a big difference. Good customer service can lead to repeat business, whereas unsatisfied customers tell all their friends. In the box opposite you will find some tips for good customer service.

## Customer relationship management (CRM)

Customer service often makes use of CRM software. This allows the company to provide a unified face to the customer, regardless of their channel of communication – telephone, email, or face-to-face. The customer may have an initial enquiry, an order, an amendment to an order, a confirmation of an order, a cancellation of an order, an enquiry about delivery details, an after-sales enquiry about using the product, or a complaint. With a good CRM system it makes no difference – in every case the details will get logged so that any member of staff can immediately see a record of the case. Having this information instantly available on-screen is a huge advantage. While talking to a customer you know which products they have bought before, to what value, how they paid, etc. You can also see a record of which questions they have asked, whether they have ever made a complaint, and if so how it was resolved.

## Active listening

A key skill for customer service staff is active listening. This means:
- Use the other person's name.
- Let the customer explain the issue and pay full attention while they're speaking. Don't interrupt, except for a) clarification questions and b) occasional brief summaries. These summaries show you're listening and are on common ground.
- Make written notes of key points.
- If there is a problem, resist the urge to argue, defend or excuse. Apologize sincerely and acknowledge any inconvenience caused.
- If the conversation is face-to-face, maintain good eye contact and an open body posture (ie leaning slightly towards the other person).

# Customer service tips

## Little things that make a BIG difference

★ If customers have to wait, offer a drink, magazines and a comfortable chair.

★ Be friendly: use names, remember preferences, send a birthday card.

★ Provide something free: coffee, biscuits, pens, samples.

★ After an expensive purchase, follow up with a quick call just to check they're happy.

★ Provide a life-time money-back guarantee. Almost no-one actually returns products.

★ Remember to provide an FAQ section on your website and sales literature.

★ Don't give customers the run-around: if you can't personally deal with something, then stay with the customer while you hand them over gracefully to a colleague.

★ Remember that the thing that makes customers most annoyed is when they're passed from person to person on the phone. Take responsibility, and if you can't deal with it, then say you'll call them back. (You may need to refer it upwards to your supervisor for a decision first.)

★ Make specific commitments: not, 'We'll get back to you in a couple of days,' but 'We'll get back to you by 5pm tomorrow.'

## Don't forget your existing customers

★ Offer them a bulk purchase discount in the future.

★ Get them to upgrade their product.

★ Every time you ship a product, include a flyer, catalogue, special offer, etc inside.

★ Have periodic promotions for 'preferred customers'.

★ Invite customers to an event: it could be a product demonstration or seminar, or it could be a social event in an art gallery / historic building / interesting location.

★ Have frequent-buyer programs, and mail frequent buyers with a periodic newsletter.

★ Ask your customers how you can improve. Use customer satisfaction surveys (and provide an incentive for them to be returned).

# Exercises

**19.1 Find a word in the text opposite that matches each definition below. The words appear in order.**

1 entered as an official record _____

**Now do the same for the words in 'Customer service tips' opposite.**

2 *(phrasal verb)* ask your boss to deal with an issue

_____

3 promises to do something _____

4 *(two words)* when you buy something in large amounts

_____

5 advertisement or announcement printed on paper; small leaflet _____

**19.2 Make phrases by matching an item from each column.**

| | |
|---|---|
| 1 follow up | a life-time guarantee |
| 2 provide | a purchase with a quick call |
| 3 be passed | any inconvenience caused |
| 4 make | the urge to argue |
| 5 include | specific commitments |
| 6 log | from person to person |
| 7 resist | a flyer inside every package |
| 8 acknowledge | details on a CRM system |

**19.3 Complete the sequence with the words in the box.**

> *a complaint     an initial enquiry     information*
> *an invoice (with the goods)     an order     the order*
> *the payment     the problem     a quotation     the quotation*

**customer**

makes
1 _____

requests
3 _____

makes
5 _____

receives the goods and pays

makes
9 _____

**customer services**

sends
2 _____

gives
4 _____

confirms
6 _____ and processes it

sends
7 _____

processes
8 _____ and sends a receipt

solves
10 _____

**19.4 Make phrases by matching an item from each column.**

| | |
|---|---|
| 1 body | customers |
| 2 channel | ground |
| 3 common | information |
| 4 on-screen | posture |
| 5 preferred | of communication |
| 6 pre-sales | claim |
| 7 bulk purchase | guarantee |
| 8 money-back | enquiry |
| 9 satisfaction | discount |
| 10 warranty | survey |

**19.5 Fill in the gaps.**

1 The words 'guarantee' and 'warranty' have very similar meanings. However a _____ usually has a time period that can be extended and the word is used in both American and British English, whereas a _____ often cannot be extended, is more common in British English, and can be used with a more abstract meaning (like 'a promise').

2 FAQ stands for Fr_____ As_____ Qu_____s.

3 If a customer asks you to do something and you avoid giving them a definite answer, then you 'give them the r_ _-a_ _ _ _d' *(informal)*.

**19.6 Complete the definitions with the words in the box.**

> *expectations     experience     feedback     loyalty     profile*
> *requirements     satisfaction     survey*

1 customer _____ = the feeling that a customer gets when they're happy

2 customer _____ = when a customer always buys from the same company

3 customer _____ = information, advice or criticism, deliberately collected from customers or given informally by them

4 customer _____ = a set of questions you ask to find out customers' opinions

5 customer _____ = what a customer feels and remembers about the service they have received

6 customer _____ = how people think they should be treated

7 customer _____ = an analysis of your customers according to age, lifestyle, etc

8 customer _____ = customer needs

**See page 148 for some discussion topics.**

## What is a market?

The phrase 'the French market' is just another way of saying 'the population of France', but marketing professionals think of a market in a more specific way. The whole population of a country can be broken down into market segments.

In a B2C (business to consumer) company, customers can be divided according to:

- Demographics: age group, gender, ethnicity, income, occupation, social class, marital status.
- Psychographics: personality, attitudes, lifestyle.
- Geographics: national or regional divisions, city-centre or suburban customers.
- Benefits looked for by the customer: price, overall value, specific features, image with peers, ease-of-use, service, etc.
- Current purchasing situation of the customer: brands used now, how and where purchased, how and when used.

For a B2B (business to business) company there may be other factors. For example, a B2B company needs to know the type of customer (eg manufacturer, retailer), the industry group of the customer (eg toy manufacturer or clothing manufacturer), their size (eg sales volume, number of retail outlets), the ownership (ie private or public), etc. B2B customers are less interested in image and more interested in things like ability to meet changing patterns of demand, consistent quality, Just-In-Time delivery, etc. They're also reached in very different ways such as trade shows and by travelling sales reps.

## Who should we target?

Once a company has decided how to segment the market, it can then do any one of the following:
- Target the mass market: the company targets one large market with a single marketing strategy. This was popular in the early days of marketing (eg consumer products in the 50s and 60s), but few companies today view this option as feasible.

- Target multiple segments: here, each segment will have its own marketing strategy. Most large consumer product firms do this – they offer multiple products at different price points with different messages, all within the same product category.
- Target one segment: a niche market. The company targets a small market, often with just one or two very specialized products.
- Target individual customers with tailor-made products: there may be a personal dialogue to establish specialized requirements, or the company may use data about previous purchases (eg Amazon's book recommendations based on what you have previously ordered from their site). The Internet has been the catalyst for this approach.

## What is marketing?

Marketing begins with 'the four Ps': product, place, promotion and price. These combine to form the marketing mix for any one product or service. Elements of 'the four Ps' are shown in the table:

| Product | Place (Distribution) |
|---|---|
| <ul><li>Features and associated benefits</li><li>Branding (ie product identity)</li><li>Packaging (eg there may be a bag inside a box)</li><li>Label (eg printed on the package)</li></ul> | <ul><li>Retailer</li><li>Wholesaler</li><li>B2B distributor</li><li>Agent</li></ul> |
| **Promotion** | **Price** |
| <ul><li>Advertising</li><li>Sales promotions (eg special offers, discounts)</li><li>Public relations</li></ul> | <ul><li>External factors (eg elasticity of demand, customer expectations, competitor's products)</li><li>Internal factors (eg profit required, market share required)</li></ul> |

As well as 'the four Ps', the term 'marketing' also includes marketing strategy. At its simplest, this includes:
- Analyzing the business environment using market research.
- Developing new products and new markets.
- Responding to external forces: the economy, activity of competitors, innovation, cultural change, etc.

'The four Ps' are covered in more detail in the next four units.

# Exercises

**20.1 Find a word in the text opposite that matches each definition below. The words appear in order.**

1 separate parts _____
2 the fact of being male or female _____
3 people of the same age or who belong to the same social group _____
4 (formal) buying _____
5 (three words) the ways that a product is needed in different amounts at different times _____
6 (informal) people who sell products for a company _____
7 try to influence; aim to hit _____
8 possible and likely to succeed _____
9 (two words) particular prices that have been specially chosen (eg €9.90 or €199) _____
10 (two words) small group of potential customers who have similar needs or interests _____
11 something that results in important changes _____

**Now do the same for the words in 'What is marketing?' opposite.**

12 important parts of a product _____
13 piece of paper (or other material) with information on it that is attached to an object (or printed on it) _____
14 (three words) how much sales volume changes when you change the price _____

**20.2 Write each of these words next to its best definition: *advertising, marketing, promotion, publicity*.**

1 all the ways used to encourage demand for a product (the most general word) _____
2 an activity that attracts people's attention to a product (one aspect of #1) _____
3 telling people about a product (eg on the television, in magazines) in order to persuade them to buy it (one aspect of #2) _____
4 any information that makes people notice a product (this may be unplanned, out of the control of the company and not part of its marketing strategy) _____

**20.3 Match each word on the left with five words on the right. Check any unknown words in a dictionary.**

|  |  |
|---|---|
|  | agency |
|  | campaign |
|  | forces |
|  | leader |
| market | mix |
| marketing | price |
|  | sector |
|  | share |
|  | strategy |
|  | tool |

**20.4 Complete each sentence with a word partnership from the previous exercise.**

1 If the government doesn't interfere, then prices are set by _____ .
2 'The four Ps' give the _____ for a particular product.
3 The percentage of the market that you have is your _____
4 Sponsored links on Google (when a customer searches for your product type) is a very effective _____ .

**20.5 Read what a marketer says about the history of a product.**

> 66 We chose to focus our strategy on people in their late teens, and so we launched the product at a series of big rock concerts over the summer. We soon gained market share, and after two years we were the market leader. But after a while consumers wanted something different. Our competitors noticed this before we did, and our sales dropped dramatically. Retailers stopped stocking our brand and we had to stop making the products. We had a big meeting and thought again about our whole strategy. We agreed that we would try one more time. 99

**The phrases below can all be used with 'the market'. Put them into order (1–8) so that they match the order in the story.**

| | |
|---|---|
| ☐ | a be forced out of |
| ☐ | b put a product onto |
| ☐ | c break into |
| ☐ | d reassess |
| 1 | e decide to target |
| ☐ | f re-enter |
| ☐ | g fail to see changes in |
| ☐ | h take over |

**20.6 Divide the phrases in the box into three groups, based on their meanings.**

| *be driven out of*    *open up*    *corner*    *withdraw from* |
|---|
| *enter*    *capture*    *penetrate*    *dominate* |

| break into | take over | be forced out of |
|---|---|---|
| _____ | _____ | _____ |
| _____ | _____ | _____ |
| _____ | _____ | _____ |

See page 148 for some discussion topics.

'Product' is the first of 'the four Ps' of marketing. In marketing terms, a product is a solution for a target market. The word covers goods and services and can also include the warranty, customer support and any complimentary products (eg add-on items such as a case for carrying the product).

## Four key factors

### 1 Features

Features are characteristics of a product that offer benefits to the customer. Take the example of a television:

| Feature | Benefit |
| --- | --- |
| screen size | allows for more distant viewing |
| screen resolution | clear, more realistic picture |
| surround sound | enhanced sensory experience |

The benefits above are called 'functional benefits'. In addition, there are psychological benefits. These address needs such as status within a group, risk reduction, sense of independence and happiness.

### 2 Branding

Branding involves establishing an identity for a product with the goal of distinguishing it from competitors' offerings. This is essential in markets where products are similar and competition is fierce. It's particularly important in helping to position the product: high-end (= upscale / up-market), mid-market, or low-end (= economy / down-market).

The brand itself may be the name of a product, or a family of products, or of the company that makes them. It usually includes a design element such as a logo or a symbol (eg Nike's 'swoosh').

Branding is traditionally associated with B2C, but recently B2B companies (eg Intel) have also started to invest in branding.

### 3 Packaging

Packaging is very important. It protects the product during shipping and handling, it gives visibility to the product (attracting attention on the shelves) and it can add value (by making the product easier to use).

### 4 Labelling

The label is attached to or printed on the package or the product. It can attract attention with graphics or catchy words and provides information to aid a purchase decision (eg size, fabric, washing instructions for clothes). It usually includes a code for use at the checkout.

For many products (eg food, pharmaceuticals) there are legal requirements for the label relating to the listing of ingredients, nutritional information and instructions for use.

## Brands: aims, advantages and strategies

### AIMS

**Stage 1 (brand=benefit):** when the customer sees the brand, they associate it with the benefits they receive.

**Stage 2 (benefit=brand):** when the customer needs a solution to a problem, they automatically think of the brand.

### ADVANTAGES

**Brand loyalty:** customers are less likely to switch to alternative brands in the future; protects company from price wars.

**Brand stretching:** new products can be added under the same 'family' brand name.

**Brand equity:** once the brand has a financial value, it can be sold or licensed.

### STRATEGIES

**Individual (stand-alone) branding:** new products are given new names, with no obvious connection to other brands or even to the company (eg Proctor and Gamble's range).

**Family branding:** new products are placed under the umbrella of an existing brand (most consumer products, eg Gillette).

**Co-branding:** partnership with another firm that has an established brand (eg Visa cards carrying the name of another organization).

**Private or Store branding:** suppliers produce for another company (eg retail stores selling own-brand items made by an outside company).

**Brand licensing:** others are allowed to produce items carrying the brand name (eg a children's movie character licensed to a toy or food manufacturer).

# Exercises

**21.1 Find a word in the text opposite that matches each definition below. The words appear in order.**

1 given free _____

2 improved _____

3 easy to remember _____

**Now do the same for the words in 'Brands: aims, advantages and strategies' opposite.**

4 change from one thing to another _____

**21.2 Complete the definitions with the words in the box.**

> association   awareness   equity   ~~image~~
> leader   loyalty   manager   stretching

1 brand ____image____ = the ideas and beliefs that people have about a brand

2 brand _____ = a person who is in charge of developing and selling a brand

3 brand _____ = the brand that has the largest number of sales in its product category

4 brand _____ = the support that people give to a brand by continuing to buy it rather than changing to other brands

5 brand _____ = the value of the brand on the balance sheet of the company

6 brand _____ = using a successful brand name to sell new types of products

7 brand _____ = what people think of when they see or hear the name of a brand

8 brand _____ = the degree to which people know about a brand

**21.3 Find a 'brand …' phrase from the previous exercise with a similar meaning to:**

1 brand recognition _____

2 brand extension _____

**21.4 Write each word in the box next to the word in italics with the closest meaning.**

> best-selling   economy   exclusive   favourite
> leading   luxury   traditional   upmarket
> upscale   value-for-money   well-known

1 a / an *high-end*, _____ , _____ , _____ , _____ brand

2 a / an *low-end*, _____ , _____ brand

3 a / an *classic*, _____ brand

4 a / an *top*, _____ , _____ , _____ brand

5 a / an *famous*, _____ brand

**21.5 Fill in the missing letters. All the words describe features.**

66 Have you seen this amazing camera? It uses an [1]inn_ _ _ive lens mechanism to get 6x optical zoom. That's amazing! It's [2]fu_ _y auto_ _ _ _c, and has a [3]bu_ _t-in flash. It's also one of the most [4]p_ _table cameras I've ever seen – it's so [5]co_ _ _ct that it easily fits in a shirt pocket. It uses own-brand, [6]rech_ _ _able batteries. It's a really [7]we_ _-m_ _e, [8]st_ _ _-of-the-a_ _ piece of kit. 99

66 I've seen an [9]integr_ _ _d fridge-freezer that I'm thinking about buying. The shelves are [10]adj_ _ _able and it's very [11]e_ _ _ to cl_ _n. It comes with an [12]opt_ _ _al icemaker. It's [13]en_ _ _ _y-eff_ _ _ _nt, so it will be [14]ec_ _ _ _ical to run, and they say the materials can be [15]rec_ _ _ed later, so that makes it very [16]env_ _ _ _ _ _ _ally f_ _ _ _ly. It's made by a [17]rel_ _ _le manufacturer, and it's [18]a_ _ _able in a r_ _ _ _ of colours. 99

66 I want a pair of [19]high-per_ _ _ _ _ce sneakers. They have to be [20]waterp_ _ _f. Also, I do a lot of jogging and I don't want to injure my knees. So, the soles should be really [21]hi_ _-t_ch – you know, [22]sh_ _k-abs_ _bent as well as being [23]h_ _d-w_ _ring. And I don't want just a [24]sta_ _ _ _d pair – my friends would just laugh at me. No, they have to be really [25]styl_ _ _ – in fact it would be good if they were a [26]lim_ _ed edition. 99

66 I'd like to get a cordless phone for my study. I want a really [27]u_ _r-fr_ _ _ _ly one, with a [28]l_ _g-la_ _ing battery. I will probably add more handsets later, so it has to be [29]exp_ _ _able, and it would be good to have a [30]one-t_ _ch speakerphone in the base for when I'm working at my desk. 99

**21.6 Match products 1–4 with their packaging a–d. The underlined vocabulary refers to packaging. Check any unknown words in a dictionary.**

1 some ceramics bought from an open-air market

2 recordable DVDs

3 meat bought from a supermarket

4 a small quantity of paracetamol tablets

a They come in a blister pack, which is itself packaged in a box (= carton) made of paperboard (thinner than cardboard). ☐

b This sits in a cardboard tray, covered by transparent cellophane. It has a label that shows the 'display until' date and the 'use by' date (or 'best before' date). ☐

c Each one comes in a plastic case, but usually you buy several in a shrink-wrapped pack. ☐

d These were wrapped in bubble wrap to protect them, and this was held in place with gaffer tape (a type of duct tape). ☐

**See page 148 for some discussion topics.**

'Place' is the second of 'the four Ps' – customers must be able to obtain the product easily and conveniently. This depends on the distribution channel.

## Distribution channels

There are three broad categories of companies involved in distribution:

1 Resellers (called distributors or dealers in some markets) who purchase products and sell them to others. There are various types of reseller: a retailer (who sells directly to the final consumer), a wholesaler (who buys from a manufacturer and sells to a retailer) and an industrial distributor (in the B2B market).

2 Intermediaries (eg agents and brokers) who don't actually purchase the product. They bring suppliers and buyers together in exchange for a fee.

3 Logistics companies. See unit 15.

Another option is direct distribution, where there are no resellers and the manufacturer sells directly to the end user. Examples here include:

● Direct marketing: the customer places an order by visiting the company's website, or ordering from a catalogue (AmE catalog), or by dialling a toll-free telephone number.

● Direct retail: where a company operates its own retail outlets (eg H&M, Zara, Apple).

● Personal selling: those cases, common in B2B, where the salesperson actually takes the order and arranges delivery.

## Coverage: mass, selective or exclusive?

Large companies want mass coverage, but only a very few can reach all potential customers with their distribution channels. It is simply unrealistic in terms of cost. A good example of a company that really can make its products available everywhere is Coca-Cola. You can find it in supermarkets, convenience stores, vending machines, restaurants, hotels, etc. Most companies have to settle for selective coverage, with fewer locations and a more focused target market. A few companies – those with high-end products – choose exclusive coverage. Here the product is only available at selected locations, perhaps international airports and a few stores in fashionable shopping districts.

To some extent the Internet has given all companies the potential to reach a mass market. However, this isn't as easy as it appears, because they still have to fight a) to distinguish themselves from other web-based firms and b) for visibility – by having good search engine optimization so that their name appears high up the search results.

## Retailing

There are a variety of retail formats:

Corner shop
(AmE Mom-and-Pop store)

Convenience store

Supermarket

Franchise

Cash and carry (AmE Warehouse store)

E-tailer

Specialty store

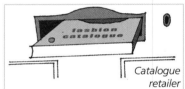
Catalogue retailer

Department store

Vending machine

Retailing is highly competitive. The following factors can all contribute to success or failure:

● Ability to identify what products customers want.
● Layout and atmosphere (eg light, sound, decor).
● Product presentation inside the store (merchandising).
● Overall customer satisfaction with the shopping experience.
● Location.
● Building 'traffic' through advertising.
● Keeping pace with technology: logistics, databases of customer buying behaviour, in-store technology at the check-out, etc.

### Channel power

Who has the power in the distribution channel? This is a key issue.

**Product power:** This is when a brand has a high level of demand and the retailer has to stock it, regardless of the cost to them.

**Wholesale power:** This is when a wholesaler buys a large quantity at low cost, and can then make a large mark-up when they resell to small, powerless retailers.

**Retail power:** This is when the retailer can choose from many suppliers and so drives down the price it pays to them.

# Exercises

**22.1 Find a word in the text opposite that matches each definition below. The words appear in order.**

1 money that you pay for a service _____

2 *(two words)* places where products are sold

_____

3 *(two words)* when a large percentage of people are reached by a distribution channel _____

4 *(phrasal verb)* accept something that isn't exactly what you want _____

5 the way in which something is arranged

_____

6 the style of decoration and furniture in a building

_____

7 *(three words)* changing as fast as something else

_____

**Now do the same for the words in 'Channel power' opposite.**

8 *(phrasal verb)* uses aggressive tactics to make prices fall

**22.2 Match each description below to one of the retail formats in the list opposite.**

1 Small store, good location, open till late, fast checkout, but limited range and expensive _____

2 A small, privately-owned, family-run store – often in a local neighbourhood _____

3 Online-only retailer such as Amazon _____

4 Large store carrying just one product category (eg sports shoes, office supplies, electronics) _____

5 Emphasis is on value-for-money; originally mainly food retailing but increasingly moving into other areas like clothing _____

6 Similar to a supermarket, but with a greater variety of products, better quality, higher prices and better service levels _____

7 Requires buyers to make large purchases; limited product selection; may restrict entry to the general public

_____

8 A company gives permission for someone to use their brand name, products, etc in exchange for part of the profits

_____

**22.3 A store buys something for €10 and sells it for €15. Fill in the gaps with one of these words: *margin*, *mark-up*.**

1 The _____ is 50%. The cost price (€10) is increased by a half (€5) to decide the selling price (€15).

2 The _____ is 33%. The profit (€5) is a third of the selling price (€15).

**22.4 Read the text about technology in retailing then answer the questions below.**

Technology is changing the face of retailing. Here are just some of the new developments:

**Electronic signage** A small LCD screen can be incorporated into a tag hanging from the merchandise, or into a stand-up sign positioned near it. The display shows price, product information, promotions, etc.

**Soft security tags** An electronic surveillance tag is incorporated into a garment at the point of manufacture. These tags are flexible and paper thin. A device at the point-of-sale (POS) automatically deactivates the tag.

**Self-scanning** Shoppers use a hand-held scanner that reads the bar codes on items they buy. They can pay automatically with the same device and have a special express lane at the checkout.

**Virtual showrooms** Customers view computerized images of room interiors and furnishings. The technology has the potential to offer thousands of items that cannot be displayed on the retail floor. Also, it can replicate the dimensions of the customer's own kitchen, bathroom, etc and show how they would look with the planned additions. Customers can mix and match colours, styles and patterns.

**Find a word in the text that means:**

1 *(formal)* the use of signs _____

2 a small label _____

3 *(formal)* things for sale in a store _____

4 *(formal)* a piece of clothing _____

5 a machine or tool that does a special job

_____

6 place where you pay in a store _____

7 things in a room such as furniture, carpets and curtains

_____

8 *(three words)* put things together in different ways

_____

**See page 148 for some discussion topics.**

# 23 Promotion

## The aims of promotion

'Promotion', the third of 'the four Ps' of marketing, can have a variety of different aims. Its classic aims are:

- To build awareness of a new product.
- To reinforce a brand.
- To stimulate demand, either by getting new customers to try a product (eg free sample, free trial), or by getting existing customers to buy more, or sooner.

But promotion can work in more subtle, often unintended, ways. For example it can create an initial interest in a product category and then convince customers that they have a need for it – before they think about specific brands.

## Promotional activities

There are four main types of promotional activity:

### 1 Advertising

This includes the whole variety of media outlets: television, radio, print (eg newspapers, magazines), Internet (ie web and email), direct mail, outdoor (eg billboards, buses), indoor (eg airports, in-store), product placement, mobile devices and sponsorship.

Large companies rarely handle their own advertising; they usually use the services of an advertising agency – perhaps using different agencies for different product lines.

### Who does what in an advertising agency?

**Account manager:**
works with the client to develop the strategy.

**Creative team:**
generate ideas and take the initial concept through to the final advertisement.

**Market researchers:**
assess the client's market situation and test creative ideas.

**Media planners:**
actually place the ads in the various media and negotiate deals with them.

### 2 Sales promotions

This includes coupons, special offers, contests, loyalty programs, etc.

### 3 Personal selling

This can be either face-to-face or via the telephone. See unit 18.

### 4 Public relations (PR)

This has various functions:

- Monitoring the media for any coverage of the company, and maintaining contacts with people in the media (eg issuing news releases as part of a press kit).
- Keeping in contact with customers and / or employees through company newsletters, in-house blogs, etc.
- Crisis management when something happens that threatens the company image.
- Organizing special events to build both brand awareness and brand loyalty. Events might include parties, product demonstrations, stunts, seminars, etc – often in unusual locations.
- Building goodwill through community programs and philanthropy.

## Other targets of promotion

Finally, it's important to remember that customers aren't the only target of promotion. Other targets of a marketing message might be news media, special interest groups (eg environmental organizations), opinion formers (eg doctors for the pharmaceutical industry), trade associations, partners in the distribution channel (eg retailers), investors, employees, etc. An often overlooked area is the importance of in-house promotion: explaining a new product to the sales force and motivating them to sell it.

### Trends in advertising

**Changing media choices:**
cellphone screens, social networking sites, podcasting (audio and video).

**Digital convergence:**
everything will connect to the network (not just computers, televisions and cellphones, but also wallets, fridges and cars).

**Audience monitoring:**
tracking and measuring how consumers respond to advertisements is becoming easier and more important.

**GPS in personal mobile devices:**
this allows businesses to push targeted, location-specific ads (eg restaurants, bars, specialist shops).

# Exercises

**23.1 Find a word in the text opposite that matches each definition below. The words appear in order.**

1 large boards for advertisements in an outside public place (BrE hoardings) _____

2 providing money for a special event or a sports team in order to advertise a brand name _____

3 news about something – on the television, on the radio, or in newspapers and magazines _____

4 *(two words)* information given to reporters that contains news plus supporting material (eg background information, photos) _____

5 silly or unusual things that are done to get public attention _____

6 *(formal)* kind feelings towards a person or organization _____

7 the practice of giving money and help to people who are poor or in trouble _____

8 a situation in which things gradually become very similar _____

9 following the development or progress of someone or something _____

10 a system that uses radio signals from satellites to show an exact position on the Earth _____

**23.2 Make phrases by matching an item from each column.**

1 build — an ad in the media
2 stimulate — in contact with customers
3 take — demand by offering a free trial
4 place — awareness of a new product
5 issue — how consumers respond to advertisements
6 keep — an initial concept through to the final advertisement
7 monitor — targeted ads to a mobile device
8 push — a news release

**23.3 Underline the verbs that make sense in the sentence.**

1 The agency *carried / placed / published / put / ran / took out* an ad in a magazine.
(5 correct answers)

2 The magazine *carried / placed / published / put / ran / took out* the ad.
(3 correct answers)

**23.4 The items in the box are all methods of sales promotion. Match each one to its definition below.**

> discount    loyalty program    contest    personal appearance
> free sample    trade-in    free product    coupon    free trial

1 a competition where the winner gets a prize _____

2 small piece of paper which you can use to buy goods at a lower price _____

3 short-term price reduction _____

4 experiencing a small quantity of a product without purchasing it _____

5 experiencing a service for a short time without purchasing it _____

6 'buy one, get one free' _____

7 where customers are offered a reward (eg discount, free product) for frequent purchasing _____

8 where a celebrity appears somewhere in order to generate customer traffic _____

9 using an older product as part-exchange for a new product _____

**23.5 Study the table below carefully. Then label each column 1–4 with one of these types of promotional activity: *advertising*, *personal selling*, *sales promotions*, *PR* (media coverage such as stories about the company or reports on special events).**

**Of course there may be exceptions!**

| | 1 _____ | 2 _____ | 3 _____ | 4 _____ |
|---|---|---|---|---|
| Intended audience | mass & targeted | mass & targeted | mass | targeted |
| Message flow | one-way | one-way | one-way | two-way |
| Payment model | paid | paid | non-paid | paid |
| Interaction type | non-personal | non-personal | non-personal | personal |
| Demand creation | lagging* | quick | lagging | quick |
| Message control | good | good | poor | very good |
| Message credibility** | low | medium | high | medium |
| Cost effectiveness | difficult to know | medium to high | high (because non-paid) | high |

*lagging = developing more slowly    **credibility = the quality of being believed and trusted

See page 148 for some discussion topics.

## The importance of price

'Price' is the last of 'the four Ps' of marketing, and is probably the one that marketers talk least about. It doesn't seem like an exciting part of the job – in fact a product's price might simply be generated by a spreadsheet. But decisions about price are important for many reasons:

- Price is the most flexible and adjustable part of the marketing mix – it can be changed very rapidly (unlike, say, product or distribution decisions).
- Pricing decisions are critical for revenue: set a price too low and you miss out on profits; set it too high and you lose sales and market share.
- Price is important for first impressions: a customer may not consider the whole product offering if they have dismissed it initially because of the price; equally a high price may say 'quality' and encourage the customer to take an interest.
- Price is an important part of sales promotions. See unit 23.

So, what are the factors that have to be taken into consideration when setting a price? Some important ones are described below.

## Internal factors that affect price

- Profitability: a company usually requires a minimum return on its investment (ie the total costs of making and marketing the product). But this return may not be important – for example with a new product that isn't yet established – as long as revenue at least covers the costs.
- Market share: a price may be set artificially low in order to gain a hold in a new market, or where there is a price war.
- Consistency with marketing strategy: if the company's overall strategy is to position itself at the high end of the market (and emphasize non-price benefits like quality, service, etc), then price will be kept high.

## External factors that affect price

- Elasticity of demand: in an elastic market, a small change in price results in a big change in demand. In an inelastic market, a small change in price has little impact on demand. The trick is to find the particular price level at which profits (or other objectives) are maximized.
- Customer expectations: remember that 'customers' here also includes distribution partners – they're often the ones who set the final price that the end user pays.
- Competitors' products: every company has to watch what competitors are charging. The market leader often sets prices in a market, and they're usually able to charge a premium.

## Setting a price

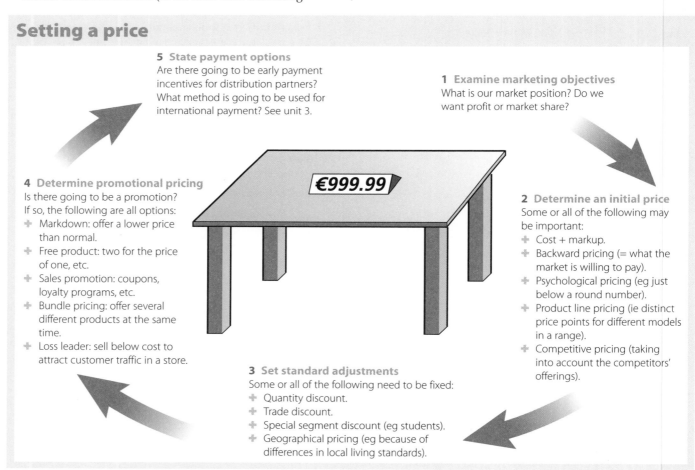

**5 State payment options**
Are there going to be early payment incentives for distribution partners? What method is going to be used for international payment? See unit 3.

**1 Examine marketing objectives**
What is our market position? Do we want profit or market share?

**4 Determine promotional pricing**
Is there going to be a promotion? If so, the following are all options:
- ✦ Markdown: offer a lower price than normal.
- ✦ Free product: two for the price of one, etc.
- ✦ Sales promotion: coupons, loyalty programs, etc.
- ✦ Bundle pricing: offer several different products at the same time.
- ✦ Loss leader: sell below cost to attract customer traffic in a store.

*€999.99*

**2 Determine an initial price**
Some or all of the following may be important:
- ✦ Cost + markup.
- ✦ Backward pricing (= what the market is willing to pay).
- ✦ Psychological pricing (eg just below a round number).
- ✦ Product line pricing (ie distinct price points for different models in a range).
- ✦ Competitive pricing (taking into account the competitors' offerings).

**3 Set standard adjustments**
Some or all of the following need to be fixed:
- ✦ Quantity discount.
- ✦ Trade discount.
- ✦ Special segment discount (eg students).
- ✦ Geographical pricing (eg because of differences in local living standards).

# Exercises

**24.1 Find a word in the text opposite that matches each definition below. The words appear in order.**

1 able to be changed slightly _____
2 income; turnover _____
3 *(phrasal verb)* lose an opportunity to do or have something _____
4 is enough to pay for _____
5 *(three words)* obtain control or power _____
6 doing things in the same way _____
7 clever and effective way of doing something _____
8 *(three words)* ask for an additional amount of money, above the standard amount _____

**Now do the same for the words in 'Setting a price' opposite.**

9 an increase in the price of something (ie the percentage by which the cost price is increased) _____
10 *(two words)* number ending in 0 _____
11 a group of products that are packaged together and sold as a set _____
12 things that encourage you to work harder, start a new activity, etc _____

**24.2 Make phrases by matching an item from each column.**

1 lose            a minimum return on your investment
2 take            sales and market share
3 require         the costs with sales revenue
4 cover           several factors into consideration

5 gain            yourself at the high end of the market
6 position        below cost to attract customer traffic
7 set             a hold in a new market
8 sell            the final price that the end user pays

**24.3 Read this short explanation of discounts and underline the correct words in italics.**

1 A *prompt / proper* payment discount is given to help with cash flow.
2 A quantity discount encourages a larger purchase – any economies of *volume / scale* can be *passed over / passed on* to the final customer.
3 Trade discounts are for partners in the distribution *channel / canal*.
4 Seasonal discounts are given during *slack / loose* periods of the year, or during the January *promotions / sales*.

**24.4 Match one verb from each column so that all three have a similar meaning. All the verbs can be used with 'a price'.**

increase        establish        work out
lower           arrive at        put up
set             raise            settle on
negotiate       figure out       bring down
calculate       cut              determine

**24.5 Write each word in the box next to the word in italics with the closest meaning.**

> attractive   bargain   budget   excessive
> exorbitant   fair   inflated   list   reasonable
> recommended   reduced   selling

1 a / an *high*, _____ , _____ , _____ price
2 a / an *low*, _____ , _____ , _____ price
3 a / an *good*, _____ , _____ , _____ price
4 the *retail*, _____ , _____ , _____ price

**24.6 Complete what a marketing manager says about prices with the verbs in the box.**

> agreed to   drop   freeze   held down   matched
> received complaints about   re-thought
> set   undercut   were forced to raise

66 Initially we ¹ _____ prices at what we thought was a reasonable level. Then our costs started to increase. We ² _____ our prices for as long as we could, but eventually we ³ _____ them. Immediately we ⁴ _____ the new prices from our customers. They told us that our prices weren't competitive any more. Up to that point we had always ⁵ _____ our competitors' prices, or even slightly ⁶ _____ them. But no more. We were in danger of losing customers, so we ⁷ _____ our whole pricing strategy. We couldn't afford to ⁸ _____ our prices back down to the previous level, and anyway this would have looked very bad in the market. Instead, we announced that we would ⁹ _____ the new prices for twelve months, to give some stability. Nearly all our customers ¹⁰ _____ this, although they weren't happy. 99

**See page 148 for some discussion topics.**

## Understanding a business

Marketers must first have a detailed understanding of their business in order to develop their marketing strategies. This is often done using a '5Cs' analysis:

1 Customer analysis: this involves breaking down the market into segments. See unit 20.
2 Company analysis: marketers need to understand their company's cost structure, look at how profits are generated from different product lines and different customer accounts, and identify core competencies in the organization.
3 Collaborator analysis: this means producing a profile of all the channel partners (eg suppliers, distributors).
4 Competitor analysis: marketers build profiles of each competitor, focusing on their relative strengths and weaknesses.
5 Context analysis: as well as the economic and social context, this includes things like potential threats in the industry (eg substitute products, new entrants) and also the changing bargaining power of suppliers and customers.

## Market research

In order to collect all this data, it's necessary to do market research. A variety of techniques are used:

- Quantitative research: the most common research tool here is a survey that captures information with a questionnaire. Information can also come from doing small-scale experiments such as looking at the effect on sales of changing price points, or moving displays within a store. Websites also offer many opportunities for collecting data – customers' behaviour on a site can be easily tracked.
- Qualitative research: the company may carry out individual interviews, or focus groups. A modern technique is to use observational research where customers are watched in a natural setting as they shop or use products at home.
- Secondary research: data can be collected from other sources such as consulting firms, trade associations, magazine articles, government statistics, etc.
- Test marketing: this involves trying out new products in certain locations.

## Developing a marketing strategy

Once a company has done the kind of research outlined in the two sections above, it's in a better position to understand its customer base and its competitive position in the industry. Marketing managers are then able to develop a strategy. This will relate to:

- Identifying new markets and gaps in the market.
- Developing new products and identifying their desired positioning.
- Developing the company's competitive advantages.
- Maximizing revenues and profits.
- Gaining market share.

The second of these, new product development, will go through a process that includes some or all of the stages in the diagram below.

## New product development

**7 Commercialization**

The distribution channels are filled with the product and it is launched.

Advertisements are produced and placed.

**1 Idea generation**

Ideas can come from R&D department, customers, competitors, focus groups, sales people, trade shows.

**2 Idea screening**

Marketers have to ask some basic questions to screen the initial ideas, eg How will customers benefit? Is it technically feasible to make? Does this early idea look like it will be profitable?

**6 Technical implementation**

The company has to allocate resources and plan engineering operations, logistics and work schedules.

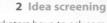

**3 Concept development**

At this stage marketers need to think in much greater detail about the concept, eg 'Who exactly is the target market?' 'How will it fit with other existing products?'

Marketers work with other colleagues to see if there are any production issues.

Some informal tests can be done by simply asking prospective customers what they think about the concept.

**5 Beta testing and market testing**

At this point the company produces a prototype and tests the product in use.

Marketers will hold focus groups.

Adjustments will be made on the basis of these tests, and a more final version of the product might be sold in a test market.

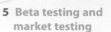

**4 Business analysis**

Here marketers work closely with colleagues from sales and finance to try to estimate the likely selling price, sales volume, profitability and breakeven point.

# Exercises

**25.1 Find a word in the text opposite that matches each definition below. The words appear in order.**

1 (two words) things that a company can do well

_____

2 things that could cause damage or harm

_____

3 set of questions that you ask a large number of people in order to find out their opinions _____

4 a written list of questions _____

5 relating to things that cannot easily be measured with numbers such as opinions or attitudes _____

6 (two words) small groups of people who are asked to discuss and give their opinions about a particular subject

_____

7 (two words) things that help a company be more successful than others _____

**Now do the same for the words in 'New product development' opposite.**

8 checking something to see if it's suitable to take forward to the next stage _____

9 (two words) time when a product earns just enough money to pay for its costs _____

10 (two words) testing something by giving it to a few customers to try so that any problems will be found

_____

11 first design of something new _____

12 decide to use a particular amount of time, money, etc for a particular purpose _____

**25.2 Make phrases by matching an item from each column.**

| 1 | cost | competencies |
|---|------|-------------|
| 2 | product | research |
| 3 | core | group |
| 4 | bargaining | structure |
| 5 | quantitative | power |
| 6 | focus | line |
| | | |
| 7 | customer | development |
| 8 | competitive | base |
| 9 | concept | test |
| 10 | breakeven | implementation |
| 11 | beta | advantage |
| 12 | technical | point |

**25.3 Use phrases from exercise 25.2 to complete the sentences below. The phrases are not in order.**

1 Their location gave them a huge _____ over other firms.

2 A supplier of specialized components has strong _____ with a manufacturer.

3 They decided to sell some small business units and just focus on their _____ .

4 After the initial ideas have been screened, we move to the _____ stage where we think about the product in much greater detail.

5 The advertising agency have produced some new ideas for outdoor posters. I want to show them to the next _____ and see what people say.

6 By the time the new product gets to the _____ stage the marketers have done their job and the operations people take over.

**25.4 One word or phrase from each group in italics does not make sense. Cross it out.**

1 We are up against, come up against, look towards, face a lot of competition.

2 This legislation will encourage, gain, promote, stimulate competition.

3 We're doing our best to cope with, handle, respond to, treat with the competition.

4 We try to avoid, carry out, stay away from, steer clear of market segments where there is too much competition.

5 We face cut-throat, fierce, intense, particular, severe, strong, tough competition.

6 We welcome fair, free, healthy, large, open competition.

**25.5 Put these verbs into the most likely chronological order: design, launch, discontinue, manufacture, sell, upgrade.**

1 _____
2 _____
3 _launch_ a product
4 _____
5 _____
6 _____

**25.6 Put these phrases into the most likely chronological order: carry out, cut back on, put money into, abandon, suggest the need for, see the limitations of.**

1 _____
2 _____
3 _carry out_ market research
4 _____
5 _____
6 _____

See page 149 for some discussion topics.

The income statement (profit and loss account/'the P&L') is one of a company's three major financial statements. (See units 27 and 28.) It measures a company's financial performance over a fiscal quarter or a fiscal year. In summary, it shows: Revenue minus Expenses = Profit. A fuller version is given in the box and then explained below.

> Revenue
> – Cost of sales
> *Gross profit*
> – SG&A
> *Operating profit*
> + Non-operating profit
> *EBITDA*
> – Interest
> – Tax
> – Depreciation
> – Amortization
> *Net profit after tax*
> – Dividends
> *Retained profit*

## What is revenue?

Revenue (= turnover) is the money that comes into the company from the sale of products or services. This figure is referred to as 'the top line' because of where it appears on the P&L. 'Top line growth' refers to sales growth.

## What are expenses?

Expenses (= costs) refers to money that the company has to spend to run the business. This can be broken down in many ways, but a basic distinction is between:
- Cost of sales (cost of goods sold/COGS): this refers to the cost of actually making the product, for example materials costs and labour costs in the factory.
- Selling, general and administrative expenses (SG&A/ operating expenses/overheads): this refers to marketing costs such as advertising, office salaries, rent, telephone, electricity.

## What is profit?

Profit (= earnings) has two components:
- Operating profit (from regular business activities).
- Non-operating profit (eg from the sale of some land or shares in another company).

## EBITDA

EBITDA stands for 'earnings before interest, tax, depreciation and amortization'. On the P&L we subtract the I, T, D and A in turn:

Interest (paid to the bank for any loans)
Tax (paid to the government)
Depreciation (= the gradual loss in value of tangible assets, eg vehicles, machinery)
Amortization (= the loss in value of intangible assets, eg patents, copyrights)

## Net profit after tax / retained profit

The figure that remains is the net profit after tax (= net income/'the bottom line'). To complete the P&L we then subtract dividends (paid to shareholders), leaving finally the retained profit (= reserves/retained earnings) that is reinvested in the business.

## Budget report

Figures for the real-life revenue, costs and profits will be different from the budgeted (= planned/forecast) figures. This analysis is presented to managers in a budget report. In its simplest form this report has the first five lines of the P&L in the box opposite, with three columns showing 1) the actual results, 2) the budgeted results and 3) the variance (= difference between the two).

Variances can be favourable or unfavourable, and individual managers may see this information for only their own product lines or geographical area.

## What causes variance?

### Causes of a change in revenue

- A change in sales volume.
- A change in the profit margin on each item (due to higher / lower selling prices).

### Causes of a change in costs

- A result of a change in sales volume (ie it simply costs more to produce more).
- A change because more is being spent to achieve each €1 of sales (ie a genuine increase in costs – a decrease in productivity).

### Causes of a change in profit

- A complex interplay of the changes in revenue and costs (including the different types of costs).

The budget report allows managers to see where the unexpected changes are, and which changes are the most significant. The reasons for any variance can be identified and any corrective action taken.

# Exercises

**26.1 Underline the correct words in italics.**

1 The term 'turnover' means the same as *revenue / profit*.

2 The term 'earnings' means the same as *revenue / profit*.

3 The term 'overheads' refers to *the direct costs of making products / the indirect costs of selling a product and running the office*.

4 The wages of factory workers and the salaries of office workers are shown *in the same place / in different places* on a P&L.

5 A company buys the patent on a piece of a technology for $30m. The patent lasts for 15 years. So $2m is recorded each year as a/an *amortization / depreciation* expense.

6 The word which means 'before other things are taken away' is *gross / net*. It can refer to profit, salary or weight.

**26.2 Complete the P&L with the words in the box.**

| EBIT    Dividends    Cost of goods sold    Income taxes |
| --- |

## *Profit and loss account*
*(figures in millions)*

| | |
| --- | --- |
| **Operating revenues** | |
| Net sales | **$10,219** |
| **Operating expenses** | |
| 1 _____ | $3,972 |
| SG&A | $4,155 |
| Depreciation and amortization | $480 |
| Total operating expenses | ($8,607) |
| **Operating profit** | **$1,612** |
| Non-operating profit | $65 |
| 2 _____ | **$1,677** |
| Interest | ($72) |
| **Earnings before income taxes** | **$1,605** |
| 3 _____ | ($514) |
| **Net profit after tax** | **$1,091** |
| 4 _____ | ($710) |
| **Retained profit** | **$381** |

Compare the P&L above with the one opposite. You will notice that there are one or two different words, and a slightly different order (particularly for 'depreciation and amortization'). This is deliberate, and is designed to show the variation that is possible in the layout of a P&L.

Notice also how figures to be subtracted are shown with a bracket.

**26.3 Find a word in the text or box opposite that matches each definition below. The words appear in order.**

1 related to government taxes and spending

_____

2 *(two words)* property that you own which can be physically touched _____

3 the way in which two or more things affect each other

_____

**26.4 Cross out the item which has a <u>different</u> meaning to the others.**

1 to *bring in, earn, generate, invest, make* a profit.

2 to *boost, plough back, reinvest* profits.

3 to *guarantee, jeopardize, put at risk* profits.

4 to *incur, make, offset, run up, suffer* a loss.

5 a *big, considerable, fat, handsome, healthy, huge, satisfactory, substantial* profit.

6 a / an *interim, modest, slight, small* profit.

**26.5 Fill in the missing letters.**

1 If a profit is bigger than any previous profit, it's a rec _ _d profit. If a profit is fair and reasonable, it's a legi_ _ _ate profit.

2 Some items which result in a profit (or loss) are not normally repeated – like the sale of a subsidiary company, or the effects of a natural disaster. These are called 'extrao_ _ _nary' or 'exc_ _ _ional' items.

3 If a company is making a loss, we can say that it's 'in the _ _d'. Eventually, it will go bank_ _ _t (= go into liqu_ _ _ _ion).

4 If a company accepts that it cannot get back money it has lost, then it wr_ _ _s o_ _ the loss.

5 To express the opposite of a 'favourable variance', accountants often say an 'adve_ _e variance'.

6 If some goods are sold (or a service is delivered) in the middle of December, but the customer only pays in the middle of January, then this is recorded in the income statement for the earlier of the two years. This fundamental principle is referred to as 'the acc_ _al basis of accounting'.

**See page 149 for some discussion topics.**

*"New from accounting, sir. Two and two is four again."*

# 27 Balance sheet

The balance sheet (BS) is another financial statement that companies have to produce as part of their accounts. (See also units 26 and 28.) The BS applies to a single point in time, and gives a picture of everything that a company owns (= its assets) and everything that it owes (= its liabilities). The basic equation of the BS is: Assets = Liabilities plus Shareholders' Equity. A fuller version is given in the box and then explained below.

| Assets | Liabilities |
|---|---|
| **Current assets** | **Current liabilities** |
| Cash | Bank debt |
| Accounts receivable | Accounts payable |
| Inventories | Liabilities for tax |
| **Long-term assets** | Short-term provisions |
| Fixed assets | **Long-term liabilities** |
| Intangible assets | Bank loans |
| Financial assets | Bonds payable |
| | **Shareholders' equity** |

## Assets

Current assets are those that can be turned into cash quickly. They include cash at the bank, accounts receivable (ie money owed by customers) and inventories (ie unsold stock).

Long-term assets are those that cannot be turned into cash quickly. They include fixed assets (eg plant and machinery, land and buildings, motor vehicles), intangible assets (eg copyrights, patents, goodwill acquired from other companies) and financial assets (eg investments in other companies).

## Liabilities

Current liabilities are those that have to be paid within the next year. They include bank debt, accounts payable (ie money owed to suppliers and utility bills), liabilities for current tax and provisions (ie money set aside for a particular purpose, eg bad debts or a court ruling).

Long-term liabilities include bank loans (including any mortgage) and money owing to bondholders. (The principal has to be paid back at the maturity of the bond.)

Shareholders' equity started as the capital originally invested to begin the business, and now it has grown through a) reinvested profits and b) any additional shares that have been issued. Think of it like this: imagine that the business had to stop, and all the assets were sold and this money used to pay off all the liabilities. What would happen to the remaining part? The answer is that it would be returned to the shareholders – it belongs to them. It is their equity (capital).

## What can a balance sheet show?

### Liquidity

- Liquidity is the degree to which an asset can be converted to cash quickly. This is often measured by using the 'current ratio', which is *current assets divided by current liabilities*. A high current ratio means that over the longer term there are plenty of assets to convert into cash to pay the debts.
- A more short-term measure of liquidity is 'working capital' ie *current assets minus current liabilities*.

### Leverage (level of debt)

- In everyday language, leverage is the use of borrowed money (ie debt) to try to increase profits.
- In accountants' language, leverage is a measure of how far a company is funded by loans (eg banks and bonds) rather than its own capital. On a BS leverage is defined as *long-term liabilities divided by shareholders' equity*.
- A highly leveraged company has taken on a lot of debt. But this isn't always bad: borrowing funds wisely to expand a growing business is good news for shareholders.

### Book value

- 'Book value' is a company's net worth (ie its financial value – what is left on the books – if it went out of business). It is an everyday term with the same meaning as 'shareholders' equity'. So book value equals *total assets minus total liabilities*.
- Anyone buying shares in a company is buying a share in the book value, plus a share in any future growth.

### Profitability

- There are several common measures of profitability, but one of the commonest is Return on Equity (ROE). Return on Equity equals *net profit after tax divided by shareholders' equity*.
- ROE shows how much profit a company generates in relation to its book value.

# Exercises

**27.1 Fill in the missing letters.**

1 Assets are things that you ow_.

2 Liabilities are things that you ow_.

**27.2 Find a word in the text opposite that matches each definition below. The words appear in order.**

1 an amount of money that a person or company owes

_____

2 documents given to people who invest money in a company, promising to pay back the money (= the principal) with interest (= the coupon) _____

3 a company's reputation, relationships with customers and collective know-how (when one company buys another, this is what it pays for above the book value)

_____

4 (phrasal verb) keep from a larger amount in order to be used later _____

5 the money that you borrow from a bank to buy a property

_____

6 (phrasal verb) give someone all the money you owe them (Note: 'paid back' isn't the answer.) _____

> **Common mistakes** Many languages use words like 'actives' and 'passives' for assets and liabilities. These words do not exist in English. Also, many languages use a word like 'obligations' for bonds. This is a false friend – the word isn't used in this way in English.

**27.3 Complete each phrase with a preposition from the box.**

| back | by | for | in | into | on |
|---|---|---|---|---|---|
| out of | over | to | through | | |

1 a current asset can be turned quickly _____ cash

2 'accounts receivable' is money owed _____ customers

3 'accounts payable' is money owed _____ suppliers

4 'financial assets' are investments _____ another company

5 'provisions' includes money set aside _____ bad debts

6 bondholders have to be paid _____ at maturity

7 shareholders' equity grows _____ reinvested profits

8 a highly leveraged company has taken _____ a lot of debt

9 'book value' is the value of a company if it went _____ business

10 _____ the long term a company needs cash to pay the debts

('in' is possible in #10, but isn't the answer here.)

**27.4 Does the term 'creditors' mean accounts receivable or accounts payable?**

**27.5 The verbs in the box can all be used with 'assets'. Divide them into three groups, based on their meanings.**

| accumulate | own | dispose of | build up |
|---|---|---|---|
| hold | acquire | possess | realize |

**have**       **buy**       **sell**

_____ _____ _____

_____ _____ _____

_____ _____

**27.6 The verbs in the box can all be used with 'debts'. Divide them into two groups. The meanings within a group are similar but not identical.**

| settle | build up | clear | honour | incur |
|---|---|---|---|---|
| pay off | repay | run up | service | |

**collect**       **pay back**

_____ _____

_____ _____

_____ _____

_____

_____

_____

**27.7 Fill in the missing letters.**

1 A business may have used all its funds to buy equipment, vehicles and inventory. If so, you can say that it has 't_ _d _ p' all its money in assets.

2 If a debt isn't paid back, then the company defa_ _ts on the debt.

**27.8 Complete the text with these words: copyright, patent, trademark.**

1 If you design a new product, or a new process, you can apply for a _____ . This gives you the legal right to be the only person to make, use or sell it. It lasts for a limited period of time.

2 If you produce an original piece of work (eg a book, design, computer program), you own the _____ on it. Other people cannot reproduce it without your permission. The right is created automatically – you don't need to apply.

3 If you have a unique name or symbol that you use for your products, you can apply to register it as a _____ . Once this has been done, other people cannot use it.

**See page 149 for some discussion topics.**

The cash flow statement (CFS) is an official financial statement – the third covered in this book. (See units 26 and 27.) Information for the CFS comes from the P&L and balance sheet, but is presented in a different way. It is concerned with real money (ie cash) – not amounts that haven't yet been received or paid. Generally speaking, investors like to see the CFS because it's less open to the use of accounting tricks.

## Cash

Cash can come from (or be used for) three areas:
- **Operations:** this is money received (or lost) from actual business activity.
- **Investing:** this includes money spent on physical property (eg plant and equipment), money received (or lost) by investing in stocks and bonds, and money made (or lost) from buying or selling subsidiaries.
- **Financing:** this includes money made by issuing new shares, money spent by buying back shares from the market, dividend payments made to shareholders, money received by borrowing from the bank and money used to repay previous loans.

A simplified CFS produced at the end of a financial year might look like the one in the box.

| Cash flow from operations | |
|---|---|
| Net profit after tax | 3,600,000 |
| Depreciation | 80,000 |
| Decrease in accounts receivable | 30,000 |
| Increase in accounts payable | 30,000 |
| Increase in taxes payable | 10,000 |
| Increase in inventory | - 60,000 |
| Net cash from operations | 3,690,000 |
| | |
| **Cash flow from investing** | |
| Plant and equipment | - 800,000 |
| | |
| **Cash flow from financing** | |
| Issuing new stock | 300,000 |
| Stock dividends paid | - 630,000 |
| Bank repayments | - 400,000 |
| **Free cash flow** | **2,160,000** |

See units 26 and 27 for vocabulary in this box.

## Cash flow statement breakdown

Looking at each figure in turn:

**Net profit after tax** This figure comes from the P&L. See unit 26.

**Depreciation** This was subtracted on the P&L to arrive at the net profit, but in fact it was a 'paper' expense and the profit wasn't really reduced by this amount. So it is added back here to make the sums right.

**Decrease in accounts receivable** A decrease means that more customers have paid off their credit accounts, and so more cash has entered the company.

**Increase in accounts payable** An increase means that the company owes more money to suppliers. This is available temporarily as cash inside the company.

**Increase in taxes payable** The same logic applies. If there is an increase in taxes owed, it is added on the CFS as there is more cash still inside the company until it's paid. If taxes have been paid off, then the amount is deducted – there is less cash in the company.

**Increase in inventory** The company has spent money to purchase materials. If this is done with cash, the amount is shown as a deduction. Notice that if the purchase was made on credit and the amount is still outstanding at the end of the year, then there would be an increase in Accounts Payable and the amount would show as an addition on the CFS.

**Plant and equipment** If the company invests money in assets such as buildings or equipment, then this shows as 'cash out' (ie a deduction). If the asset had been sold, it would be 'cash in'.

**Issuing new stock** This company has raised capital by issuing new shares.

**Stock dividends paid** Cash has been used to pay a dividend to existing shareholders.

**Bank repayments** Cash has been used to repay part of a bank loan.

The amount that remains is the 'free cash flow'. This is what a company has left after it has paid all its expenses. It is often considered to be the real 'bottom line'.

# Exercises

**28.1 Find a word in the text opposite that matches each definition below. The words appear in order.**

1 large machinery used in industrial processes

_____

2 officially making something available to buy

_____

3 *(informal)* calculations _____
4 taken away from a total amount; subtracted

_____

5 not yet paid _____
6 money, especially when it's used to start a business or produce more wealth _____

**28.2 Below you will see a simplified cash flow forecast for a new business. Note that a cash flow <u>forecast</u> looks forward, unlike the cash flow <u>statement</u> opposite.**

**Study the first two columns, then add these figures in the correct place in the third column.**

| 940 | 9,560 | 10,500 | 26,960 | 27,900 |

*Cash flow from operations*

|  | Open | Jan | Feb |
|---|---|---|---|
| **Opening balance** |  | 30,000 ¹_____ |  |
| Income |  |  |  |
| Sales |  | 9,000 | 10,500 |
| Capital in | 30,000 |  |  |
| **Total income** | 30,000 | 9,000 ²_____ |  |
| Finances |  |  |  |
| Loan repayments |  | 200 | 200 |
| Interest paid |  | 40 | 40 |
| Direct costs |  |  |  |
| Inventory |  | 6,500 | 4,000 |
| Labour |  | 1,800 | 1,800 |
| Expenses |  |  |  |
| Salaries |  | 2,400 | 2,400 |
| Office rent |  | 400 | 400 |
| Web services |  |  | 400 |
| Office supplies |  | 200 | 80 |
| Utilities |  |  | 240 |
| Insurance |  | 500 |  |
| **Total outgoings** |  | 12,040 ³_____ |  |
| **Net cash flow** | 30,000 | (3,040) ⁴_____ |  |
| **Ending balance** | 30,000 | 26,960 ⁵_____ |  |

**28.3 Refer to the cash flow forecast from the previous exercise and mark these statements True (T) or False (F).**

1 Most of the capital to start this business probably came from the bank, not the personal funds of the business owner. **T / F**
*(Clue: look at the size of the loan repayments in relation to the 'capital in')*

2 The wages of staff who actually make the product (or serve customers) are shown separately from the salary of the manager. **T / F**

3 Rent is probably paid monthly, in advance. **T / F**

4 The gas and electricity companies are probably paid monthly, in advance. **T / F**

5 It is a convention in accounting to show negative figures in brackets. **T / F**

6 The fact that cash flow was negative in January is a bad sign for this new business. **T / F**

**Continue in the same way, answering questions about cash flow in general.**

7 On a spreadsheet, there would probably be two columns for each month: one for forecast figures and one for actual figures. **T / F**

8 If you make a sale in January, but the customer takes advantage of one month's credit, the sales figure would be entered in January. **T / F**
*(Clue: remember that cash flow statements use cash accounting, unlike income statements which use accrual accounting – see 26.5 #6.)*

9 The cash flow statement contains a lot of new information that isn't available from the P&L or balance sheet. **T / F**

10 A 12-month cash flow forecast is a key element in any business plan. See unit 9. **T / F**

**28.4 Make phrases by matching an item from each column.**

| 1 | record | the same logic |
| 2 | pay off | something as an expense |
| 3 | apply | capital by issuing new shares |
| 4 | raise | a credit account in full |
| 5 | present | money from the bank |
| 6 | subtract | shares from the market |
| 7 | buy back | one figure from another |
| 8 | borrow | information in a certain way |

**28.5 Fill in the gaps using these words: *as, by, in, on, on.***

1 spend money _ _ plant and equipment
2 invest money _ _ plant and equipment
3 have money available _ _ cash
*['in' is possible in #3, but isn't the answer here.]*
4 make a purchase _ _ credit
5 raise capital _ _ issuing new shares

**See page 149 for some discussion topics.**

## Cash inflows and outflows

A healthy cash flow is obviously important for a business: it enables the bills to be paid, the business to be expanded, and lenders and investors to be reassured. For a well-established company, cash will also be needed to pay a dividend to shareholders.

Sources of cash inflows are:
- Payments from customers.
- Shareholder investments.
- Bank loans.
- A bank overdraft.
- Interest on bank savings.

Sources of cash outflows are:
- Purchase of stock and raw materials.
- Purchase of fixed assets: IT equipment, machinery, office furniture, etc.
- Daily operating expenses such as office supplies.
- Payments of salaries, rent, utilities.
- Loan and overdraft payments.
- Dividends to shareholders.
- Payment of taxes.

## Controlling cash flow

Some of the items above are under direct control and can be managed on a day-to-day basis, others less so. For example, the first item under cash inflows (ie accounts receivable) and the first three items under cash outflows (ie accounts payable) are areas where there is real control as to when cash enters or leaves the company. Other items are less manageable on a day-to-day basis: a bank loan is a strategic decision with a one-off impact, payments of salaries and utilities happen at fixed times in fixed amounts.

A key item that directly impacts cash flow is inventory management. (See units 15 and 16.) 'Dead' inventory sitting on a shelf, in a storeroom or in a warehouse equals dead cash flow. Cash has been taken out of circulation. Reducing 'dead' inventory is a major way that managers can control cash flow.

## Cash flow problems

More businesses fail due to cash flow problems than due to lack of profitability, particularly in the early years. This is because of overtrading, in other words accepting new work without having sufficient resources to complete it and keep the business running. A key concept here is 'working capital'. From a strict accounting viewpoint, this is defined as 'current assets minus current liabilities'. (See unit 27.) But from an everyday management viewpoint, it's simply having enough cash to pay the bills.

## Top 10 tips for improving cash flow

### Managing receivables

1. Offer discounts to customers who pay rapidly.
2. Ask customers to make an initial deposit at the time the order is taken.
3. Run credit checks on all new customers.
4. Have heavily discounted special offers on sales of old inventory to generate cash now.
5. Issue invoices promptly and follow up immediately if payments are slow in coming.
6. Look for options with persistent slow-paying customers such as a percentage prepayment, or cash on delivery (c.o.d.).

### Managing payables

7. Negotiate extended credit terms.
8. If you need to delay a payment, communicate with suppliers and warn them.
9. Look carefully at your suppliers' early payment discounts. Will they really help you to reduce overall costs? How much discount will they give you in exchange for taking more of your cash earlier? The devil is in the detail.
10. Lease assets, rather than buy them.

The problem is this: new work involves buying stock, using equipment, paying staff, and paying the fixed costs of rent and utilities, all before any payments come in. You need cash (ie working capital) to do all that, and cash has to come from somewhere. If you have given a new customer a long credit period in order to win their business, or if an existing customer is late in paying at a critical time, then you might have very serious problems.

So what can a business do if it has followed all the tips in the box above and still finds that it has a shortfall with cash? The first step is to take advantage of any emergency line of credit arranged at the bank. The second step is to make partial payments on less important bills. And a final option is to use a third party to buy your invoices in return for them taking a percentage of the total (called 'factoring').

# Exercises

**29.1 Find a word in the text opposite that matches each definition below. The words appear in order.**

1 made to feel less worried about something

_____

2 arrangement with a bank that allows you to have a temporary negative balance _____

3 continuing to do something, especially something bad or annoying _____

4 *(two words)* costs that don't change when production goes up or down _____

5 the difference between the amount you have and the amount you need _____

**29.2 In the 'Tips' box you will see the common and useful phrase 'the devil is in the detail'. From the context, does this mean …?**

1 if you look at the details, you will see lots of bad things ☐

2 you need to look at the details to see the real situation ☐

**29.3 Make phrases by matching an item from each column.**

| | |
|---|---|
| 1 have a healthy | expenses |
| 2 be a well-established | cash flow |
| 3 have daily operating | on a day-to-day basis |
| 4 be managed | accounting viewpoint |
| 5 take advantage | company |
| 6 see something from a strict | of a line of credit |
| | |
| 7 make an initial | checks |
| 8 run credit | payment discount |
| 9 have heavily | credit terms |
| 10 have persistent | deposit |
| 11 negotiate extended | slow-paying customers |
| 12 give an early | discounted offers |

**29.4 Make pairs of words with a similar meaning from the list below. All the words and phrases are used with 'cash'.**

~~be short of~~, in advance, inflows, infusion, injection, generate, holdings, loose, needs, payment (in full), raise, receipts, requirements, reserves, ~~run out of~~, settlement, shortage, shortfall, spare, up front

**Pairs:**

*be short of = run out of*

**29.5 Complete the story about overtrading with these words:** *clear, delivery, fulfil, limit, outstanding, overdraft, squeeze, turnover.*

### Background

Manuela's business is three years old. Her annual [1] _____ is €180,000, of which €20,000 is profit. She operates with a bank overdraft of up to €25,000.

Manuela succeeds in winning an important contract to supply Novatech. The order is for €40,000 a month for two years. She will be paid 60 days after [2] _____ . *(Note: sixty working days = three months.)*

She calls her suppliers. She orders everything she needs to fulfil the contract in the first few months.

### The first month

Things go well. Manuela receives her supplies and begins to make the items for Novatech.

### The second month

Manuela makes her first delivery to Novatech and she's happy. Her suppliers continue to supply materials, but to pay them all she has to increase her [3] _____ .

### The third month

Manuela makes more deliveries to Novatech, but her overdraft is now at the [4] _____ .

### The fourth month

Manuela is worried. She can't pay all her suppliers. However, she thinks she'll be fine because she's still delivering to Novatech, and they're pleased with her quality.

### The fifth month

The first payment from Novatech arrives on time. This helps Manuela to pay the most [5] _____ bills, but her overdraft is still €4,000 over the limit. Some suppliers are becoming uneasy, and one is threatening legal action. The bank refuses to [6] _____ any more cheques.

### The sixth month

Novatech are having cash flow problems of their own, and decide to [7] _____ their smallest and newest suppliers. They write to Manuela to say that unfortunately their payment this month will be delayed. A few days later her bank demands that the overdraft is repaid within seven days. Manuela decides that she can't [8] _____ any more orders. She closes the business and blames the bank.

**See page 149 for some discussion topics.**

*"What are our most profitable product lines?"*

**"What will happen to profits if our sales volume drops?"**

*"How far can volume drop before we start to actually lose money?"*

*"If we lower our prices in order to sell more, how much more volume will we need to compensate for the lower price?"*

"If we take out a loan, what extra sales volume will we need to cover the cost of the loan?"

All the questions above can be answered by knowing one simple thing: the relationship between fixed and variable costs.

## Fixed costs and variable costs

**Fixed costs** remain more or less the same regardless of the level of sales. Typical examples are salaries of permanent employees, advertising, R&D, rent, interest on bank loans, insurance, heating and lighting, etc.

**Variable costs** increase directly in proportion to the level of sales. Typical examples are parts and materials, wages of temporary employees, sales commissions, delivery charges, etc.

There are items that are difficult to categorize, and all costs vary to some degree. But advertising for example is usually considered to be a fixed cost because a) it has a fixed budget for each accounting period and b) advertising costs for a whole brand will not be increased or decreased immediately in proportion to the sales of individual product lines.

## Breakeven analysis

Once you know specific values for the various costs, the first thing you're able to do is a breakeven analysis.

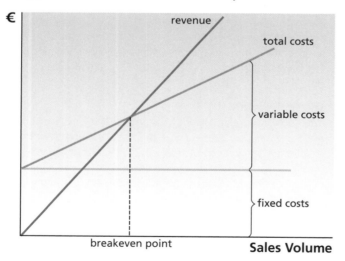

Every business student knows the classic graph of how costs and revenue rise at a different rate as sales increase, and how there is a breakeven point where they cross. The breakeven point is the sales volume you need to exactly cover all your costs.

Breakeven analysis can be used for deciding whether a new product idea is worth developing, and for computing the new sales figures that would be necessary if you decide to increase fixed costs (eg by renting more office space).

## Operating leverage

Operating leverage is the extent to which a business uses fixed costs (as compared to variable costs) in its operations. If a business has high fixed costs, then a small rise or fall in sales will produce a large rise or fall in profits. Profit is more sensitive to a change in sales volume.

Knowing the operating leverage gives managers a more accurate analysis than looking simply at the breakeven point. It also reminds them to keep fixed costs low in order to limit downside risk, and helps them to see the effects of substituting machinery (with higher fixed costs) for labour (with higher variable costs).

## Contribution margin analysis

The contribution margin is the percentage of each euro of sales that remains after the variable costs are subtracted. This is the amount that is available to contribute towards fixed costs and profit. Contribution margin is used to:
● Compare the profitability of different product lines.
● Decide whether to add or subtract a product line.
● Decide how to price a product.
● Decide how to structure any commissions (so that sales staff are encouraged to push more profitable lines).

# Exercises

**30.1 Look at the graph then underline the correct words in italics in the statements below.**

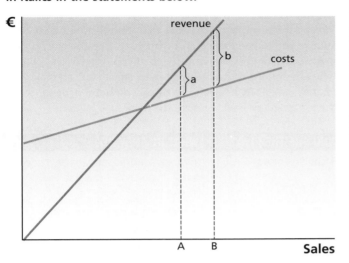

1 If point A represents sales of 100 units, then point B represents sales of *120 / 200* units.
2 If bracket 'a' represents a profit of €100,000, then bracket 'b' represents a profit of *€120,000 / €200,000*.
3 This means that an increase in sales of *20% / 100%* produces an increase in profit of *20% / 100%*.
4 This is the phenomenon of *operating leverage / contribution margin*.

> The graph above shows that this company has high operating leverage. A **small** rise in sales (from A to B) produces a **large** rise in profits (from 'a' to 'b').
> Similarly, a **small** fall in sales from B to A produces a **large** fall in profits from 'b' to 'a'.

**30.2 The two graphs below are for the same company, six months later. Notice that the revenue is unchanged.**

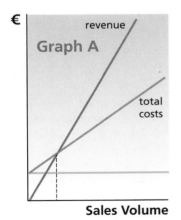 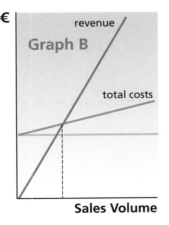

1 In which graph, A or B, have managers reduced the advertising budget (a fixed cost)? ☐
2 In which graph, A or B, have managers found another supplier with cheaper materials (a variable cost)? ☐

**30.3 Refer to the graphs in 30.2. Underline the correct words in italics below.**

1 Reducing fixed costs (Graph A) means that *more / fewer* sales are needed to break even. Reducing variable costs (Graph B) does not have such a big effect on the breakeven point.
2 Look at the increasing gap between revenue and costs as sales increase in both graphs – this is the operating leverage. Reducing variable costs (Graph B) gives *more / less* operating leverage than reducing fixed costs (Graph A).

**30.4 Study the top half of an income statement below. It is in 'contribution format', so a) the variable costs and fixed costs are listed separately and b) figures for different product lines (A, B and C) have been separated out.**

| Income statement (figures in €000) | line A | line B | line C |
|---|---|---|---|
| Sales revenue | **500** | **765** | **830** |
| *Less variable costs* | | | |
| Cost of goods sold | 275 | 325 | 370 |
| Sales commission | 80 | 105 | 140 |
| Shipping costs | 35 | 30 | 55 |
| Total variable costs | (390) | (460) | (565) |
| Contribution margin | 22% | 40% | 32% |
| *Less fixed costs* | | | |
| Salaries | xxx | xxx | xxx |
| Advertising | xxx | xxx | xxx |
| Etc | | | |
| Operating profit | xxx | xxx | xxx |

Check the definition of 'contribution margin' opposite to see how the % figures in the table are calculated.

Example (line A):
500 – 390 = 110
$\frac{110}{500}$ x 100 = 22%

**Underline the correct letters in italics.**
1 In order to maximize profits, the company should emphasize line *A / B / C* in its product mix.
2 Sales commissions on line *A / B / C* may be a little too generous.
3 The selling price of line *A / B / C* is probably too low.

See page 149 for some discussion topics.

## Stock and bond markets

Stock markets are the best-known financial market, and their function is firstly to raise capital when a company goes public (ie issues shares for the first time), and secondly to provide a place where buyers and sellers of those shares can then exchange them.

When a business reaches a certain size, the original owners might decide that they want to go public and list their shares (AmE stocks) on a stock market. With the help of an investment bank, they sell these shares to the market at an IPO (initial public offering). A huge sum of money enters the business as a one-time event and can be used to expand the business. Ownership of the business passes from the original founders to the shareholders.

The bond market is also used to raise capital, but in this case the capital is raised as a loan. Bonds can be issued by companies, governments and some municipal or state authorities. The investor – the bondholder – provides money, and this is paid back with interest over the term of the loan.

Stocks and bonds, which are collectively known as 'securities', are actively traded on the markets after they have been issued.

## Money market

The money market is less well-known, but it provides important short-term liquidity for the financial system. Companies can fund their short-term needs with a range of debt instruments, often referred to as 'commercial paper'. Banks use this paper to borrow and lend amongst themselves. Governments, states and local governments also have access to money market instruments to fund their short-term debt.

## FX market

By far the largest financial market in the world is the foreign exchange (forex/fx) market. Companies need currencies to pay their foreign bills. Central banks buy and sell currencies to manipulate the exchange rate. Governments use currencies to buy the bonds of other countries. Pension funds need currencies to make investments overseas. Speculators buy and sell currencies as they chase short-term trends, adding a lot of volatility to the system. And everybody wants to hold their spare cash in a currency with a good rate of interest.

## Commodity markets

Commodity markets exist to trade physical products such as oil, gas, metals, grains and meat.

## Derivative markets

Finally, there are derivatives markets. A derivative is a financial instrument whose value is derived from (= depends on) another asset. For example, an options contract on a stock allows you to make money if the value of the underlying stock rises (or falls) to a certain level by a certain date. If it

does, you gain more as a percentage than the movement of the underlying stock. If it doesn't, you lose everything.

So, in exchange for some risk, you can increase your potential return. But notice that an options contract also allows you to be more careful with your investments: if you own a stock and it falls in value then you lose money – but with an options contract on the same stock you can make money as the stock falls. In this way you have 'hedged' (ie protected yourself against) the risk.

| WHO ARE THE PLAYERS? | WHAT DO THEY DO? |
|---|---|
| **Retail investors** | These are individuals who purchase small amounts of securities for themselves. |
| **Institutional investors**<br>– investment banks<br>– pension funds<br>– insurance companies<br>– mutual funds | **Investment banks** buy and sell securities on behalf of their clients (large companies), and on their own behalf.<br>**Pension funds** invest money that people are saving for their retirement.<br>**Insurance companies** invest the money they receive from policyholders.<br>**Mutual funds** (BrE unit trusts) pool the money of many small investors to invest in selected companies in a particular field. |
| **Hedge funds** | Often quite secretive, these are companies that pool the money of wealthy investors and act in an aggressive way: speculating on a short-term basis, using leverage (ie borrowing money to increase potential profits), using derivatives, etc. |
| **Private equity firms** | These firms typically invest in private companies, not publicly listed companies. There are two very different types of activity:<br>+ venture capital to support start-ups.<br>+ buy-outs (where a company is taken over, restructured, and then sold). |
| **Sovereign wealth funds** | These are investment vehicles owned by national governments with a large budgetary surplus (eg because of oil revenues). They invest in a range of assets (eg stocks, bonds). |

# Exercises

**31.1 Find a word in the text opposite that matches each definition below. The words appear in order.**

1 people who start a business _____
2 documents given to someone who invests money in a government or company, which promises to pay back the money with interest _____
3 *(two words)* the relation in value between one currency and another (eg € / $) _____
4 people who buy and sell assets (eg shares, bonds, currencies, raw materials) in the hope of making a quick profit _____
5 sudden, often dangerous, changes _____
6 primary, existing under the surface _____

**Now do the same for the words in 'Who are the players?' opposite.**

7 *(three words)* acting as the representative of; instead of
_____
8 people who own insurance _____
9 combine people's money so that it can be used more effectively _____
10 *(two words)* money invested in a new company to help it develop _____
11 situations in which a person or group gains control of a company by buying all or most of its shares
_____
12 *(two words)* when a government receives more than it spends over a particular period of time
_____

**31.2 Put the words in each box into two groups, based on their meaning.**

a | *bear, booming, bull, depressed, falling, healthy, rising, strong, weak* | market

a | *good, high-risk, profitable, risky, secure, sound, speculative, worthwhile* | investment

**31.3 Make phrases by matching an item from each column.**

1 go — capital by issuing bonds
2 list — short-term debt with 'commercial paper'
3 raise — shares on a stock market
4 pay back — public with an IPO
5 fund — a loan with interest

6 manipulate — a start-up with venture capital
7 chase — the exchange rate
8 buy shares — short-term trends in the market
9 support — a company, then restructure it
10 take over — on behalf of a client

**31.4 Complete the sentences about currencies with these words: *appreciates, depreciates, floats, pegs, props up*.**

1 If a government _____ its currency to another, then it keeps it at the same level.
2 If a government _____ a currency, then it supports it and prevents it from falling.
3 If a currency _____ freely, then its value is allowed to change against other currencies.
4 If the € rises against the $, it _____ .
5 If the € falls against the $, it _____ .

**31.5 Fill in the missing letters in these commodities.**

1 Energy: cr_ _e oil, na_ _ _ _l gas
2 Food and fibre: c_ _oa, co_ _on
3 Grains and oilseeds: wh_ _t, soyb_ _ _s
4 Meat: ca_ _le, h_gs (BrE pigs)
5 Metals: co_ _er, ir_ _ ore

**31.6 Complete the text with the words in the box.**

| *commodity contracts* | *downside risk* |
| *hedging* | *leverage* | *underlying asset* |

Two concepts that are fundamental to modern finance are leverage and hedging.

1 _____ is using borrowed money to buy an investment. You invest €100 of your own money and €100 – or €1,000 – of the bank's. This gives you enormous profits if your investment is a good one, but also magnifies the 2 _____ . A lot of leverage in a market increases volatility. If the market moves against you, it's not just your own money you're losing, but the borrowed money as well. So you have to sell shares quickly to minimize losses, and this drives down the market very quickly.

3 _____ means trying to protect yourself against risk. If you hold a lot of shares, foreign currency or 4 _____ , you'll clearly make money if the price of the asset goes up. But if the price goes down, you'll lose. You can hedge this risk by buying a derivative that is structured to make money as the price of the 5 _____ falls. So if the market moves against you, at least you have some protection.

**See page 149 for some discussion topics.**

## Stocks and shares

The word 'stocks' is used in the US, both 'stocks' and 'shares' in the UK, and 'equities' inside the industry. The people who own them are known as stockholders/shareholders. (Players in the market are shown in unit 31.)

A company's shares first appear on a stock exchange at the IPO (initial public offering). (See units 4 and 31.) From this point, they begin to be actively traded on the exchange. People buy stocks for two reasons:

1 Stocks pay a dividend. You can see from the income statement in unit 26 that some of the profit that a company makes is returned to the shareholders every year as a dividend payment.

2 The price of the stock on the market can go up. If you buy low and sell high, you make a profit (ie a capital gain). Obviously you can also make a loss.

Notice that dividends and capital gains are quite independent. There might be a well-established company in the healthcare or food retailing area that pays a high, consistent dividend every year, but whose stock price changes very little. Equally, there might be a smaller company in the technology sector whose stock price is going up rapidly, but they pay no dividends at all, because all their profits are reinvested to help expand the business.

## Exchanges and indices

Nearly every country has a stock exchange, and on the exchange certain shares can be grouped together to make an index. In the US there is the Dow Jones, the S&P and the NASDAQ; in Europe the FTSE, the DAX and the CAC; in Asia the Nikkei, the Hang Seng and the Sensex. An index can be used as a benchmark for individual stocks: is the stock outperforming or underperforming the index?

Every stock is quoted with two prices: a bid price (= the buying price) and an offer price (= the selling price). The difference between these two (= the 'bid/offer spread') is the profit that goes to the exchange and other people who handle the transaction.

## Funds

Instead of buying stocks in an individual company, you can buy stocks in a fund. Funds hold a range of shares and a diversified portfolio helps to spread risk. The fund manager picks stocks with the help of analysts who have expertise in particular areas, for example Chinese banks, or small biotech companies, or dividend-paying companies.

Investors choose funds on the basis of their holdings, their past performance, their manager, their risk profile and their marketing.

## Evaluating a stock

Professional investors look at a whole range of factors when deciding which stocks to buy:

## EVALUATING A STOCK

| | |
|---|---|
| **SWOT of the company** | – Existing products and pipeline<br>– Growth prospects<br>– Existing competitors and barriers to entry<br>– Strategy of senior management<br>– Quality of senior management |
| **Financial situation of the company** | – Revenue and net profit<br>– Cash flow<br>– Level of debt<br>– Dividends paid in recent years<br>– Financial ratios with figures taken directly from the income statement and balance sheet.<br>Examples: EPS (earnings per share), P/E ratio (price/earnings ratio), ROE (return on equity), etc |
| **Market conditions** | – Prospects for that particular industry<br>– General economic situation: growth in the economy, consumer spending etc |
| **Technical analysis** | – Studying chart patterns: support and resistance, trading channels, breakouts etc<br>– Studying investor sentiment (eg prices are lowest when sentiment is at its most bearish)<br>– Cycle analysis: seasonality (eg stocks do better from Oct–May) and 'the Presidential cycle' (ie stocks do better in the second half of a US President's term in office) |

# Exercises

**32.1 Find a word in the text opposite that matches each definition below. The words appear in order.**

1 *(two words)* accounting a profit that is made from the sale of an investment _____
2 a number that shows the value or level of something, so that you can measure changes _____
3 an amount or standard that you can use for judging how good or bad other things are _____
4 doing better than _____
5 *(two words)* a range of different types of stocks _____
6 chooses _____

**Now do the same for the words in 'Evaluating a stock' opposite.**

7 a method used to study an organization by analyzing its strengths and weaknesses, the opportunities it has and the threats it faces _____
8 products being planned or developed that will be available in the future _____
9 possibilities (especially good things that might happen) _____
10 *(three words)* things that make it difficult for a new company to enter a market, for example the need for a lot of capital or specialized know-how _____
11 a price level on a stock chart that has stopped previous declines _____
12 *(two words)* two parallel lines drawn on a stock chart that contain the price movements over a period of time _____
13 how players in the market feel about an individual stock or the economy _____
14 a series of events that happen again and again in the same order or at the same times _____

**32.2 Make phrases by matching an item from each column.**

1 make a dividend          portfolio
2 quote a bid              profile (of a fund)
3 have a diversified       payment
4 past                     sentiment
5 risk                     patterns
6 growth                   /offer spread
7 chart                    performance (of a fund)
8 investor                 prospects

**32.3 Complete the text about financial ratios with the words in the box. Check any unknown words in a dictionary.**

| assets | bluff your way | capital gain | earnings |
|---|---|---|---|
| metrics | overpriced | profitability | share price |

Investors need a way to analyze a company objectively, and senior managers inside the company also need
¹ _____ (= performance indicators) to monitor its financial health. This is where financial ratios have a role: they use figures taken directly from the company accounts to give information about ² _____ (= profits), growth and value in the market. These ratios also appear in news reports, and if you want to ³ ' _____ ' in finance, you should at least recognize the words passively! Here are some important ones:

1 **EPS** Earnings per share. This is the net profit after tax divided by the number of shares that have been issued. It is a basic measure of ⁴ _____ (= the ability to make money).
2 **P/E** Price-to-earnings ratio. This is the company's share price divided by the EPS. For an investor, it's probably the single most important indicator. It shows what the market is willing to pay for the company's earnings. It is used to compare companies in the same market: a high P/E means that the market has high hopes for the company's future, but it may also indicate that the stock is ⁵ _____ .
3 **P/S** Price-to-sales ratio. This is similar to the previous ratio, but here the ⁶ _____ is divided by the annual sales per share. It is useful when evaluating young companies with lots of sales but little or no profits.
4 **ROE** Return on equity. This is the net profit after tax divided by the shareholders' equity. It is a measure of how efficiently a company uses its ⁷ _____ to produce earnings.
5 **Dividend Yield** This is the annual dividend per share divided by the share price. It shows you the return in dividends that you get when you buy a stock. You need to know this if you're looking for regular dividends from an established company rather than the chance of a ⁸ _____ from a high-risk growth stock.

**See page 149 for some discussion topics.**

Recruitment (hiring) is a key area within human resources. The process involves many decisions:

### Should you hire a full-time employee on a permanent contract?

A full-time employee is likely to have a better skillset, more experience, more loyalty, and you will have more control over their time. On the other hand, you're taking some risk with your commitment to this individual, and you will have extra costs (eg paid vacation) to consider. Other options might include:

- Fixed-term contracts.
- Part-time employees (eg students, retirees, individuals with children).
- Temporary help ('temps', recruited through an agency).
- Independent contractors and freelancers (who might work off your premises).
- Reorganizing the department to allocate work in a different way.

### What job will the new employee do?

There will be certain job skills that the organization needs. If you're replacing an existing employee, then an exit interview could help to clarify some of the issues. After some analysis you may produce:

- A job description that gives the job title, a summary of the job and a list of the main tasks or duties.
- A person specification that lists the knowledge, experience, qualifications and skills that you would like a candidate to have. These are often divided into 'essential' and 'desirable specifications'.

### How will you attract applicants?

Once you have a job opening, your first thoughts are likely to be internal applicants. If you don't offer opportunities to existing employees, they're likely to become demotivated and start looking elsewhere. But if you do need to recruit externally, then you can use a variety of electronic and print media such as an online posting on a jobs website, or a classified ad (or a display ad) in a newspaper. You can also use the services of a specialist employment agency, including headhunting firms for senior managers.

Another source of new recruits is referrals, ie suggestions made by colleagues, existing employees, etc. But beware: a workplace with too many friends results in a group that resists supervision, covers up for its members, socializes too much, ignores those not in the group, and causes problems if conflicts arise.

### What kind of interview and selection process will there be?

You will begin by asking for and looking through CVs (BrE) or resumes (AmE), unless you have a special template or application form designed by the company. You will then draw up a shortlist of candidates and call these people for interview.

At the interview there are a number of stages that you will probably go through:

1 Begin by establishing rapport with the candidate. They will be nervous, and you want to put them at their ease so that they can answer questions properly. You can also check their ability to socialize and be friendly.
2 Outline the company background and where the job fits.
3 Encourage the candidate to talk about how their skills and experience are relevant. Ask open-ended questions and keep the interview moving and on track.
4 Close the interview, and indicate to the candidate the next step and the timeframe.
5 Rate the candidate while they're fresh in your mind. Keep a record.

After the interview, and depending on the job, there may be further tests. These can include practical tests (of manual skills or computing skills) and psychometric tests (eg problem-solving, decision-making, interpersonal skills). Some large companies have special assessment centres to do these tests.

Finally, before selecting the best candidate and making a job offer, you may want to do some background checks. At a minimum this involves calling former employers who were listed by the candidate as references.

### Tips for a CV (resume)

- ✔ Put a 'Summary' in a box at the top – one short paragraph with your current position and objectives.
- ✔ Put 'Work experience' before 'Education', with the most recent job first. Include references at the end, or at least a line saying they're available on demand.
- ✔ Be specific in your descriptions of responsibilities in previous jobs.
- ✔ Include lots of action verbs.
- ✔ Focus on achievements (ie important things you have done) rather than skills.
- ✔ DON'T leave gaps in your employment record, and DON'T put down many jobs in a short time.

### Tips for a cover letter

Include a cover letter with your CV. This could be the body of an email if you're sending the CV as an attachment. In the cover letter:

- ✔ Refer to the particular vacancy (eg where you saw it advertised).
- ✔ Show how your skills and experience would be relevant.
- ✔ Highlight a couple of points from your CV.
- ✔ Say when you're available for interview.
- ✔ Generally 'sell' yourself.

For more help, use an Internet search engine. First choose a word like 'CV' or 'resume' or 'cover letter', then add a word like 'tips' or 'example' or 'advice' or 'writing guide'.

# Exercises

**33.1 Find a word in the text opposite that matches each definition below. The words appear in order.**

1 *(human resources)* range of skills _____
2 buildings that a business uses _____
3 decide to use a particular amount of money, time, etc for a particular purpose _____
4 examinations that you have passed _____
5 finding somebody who has the right skills for a senior job and persuading them to leave their present job _____
6 *(two words)* people who have recently joined an organization _____
7 *(phrasal verb)* protects someone by hiding unpleasant facts about them _____
8 *(phrasal verb)* reading something to find the information you want _____
9 a pre-designed document formatted for a particular purpose _____
10 relationship of understanding, friendliness and respect _____
11 decide that someone has a particular standard or level _____

**Now do the same for the words in 'Tips for a cover letter' opposite.**

12 a job that is available _____

**33.2 Make phrases by matching an item from each column.**

1 be on — work in a different way
2 recruit — a permanent contract
3 work — looking elsewhere for a job
4 allocate — off the premises as a freelancer
5 start — temps through an agency

6 ask — an interview on track
7 focus — a shortlist of candidates
8 keep — on achievements rather than skills
9 do — open-ended questions
10 draw up — some background checks

**33.3 Divide the words in the box into three groups, based on their meanings.**

| appoint | fire | hire | lay off | make redundant (BrE) | quit |
| recruit | resign | stand down | take on | terminate (AmE) | |

**employ**
_____
_____
_____
_____

**dismiss**
_____
_____
_____
_____

**hand in your notice**
_____
_____

**33.4 Find two words in the second column in exercise 33.3 that are used when the employee does something wrong, not when the company needs to save money.**

_____ / _____

**33.5 Underline the correct words in italics.**

1 *A candidate / An applicant* has simply asked for a job (eg by sending a CV); *a candidate / an applicant* is being actively considered for the job by the company.
2 A *classified ad / display ad* is a short piece of text; a *classified ad / display ad* has a box around it and can have artwork.
3 If you *outline / highlight* a point, you make people notice it and think about it; if you *outline / highlight* a point, you describe the main ideas.

**33.6 Cross out the item which has a <u>different</u> meaning to the others.**

1 to *complete, fill in, fill out, submit* an application form
2 to *attend, be called for, carry out, get, go for* an interview
3 to *allocate, assign, delegate, give somebody, set somebody, succeed in* a task
4 to *be faced with, carry out, do, fulfil, perform* a task
5 to have a *challenging, daunting, difficult, hard, thankless, uphill* task
6 to talk about a candidate's employment *contract, history, record*
7 to have an established recruitment *method, policy, procedure, process*
8 to have the required *expertise, know-how, mindset, skillset*

**33.7 Match pairs with a similar meaning, one from each box. All the words can be used with 'experience'.**

| considerable | direct | practical |
| previous | limited | relevant |

| appropriate | extensive | first-hand |
| hands-on | little | prior |

**33.8 Match pairs with a similar meaning, one from each box. All the words can be used with 'job'.**

| boring | challenging | decent |
| ideal | manual | regular |

| blue-collar | dead-end | demanding |
| dream | steady | worthwhile |

**See page 150 for some discussion topics.**

Pay is often referred to as 'salary' in white-collar jobs and 'wages' in blue-collar jobs. A company offers a compensation package (= pay + benefits) to employees, and this is the main way to attract and retain them.

## Levels of pay

How do you decide what level of pay is appropriate? You can start by finding out what other employers are paying. The best way to get this information is probably networking: ask existing staff, counterparts from other companies, people already doing that job, etc. You could also look at the job advertisements in local newspapers and agencies, or perhaps consult with your chamber of commerce.

Sometimes the salary for a job is fixed; at other times it may be open to discussion, for example at interview or when a job offer is made. A student looking for their first job probably won't have much bargaining power over pay, but other people might. In particular, you have a position of strength if you have specialized skills, an existing job, and you can see that the company needs you.

Besides deciding how much to pay new hires, the other major concern of employers is how much of a rise (AmE raise) to give existing employees. The three basic approaches, which are often mixed, are:

1 Give everyone the same percentage rise.
2 Offer annual increments based on length of service.
3 Have an incentive scheme where part of the rise is a bonus based on performance, results or profits.

## Performance-related pay

The pros and cons of option 3 above (ie performance-related pay), are well-known:

**Pros** It provides a strong motivation to work well; colleagues know who isn't pulling their weight and resent it if these people are paid the same.

**Cons** It creates tension between colleagues; performance may be difficult to measure; employees stop focusing on quality of work and instead just focus on those factors that affect pay.

It is of course possible to give a bonus to everyone at the end of the year if certain targets are met, and this overcomes the objection about competition undermining teamwork.

## Laws that affect pay

From the human resources point of view, another important issue is compliance with the laws that affect pay. There may be laws about:

- The minimum wage (an hourly rate for low-paid workers).
- Overtime ('time-and-a-half' may be mandatory for some workers).
- Equal pay for equal work (to combat discrimination based on gender, age, race, etc).

## Benefits

Benefits, the second area of compensation, are covered in the table below. Many of these have a minimum level that is required by law, but an option is for the company to offer more.

| | |
|---|---|
| **Time-off benefits** | Annual leave days (paid vacation)<br>Sick leave<br>Time off for pregnancy (maternity leave), birth, moving house, etc |
| **Insurance** | Life insurance – attractive to people with families<br>Private health insurance<br>Disability insurance (for serious, permanent injuries that cause long-term loss of income) |
| **Pension plan (for retirement)** | The employer usually sets up the plan and makes payments into it, but the employee can also make contributions |
| **Workers' compensation** | Protection against loss of income (and for medical payments) due to a work-related injury, accident or illness |
| **Fringe benefits** | Car<br>Laptop, mobile device, etc<br>Membership of a health club<br>Employee discount on the company's own products<br>Relocation expenses |

Extra benefits offer great flexibility in how you reward employees. Research in the UK has shown that the most common benefits offered by large companies are employer pension plans, life insurance, and an increased number of annual leave days. Other popular benefits include professional development opportunities such as seminars, conferences and courses.

# Exercises

**34.1 Find a word in the text opposite that matches each definition below. The words appear in order.**

1 *(two words)* office jobs rather than factory jobs
_____

2 *(human resources)* continue to employ; keep
_____

3 a series of regular, small increases _____

4 *(three words)* advantages and disadvantages
_____

5 *(three words; idiom)* doing their share of the work
_____

6 feel angry because you aren't treated fairly
_____

7 gradually making something less effective
_____

8 the practice of obeying a law _____

9 ordered by law _____

10 unfair treatment _____

**Now do the same for the words in the box opposite.**

11 a condition in which someone isn't able to use a part of their body properly _____

12 *(two words)* things that you get in addition to your basic compensation package _____

**34.2 Make phrases by matching an item from each column.**

| | |
|---|---|
| 1 compensation | scheme |
| 2 bargaining | package |
| 3 incentive | wage |
| 4 life | power |
| 5 minimum | bonus |
| 6 maternity | plan |
| 7 pension | leave |
| 8 end-of-year | insurance |

**34.3 Write each item next to the correct definition below: *life insurance, pension, retirement*.**

1 the time after you permanently stop working
_____

2 money paid to your family when you die
_____

3 money that you receive regularly when you no longer work because of your age _____

**34.4 Match each word in the box to its closest definition.**

> bonus   commission   income   overtime   perk
> remuneration   royalty   salary   wage   weighting

1 a regular amount of money that you earn – used for hourly / daily / weekly payments and blue-collar jobs *(usually used in the plural)* _____

2 a regular amount of money that you earn – used for monthly payments and white-collar jobs
_____

3 money earned by a person, an organization or a country
_____

4 *(formal)* payment that you get for your work
_____

5 the money that someone is paid for the extra hours that they work _____

6 an amount of money that is paid to somebody every time they sell a product _____

7 a payment that someone such as a writer or musician gets each time their work is sold or performed
_____

8 extra money that you're paid in addition to your usual salary, especially as a reward for good performance
_____

9 extra amount of pay given because you work in an area where it's expensive to live _____

10 something extra that you get from a job, very much like a fringe benefit, but it can have no monetary value – for example the chance to travel _____

**34.5 Cross out the <u>one</u> word in italics that does <u>not</u> make a word partnership with the key word. Check any unknown words in a dictionary.**

| | | |
|---|---|---|
| 1 a / an | *attractive, average, basic, competitive, generous, gross, incentive, monthly, net, starting, substantial* | salary |
| 2 a salary | *award, band, benefit, cut, increase, level, package, range, review, scale* | |
| 3 | *back, low, maternity, overtime, performance-related, reward, severance, sick, take-home* | pay |

**34.6 Fill in the missing letters of the prepositions below. Here are the letters you need: *deeffinnnooooorrrtuv*.**

1 I have a good job. I'm _ _ a salary _ _ €40,000.
2 I'm not paid enough. It's not fair. I'm _ _ _ _ paid.
3 He's paid too much. He doesn't deserve it. He's _ _ _ paid.
4 They pay my salary _ _ _ _ my account at the end of the month.
5 The company paid _ _ _ my laptop.

**See page 150 for some discussion topics.**

**Issues in the workplace**

The previous two units covered recruitment, salary and benefits. These are the core areas of human resources (HR). But there are a whole variety of other workplace issues, both big and small, that HR managers have to deal with. Small firms often sort these things out informally, but in a large organization a union representative might become involved. Most of these areas have legal requirements that HR has to monitor, and the paperwork required for this may be a large part of the work of the HR department.

### WORKING HOURS AND OVERTIME

These are usually clear in principle – but what about a situation where there is too much unpaid, unofficial overtime? And is it always clear whether training and travel count as part of the job, and whether working lunches count as 'working hours'? HR could become very unpopular with other managers if it tries to enforce the rules in these areas too strictly.

### *Leave and absence*

Again, the principles are clear – but what happens when a sick child needs looking after for several days? What happens if someone is missing work because of serious personal problems? What happens if everyone wants to take their holidays at the same time in the summer and there is no-one left in the office? What happens if it has become the norm for people to leave work early on Friday afternoon – but now the new CEO doesn't like it and wants HR to do something about it?

### Health and safety

There are statutory rules in this area, and every company has to maintain minimum levels of hygiene and comfort. But again there are issues that HR might have to deal with. Do all factory workers know the health and safety regulations? Are all the procedures being followed? The answer to the last question is probably 'no' in most factories – after some time people start to cut corners and pay less attention. Remember that if there is a serious workplace accident, then the employee affected might have a major claim against the company.

### *Dealing with harassment and bullying*

This can begin in very subtle ways – and lead to a large compensation award against you if not dealt with properly.

### GRIEVANCE PROCEDURES

An employee may have concerns or complaints about their work, employment terms, working conditions or relationships with colleagues. If so, they may want to discuss them or bring them formally to the attention of HR. They will expect HR to address and resolve these grievances. Is the procedure for doing this clear?

### *Disciplinary and dismissal procedures*

Some types of behaviour – called 'gross misconduct' – are so serious that they're likely to lead to dismissal without notice. These might include fighting, fraud, theft, etc. But what happens if an employee wants to appeal against the decision ('It wasn't my fault – he hit me first …')? What is the appeals procedure? For other less serious types of behaviour, there may be a series of warnings given to the employee before dismissal is an issue. How are those warnings given?

### Equal opportunities and diversity

Usually there is protection under the law from discrimination on the grounds of sex, race, ethnic origin, nationality, disability, sexual orientation, religion, age and marital status. But should the company go one step further and be actively promoting diversity? HR will have to implement such a policy if it has been decided, and it could well be divisive in the workforce. Groups that are currently favoured will feel threatened, and there might be comments behind people's backs that, 'they only got the job because they're …'

### *Work–life balance*

Are there opportunities for working flexible hours or job sharing? This might be important for someone wanting to work from home, or a parent returning to work after a new baby. If HR creates the precedent that one person can work from home one day a week, how do you stop everyone wanting to do it?

### *Whistle-blowing*

What happens if an employee sees evidence of fraud or bribery? Is there a procedure for them to report this confidentially? What happens if they do report it, and then feel they're being victimized afterwards for betraying their colleagues? What happens if they feel it's being covered up by the company, that there is no use reporting it internally, and so they want to make it public? Increasingly, governments are putting in place legislation to protect whistle-blowers, and HR will have to enforce this.

# Exercises

**35.1 Find a word in the text opposite that matches each definition below. The words appear in order: first down the left column, then down the right.**

1 an organization that represents the workers in a particular industry _____

2 make people obey a rule or law _____

3 a period of time when you're allowed to be away from work _____

4 *(always used with 'the')* what is usual, average or expected the _____

5 fixed by law _____

6 the practice of keeping things around you clean _____

7 *(two words; idiom)* do something quickly and carelessly, because you want to save time or money _____

8 behaviour which is deliberately unpleasant, and which causes somebody to feel upset _____

9 frightening someone or threatening to hurt them, especially if they're smaller or weaker _____

10 *(two words)* money that a court decides should be given to someone because they have suffered harm _____

11 *(formal)* a complaint that an employee makes to an employer about unfair treatment _____

12 *(formal)* pay attention to a problem and try to deal with it _____

13 formally ask someone in authority to change their decision _____

14 the fact that very different people exist within a group _____

15 an action in the past that is used as an example when someone wants to do the same thing again _____

16 reporting illegal activities within your own organization to someone in authority _____

**35.2 Make phrases by matching an item from each column.**

1 become — a precedent
2 sort — in principle
3 involve — the norm
4 create — something out informally
5 be clear — a union representative

6 appeal — and resolve a grievance
7 give — the rules strictly
8 promote — warnings to an employee
9 address — diversity
10 enforce — against a decision

**35.3 Make phrases by matching an item from each column.**

1 grievance — misconduct
2 work-life — requirements
3 health and — balance
4 legal — procedures
5 equal — safety
6 gross — opportunities

**35.4 Underline the correct words in italics.**

1 The words 'legal' and 'statutory' are very similar, but *legal / statutory* is more formal.

2 The words 'laws' and 'legislation' are very similar, but *laws / legislation* is more formal.

3 The words 'rules' and 'regulations' are very similar, but *rules / regulations* is more formal.

4 If you say you aren't satisfied, you make a *claim / complaint*. If you make a demand for something that you have a right to receive, you make a *claim / complaint*.

5 An *incident / accident* is just something that happens, whereas an *incident / accident* is a sudden event in which someone is hurt.

**35.5 Read the text about dealing with misconduct, then answer the questions below.**

What should you do if an employee's conduct is becoming a cause for concern? First, carry out a full investigation. Consider:

● The circumstances and consequences of the alleged breach of discipline.
● The employee's job, length of service and disciplinary record.
● The evidence of witnesses.
● Any previous incidents.
● Any mitigating circumstances, eg health or domestic problems, or provocation.

Now review this evidence to determine whether the case is serious enough for disciplinary measures, or whether there is an alternative, eg an informal chat or redeployment. For certain serious offences you may need to suspend an employee while a full investigation takes place.

Disciplinary measures begin with a meeting, and following that a written warning. After giving a warning, you must allow the employee time to improve their behaviour. Only move on to the next stage of the procedure – issuing a further warning or holding a formal disciplinary hearing – if the previous warning has no effect.

**Find a word in the text that means:**

1 *(three words)* reason to worry _____

2 *(four words; formal)* a situation in which it's claimed (but not proved) that someone has behaved against the rules _____

3 *(two words; formal)* facts that help to explain a mistake and make it seem less bad _____

4 moving someone to a different place or a different job _____

5 officially stop someone from working because they have broken the rules _____

6 meeting of a committee or official organization to find out the facts about something _____

**See page 150 for some discussion topics.**

" I enjoyed high school – my grades were good and I got involved in a lot of extracurricular activities. At the age of eighteen I went to university (AmE college/ university). I got a place at the university in my home town, although some of my friends moved away to other universities and lived on campus. At first I hated it, and I nearly dropped out after a few months. But after a while I made friends and got used to writing all the essays (AmE papers). Money was a problem – I had no grant or other financial aid – and I worked my way through college by doing a little part-time work whenever I could.

My degree was in economics, and my main subject (AmE major) was international trade. The lecturers (AmE professors) were good and I enjoyed the course (AmE program) very much. I spent the middle year of the course working as an intern in a bank – that was really useful. It was the only part where I got some real vocational training. At the end of the course I thought about staying on to do a Masters, but I decided that the life of a postgraduate didn't really interest me. It was time to enter the world of work.

After graduating, it took me several months to find a job. I was short-listed for a few jobs, but they never called me back for a second interview. Eventually I was offered a junior position in the international department of a bank. Because of my internship (work placement) I knew more or less what to expect in terms of the working environment. I spent five years there, learning the business and was promoted to Senior Analyst in my late twenties.

That time in my life was really hectic – I was living the life of a typical young, single person in the financial services sector. I worked hard and partied hard. I often stayed at the office until eight in the evening, and was exhausted at the weekends. By the age of thirty I was burnt out. I needed some personal space to decide where my life was going, and I decided to take a year off. I gave in my notice and quit my job.

I had saved up quite a lot of money from the job in the bank, and so I was able to go travelling. I backpacked my way around India and South-East Asia and had some crazy times. But I knew that I had to settle down one day, and I wanted to start a family. So I came home and started to look for work again.

I registered with some online employment agencies, and they found a vacancy almost immediately. It was in a similar field as before, but less high-pressure. "

## Verb forms for talking about your career

**Past simple: completed actions and situations in the past**
Single actions: I **got** a place at university.
A sequence of single actions: I **joined** the company in February, **finished** my training after four weeks, and **started** the job properly in March.
Situations that lasted for some time: I **lived** on campus.

**Past continuous: actions and situations in progress in the past (ie background events)**
I **was living** the life of a typical young person in the finance sector.
I **was working** as a waitress in a cocktail bar.

**Past perfect: making it clear that one action or event in the past happened before another**
I **had saved up** money from the job in the bank, and so …
I **had already quit** my job when they …

**Combination: background situation + actions during this time**
My salary **was increasing** year by year and so I **bought** an apartment.
While I **was working** as a sales assistant, another company **invited** me to join them.

**Combination: one action before another**
I **had saved up** money and so I **was able to** go travelling.
I **had already quit** my job when they **announced** the job cuts.

# Exercises

**36.1 Find a word in the text opposite that matches each definition below. The words appear in order.**

1 letters or numbers that show the quality of a student's work _____

2 *(two words)* things that a student does at school or college that are not part of the course _____

3 *(phrasal verb)* left university before the course had finished _____

4 money given by someone, especially the government, for a particular purpose (similar to 'scholarship', which only refers to money for study) _____

5 a course of study at a university, or the qualification that you get _____

6 a student who works in a job in order to get experience _____

7 relating to the skills you need for a particular job _____

8 *(phrasal verb)* continuing to do a job or a course after the expected time of leaving _____

9 completing your studies at university and getting a degree _____

10 busy; full of activity _____

11 *(two words)* very tired and with no energy because of working too hard for too long _____

12 *(four words)* told my employer that I would be leaving my job soon; resigned _____

13 travelled for pleasure, without much money, carrying everything needed for life in one bag _____

14 *(phrasal verb)* start living a quiet life in one place, especially when you get married _____

15 an available job _____

**36.2 Make phrases by matching an item from each column.**

| | |
|---|---|
| 1 get a place | through college |
| 2 drop out | at university |
| 3 work your way | a year as an intern |
| 4 spend | after a few months |
| 5 be short-listed | to Senior Analyst |
| 6 be promoted | a vacancy almost immediately |
| 7 register | for a job |
| 8 find | with an online agency |

**36.3 The third paragraph opposite uses the word 'eventually'. This is a false friend in many languages. Tick (✓) the one correct meaning of 'eventually' from the choices below.**

1 by accident ☐  3 possibly ☐

2 alternatively ☐  4 after a long time ☐

**36.4 Complete the sentences with the words in the box. All the words are used with 'career'.**

| | | | | |
|---|---|---|---|---|
| be over | break | chosen | concentrate on | ladder |
| make | move | opportunities | promising | take off |

1 You can _____ a good career for yourself as a lawyer. But you'll have to work a lot. For the next few years you'll have to _____ your career, not your social life.

2 If you have children, you'll need to take a career _____ . But don't worry – your skills are always in demand, and I'm sure that your career will _____ when you're in your forties.

3 Changing from financial consultant to yoga teacher is a very drastic career _____ . It means that your career in finance will _____ .

4 He's a bright young man with a very _____ career in front of him. I'm sure he'll move up the career _____ very quickly.

5 She achieved a lot in her _____ career. She took advantage of the many career _____ available in IT project management and went right to the top of her profession.

**36.5 Complete these memories by putting the verbs into the correct form: past simple, past continuous or past perfect.**

❝ I remember that occasion very well – it was while I 1 _____ (work) at Omnitel. It was in the afternoon – I 2 _____ (just / finish) lunch – and I 3 _____ (write) a report at my desk. I 4 _____ (get) an SMS on my mobile phone – it was from a headhunting agency, inviting me to call them. I 5 _____ (be) very surprised because I 6 _____ (not / contact) any agencies like that. Anyway, I 7 _____ (wait) until no-one 8 _____ (listen) and then I 9 _____ (call) them. I'm sure they 10 _____ (wait) for my call because they were immediately very friendly. They said they 11 _____ (already / find out) a lot about me by doing a Google search on my name, and that they 12 _____ (want) to have a meeting with me. ❞

See page 150 for some discussion topics.

When you describe your company, you may choose to give a brief, informal introduction or a full, formal presentation, depending on the context. The five headings below cover the important areas to include in a full presentation.

## 1 History, size and structure

Start with the name and main business activity of your company, and the sector in which you operate (eg the consumer goods sector, the business-to-business sector). Say where the head office is located. Briefly mention the company's origins, then cover key milestones (including any major restructuring) and its size and structure today.

'Size' might include the number of employees, or things like the number of stores. A technical indication of company size is your market capitalization (market cap). 'Structure' might include reference to a business group that owns several companies, or to subsidiaries, or to separate divisions (eg organized by product categories).

At this point you may want to briefly describe the organization chart (organigram) of your company. Be careful: this can be very boring!

## 2 Main products / services

Give an overview of your product range, including any competitive advantages. Note that nowadays there is little difference between the words 'product' and 'service' (eg you can have 'financial products').

## 3 Market

Talk about the countries in which you operate. Also talk about your typical customers (for a standard product) or clients (when the product is specially tailored). This may include a reference to the market segment in which you operate. See unit 20.

## 4 Key numbers

Key numbers include your annual turnover (= revenue), your net profit after tax (= net income), and your market share. For an international company, break down the revenue according to regions or countries. It's also interesting to know which lines contribute most to your revenue.

## 5 Trends and plans

This is likely to be the part of the presentation that will generate the most interest. Is the overall market growing or shrinking? Why? What new technologies or social trends are shaping your market? What are your company's plans for the future?

Finally, you may want to talk about your own job. See unit 38.

## SWOT analysis

A different way to profile a company is by means of a SWOT analysis. An example is given below, but it will be different for every company.

## SWOT analysis

| STRENGTHS of the company | WEAKNESSES of the company |
|---|---|
| products: quality, value, reliability<br>promising product pipeline<br>modern equipment and efficient manufacturing process<br>efficient distribution network<br>strong cash flow<br>cost advantages due to location<br>morale, commitment, leadership | small market share<br>weak brand image<br>gaps in product range<br>poor management information systems<br>insufficient sales people<br>low spending on innovation and R&D |
| OPPORTUNITIES in the market | THREATS in the market |
| major new contracts<br>growth in the existing market<br>new markets<br>developments in technology<br>competitors' mistakes<br>partnerships, agencies, distribution | market saturation<br>cheaper substitute products<br>changing consumer tastes<br>slowdown in the economy<br>success of existing competitors<br>entry of new competitors<br>political / legislative effects<br>a shortage of key raw materials / parts / components |

# Exercises

**37.1 Find a word in the text opposite that matches each definition below. The words appear in order.**

1 events that mark an important stage in a process

_____

2 organizing a company in a different way to make it more efficient _____

3 (two words; finance) the total value of a company's shares (= number of shares × their market price)

_____

4 companies owned or controlled by other, larger companies

_____

5 a short description that gives the main ideas without explaining all the details _____

6 (two words) things that help a company be more successful than its competitors _____

7 made for a particular purpose or person

_____

8 considering something as a whole; including everything

_____

9 becoming smaller _____

**Now do the same for words in the SWOT table.**

10 (two words) products that are planned and will be launched soon _____

11 the level of confidence and positive feelings that people have, especially people who work together

_____

12 the hard work and loyalty that someone gives to an organization _____

13 (two words) a situation when few new buyers can be found _____

14 not having enough of something; lack _____

**37.2 Make phrases by matching an item from each column.**

| | | | |
|---|---|---|---|
| 1 | market | | product |
| 2 | product | | trends |
| 3 | a standard | | D |
| 4 | social | | share |
| 5 | R& | | range |
| | | | |
| 6 | SWOT | | network |
| 7 | distribution | | analysis |
| 8 | cost | | products |
| 9 | substitute | | turnover |
| 10 | annual | | advantages |

**37.3 Complete the company presentation about Zara with the words and phrases in the box. Check any unknown words in a dictionary.**

> affordable    business model    consumer tastes
> continued expansion    founder    income    industry standard
> prime locations    state-of-the-art    turnover

Zara, part of the Inditex Group, is one of the world's fastest growing retailers, with an innovative [1] _____ that allows it to compete with quality brands but at much more [2] _____ prices.

The [3] _____ of Zara, Amancio Ortega, opened the first Zara store in A Coruña, Spain, in 1975. It was a great success, and Ortega started opening more Zara stores in Spain. Working with computer expert José Maria Castellano they created 'instant fashions' – the company reduced the time from design to distribution to just 10 to 15 days. (The [4] _____ at that time was several months.) They used [5] _____ production and warehousing procedures, and installed computerized inventory systems to link the stores to the factories. All of this meant that they were able to respond very quickly to changes in [6] _____ .

During the 1990s Inditex entered a steady stream of new markets, and by 2000 had covered most of Europe. Today, Zara is present in over 70 countries, with a network of 1,200 stores in [7] _____ in major cities.

For the whole Inditex Group (which includes Massimo Dutti, Pull and Bear, Bershka and other chains) annual [8] _____ is around 10,000 million euros, with a net [9] _____ of about 1,000 million. The total retail area of the Group is approaching 2,000,000 square metres. As a measure of the company's success, market capitalization has increased by 200% since it was first quoted. Plans for the future include [10] _____ in the Asia-Pacific Region, and the opening of more 'Zara Home' stores, selling bedroom, bathroom and living room products.

**See page 150 for some discussion topics.**

I work for a medium-sized, family-owned business. We offer specialized services to the construction industry. I personally specialize in lighting installations inside buildings – my background is in electrical engineering. I'm responsible for the initial contact with the client – I visit them at their offices and discuss their needs. My role is to talk to the architects and the developers, to try to persuade them of the importance of modern lighting design inside a building. I show them how it can create a good working atmosphere and add to a company's image. I explain our track record in this field and show them a portfolio of other lighting installations that we've done.

Once the initial contact has been made and the client is ready for a detailed proposal, I take a back seat for a while. Somebody else looks at the detailed specifications for the installation and then another colleague researches the cost of the labour and materials. Those two people work under me, and I supervise their work quite closely. Finally our legal department draws up the proposal. I oversee the whole process and sign off the proposal before it's sent to the client.

There are a number of other people that I liaise with on a day-to-day basis. We have an Office Manager who handles incoming calls, organizes my schedule and keeps on top of the filing and administration. And then outside the company I have close contact with the architects and with the project management team responsible for the whole construction.

I report to the Head of Business Development, and she reports directly to the CEO, so there are not many layers in the company and it's not at all bureaucratic.

My work is challenging, of course, because it involves both a sales function and a technical function – and every project is different. But the atmosphere in the office is great. It's very informal and I'm on first-name terms with everyone, even the CEO.

So that's me. Now about my wife. Well, she works for a large, multinational bank with its head office in Switzerland. It's a back-office function – she works in the loans department. Her job involves checking the credit history of companies who want to borrow money, and then assessing the risk of the loan. She deals with both small and medium enterprises. She's doing well – she was promoted last year. Now she's in charge of a small team of four people, so there's a management dimension to her job as well; it's not simply number-crunching.

## Describing your job

### Adjectives to describe jobs
*fascinating, rewarding, satisfying, stimulating*
*boring, dull, repetitive, routine, uninteresting*
*challenging, demanding, hard, hectic, tiring, tough*

### Contacts at work
*boss, CEO, colleague, coworker, counterpart, customer, line manager, opposite number, project leader, supplier*

### Collocations with 'task'
*approach / get down to / tackle a task*
*carry out / do / get on with / perform a task*
*complete / fulfil / succeed in (doing) a task*
*assign somebody / give somebody / set somebody a task*
*be tasked with doing something*

### Collocations with 'work'
I **work for** … (a company)
I'm **work**ing **on** … (a project)
I **work with / alongside** … (colleagues)
I **work on my own**.
I **work from home**.
to be **in work / out of work**
to be **off work** (because you're ill)
I **leave for work** at 7.30am, I **go to work** by train,
I **get to work** at about 8.45am, I'm **at work** until 6pm.

# Exercises

**38.1 Find a word in the text opposite that matches each definition below. The words appear in order.**

1 (two words) the things that a person or organization has done in the past which show how well they have done

_____

2 (phrasal verb) prepares a written document (eg a list, plan, contract) _____

3 be in charge of a group of workers and check that their work is done satisfactorily (= supervise) _____

4 (phrasal verb) officially agree to something

_____

5 exchange information so that everyone knows what is happening _____

6 (two words) the process of working with a lot of numbers and calculating results _____

**38.2 Underline the correct words in italics.**

1 A job that is challenging / demanding is difficult, but also interesting because you have to use a lot of skill; a job that is challenging / demanding needs a lot of your time and attention, but isn't necessarily either difficult or interesting.

2 The phrase 'my line manager' / 'my boss' could be a little informal, particularly if that person is present (eg being introduced by you), so instead we can say 'my line manager' / 'my boss'.

3 The word colleague / coworker is more common in Europe; the word colleague / coworker is more common in the US and Asia.

4 The word counterpart / opposite number refers to someone with the same job as you in another organization; the word counterpart / opposite number may have the same meaning, but is also commonly used for someone in your own organization who has the same job but in a different place (eg a different country).

**38.3 Complete 1–3 with endings a–c.**

1 If you get down to a task, you … ☐
2 If you get on with a task, you … ☐
3 If you fulfil a task, you … ☐

a complete it successfully.
b start doing it seriously or with effort.
c continue after stopping for a short time.

**38.4 Make phrases by matching an item from each column.**

| | |
|---|---|
| 1 make | the whole process |
| 2 take | on top of the filing |
| 3 oversee | a back seat for a while |
| 4 handle | initial contact with a client |
| 5 keep | first-name terms |
| 6 be on | incoming calls |

**38.5 Cover the opposite page with a piece of paper. Underline the correct words in italics.**

1 I work for / on / to a family-owned business.
2 I specialize in / on / to lighting installations.
3 My background is for / in / with engineering.
4 I'm responsible about / for / of the initial contact with the client.
5 My role is for / in / to talk to the architects.
6 Somebody else looks at / on / to the detailed specifications.
7 There are a number of other people that I liaise from / to / with on a day-to-day basis.
8 I report for / to / under the Head of Business Development.
9 My wife works in / on / to the loans department.
10 She deals of / on / with both small and medium enterprises.
11 She's in charge from / of / to a small team.
12 I'm working for / on / to an interesting project.
13 I'm a journalist – I spend a lot of time working at / for / on my own, from home / from the home.
14 My brother is off work / out of work – he's been unemployed for two months. My sister is off work / out of work today – she's got a bad cold.
15 Every morning I leave for work / the work at 7.30am. I arrive to / get to work at about 8.45am. I'm at / in work until 6pm.
16 Her job involves checking / to check the credit history of companies.

**38.6 Write a tick (✓) if the sentence is grammatically correct. Write a cross (✗) if it is not.**

1 I'm responsible for this. ☐
2 I'm the responsible for this. ☐
3 I'm the person responsible for this. ☐
4 This is my responsible. ☐
5 This is my responsibility. ☐

**See page 150 for some discussion topics.**

# 39 Telephoning – making and taking calls

In the dialogue below Celine Perez (CP) calls Maurice Cassidy (MC) on his direct line.

> MC: Maurice Cassidy.
> CP: Hello Maurice, this is Celine Perez speaking.
> MC: Celine – how nice to hear from you! How are things over in Paris?
> 5 CP: Fine, fine. Maurice – is this a good time to talk? Are you in the middle of something?
> MC: No, now is good. Just let me close down this document I've been working on. OK – what can I do for you?
> 10 CP: The reason I'm calling is because of the first quarter sales figures. Have you seen them?
> MC: Yes, I have. Sales in France were below target, right?
> CP: Exactly. The sales report doesn't give any explanation for that. I thought you might have some ideas.
> 15 MC: I do have some ideas, but I'd like to speak to Anna in Marketing about it. Can I get back to you tomorrow about this?
> CP: Sure.
> MC: OK, leave it with me. I'll call you tomorrow afternoon.
> 20 CP: Great – I'd appreciate that. Thanks for your time. Bye.

- Notice how Maurice starts the conversation in a friendly way at line 3.
- Notice how Celine checks that the other person has time to talk.
- Notice at line 14 how Celine uses indirect language (ie past forms: *thought/might*) to encourage MC to give information – she doesn't want him to feel under any pressure.

In the second dialogue below Monika phones a company to ask about their market research services. She speaks first to the receptionist.

> Receptionist: Good morning, ICT Communications. Teresa speaking. How can I help you?
> Monika: Oh, good morning. I'd like to speak to someone in your market research department.
> 5 Receptionist: Can I have your name, please?
> Monika: Yes, it's Monika Weber.
> Receptionist: OK, Monika, please hold while I try to connect you.
> Gianfranco: Market Research. Gianfranco speaking.
> 10 Monika: Oh, hello. My name is Monika Weber from Springer Media and I'm calling to ask a few questions about your market research services.
> Gianfranco: Of course, Monika. How can I help you?
> Monika: I'd like to know …

- Notice at line 1 how the receptionist gives a very full answer.
- Notice at line 9 how Gianfranco answers his internal phone.

## The phrases you need ☞

### Answer the phone
(receptionist) *Good morning, ICT. Teresa speaking. How can I help you?*
(internal phone) *Hello. / Sales Department. / Nick Hamilton.*

### Connect the caller
*Please hold while I try to connect you.*
*I'll try her number for you.*

### Say who's calling + why
*This is … speaking / My name is …*
*This is … (here).*
*Can I speak to …, please?*
*I'd like to speak to someone about …*
*The reason I'm calling is …*
*I'm calling to ask a few questions about …*
*I'm calling in connection with …*

### Greetings
*Hello! How are you!*
*How nice to hear from you! How are things in Paris?*
*Oh! I didn't recognize your voice!*
*Thanks for calling – did you get my email?*

### Check it's a good time
*Is this a good time to talk?*
*Are you in the middle of something?*
*Do you have a second?*

### End the call
*Is there anything else I can help you with today?*
*Thanks for calling / It's been nice talking to you. Bye.*
*Thanks for your time.*
*OK, leave it with me. I'll call you tomorrow afternoon.*

# Exercises

**39.1 Cover the opposite page with a piece of paper. Now try to remember the words below. (The last letters have been given.)**

1 Hello Maurice, _ _ _s is Celine Perez _ _ _ _ _ _ _g.
2 Celine – how _ _ _e to _ _ _r from you!
3 Is this a _ _ _d _ _ _e to talk? Are you in the _ _ _ _ _e of something?
4 Just let me _ _ _se _ _ wn this document I've been working on.
5 The _ _ _ _on I'm calling is _ _ _ _se of the first quarter sales figures.
6 The sales report doesn't give any explanation for that. I _ _ _ _ght you _ _ght have some ideas.
7 Can I _ _t _ _ck _o you (= contact you again) tomorrow about this?
8 OK, _ _ _ve it _ _ _th me.
9 Great – I'd _ _ _ _ _ _ _ate that.

**Remove the paper and check your answers.**

**39.2 At line 5 Celine checks that it's a good time to talk. Put the words below into order to make similar phrases.**

1 have you a second Do?
2 me Do want later you to back call?
3 now right you Are busy?

**39.3 We often use a past tense to make our language polite or indirect (to make the other person feel they are under no pressure).**

I *wanted* to speak to someone about my order.
(= I'd like to)
I *was* just *calling* about the sales figures.
(= I'm calling)
I *thought* you *might* have some ideas.
(= Do you have any ideas?)

**Rewrite each sentence using one of the structures above.**

1 I'm calling to see if everything's OK for Friday.

_____

2 I'd like to ask you a question about Simon.

_____

3 I know you'll be interested in this.

_____

**39.4 Cover the opposite page with a piece of paper. Underline the alternative in italics below that is more natural.**

1 Good morning, ICT. Teresa speaking. *Can I help you? / How can I help you?*
2 *I want to speak / I'd like to speak* to someone in your market research department.
3 *Please can I have your name? / Can I please have your name? / Can I have your name, please?*
4 *I'm / It's* Monika Weber.
5 OK, please *hold / wait in line* while I try to connect you.
6 *Gianfranco speaking / I'm Gianfranco.*
7 I'm calling to *know / ask* a few questions *of / about* your market research services.
8 Of course, Monika. How *can / would* I help you?

**39.5 Look at phrases a–e then mark the statements below True (T) or False (F).**

a I'd like to speak to …
b Can I speak to …?
c Could I speak to …?
d I must speak to …
e I need to speak to …

1 In practice, phrases a–c are more or less the same – the listener probably won't even notice. **T / F**
2 Phrase d is direct and urgent, but is OK in business. **T / F**
3 Phrase e is direct and urgent, but is OK in business. **T / F**

**39.6 Look at phrases a–d then answer the questions below.**

a The reason I'm calling is …
b Perhaps you could help me. I'd like to speak to someone about …
c I'm calling in connection with …
d I don't know if I'm through to the right department, but I'm calling to ask a few questions about …

1 Which two phrases immediately give the reason for your call? ☐ ☐
2 Which two phrases ask for help or general information? ☐ ☐

Read the dialogues on page 82 aloud. Do it by yourself or with a colleague (changing roles at the end). Practise several times until you're fluent.

**39.7**  **1 Speaking practice: listen and repeat. Repeat each phrase you hear and then listen to check.**

In the dialogue below the caller (C) wants to speak to someone who isn't available. The receptionist (R) takes the call.

> R: ICT. Teresa speaking. How can I help you?
> C: I'd like to speak to Stefan Lipska, please.
> R: I'll try his number for you. ♪ ♪ ♪ Hello?
> C: Hello.
> 5 R: I'm not getting any reply. Just bear with me for a moment while I try another number.
> C: OK.
> R: I'm sorry, I'm not having any luck – he must be in a meeting. Would you like his voicemail?
> 10 C: No, I need to talk to him personally.
> R: I can ask him to call you back.
> C: Yes, please do that. It's Frank Hayden here. He knows me.
> R: OK, I'll just make a note of your name. Frank Hayden.
> 15 Is that with an 'i' or an 'e' at the end?
> C: It's an 'e', 'e' as in Egypt. H-A-Y-D-E-N.
> R: OK, Mr Hayden, I'll tell him as soon as he comes out of the meeting.
> C: Thank you. Goodbye.

● Notice how the caller clarifies the spelling by using a place name.

In the next dialogue the caller (C) gets through to a secretary (S).

> C: Hello, can I speak to Stefan Lipska, please?
> S: I'm sorry, Stefan Lipska is out of the office this afternoon. This is his secretary speaking. Would you like to leave a message?
> 5 C: Yes please. Can you ask him to call me back?
> S: OK. Let me just get a pen. Right. Can you give me your name and number?
> C: Yes, it's Ella Vogelaar.
> S: Can you spell that?
> 10 C: It's Ella, E-double L-A, Vogelaar, V-O-G-E-L-double A-R.
> S: And the number?
> C: It's 0031, that's the code for the Netherlands, 20 512 6149.
> S: OK, so that's Ella Vogelaar on 0031 20 512 6149.
> 15 C: That's right.
> S: Anything else?
> C: No, that's all. Just ask him to call me as soon as possible. It's an urgent matter.
> S: I understand. I'll make sure he gets the message.
> 20 C: Thank you. Goodbye.
> S: Goodbye. Thank you for calling.

● Notice at line 10 how the caller says the names before spelling them. Hearing the whole word first helps the listener.
● Notice at line 14 how the secretary checks by repeating the name and number.
● Notice how the receptionist and the secretary finish the dialogues by promising action (*I'll …*).

## The phrases you need ☞

**Ask the caller to wait**
*Just bear with me for a moment.*
*Can I put you on hold?*
*Right, sorry to keep you waiting.*

**Explain someone is unavailable**
*He must be in a meeting.*
*Sorry, she's out of the office / on another call.*

**Ask for information**
*What's it in connection with?*
*Can you give me your name?*
*Can I take your number?*

**Leave a message**
*Do you know how long he'll be?*
*Can I leave a message?*
*This is … / It's … / My name is Frank Hayden.*
*Can you ask him to call me back?*

**Take a message**
*Would you like to leave a message?*
*Let me just get a pen.*
*OK. Go ahead.*
*Can you spell that (for me)?*
*Is that with an 'i' or an 'e'?*
*Is that 'i' as in Italy, or 'e' as in Egypt?*
*Let me read that back to you.*

**Promise action**
*I'll tell him as soon as he comes out of the meeting.*
*I'll make sure he gets the message.*

# Exercises

**40.1 Cover the opposite page with a piece of paper. Now complete each sentence below with a verb, a preposition, or both. The longer lines are for verbs and the shorter ones are for prepositions. ('out of' is one item.)**

| | | | | | |
|---|---|---|---|---|---|
| ask | bear | call | leave | let | make |
| make | must | need | put | read | ~~speak~~ |

| | | | | | |
|---|---|---|---|---|---|
| back | back | for | for | in | in | of |
| on | on | on | out of | ~~to~~ | with |

*(first dialogue opposite)*

1  C: I'd like to _____*speak*_____ _____*to*_____ Stefan Lipska, please.
2  R: I'll try his number _____ you.
3  R: Just _____ _____ me for a moment.
4  R: I'm not having any luck – he _____ be _____ a meeting.
5  C: I _____ to talk to him personally.
6  R: I can ask him to _____ you _____.
7  R: I'll just _____ a note _____ your name.
8  C: It's 'e' as _____ Egypt.

*(second dialogue opposite)*

9  S: Stefan Lipska is _____ the office this afternoon.
10  S: Would you like to _____ a message?
11  S: _____ me just get a pen.
12  C: That's the code _____ the Netherlands.
13  S: OK, so that's Ella Vogelaar _____ 0031 20 512 6149.
14  C: Just _____ him to call me as soon as possible.
15  S: I'll _____ sure he gets the message.

*(The phrases you need)*

16  Can I _____ you _____ hold?
17  Sorry, she's _____ another call.
18  Let me _____ that _____ to you.

**40.2 Underline the correct words in italics.**

1  I'll tell him *as / so* soon as I see him.
2  Can you spell *it / that*?
3  Is there *anything / something* else?
4  Thank you for *your calling / calling*.

**40.3 Put the words in the right order. Write the answers under the correct heading below.**

a  Can me to ask you back him call?
b  Do you be he'll know how long?
c  Hold check . just on a moment I'll.
d  I'll sure the message make she gets.
e  I'm sorry she's maternity leave but on.
f  Right, you waiting to keep sorry.
g  She's at desk her at the moment not.
h  What's connection with it in?

**Ask the caller to wait**
1  _____
**After waiting**
2  _____
**Explain someone is unavailable**
3  _____
4  _____
**Ask for information**
5  (caller) _____
6  (secretary) _____
**Leave a message**
7  *Can you ask him to call me back?*
**Promise action**
8  _____

**40.4 Put the dialogue between secretary and caller into the correct order.**

*(Secretary's phrases)*

a  Sorry, she's out of the office right now.
b  Of course. Can you give me your name?
c  Good morning, Logistica.
d  Right, I've got that. It's James Matthews about the containers in Hamburg.
e  Is there anything else?
f  And what's it in connection with?

*(Caller's phrases)*

g  No, that's all. Thank you for your help. Goodbye.
h  Hello. I'd like to speak to Lena, please.
i  It's about the containers in Hamburg.
j  Could you ask her to call me back?
k  Yes, that's right.
l  Yes, it's James Matthews. Lena knows me.

1 (S) [c]  2 (C) ☐  3 (S) ☐  4 (C) ☐  5 (S) ☐  6 (C) ☐
7 (S) ☐  8 (C) ☐  9 (S) ☐  10 (C) ☐  11 (S) ☐  12 (C) ☐

> Read the dialogues on page 84 aloud. Do it by yourself or with a colleague (changing roles at the end). Practise several times until you're fluent.

**40.5 ⊕ 2 Speaking practice: listen and repeat. Repeat each phrase you hear and then listen to check.**

Erik (E) is on a business trip. In the dialogue below he calls his colleague Maria (M) from the local office.

E: Maria? I'm on a train from the airport. My flight arrived late.
M: Erik? It's a really bad line. You keep breaking up.
E: We're going through tunnels. I was saying that my flight arrived late. I'll have to change plans.
5 M: Right.
E: Instead of going to the hotel to change, I'll go straight to the conference venue.
M: Sorry, I didn't catch that. Do you want to change the
10 hotel?
E: No, no. I was saying I don't have time to change my clothes at the hotel. I need to go straight to the conference venue. But I … Hello?
M: Hello?
15 E: We got cut off. I don't know what happened. Yes, I need to go straight to the venue. I'll see you at the registration desk at two.
M: I understand. I'll meet you at two o'clock at the registration desk.
20 E: Exactly.
M: Thanks for letting me know.
E: OK, I have to go now. I have another call to make. See you at two. Bye.

- Notice at line 6 how Maria uses active listening.
- Notice at line 9 how Maria asks for repetition and then says what she thinks she heard.
- Notice at line 18 how Maria repeats the important information.

In the next dialogue Erik has some good news for Maria.

E: Hello? Maria? It's Erik here.
M: Hi Erik. Nice to hear from you. It sounds like you're having a party! Can you speak up a bit?
E: I'm calling from a restaurant. It's very noisy in here – I'll
5 just go outside. (…) Can you hear me now?
M: Yes, that's fine now.
E: Good. I was just calling to tell you the news about the contract. We got it! We got the contract!
M: Fantastic! That's wonderful!
10 E: They're going to pay two hundred and fifteen thousand.
M: Did you say two hundred and fifty – five, zero?
E: In your dreams! No, two hundred and fifteen – one, five. It still gives us a very good margin.
15 M: And did they agree to the time schedule we proposed?
E: Well, I had to move a little on that in the discussions.
M: What exactly do you mean by 'move a little'?

E: I said that we could start work in early March and finish the installation by the middle of April.
20 M: Now, wait a minute. Let me just check that I understand. Are you saying that we have just six weeks to do the whole job?
E: That's right.
M: I see. That's going to be difficult, you know.
25 E: Well, there is a way we can do it. Look, my battery is very low. I think we're going to get cut off. I'll give you a call tomorrow.
M: OK. Great news anyway. Thanks for calling. Bye.

- Notice at line 12 how Maria checks the figure by saying the individual numbers (it is very easy to get confused by *thirteen/thirty, fourteen/forty,* etc).
- Notice at line 17 how Maria clarifies a very specific point.
- Notice at line 20 how Maria checks by rephrasing the idea in a different way.

## *The phrases you need* ☞

**Comprehension problems**
*I'm sorry, I don't understand.*
*Can you speak more slowly, please?*

**Ask for repetition**
*Can you repeat that?*
*Sorry, I didn't catch that.*
*Would you mind saying that again?*
*Did you say fifty, five-zero?*

**Clarify**
*What exactly do you mean by …?*
*Let me just check that I understand. Are you saying that …?*
*Can I just go over that again?*

**Active listening**
*Right. / I see. / I understand. / OK.*
*Really? / That's interesting.*
*(confirming) Exactly. / Yes, that's right. / Correct.*
*(pleasure) Great! / Fantastic! / That's wonderful!*

**Technical problems**
*Can you speak up a bit?*
*It's a really bad line. You keep breaking up.*
*My battery is very low. I think we're going to get cut off.*
*It's very noisy in here – I'll just go outside. Can you hear me now?*

**Returning after problems**
*We got cut off. I don't know what happened.*
*Sorry about that. Where were we?*

# Exercises

**41.1 Cover the opposite page with a piece of paper. Now make phrases by matching an item from each column.**

*(first dialogue opposite)*

| | |
|---|---|
| 1 It's a really | breaking up. |
| 2 You keep | cut off. |
| 3 I didn't | go now. |
| 4 We got | letting me know. |
| 5 Thanks for | bad line. |
| 6 I have to | catch that. |

*(second dialogue opposite)*

| | |
|---|---|
| 7 Can you speak | hear me now? |
| 8 I'll just go | up a bit? |
| 9 Can you | check that I understand. |
| 10 What exactly | outside. |
| 11 Let me just | do you mean by …? |
| 12 Are you saying | get cut off. |
| 13 My battery | a call tomorrow. |
| 14 We're going to | that …? |
| 15 I'll give you | for calling. |
| 16 Thanks | is very low. |

**41.2 Fill in the letters to make phrasal verbs. The definitions are given to help you.**

1 We got _ _ _   _ _ _ . I don't know what happened.
(= interrupted in the middle of the call because the telephone line stopped working)

2 Can you _ _ _ _ _   _ _ a bit?
(= talk more loudly)

3 It's a really bad line. You keep _ _ _ _ _ _ _ _   _ _ .
(= your voice is dividing into short separate noises)

4 Can I just _ _   _ _ _ _ that again?
(= repeat a series of things in order to understand them)

5 Please _ _ _ _   _ _ while I get a pen.
(= wait a moment)

6 I've been trying to call Erik but I can't _ _ _   _ _ _ _ _ _ _ .
(= succeed in talking to him by phone)

*Clues: If you didn't know any of the phrasal verbs above, here are the missing letters to help you: 1 cffotu  2 aekppsu 3 abegiknpru  4 egoorv  5 dhlnoo  6 egghhorttu*

**41.3 'Active listening' is very important in a telephone call. Put the phrases in the box under the most appropriate heading in the table at the top of the next column.**

| |
|---|
| And why was that?    Did you?    Exactly. Great!    Half a million euros!    Has she? Right / I see / Sure.    So what did you do?    That's right. That's wonderful!    Vietnam!    Yuh / Mmm / Uh-huh. |

| Little words and noises | Auxiliary + pronoun |
|---|---|
| 1 _____ | 7 _____ |
| 2 _____ | 8 _____ |
| **Confirming** | **Key words (as an echo)** |
| 3 _____ | 9 _____ |
| 4 _____ | 10 _____ |
| **Showing pleasure** | **Asking for details** |
| 5 _____ | 11 _____ |
| 6 _____ | 12 _____ |

**41.4 Use a word or phrase from exercise 41.3 to complete these telephone responses. Find a solution that uses one example from each category except 'Little words and noises'.**

1 Guess what! We got the contract! → *Great!*

2 Well, I've heard that they're moving all their production to Vietnam. → _____

3 Before we finish, did you know that Laura has been promoted to Marketing Director? → _____

4 So what you're saying is that sales are probably going to be below target this quarter. → _____

5 Anyway, I looked everywhere but I couldn't find the USB stick with my presentation on it. → _____

**41.5 Erik ends the first dialogue opposite by saying 'OK, I have to go now. I have another call to make'. Put the words below into order to make other phrases to end a call.**

1 I'll stop to have there. I have to see me waiting someone.

2 It's talking to you nice been. And I'll send the email you wanted by details. Bye.

3 Anyway, you I won't any keep longer. I'm busy you're sure.

4 Is there help you with I can anything else today?

| |
|---|
| Read the dialogues on page 86 aloud. Do it by yourself or with a colleague (changing roles at the end). Practise several times until you're fluent. |

**41.6 ● 3 Speaking practice: listen and repeat. Repeat each phrase you hear and then listen to check.**

# 42 Telephoning – arranging a meeting

In the dialogue below Monika (M) calls Liviu (L) to arrange a meeting.

> M: Hello. I'd like to speak to Liviu Balanescu, please.
> L: Speaking.
> M: Oh, good morning. My name's Monika Dannemann
> and I sent you an email last week about the
> 5 construction project in Bucharest.
> L: Oh, yes, of course. Nice to hear from you, Monika.
> Your email sounded very interesting. And I'd like very
> much to meet you to discuss it further.
> M: That's great. What day would suit you? I'll be in
> 10 Bucharest from the eighteenth to the twenty-first.
> L: Let me just check. What about Tuesday the nineteenth?
> M: That sounds fine. What time would be good for you?
> L: Shall we say two pm?
> M: I'd prefer a bit later if you don't mind. Could we make
> 15 it three?
> L: Perfect. We can meet here in my office on Tuesday the
> nineteenth at three o'clock.
> M: And where exactly is your office?
> L: It's in the centre – it's very easy to get to. I'll send
> 20 an email to confirm the meeting and with a link to
> our website. You'll find a map and a lot of other
> information on there.
> M: Very good. I look forward to meeting you on the
> nineteenth.
> 25 L: Bye, and thanks for calling.

- ● Notice at line 4 how Monika begins by referring to the last contact.
- ● Notice at line 16 how Liviu confirms the details.

In the next dialogue Liviu's secretary (S) calls Monika (M) to change the arrangements.

> S: Good morning. Is that Monika Dannemann?
> M: Yes.
> S: Oh, hello Monika. This is Mr Balanescu's secretary. He
> asked me to call you. Unfortunately Mr Balanescu can't
> 5 make the meeting with you on Tuesday the nineteenth.
> M: Oh, I see.
> S: Yes. He apologizes – he has to be out of the office
> all day. He suggests that you meet the following day
> instead.
> 10 M: The day after? OK, that's no problem. What time are
> you thinking of?
> S: Any time in the afternoon – whenever is convenient for
> you.

> M: How about three o'clock again?
> 15 S: That sounds fine. Three o'clock on the twentieth.
> Just give your name at reception and I'll come down
> to meet you. And I'm sorry again about the change.
> M: No problem at all. Goodbye.

- ● Notice at line 17 how the secretary apologizes again at the end of the call.

## The phrases you need ☞

**Refer to last contact**
*I sent you an email last week.*
*We met at the conference and you gave me your card.*

**Open suggestions**
*Can we meet up?*
*What time would be good for you?*
*What time are you thinking of?*

**Concrete suggestions**
*What about next Tuesday?*
*How about 9 February?*
*Shall we say …?*
*Could we make it … (instead)?*
*Would eleven-thirty suit (= be convenient for) you?*

**Responses**
*Yes, that's fine. / That sounds fine.*
*I'd prefer a bit later if you don't mind.*
*No, sorry, (BrE I'm afraid) I can't make it then.*
*My schedule is quite full that day.*

**Confirm**
*Perfect. We can meet here on … (day) at … (time).*
*I'll send an email to confirm the details.*

**Change arrangements**
*Unfortunately I can't make next Tuesday. I'm out of the office all day. How about …?*
*We have an appointment for two, but I can't make it at that time.*
*Something urgent has come up. Can we reschedule?*
*I'm sorry again about the change. I hope it's not a problem for you.*

# Exercises

**42.1 In the telephone call below, Andy (A) calls Bulent (B) to arrange a meeting. Complete the dialogue with the words in the box.**

> a little more depth    be my guest    by the way
> if you don't mind    instead    meet up    shall we say
> sounds fine    suit you    thinking of    this is
> two blocks away

A: Good morning, is that Bulent Gul?

B: Yes.

A: Oh hello, [1] _____ Andy Cutting here. We met at the conference in Istanbul last week. We were introduced by Mr Arif.

B: Of course, I remember very well, we exchanged business cards. How are you Andy?

A: Fine. Fine. Look, I'm going to be in Istanbul again at the end of next month. Can we [2] _____ sometime? We can talk about your plans for the future in [3] _____ , and I can show you how our company can add value to your ideas.

B: Yes, it would be a good opportunity to talk some more. What day are you [4] _____ ?

A: I'll be over there from the twenty-eighth to the thirtieth of October.

B: Which of those days would [5] _____ best?

A: [6] _____ Tuesday the twenty-ninth?

B: That [7] _____ . What about the time? Is nine o'clock OK?

A: I'd prefer a bit later, [8] _____ . Could we make it eleven [9] _____ ?

B: Perfect. I'll see you here at my office at eleven o'clock on Tuesday the twenty-ninth. And afterwards I hope that you will [10] _____ for lunch.

A: That's very kind of you. I would really like that. Thank you very much.

B: OK. Oh, [11] _____ , do you know how to find our offices?

A: If I give your card to the taxi driver, will they know the address?

B: Yes, they will. It's in the business district – just [12] _____ from the Marriott.

A: OK, I'll find it. Goodbye.

**42.2 In the next call, Bulent calls Andy to change the arrangements. Complete the dialogue with the words in the box.**

> can't make it    come up    fits my plans    for the time of year
> 'll    look    over there    reschedule    sorry again
> still open    these things happen    would be good

B: Hello Andy. This is Bulent Gul here – from Istanbul.

A: Oh, hello Bulent. How nice to hear from you! How are things [1] _____ in Turkey?

B: It's very hot – much hotter than usual [2] _____ . What about the UK?

A: We're having a lovely autumn. I can see the trees from my window.

B: Very nice. [3] _____ , Andy, I'm calling about our meeting at the end of the month. Unfortunately I [4] _____ on the twenty-ninth. Something urgent has [5] _____ .

A: Don't worry about that. [6] _____ .

B: Can we [7] _____ ? Are you free the previous day – the Monday?

A: Let me just check. Yes, that's fine. I have an appointment but the timing is [8] _____ . What time [9] _____ for you?

B: The same time? Eleven?

A: Yes, that's fine.

B: Good. I'm [10] _____ about the change. I hope it's not a problem for you.

A: No, no problem, I can make it on the Monday. Actually it [11] _____ quite well.

B: OK. I [12] _____ see you on the twenty-eighth and I'll send an email to confirm.

A: See you then. Bye.

**42.3 Can you fill in the missing word?**

An _____ is an arrangement to see someone at a particular time, especially for a business meeting or a professional service.

> Read the dialogues on page 88 aloud. Do it by yourself or with a colleague (changing roles at the end). Practise several times until you're fluent.

**42.4 🌐 4 Speaking practice: listen and repeat. Repeat each phrase you hear and then listen to check.**

Read the dialogue below. A customer (C) calls a supplier (S) to make a complaint.

> C: I'm calling in connection with my order, reference number LN0064.
> S: Thank you. Please wait one moment while I bring your details up on the screen. … OK. For security purposes, can you confirm your name and the company name please?
> C: Yes, it's Mr. Chen from Zed Technika.
> S: That's fine. How can I help you today?
> C: I have a complaint. We received the order this morning but you only shipped 80 pieces. The order was for 100 pieces.
> S: I'm sorry to hear that. Can you leave it with me? I'll look into it and get back to you this afternoon.
> C: No, I'm sorry, that isn't good enough. We need those items urgently. I want you to authorize the shipping of the missing 20 pieces and then send them today.
> S: I understand how you feel. But I do need to check at this end and see what's going on. I'll call you back within an hour, and of course we can send the pieces again if necessary.
> C: What do you mean 'if necessary'? Can I have your name please?
> S: Yes, of course, it's Sandra Lewis.
> C: OK, Sandra, I expect your call by twelve o'clock at the latest. Goodbye.

- Notice how the customer waits until the supplier has all the order details on the screen before beginning the complaint.
- Notice at line 9 how the customer states the complaint very simply and clearly.
- At line 14 the customer insists on action. The supplier shows understanding at line 17 but resists the pressure.
- At line 18 the supplier promises action with 'I'll'.
- At line 21 the customer shows signs of anger. This is not good. However, getting the name of each employee you deal with is a very powerful tool.

In the next dialogue Sandra returns the customer's call.

> S: Oh hello, is that Mr. Chen?
> C: Speaking.
> S: This is Sandra Lewis here, from Shiro Semiconductors, calling you back about the missing pieces.
> C: Oh yes.
> S: I do apologize once more, Mr. Chen, but I have good news for you. I've had a word with the warehouse and it seems they sent a partial order – they only had 80 pieces in stock. However they do now have more pieces. I'll make sure that the missing items are sent to you this afternoon by special delivery.

> C: OK.
> S: I'm sorry again for any inconvenience this has caused.
> C: OK, it's sorted out now. Thank you for your help.
> S: Is there anything else?
> C: No, that's all. Goodbye.

- At line 10 Sandra promises action with 'I'll'.
- At line 13 Sandra apologizes again in a full and formal way.
- At line 14 the customer remembers to thank Sandra, even though he is probably not very happy. He needs to keep a good relationship with Sandra for future occasions.

## The phrases you need ☞

### Make a complaint
*I'm calling in connection with my order, reference number …*
*We received the order this morning but you only shipped … pieces.*
*We still haven't received the …*
*There's a fault with the …*
*There seems to be a problem with the invoice.*
*I'm sorry, that isn't good enough.*

### Show understanding
*I'm sorry to hear that.*
*I do apologize.*
*I understand how you feel.*
*I'm sure we can sort it out.*

### Get the facts
*What exactly is the problem?*
*Do you have a reference number?*
*I need to ask you a few quick questions.*

### No action
*It's not our policy to …*
*I understand exactly how you feel, but it's not our responsibility to …*

### Promise action
*Can you leave it with me? I'll look into it and get back to you this afternoon.*
*I need to check at this end and see what's going on.*
*I'll call you back within an hour. Is that OK?*
*I'll send a replacement immediately by special delivery. It should be with you tomorrow.*
*I'll make sure that …*

### End the call
*I'm sorry again for any inconvenience this has caused.*
*If you have any more problems, please let me know.*

# Exercises

**43.1 Make phrases by matching the beginning of each sentence 1–12 with its correct ending a–l. Not all the phrases appear opposite.**

Making a complaint

1 I'm calling in … [b]
2 We received the order but you only … ☐
3 The machine arrived but there's … ☐
4 We still … ☐
5 The printer isn't working … ☐
6 One of the items was damaged … ☐
7 There's an intermittent fault … ☐
8 The quality isn't as good as … ☐
9 You sent me a new part … ☐
10 There seems … ☐
11 I keep emailing you but … ☐
12 I'm sorry, that isn't good … ☐

a on the control panel.
b connection with my order number LN0064.
c to be a problem with the invoice.
d your original sample.
e I just get automatic replies.
f shipped 80 pieces.
g in transit.
h haven't received the goods we ordered.
i enough.
j but it doesn't fit.
k properly. It's been fine up to now.
l no instruction manual.

**43.2 Match each complaint above to a response below. Write the answer as 'number + letter'. (See #1.)**

1 ___1b___ → Thank you. Please wait one moment while I bring your details up on the screen.
2 _____ → I see. Is it still under warranty?
3 _____ → I'm sorry about that. I'll put you through to the accounts department and I'm sure they can sort it out.
4 _____ → Really? That's very strange. I'll send you a pdf by email right now and put a paper copy in the post as well.
5 _____ → I understand how you feel. But I do need to check at this end and see what's going on. I'll call you back within an hour.
6 _____ → OK. I need to ask you a few quick questions to try to diagnose the problem. Do you see any flashing lights on the display while the fault occurs?

**43.3 Make phrases by matching an item from each column.**

Dealing with a complaint

1 Can you leave — to you this afternoon.
2 I'll look — apologize once more.
3 I'll get back — it with me?
4 I understand — to check at this end.
5 I need — how you feel.
6 I do — into it.

7 I'm sure we can — word with the warehouse.
8 What exactly — sure the items are sent to you.
9 Sorry again — sort it out.
10 I'll send a — is the problem?
11 I'll make — replacement immediately.
12 I've had a — for any inconvenience this has caused.

**43.4 In the second dialogue Sandra tries to minimize the problem by using 'seems': *It seems they sent a partial order*. Rewrite the sentences below so that they minimize a problem. Use the words in brackets.**

1 There's a problem with our suppliers. (I think / may be / issue)
_____

2 It's going to be difficult to send a technician today. (not / easy)
_____

3 There will be a delay while we process the new order. (might / short)
_____

4 There is a problem with the invoice. (there / seems / be / small)
_____

5 I need to speak to my level two supervisor about this. (just / have a quick word with)
_____

6 It would be easier for you if we simply issued a new invoice. (wouldn't?)
_____

**43.5 This sentence refers to promising action: *I'll investigate it, find an answer, and call you again tomorrow*. Fill in the missing letters to write a sentence with the same meaning using phrasal verbs.**

I'll l _ _ _  i _ _ _ it, s _ _ _  it o _ _ , and g _ _  b _ _ _  t _  you tomorrow.

> Read the dialogues on page 90 aloud. Do it by yourself or with a colleague (changing roles at the end). Practise several times until you're fluent.

**43.6 🌐 5 Speaking practice: listen and repeat. Repeat each phrase you hear and then listen to check.**

# 44 Telephoning – review

## 44.1 Fill in the gaps with the words in the box.

| back | back | for | from | in | in |
|---|---|---|---|---|---|
| on | on | out of | over | with | |

1 I'm calling _____ connection _____ your job advertisement.
2 How nice to hear _____ you!
3 Thanks _____ calling.
4 Can I put you _____ hold?
5 Sorry, she's _____ the office.
6 Sorry, she's _____ another call.
7 Can you ask him to call me _____ ?
8 Is that 'i' as _____ Italy?
9 Let me read that _____ to you.
10 Can I just go _____ that again?

| back | by | for | for | into | of |
|---|---|---|---|---|---|
| off | on | up | up | with | with |

11 Just bear _____ me _____ a moment.
12 Can you speak _____ a bit?
13 It's a bad line. You keep breaking _____ .
14 We got cut _____ . Where were we?
15 What time would be good _____ you?
16 What time are you thinking _____ ?
17 Can you leave it _____ me?
18 I'll look _____ it and get _____ to you.
19 I need to check and see what's going _____ .
20 I'll send a replacement _____ special delivery.

## 44.2 Match each phrase 1–8 with a phrase a–h with a similar meaning.

1 Yes, this is (your name) here. ☐
2 Please wait a moment. ☐
3 I'll ask her to get back to you. ☐
4 Would you like to speak to …? ☐
5 Can I take a message? ☐
6 Can I just repeat everything to check? ☐
7 Can you repeat that? ☐
8 Yes, that's right. ☐

a Let me just read that back to you.
b Shall I put you through to …?
c Just bear with me.
d Sorry, I didn't catch that.
e Would you like to leave a message?
f Speaking.
g I'll ask her to call you back.
h Exactly.

## 44.3 Complete the conversation below using phrases a–h from the previous exercise. The conversation is between a receptionist (R), secretary (S) and caller (C).

**Write the phrases in full (rather than just the letters) – it will help you to remember them.**

R: Good afternoon, Pharma International. How can I help you?
C: Can I speak to Roberta Jarvik, please?
R: I'll try her number for you. … Sorry, there's no answer.
   [1]_____ for a moment while I try another extension. … No, still no answer.
   [2]_____ her secretary?
C: Yes please.
S: Good afternoon, R&D department.
C: Oh, hello, is that Ms. Jarvik's secretary?
S: [3]_____ .
C: I was hoping to speak to Ms. Jarvik today. Do you know when she will be available?
S: I'm afraid she's out of the office all day.
   [4]_____ ?
C: Yes, please. Can you tell her that Yi Sang called, from Seoul Hospital. It's about your new heart drug.
S: [5]_____ . Can you give me your name again please?
C: Yes, it's Yi Sang. That's Y-I, new word, S-A-N-G.
S: OK, got that. And the message?
C: I'd like to talk to her about your new heart drug. The one that has just passed phase three clinical trials. We might be interested in getting involved in phase four trials. I need to speak to her personally about this.
S: Right. [6]_____ . Yi Sang called from Seoul Hospital about the new heart drug. It's about the phase four clinical trials.
C: [7]_____ .
S: Does she have your number?
C: Yes, she does.
S: Fine. [8]_____ tomorrow.
C: Thank you very much for your help. Goodbye.

**When you finish, read the conversation aloud. Do it by yourself, or with a colleague (changing roles at the end). Practise several times until you're fluent.**

**44.4 Complete the conversation using the words in brackets. Nikos (N) calls Mr Slavicek (S). The receptionist (R) answers.**

R: Good morning, NutriFruits. Ivana speaking.
_How can I help you_? (how / help)

N: ¹ _____ (I / like / speak) to Mr Slavicek, please.

R: Please hold ² _____ (while / try / connect).

♪ ♪ ♪

S: Milan Slavicek.

N: Hello Mr Slavicek. This is Nikos Karouzos from Seven Seas Shipping.

S: Nikos! ³ _____ (how / nice / hear from)!
⁴ _____ (how / things / Athens)?

N: Fine, fine. And in Zagreb?

S: Good. We're very busy at the moment – lots of new business. It seems that everyone wants fruit from Croatia these days.

N: That's good to hear. Look, ⁵ _____ (this / good time / talk)? Do you have a second?

S: ⁶ _____ (just / give / moment) while I finish something. OK. ⁷ _____ (ahead).

N: ⁸ _____ (reason / calling) because of your next shipment that we're handling. It's for four containers, at the end of November.

S: Yes, that's right.

N: Well, ⁹ _____ (thought / might) interested in a way to save a bit of money.

S: ¹⁰ _____ (course), Nikos, I'm always interested in saving money.

N: We have a small ship leaving Dubrovnik one week earlier. We have some space on that ship for your containers.

S: ¹¹ _____ (let / just check / understand). Are you saying that if we can send the containers one week earlier, there will be a different price?

N: Exactly. For every container that you send on the earlier ship, we'll give you a 2% discount on the price we quoted.

S: ¹² _____ (just / go over / again)? You mean that if we send all four containers in mid November, we will get a total discount of 8%?

N: That's right.

S: OK, that's very interesting, but I can't give you an answer right now. ¹³ _____ (I / get back / you) in a day or two.

N: That's fine.

S: ¹⁴ _____ (is / else) we need to discuss while you're on the line?

N: No, I don't think so. That's all.

S: OK, Nikos, ¹⁵ _____ (thanks / calling). Nice talking to you.

N: ¹⁶ _____ (It's / nice / talking / too). Bye.

**When you finish, read the conversation aloud. Do it by yourself, or with a colleague (changing roles at the end). Practise several times until you're fluent.**

**44.5 Read the dialogue about arranging a meeting. Choose the best word/s to fill each gap from A, B, C or D below.**

Ann: Hi Jim – ¹ _____ Ann.

Jim: Hi.

Ann: Jim – we need to meet up sometime to discuss the Frankfurt Trade Fair.

Jim: OK. What time ² _____ be good for you?

Ann: What about ³ _____ Monday?

Jim: Let me see. No, sorry, I can't ⁴ _____ then. Could we meet on Tuesday ⁵ _____ ?

Ann: My schedule is quite ⁶ _____ on Tuesday, but I'm free later in the afternoon.

Jim: OK. What time would ⁷ _____ you best?

Ann: ⁸ _____ we say 6pm? Or is that too late?

Jim: Well, it is really. I'd prefer a bit earlier if you don't ⁹ _____ .

Ann: Is five OK?

Jim: Yes, that ¹⁰ _____ fine. That's much better.

Ann: Perfect. ¹¹ _____ send an email to confirm.

Jim: OK. ¹² _____ calling.

| | A | B | C | D |
|---|---|---|---|---|
| 1 | I'm | This is | Here is | Speaking |
| 2 | should | could | would | can |
| 3 | the next | at next | on next | next |
| 4 | make | make it | be | arrange |
| 5 | alternative | in place | instead | instead of |
| 6 | full | occupied | complete | engaged |
| 7 | convenient | suit | prefer | advantage |
| 8 | will | shall | how | what |
| 9 | mind | care | worry | trouble |
| 10 | could be | seems me | feels | sounds |
| 11 | I | I'd | I'll | I'm |
| 12 | Thanks for | Thanks for your | I thank your | Nice |

Marija Novak is looking for a job through an online recruitment agency. She sends an email with her CV and a few comments:

> Dear Sir or Madam
>
> [1] I'm writing with regard to job vacancy ref. no. LON009627 on your website. As requested, I attach my CV.
>
> [2] I feel confident that my skills and achievements are a very good fit for this job profile.
>
> [3] Please feel free to contact me if you have any questions.
>
> [4] I look forward to hearing from you.
>
> Marija Novak

A recruitment consultant replies:

> Dear Marija
>
> [1] Thank you very much for sending your CV. We will look through it carefully and contact you again if necessary.
>
> [2] Please be aware that the job market is extremely competitive and that we receive many applications for our vacant positions.
>
> [3] If I can offer any further advice or assistance, please don't hesitate to contact me.
>
> Kind regards
>
> Lotte Mueller

The emails above use polite, formal language. Compare them with the emails between Marija and a friend on the right.

> Steven
>
> [1] Hi! I hope you're well.
>
> [2] This is just a quick note to ask for some help. I've been applying for jobs in London using online agencies, but I've had no luck at all. They just send back these standard emails – it's really depressing.
>
> [3] Anyway, I was wondering if you could help me? I thought you might know of some London recruitment agencies that have jobs in the finance area. Can you send me some names? I'd really appreciate it.
>
> [4] Thanks for your help.
>
> [5] Best wishes to Tessa.
>
> Marija

> [1] Hi Marija, great to hear from you again. I'm fine – just got back from vacation in Morocco. Amazing!
>
> [2] Anyway, thanks for your email. I'm happy to help – I'll ask a few people and try to think of some agencies you could try.
>
> [3] Shall I also send you a copy of the London 'Yellow Pages' in the mail? Sometimes it's better than online – it's very comprehensive and lists loads of agencies and other information all in one place.
>
> [4] Good luck with the job hunting!
>
> Steve

These last two emails are friendly and informal, but note how Marija starts paragraph 3 of her email to Steven – she uses polite, formal language with her friend because she's asking for a favour.

## The phrases you need ☞

| | More formal | More informal |
|---|---|---|
| **First line** | *Dear Sir or Madam / Dear (name)* | *Hi … / (just the name) / (nothing at all)* |
| **Friendly open** | *It was a great pleasure to meet you in …* | *How's it going? / I hope you're well*<br>*Great to hear from you again!* |
| **Previous contact** | *Thank you very much for sending …*<br>*Further to our earlier conversation, …* | *Thanks for your email.*<br>*Following your call, …* |
| **Reason for writing** | *I'm writing with regard to …*<br>*I'm writing to find out more information about …* | *This is just a quick note to say / ask for …*<br>*Re your email below, …* |
| **Request** | *I was wondering if you could …*<br>*I would be grateful if you could …* | *Please …*<br>*Can you …?* |
| **Offer help** | *Would you like me to …?*<br>*If you wish, I would be happy to …* | *Shall I …?*<br>*Do you want me to …?* |
| **Final comments** | *If I can offer any further assistance, please don't hesitate to contact me.*<br>*Please feel free to contact me if you have any questions.* | *If you need any more information, just let me know.*<br>*Just give me a call if you have any questions.* |
| **Friendly close** | *I look forward to hearing from you.*<br>*Give my regards to …* | *See you soon. / Thanks for your help.*<br>*Good luck with … / Best wishes to …* |
| **Last line** | *Yours sincerely / Kind regards / Best wishes* | *Best wishes / All the best / (just the name)* |

# Exercises

**45.1 Cover the opposite page with a piece of paper. Now make phrases by matching an item from each column.**

*(first two emails)*

| | | |
|---|---|---|
| 1 | I'm writing | to hearing from you. |
| 2 | Please feel free | further assistance, please … |
| 3 | I look forward | to contact me if … |
| 4 | Thank you very much | with regard to … |
| 5 | If I can offer any | for sending your CV. |

*(second two emails)*

| | | |
|---|---|---|
| 6 | I hope you're | you could help me. |
| 7 | This is just a | hear from you again. |
| 8 | I was wondering if | well. |
| 9 | I'd really | send you a copy of …? |
| 10 | Great to | quick note to … |
| 11 | Shall I | appreciate it. |

**45.2 Look at the numbered paragraphs in the four emails opposite. Write one of the paragraph types in the box on each line below. The paragraph types can be used more than once.**

> Body of email    Final comments    Friendly close
> Friendly open    Offer help    Previous contact
> Reason for writing    Request

## First email
1st para _____
2nd para *Body of email*
3rd para _____
4th para *Friendly close*

## Second email
1st para _____
2nd para _____
3rd para *Final comments*

## Third email
1st para *Friendly open*
2nd para _____
3rd para _____
4th para *Friendly close*
5th para _____

## Fourth email
1st para _____
2nd para _____
3rd para *Offer help*
4th para _____

> Notice how the body of the email (including requesting and offering help etc) is framed on either side by the opening and closing paragraphs. It is rare to have only the body of the email with no framing.

**45.3 Complete the three emails below with words from the box.**

> an attachment    as requested    don't hesitate
> do you want    further assistance    get back    grateful for
> great pleasure    hearing from    please    re
> relation to    useful discussion    very impressed
> wondering if    with regard

---

✉ | To... | Abu Abdullah
Send | Subject: | Investment fund for India

Dear Mr Abdullah

It was a ¹ _____ to meet you and your team in Dubai last month. Your hospitality was very generous and I was ² _____ by your new offices.

I'm writing ³ _____ to your plans to set up an investment fund for India. After our very ⁴ _____ on this issue I now need a little more background information.

I was ⁵ _____ you could send me a copy of the consolidated accounts for your group of companies? Also, I would be ⁶ _____ any information that you have about regulation of the Dubai Stock Exchange.

I look forward to ⁷ _____ you soon.
Sanjay Gulati

---

✉ | To... | Sanjay Gulati
Send | Subject: | Dubai info

Dear Sanjay
Many thanks for your email and for your kind words. It was a pleasure for us to welcome you here in Dubai.

⁸ _____, I'm sending you a copy of our accounts as ⁹ _____ . In ¹⁰ _____ the Exchange, their website is www.difx.ae and this has all the information you need.

Please ¹¹ _____ to contact me if I can be of any ¹² _____

Best wishes
Abu Nasser Abdullah

---

✉ | To... | Mukesh
Send | Subject: | Accounts to check (Dubai)

Mukesh – ¹³ _____ your email, I contacted Mr Abdullah and he sent me their accounts. They're attached here.

¹⁴ _____ have a good look and ¹⁵ _____ to me if there are any issues. I'm leaving this to you – I have no clue how to read accounts.

¹⁶ _____ me to call a meeting with Bhaskar in a week or so to discuss all this?

Good luck with the accounts!
Sanjay

---

See page 151 for some writing tasks.

Emails used inside a company are often short and direct. Look at the following example:

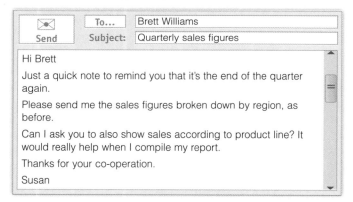

**To...** Brett Williams
**Subject:** Quarterly sales figures

Hi Brett

Just a quick note to remind you that it's the end of the quarter again.

Please send me the sales figures broken down by region, as before.

Can I ask you to also show sales according to product line? It would really help when I compile my report.

Thanks for your co-operation.

Susan

Here is the reply to the above email:

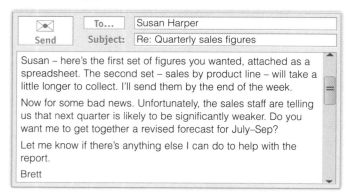

**To...** Susan Harper
**Subject:** Re: Quarterly sales figures

Susan – here's the first set of figures you wanted, attached as a spreadsheet. The second set – sales by product line – will take a little longer to collect. I'll send them by the end of the week.

Now for some bad news. Unfortunately, the sales staff are telling us that next quarter is likely to be significantly weaker. Do you want me to get together a revised forecast for July–Sep?

Let me know if there's anything else I can do to help with the report.

Brett

The level of formality of internal emails depends on the audience and reason for writing. Usually the style is just neutral, but here is an example of a formal and an informal email:

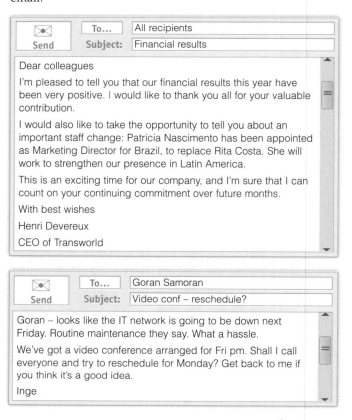

**To...** All recipients
**Subject:** Financial results

Dear colleagues

I'm pleased to tell you that our financial results this year have been very positive. I would like to thank you all for your valuable contribution.

I would also like to take the opportunity to tell you about an important staff change: Patricia Nascimento has been appointed as Marketing Director for Brazil, to replace Rita Costa. She will work to strengthen our presence in Latin America.

This is an exciting time for our company, and I'm sure that I can count on your continuing commitment over future months.

With best wishes

Henri Devereux
CEO of Transworld

**To...** Goran Samoran
**Subject:** Video conf – reschedule?

Goran – looks like the IT network is going to be down next Friday. Routine maintenance they say. What a hassle.

We've got a video conference arranged for Fri pm. Shall I call everyone and try to reschedule for Monday? Get back to me if you think it's a good idea.

Inge

## The phrases you need ☞

**Remind**
*Just a quick note to remind you that …*
*I'd like to remind everyone that …*

**Request**
*Please … / I need you to … / I'd be grateful if you could …*
*I wonder if you could give me some information?*
*Can I ask you to …? / I would appreciate your help with this.*

**Be helpful**
*Here's the … you wanted. / I've attached …*
*I'll … / I'll get onto it right away.*
*Shall I …? / Do you want me to …?*

**Thank**
*I would like to thank you very much for …*
*Well done! You've done a great job.*

**Give news**
*I'm pleased to tell you that … / I'm sure you will be pleased to hear that …*
*The bad news is that … / Unfortunately, …*
*Would all staff please note that …*
*I would like to take the opportunity to tell you about …*
*The reasons for the changes are as follows: …*

**Friendly close**
*Please get back to me if you need any more information.*
*Let me know if there's anything else I can do.*
*Thanks again for all your help. I really appreciate it.*
*Thanks for your co-operation.*

# Exercises

**46.1 Complete the very short emails below using these words:** *advance, co-operation, know, let, 'll, quick note, please, remind, say.*

1 Just to _____ that I got your email and
I _____ speak to Fernanda about it when I see her.
2 Just a _____ to _____ you that
the team meeting is tomorrow at 9am. _____
bring copies of my report with you.
3 Just to _____ you _____ that
there will be a fire drill at some point next week. Thank you
in _____ for your _____ .

> The emails above, like the first one opposite, begin with 'just' to show a short message.~

**46.2 Cover the opposite page with a piece of paper. Now try to remember the words below. (Some letters have been given.)**

1 Susan – _ _ _ _'s the first set of figures you wanted,
a_ _ _ _ _ed as a spreadsheet.
2 Now for some bad news. U_ _ _ _ _ _ _ _ _ly, the
sales staff are telling us that next quarter is likely to be
signi_ _ _ _ _ly weaker.
3 Do you _ _ _t me _ _ get together a revised forecast for
July–Sep?
4 _ _t me _ _ _w if there's anything _ _ _e I can do to help
with the report.
5 _ _ _ll I call everyone and try to reschedule for Monday?
6 _ _t _ _ _k to me if you think it's a good idea.

**46.3 Put the words below into the correct order. Write all the answers under the correct heading below.**

I'm to tell you that pleased …
I would also like the opportunity to take to tell about you …
I would like to thank for you all your valuable contribution.
Thanks for all your again help. I appreciate it really.
I'm pleased you will be sure to hear that …
I be interested you'd thought to know that …
Would all staff note please that …
I'm everything you have done very grateful for.

**Announcing good news**
1 *I'm pleased to tell you that …*
2 _____

**Announcing general news**
3 _____
4 _____
5 _____

**Thanking**
6 _____
7 _____
8 _____

**46.4 Complete each sentence 1–8 with the best ending a–h.**

1 I'm sure you will be … c
2 Following … ☐
3 I'd like to remind …☐
4 Can I ask you …☐
5 I would appreciate …☐
6 The reasons …☐
7 Please …☐
8 Please note …☐

a to let Paula in HR know your holiday plans for the summer asap?
b everyone that redecoration of staff offices will begin on Monday.
c pleased to hear that I have negotiated a discount for all employees at the local fitness centre.
d a meeting of the senior management team last month, it has been decided to reorganize the department.
e that anyone wishing to benefit from this discount should register at the centre before the end of August.
f move all tables and desks away from the walls to allow access to areas that need to be painted.
g for the changes and the proposed new structure are in the attached document. I would be grateful for any comments or feedback.
h your help with this as we need to make sure that everyone doesn't go away on vacation at the same time.

**46.5 Make four short, complete emails using the answers to the previous exercise.**

Email 1: 1c + 8e
Email 2: 2d + ☐
Email 3: ☐ + ☐
Email 4: ☐ + ☐

**See page 151 for some writing tasks.**

## 47 Emails – commercial

In the exchange of emails below a customer makes an enquiry and the supplier replies:

### Email 1

| | To... | info@powerpack.com |
| --- | --- | --- |
| Send | Subject: | Specifications for power packs |

I visited your stand at the Energy Trade Fair in Hanover and was impressed by your range of power packs based on fuel cell technology.

I picked up a brochure at the fair, and would now like some more detailed technical specifications for your range of fuel cells for small handheld devices.

In particular, I would like to know about power packs suitable for a portable DVD player.

Please send details of size, energy output, etc.

I look forward to hearing from you.

### Email 2

| | To... | Dan Bailey |
| --- | --- | --- |
| Send | Subject: | Info re power packs |

Thank you for your email. I'm attaching a document that gives full details of our range of power packs.

Can I draw your attention to models FC68 and FC72? These would be ideal for a small handheld device.

I would welcome the opportunity to discuss your needs in more detail. May I suggest that I call you in a day or two?

In the meantime, please don't hesitate to contact me personally if you have any questions. My direct line is given below.

Best wishes

● The person writing email 2 will be a sales consultant, and they use the enquiry as a chance to enter into a sales dialogue. In the follow-up conversations this person will use sales language from units 18–24.

After further telephone conversations and emails the customer now places an order:

### Email 3

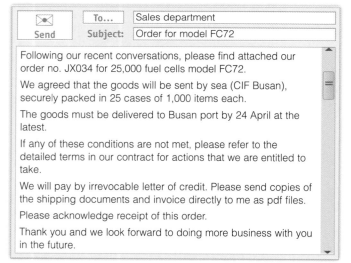

| | To... | Sales department |
| --- | --- | --- |
| Send | Subject: | Order for model FC72 |

Following our recent conversations, please find attached our order no. JX034 for 25,000 fuel cells model FC72.

We agreed that the goods will be sent by sea (CIF Busan), securely packed in 25 cases of 1,000 items each.

The goods must be delivered to Busan port by 24 April at the latest.

If any of these conditions are not met, please refer to the detailed terms in our contract for actions that we are entitled to take.

We will pay by irrevocable letter of credit. Please send copies of the shipping documents and invoice directly to me as pdf files.

Please acknowledge receipt of this order.

Thank you and we look forward to doing more business with you in the future.

● In email 3 the customer confirms details that have been covered in previous discussions.

● See unit 3 for the language of international trade (CIF / letter of credit etc).

### The phrases you need ☞

**Enquiry**

*I visited your stand at … and was impressed by …*
*I would like some detailed specifications for …*
*In particular, I would like to know …*
*Please send details of your product range and prices / discounts / delivery times / terms of payment, etc.*

**Reply to enquiry**

*Thank you for your email of 12 February enquiring about …*
*I'm attaching a document that gives full details of …*
*Can I draw your attention to …?*
*Our standard terms are payment within 28 days, but we offer discounts for prompt payment. We also offer quantity discounts for large purchases.*
*We can ship within one week of a firm order.*
*I would welcome the opportunity to discuss your needs in more detail.*
*We hope that you find our quotation satisfactory and look forward to receiving your order.*
*Please don't hesitate to contact me personally if you have any questions.*

**Placing an order**

*Following our recent conversations, please find attached our order no. … for …*
*If you don't have the items requested in stock, please advise us immediately.*
*The goods must be delivered by … at the latest. / Please confirm your delivery date.*
*If any of these conditions are not met, please refer to the detailed terms in our contract for actions that we are entitled to take.*
*Please acknowledge receipt of this order.*

**Shipping an order**

*The goods will be sent by sea / air / road / rail and will be securely packed in boxes / cases / crates.*
*We look forward to doing more business with you in the future.*

# Exercises

**47.1 Cover the opposite page with a piece of paper. Now try to remember the words below. (Some letters have been given.)**

1 I visited your st_ _ _ at the Energy Trade Fair.

2 I picked up a bro_ _ _ _e at the fair, and would now like some more detailed technical spe_ _ _ _ _ _ _ _ _s for your ra_ _ _ of fuel cells.

3 In p_ _ _ _ _ _ _r, I would like to know about power packs sui_ _ _le for a portable DVD player.

4 Can I d_ _w your a_ _ _ _ion to models FC68 and FC72?

5 In the mea_ _ _me, please don't hes_ _ _ _e to contact me personally if you have any questions. My d_ _ _ _t l_ _e is given below.

6 Fo_ _ _ _ing our recent conversations, please find a_ _ _ _ _ed our order no. JX034.

7 The goods must be d_ _ _ _ _ _ed to Busan port by 24 April at the l_ _ _ _t.

8 If any of these con_ _ _ _ _ns are not met, please refer to the detailed t_ _ _s in our contract for actions that we are entitled to take.

9 Please send copies of the sh_ _ _ _ng documents and inv_ _ _ _ directly to me.

10 Please ack_ _ _ _edge receipt of this order.

**47.2 Write one of the sets of initials in the box next to each phrase below.**

> PR (product range)    DT (delivery times)
> PD (prices & discounts)    P (payment)

1 CIF Busan _____PD_____

2 the goods must arrive by ... at the latest _____

3 available in six colours _____

4 by bank transfer to our account number ... _____

5 there will be an additional supplement for ... _____

6 the executive model features ... _____

7 we will make a promotional allowance if you maintain an in-store display _____

8 we offer everything from ... to ... _____

9 late payments will incur a penalty of ... _____

10 we will ship within 10 working days of ... _____

11 our in-house design team has developed ... _____

12 letter of credit (l/c) _____

13 you can trade in your existing model and receive up to €1,000 cash back _____

14 payment is 60 days after invoice _____

15 a deposit of 25% is required for ... _____

**47.3 Make phrases by matching an item from each column.**

1 if you have any ———— can personalize
2 I'm confident ———— further questions
3 I also notice that you     discounts
4 I would be happy     of discounts
5 we do offer quantity     up a trade account
6 I have been looking     that we can supply
7 I can find no mention     to make a sample
8 you need to set     at your website

**47.4 Use the phrases from 47.3 to complete the exchange of emails below.**
**Write the phrases in full – it will help you to remember them.**

| ✉ | To... | Sales |
|---|---|---|
| Send | Subject: | Office supplies order |

¹ _____ and am interested in ordering some office supplies.

In particular, I need paper and cartridges for Canon photocopiers, and various mailing and packaging supplies.

² _____ desk and wall calendars with a company logo, but I would need some assurance about the quality of these items.

Your prices are shown on the site, but ³ _____ and extended payment terms for large purchases. Please send full details of these.

I look forward to an early reply.

| ✉ | To... | Michelle Young |
|---|---|---|
| Send | Subject: | Re: Office supplies order |

Thank you for your email enquiring about office supplies. ⁴ _____ all your product needs and look forward to welcoming you as a regular customer.

⁵ _____ for large orders. These are on a sliding scale, beginning at 2% for orders over €500 and going up to 8% for orders over €10,000.

Trade customers such as yourselves are given 30 days to pay our invoices, but ⁶ _____ first. We also offer attractive early payment discounts on these accounts. For further information on trade accounts please click on the link below.

In relation to our personalized calendars, ⁷ _____ product for you to look at. Please send me some artwork with your logo as a gif file, and specify whether you want a desk or wall calendar.

Thank you once again for your enquiry. ⁸ _____ please feel free to contact me.

See page 151 for some writing tasks.

In the email below a supplier is forced to give some bad news to a potential customer:

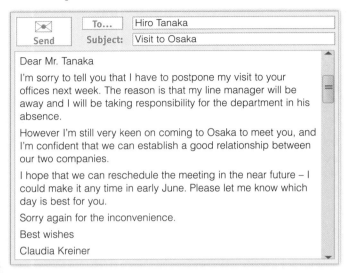

To... Hiro Tanaka
Subject: Visit to Osaka

Dear Mr. Tanaka

I'm sorry to tell you that I have to postpone my visit to your offices next week. The reason is that my line manager will be away and I will be taking responsibility for the department in his absence.

However I'm still very keen on coming to Osaka to meet you, and I'm confident that we can establish a good relationship between our two companies.

I hope that we can reschedule the meeting in the near future – I could make it any time in early June. Please let me know which day is best for you.

Sorry again for the inconvenience.

Best wishes

Claudia Kreiner

- Notice how Claudia apologizes and explains at the beginning, and then apologizes again at the end.
- Notice how Claudia reassures Mr. Tanaka with positive language: *I'm still very keen on … / I'm confident that … .*

In the next email a customer makes a complaint. In reply, the supplier apologizes and promises action.

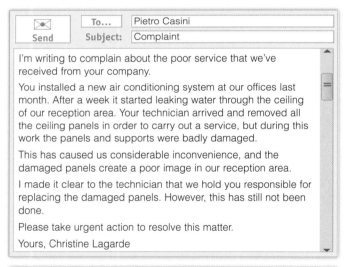

To... Pietro Casini
Subject: Complaint

I'm writing to complain about the poor service that we've received from your company.

You installed a new air conditioning system at our offices last month. After a week it started leaking water through the ceiling of our reception area. Your technician arrived and removed all the ceiling panels in order to carry out a service, but during this work the panels and supports were badly damaged.

This has caused us considerable inconvenience, and the damaged panels create a poor image in our reception area.

I made it clear to the technician that we hold you responsible for replacing the damaged panels. However, this has still not been done.

Please take urgent action to resolve this matter.

Yours, Christine Lagarde

To... Christine Lagarde
Subject: Re: Complaint

Dear Ms Lagarde

I'm very sorry to hear that you've had problems with your air conditioning system. We'll be at your office tomorrow to fit new panels.

I understand completely that your reception area needs to be of the highest standard, and I can assure you that we will leave the ceiling looking as new.

Once again, please accept my sincere apologies for any inconvenience caused.

Pietro Casini

- The tone of Christine's complaint is direct, strong and factual – but not angry.
- Pietro's reply is short and simple, avoiding conflict.
- Notice the first paragraph of Pietro's reply. After apologizing he immediately promises action.
- Notice how Pietro ends by apologizing again.

## *The phrases you need* ☞

**Customer complains**
*I'm writing with reference to …*
*I'm writing to complain about the poor service we've received from …*
*There seems to be an error / mistake / misunderstanding.*
*There's a serious fault with the …*
*This has caused us considerable inconvenience.*
*This has hurt our sales and our reputation.*
*I made it clear that …*

**Customer demands action**
*I must insist that you give this matter your urgent attention.*
*Please take urgent action to …*
*Let me remind you that this product is still under warranty. So, the best solution would be to …*

**Supplier gives bad news**
*I'm sorry to tell you that … / Unfortunately, …*
*The reason is that … / This is due to …*

**Supplier apologizes**
*I'm very sorry to hear that …*
*I would like to apologize for …*
*I was very concerned to learn about …*

**Supplier reassures and promises action**
*I'm confident that …*
*I can assure you that …*
*I will make sure that …*

**Supplier ends**
*Sorry again for the inconvenience.*
*Once again, please accept my sincere apologies for any inconvenience caused.*
*Thank you very much for bringing this matter to my attention.*

# Exercises

**48.1 Rewrite the sentences below with the correct word order, beginning as shown.**

1 I'm to tell you sorry that I have to postpone next week our meeting.

I'm _____

_____

2 Once again, please apologies for accept my sincere any inconvenience caused.

Once again, _____

_____

3 I'm ordered to tell you that the items are now in stock you pleased. We'll your order be shipping today.

I'm _____

_____

_____

4 I can doing everything possible assure you that we are to resolve this issue as possible as quickly.

I can _____

_____

_____

5 You'll be extending our online sale that we are pleased to hear for another week.

You'll be _____

_____

6 I've talked to the involved staff and I'm confident that our procedures are robust and properly working.

I've talked _____

_____

_____

7 We inform you that we regret to cannot process your order due to on your account a large outstanding balance.

We _____

_____

_____

8 Thank very much you to my attention for bringing this matter.

Thank _____

**48.2 Write sentence numbers 1 to 8 from the previous exercise in the boxes below.**

a Good news ☐ ☐
b Bad news ☐ ☐
c Reassurance ☐ ☐
d End ☐ ☐

**48.3 Study the strong complaint below. Try to guess the single missing word in each gap. Write your answers lightly at the side. Several answers may be possible.**

| | To... | Andrew Wilkinson |
| Send | Subject: | Delay to order |

Dear Mr Wilkinson

I'm writing with ¹ _____ to our order no. 05782 made on 3 July. We're ² _____ waiting for ³ _____ of these parts.

I phoned you last week about this and you ⁴ _____ me that the order would be ⁵ _____ within 48 hours.

This delay is causing us considerable ⁶ _____ as we're unable to continue our operations without the parts. This has hurt our ⁷ _____ and our reputation.

I must ⁸ _____ that you give this matter your urgent ⁹ _____ .

I'll be phoning you again later this afternoon and I hope that by then you have some good news for me. If I don't receive a ¹⁰ _____ response from you, I'll be ¹¹ _____ to reconsider our ¹² _____ business relationship.

Yours

Gloria Salinas

**Now fill in the gaps above with the suggested words in the box below.**

| attention | assured | delivery | forced |
| inconvenience | insist | long-term | reference |
| sales | satisfactory | shipped | still |

**48.4 The reply below has ten extra words. They're either grammatically wrong or don't make sense. Cross them out.**

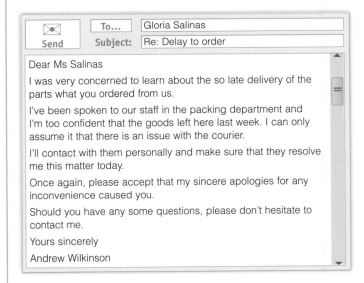

| | To... | Gloria Salinas |
| Send | Subject: | Re: Delay to order |

Dear Ms Salinas

I was very concerned to learn about the so late delivery of the parts what you ordered from us.

I've been spoken to our staff in the packing department and I'm too confident that the goods left here last week. I can only assume it that there is an issue with the courier.

I'll contact with them personally and make sure that they resolve me this matter today.

Once again, please accept that my sincere apologies for any inconvenience caused you.

Should you have any some questions, please don't hesitate to contact me.

Yours sincerely

Andrew Wilkinson

**See page 151 for some writing tasks.**

Much of the language used for making arrangements by email is similar to that used for making arrangements by telephone in unit 42.

Below is a typical exchange of emails for arranging a business trip. Only short extracts are shown.

## Host makes an invitation

It was a great pleasure to meet you in … . The next time you're in China we'd be very pleased if you could visit our company. It would be a great opportunity for you to look around our new factory.

## Guest accepts

Thank you for the kind invitation to visit your company. I'd be very interested in seeing your factory and seeing the production line in operation.

In fact I'll be in China from … to … . Please let me know if any of these dates are convenient for you.

## Host suggests an itinerary

I was very pleased to hear that you'll be here in China in January. Of course we'd be delighted to welcome you on one of those days.

I've put together a provisional itinerary – please see the details below.

…

How does this sound? Please let me know what you think.

Also, we'd be happy to arrange a local hotel for you if you wish.

## Guest replies

Thank you so much for the careful thought you put into planning an itinerary for me. It looks fine – there's just one small change that I would suggest. …

In relation to the hotel, I'll make my own arrangements.

I look forward very much to seeing you in …

## Guest contacts a hotel

I'm mailing you off your website. Do you have a room available for one person on the night of Wednesday 22 January? Please let me know the price of this, including breakfast.

I'd also like to know if you …

## Guest tells host the details

Yes, everything is finalized now.

I'm travelling on flight LH788, from Frankfurt to Guangzhou. It's due in at 11.30am. I'll be arriving at Terminal 2.

I'm staying at the Marriott. When I get there I'll need just half an hour or so to freshen up, then I can come straight to your offices.

## Host confirms everything

Just to confirm your visit to us on … at … . A driver will be waiting for you at the airport, holding a sign with your name on it.

The driver will take you to your hotel, and then bring you here.

Should you have any problems, my mobile phone number is …

## *The phrases you need*

### Host to guest

*We'd be very pleased if you could visit our company.*
*I've put together a provisional itinerary.*
*A driver will pick you up from / drop you off at the airport.*
*Do you know when you're planning to arrive?*
*Go straight to the reception desk and ask for me.*
*Should you have any problems, my mobile phone number is …*
*I'm attaching a map.*

### Guest to host

*Thank you for your kind invitation. I'd be very happy to visit your offices.*
*I'm travelling on flight number LH788, due in at 11.30am.*
*I'll need just half an hour at the hotel to freshen up.*

### Guest to hotel

*I'm mailing you off your website. Do you have a room available for the night of Wednesday 22 January?*
*I'd also like to know if you have a swimming pool and gymnasium / 24 hour reception / a courtesy shuttle bus from the airport.*
*I need a view of the … / wireless Internet access / an iron in my room when I arrive.*

### Other vocabulary

*a window seat / an aisle seat*
*a single / return trip (BrE); a one way / round trip (AmE)*
*a booking / to book (BrE); a reservation / to reserve (AmE)*
*Leave the motorway (AmE freeway) at exit 12.*
*Keep going for three blocks, then turn left.*

# Exercises

**49.1 Complete each sentence 1–8 with the best ending a–h.**

1 It was a great pleasure to … ☐ *d*
2 We'd be very pleased if … ☐
3 I'd be very interested … ☐
4 I've put together … ☐
5 A driver will pick you … ☐
6 A driver will drop you … ☐
7 Go straight … ☐
8 I'll need to freshen up … ☐

a a provisional itinerary.
b at the hotel first.
c in seeing your factory.
d meet you in Germany.
e off at the airport.
f to the reception desk and ask for me.
g up from the airport.
h you could visit our company.

**49.2 Fill in the gaps with the prepositions in the box.**

| at | at | at | at | for | for | from | in |
|----|----|----|----|-----|-----|------|-----|
| in | in | off | on | on | to | with | |

1 I was very pleased to hear that you will be here _____ China _____ January.
2 I'm mailing you _____ (or from) your website. Do you have a room available _____ one person on the night of Wednesday 22 January?
3 I'm travelling _____ flight LH788, _____ Frankfurt _____ Guangzhou.
4 The flight leaves _____ 11.15am _____ Tuesday 21 January.
5 It's due _____ at 9.30 on Wednesday 22 January.
6 It arrives _____ Terminal 2.
7 I'm staying _____ the Marriott.
8 A driver will be waiting _____ you _____ the airport, holding a sign _____ your name on it.

**49.3 Cross out the one word in each group that is not correct. Check any unknown words in a dictionary.**

1 You can *get / catch / take / miss / lose / be booked on / board / book / reserve* a flight.
2 A flight can *be overbooked / be delayed / be held up / be diverted / be bound for somewhere / leave / depart / take off / arrive / land / be full / be half-empty / be on time / be cancelled / be annulled.*

**49.4 Marcus is telling a story about his business trip. Fill in the missing letters.**

❝The taxi driver dro_ _ed me o_ _ at the wrong terminal, and it took me some time to find the right ch_ _ _-_ area for my airline. Then I had to pay an exc_ _ _ baggage cha_ _ _ because my suitcase was so heavy. Anyway, I went thr_ _ _ _ passport control and then waited for ages at security – there was a long qu_ _ _ (AmE *line*). While I was waiting for my g_ _e to be called, I decided to do some shopping. I didn't notice the time go by and I had to _ _sh to b_ _ _d the flight. During the flight we had a lot of really bad turb_ _ _ _ce – when we tou_ _ _d d_ _ _ I was shaking like a leaf. I pi_ _ed up my baggage and went to the cab r_ _k outside the terminal. On the way to the hotel we got st_ _ _ in traffic, and then at the end the driver tried to ri_ me o_ _ . I asked for a re_ _ _ _t and he wasn't very pleased. I checked into the hotel and I was looking forward to an e_ _ly ni_ _ _ _, but the disco in the hotel basement made that impossible. ❞

**49.5 The email below gives directions. Fill in the gaps with the words in the box.**

| blocks | exit | follow | main | miss | freeway | past |
|--------|------|--------|------|------|---------|------|
| signposted | turn | down | for | for | on | on | on |

Leave the ¹ _____ at ² _____ 12. Follow the main road, ³ _____ for the city centre. Stay ⁴ _____ this road ⁵ _____ about four miles until you come to a large Shell gas station on your right. You can't ⁶ _____ it.
⁷ _____ right just ⁸ _____ the gas station and keep going straight. Our offices are a short distance ⁹ _____ this road – about three ¹⁰ _____ . You'll see them ¹¹ _____ your right.
When you arrive at the ¹² _____ gate, Security will give you a visitor's pass. ¹³ _____ the road round to the main reception where there is a visitor's parking lot. When you get to reception, just ask ¹⁴ _____ me – they'll be expecting you.
If you have any problems, give me a call ¹⁵ _____ my cell phone.
Looking forward to meeting you next week.
Regards

**See page 151 for some writing tasks.**

**50.1 Fill in the gaps with verbs from the box.**

| | | | | | | |
|---|---|---|---|---|---|---|
| appreciate | contact | do | feel | hesitate | know | note |
| offer | postpone | remind | shall | take | wonder | would |

1 Please _____ free to _____ me if you have any questions.

2 _____ we reschedule the meeting for Monday?

3 I _____ if you could give me some information?

4 If I can _____ any further advice or assistance, please don't _____ to contact me.

5 Just a quick note to _____ you that it's the end of the quarter and the sales figures are due.

6 Let me _____ if there's anything else I can _____ .

7 I _____ like to _____ the opportunity to tell you about an important staff change.

8 I would _____ your help with this.

9 Please _____ that I will be away from the office for the whole of next week.

10 I'm sorry to tell you that I have to _____ my visit to your offices next week.

**Continue as before.**

| | | | | | |
|---|---|---|---|---|---|
| accept | acknowledge | assure | click | discuss | insist |
| notice | offer | resolve | send | take | welcome |

11 Can I call you in a day or two? I would _____ the opportunity to _____ your needs in more detail.

12 Please _____ copies of the shipping documents and invoice directly to me.

13 Please _____ urgent action to _____ this matter.

14 I _____ on your website that you can personalize desk and wall calendars.

15 I can _____ you we are doing everything we can.

16 We do _____ quantity discounts for large orders.

17 I must _____ that you give this matter your urgent attention.

18 For further information please _____ on the link below.

19 Please _____ receipt of this order.

20 Please _____ my sincere apologies for any inconvenience caused.

**50.2 Write the numbers of sentences 1–10 from exercise 50.1 in the boxes below.**

a Three phrases used to give information (a fact or some news) ☐ ☐ ☐

b Two phrases used as part of a request ☐ ☐

c Two phrases used for making arrangements ☐ ☐

d Three final, friendly comments ☐ ☐ ☐

**Now do the same for sentences 11–20.**

e One phrase used in a customer's initial enquiry ☐

f Three phrases used in the supplier's reply to this initial enquiry ☐ ☐ ☐

g Two phrases used by the customer after they have decided to buy ☐ ☐

h Two phrases used by a customer as part of a complaint ☐ ☐

i Two phrases used by a supplier as part of a reply to a complaint ☐ ☐

**50.3 Complete this internal email and the reply with the words in the box.**

| | | | | |
|---|---|---|---|---|
| attached | attend | circulate | co-operation | done |
| event | finalized | get back | make sure | note |
| | put | re | remind | tell |

---

✉ To... _____
Send Subject: _____

Just a quick [1] _____ to all line managers to [2] _____ you that the arrangements for the Online Marketing seminar have now been [3] _____ . It will take place on 28 April – full details are [4] _____ as a pdf.

This [5] _____ is part of our ongoing staff development program – please encourage people to [6] _____ .

I need to know approximate numbers asap – [7] _____ to me on this by the end of next week if possible.

Thank you for your [8] _____ .

Miguel Hernandez

---

✉ To... _____
Send Subject: _____

Miguel – thanks for the info [9] _____ the seminar. You've [10] _____ a lot of work into organizing this. Well done!

I'll [11] _____ the pdf to everyone concerned and [12] _____ that everyone knows about it.

Can you [13] _____ me if there is any limit on numbers? I'm sure there will be a lot of interest in our department.

Thanks again. You've [14] _____ a great job!

**50.4 Match each formal phrase 1–14 with an informal phrase a–n.**

1 I'm writing with regard to your last email. ☐
2 Further to our earlier conversation, … ☐
3 I would like to apologize for … ☐
4 I would be grateful if you could send me … ☐
5 Is next Friday convenient for you? ☐
6 Please don't hesitate to contact me if … ☐
7 Thank you for the kind invitation. ☐
8 I was wondering if you could …? ☐
9 I would be very pleased to come. ☐
10 I would like to remind everyone that … ☐
11 I will contact you again in the near future. ☐
12 We wish you every success in the future. ☐
13 Please find attached … ☐
14 I would like to thank you very much for … . I really appreciate it. ☐

a Thanks for asking me.
b Good luck with everything!
c Can you …?
d Please contact me if …
e Re your last email, …
f I'll get back to you very soon.
g Sorry about …
h Following up your earlier call, …
i Let me know if you can make it next Friday.
j I'd love to come.
k Thanks again for all your help. Much appreciated.
l Just a quick note to remind you that …
m I've attached …
n Please send me …

**50.5 Fill in the gaps with words from the box.**

| about | at | at | back | by | for | for | for | for |
|---|---|---|---|---|---|---|---|---|
| from | in | in | in | in | in | of | on | |
| on | over | ~~to~~ | to | to | ~~with~~ | with | | |

1 I'm writing _with_ regard _to_ job vacancy ref. no. TH729.
2 I'm writing _____ relation _____ job vacancy ref. no. TH729.
3 Many thanks _____ all your help.
4 I would be grateful _____ any information you have on this.
5 Have a good look at the report and get _____ _____ me if you have any questions.

6 I'm sure that I can count _____ your continuing commitment _____ (= during) future months.
7 We will contact you again _____ the near future.
8 I have been looking _____ your website and am interested _____ ordering some office supplies.
9 _____ particular, I need paper and cartridges suitable _____ Canon photocopiers.
10 I'm writing to complain _____ the poor service we've received _____ your company.
11 _____ the meantime, please don't hesitate to contact me if you have any questions.
12 We are still waiting _____ delivery _____ these parts.
13 The goods must be delivered to Busan port _____ 24 April _____ the latest.
14 Please call me _____ my direct line, 123 456 7890.
15 Good luck _____ everything.

**50.6 Complete the sentences by putting a verb in the box into either the -ing or the -ed form.**

| attach | buy | cause | concern | do | follow | forward |
|---|---|---|---|---|---|---|
| get | ~~go~~ | hear | make | request | use | wonder |

1 You can find further details by _____going_____ to our website.
2 I was _____ if you could help me?
3 As _____ , I'm sending you a copy of our accounts.
4 This has _____ us considerable inconvenience.
5 _____ our recent conversation, please find attached our order.
6 We look forward to _____ more business with you in the future.
7 I _____ it clear when I spoke to you last week that we hold you responsible.
8 I look forward to _____ from you.
9 We recommend _____ DHL, UPS or FedEx as your carrier.
10 I was very _____ to learn about the late delivery of the parts you ordered from us.
11 Thank you for _____ back to me so quickly.
12 We are interested in _____ from Fairtrade organizations such as yourselves.
13 I have _____ a copy of our brochure.
14 Your email was _____ to us.

**Presentations – opening**

There are a great variety of presentation contexts:
- Company presentation (history, structure, main products, markets, plans for the future).
- Product presentation (features and benefits of a new product).
- Internal presentation reporting financial or sales figures.
- Internal presentation analyzing a problem and suggesting solutions.
- Welcoming visitors.
- Any occasion where you speak at length in a meeting on a prepared topic.

In addition, there are a variety of presentation styles:
- Formal, structured, rehearsed, taking questions at the end.
- Informal, partly improvised, interacting with the audience.
- Somewhere between the two: using a basic structure, but allowing occasional opportunities for questions and interaction.

Which style you use depends not only on your audience and its expectations, but also on you and your personality.

Read the opening to a 'welcoming visitors' presentation in the next column. (The main body and close of a presentation are covered in units 52–53.)
- Notice how the presenter begins by giving answers to all the practical questions that might be in the audience's mind (eg What is the aim of this talk? How long will it last? Will there be a break? Who is the person speaking? Who is that man in the corner?)
- The presenter then gives an outline of the structure of the presentation.
- Finally, before beginning, the presenter makes it clear whether audience members can interrupt with questions, or keep them until the end.

> **66** Well, good morning, everyone. On behalf of BCC International I'd like to welcome you here to our offices.
>
> Can everyone see at the back? OK.
>
> The aim of this short talk is to give you an overview of our company and its products. I'll speak for about thirty minutes, and then we'll take a break for coffee and biscuits. After that, at around ten thirty, we'll take you on a tour of the factory.
>
> Before we begin, just a few words about myself. My name is Anna Edelmann and I'm in charge of public relations here at BCC. I've been with the company for twelve years, and I worked in the sales area before moving into PR.
>
> I should also introduce my colleague Mr Andersen over there in the corner. Mr Andersen is our plant manager and he will be leading the factory tour.
>
> I've divided this presentation into four sections. First I'd like to show you a timeline of our company so you can see how we've grown and developed over the years. Then I'll talk a little about our market and how it's changing. After that I'll move on to discuss customization, and how we focus on tailoring our products to our customers' needs.
>
> Finally, I'll give you a little technical background to help you understand the new technology that you'll be seeing on the factory tour.
>
> If you have any questions, please feel free to interrupt.
>
> OK, let's begin with this first slide, which shows … **99**

## The phrases you need ☞

### Welcome
*OK, let's get started. Good morning everyone and welcome to …*
*Can everybody see?*
*Before I begin, I'd like to thank (name) for inviting me here today.*
*On behalf of BCC International I'd like to welcome you here to our offices.*
*It's good to see so many people here today.*
*I'm very happy to be here.*

### Personal introductions
*Let me start by introducing myself. My name is …*
*Just a few words about myself, …*
*Perhaps I should just introduce one or two people in the room.*

### Objective
*The title of my presentation is …*
*This morning I'm going to talk about …*
*The aim of this short talk is to …*

### Get attention and interest
*Let me ask you a question. (+ rhetorical question)*
*Take a look at this picture. What does it tell you about …?*
*Somebody once said … (+ quotation)*
*Did you know that …? (+ surprising statistic)*

### Audience benefit
*I hope this presentation will enable you to …*
*By the end of my talk you will …*

### Structure
*I'll speak for about thirty minutes.*
*I've divided my talk into four main parts / sections.*
*First, I'd like to …*
*Then I'll talk a little about …*
*After that I'll move on to …*
*Finally I'll …*
*If you have any questions, please feel free to interrupt.*
*OK, let's begin with the first point / slide, which is …*

# Exercises

**51.1 Cover the page opposite with a piece of paper. Make phrases from the presentation by matching an item from each column.**

| | | |
|---|---|---|
| 1 | On behalf | see at the back? |
| 2 | Can everyone | of public relations |
| 3 | Just a few | of BCC I'd like to … |
| 4 | I'm in charge | to show you … |
| 5 | I'd like | words about myself |
| 6 | I'll talk | with this first slide |
| 7 | I'll move | on tailoring our products … |
| 8 | We focus | on to discuss customization |
| 9 | I'll give you | about our market and how … |
| 10 | Let's begin | a little technical background |

**51.2 There are many ways to create an impact in the first few minutes of a presentation. Match techniques 1–8 with phrases a–h.**

| | | | | |
|---|---|---|---|---|
| 1 | rhetorical question ☐ | | 5 | personal story ☐ |
| 2 | thank the organizers ☐ | | 6 | audience benefit ☐ |
| 3 | surprising statistic ☐ | | 7 | use of visuals ☐ |
| 4 | audience involvement ☐ | | 8 | quotation ☐ |

a Take a look at this picture. What does it tell you about teenage fashion?

b Everybody who thinks the Internet will kill traditional advertising – put your hands up.

c Wouldn't you like to double your sales in just twelve months?

d Charles Darwin once wrote, 'It is not the strongest of the species that survive, but the ones most responsive to change.'

e I'd like to thank Olga for all the hard work she has done to make this event possible.

f I want to share something with you.

g I hope this presentation will enable you to choose the most cost-effective IT solution.

h 70% of all Americans say that they're carrying so much debt that it's making their home lives unhappy.

**51.3 Make presentation phrases by using a verb 1–12 with the words a–l.**

| | | | | | |
|---|---|---|---|---|---|
| 1 | be … ☐ $h$ | 5 | give … ☐ | 9 | start … ☐ |
| 2 | take a break … ☐ | 6 | introduce … ☐ | 10 | take … ☐ |
| 3 | divide … ☐ | 7 | say … ☐ | 11 | thank … ☐ |
| 4 | feel … ☐ | 8 | speak … ☐ | 12 | welcome … ☐ |

a a few words about myself

b any questions at the end

c you an overview

d for about thirty minutes

e for coffee and biscuits

f *(name)* for inviting me here today

g free to interrupt

h happy to be here

i my talk into four parts

j one or two people in the room

k by introducing myself

l you here today

**51.4 Create different ways to open a presentation, using the verbs in the box.**

| | | | | | |
|---|---|---|---|---|---|
| bring | deal | ~~discuss~~ | fill | give | look |
| make | outline | report | show | take | talk |

*Good morning everyone and thanks for coming. This morning I'm going to …*

1 _____*discuss*_____ the issue of risk, and what you can do to minimize it.

2 _____ you an overview of the company and its products.

3 _____ you how to sell more effectively to your existing customer base.

4 _____ about investment funds: how to choose them, when to buy them and when to sell them.

5 _____ back to you on our progress with the Milestone project.

6 _____ at a variety of green technologies that are helping to combat the threat of global warming.

7 _____ you in on the background to our involvement in the Brazilian market.

8 _____ a look at how we got into the problem with our local agents in the UK and how we can get out of it.

9 _____ you up to date on the latest results from our consumer survey.

10 _____ some detailed recommendations about how to reorganize the department.

11 _____ our new marketing strategy.

12 _____ with the item outstanding from our last meeting: funding our R&D activities.

**51.5 ⊙ 6 Speaking practice: listen and repeat. Repeat each phrase you hear and then listen to check.**

'The phrases you need' below shows some phrases that can make your presentation easier to follow. You will have to supply the content yourself of course!

- Signposts: these are phrases that say where you're going in terms of the main topics of your talk.
- Develop a topic: these phrases are mini-signposts within a topic. By explicitly saying what you're going to talk about next, the audience can follow easily.
- Focus: these phrases are also mini-signposts. You're saying to the audience: 'please pay extra attention for the next few moments'.
- Question–answer: asking a question and then answering it yourself is a standard technique in public speaking. The question creates interest in the mind of the listeners, the answer provides the satisfaction of closure.
- Refer to visuals: be careful not to rely too much on your slides as they can send people into a trance of boredom. Direct attention back to yourself often.
- Ask for contributions: stop at several points during the main presentation to take questions – it creates interest and makes the presentation more interactive.

Read the presentation extract in the next column, which shows some of these techniques and phrases in context. The content in this case is technical – about wind energy technology.

- Looking just at the first half of this extract, notice how the presenter guides the audience: signposting the main topic, stating that some background is coming next, directing attention to a slide, raising a question to create interest, focusing on two issues. All of this makes the presentation easier to follow.

66 … OK, let's move on to the next point, which is wind energy technology. The market for wind turbines* is shifting from onshore to offshore. It might be useful to give a little background here. As you can see on this next slide, onshore wind farms have several drawbacks: first you need a reliably windy location, second the farms can cause visual pollution, and third there are some serious engineering questions.

What are these engineering questions? Basically there are two issues. Firstly, the stability of the structure as you make it bigger, and secondly the problem of having the blades always facing the wind.

So the trend is towards offshore wind farms, and there are some engineering challenges here. Have a look at this slide – it shows the design for an offshore turbine that sits on the surface of the sea.

It's three times more efficient than an onshore turbine of equivalent size. What is the reason for this? The reason is that it uses a completely different design that isn't dependent on the wind direction. There is a large V-shaped structure with rigid 'sails' mounted along its length. As the wind passes 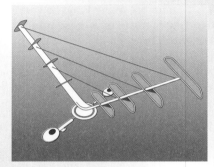 over these they act like airfoils** and this generates lift and turns the structure as a whole.

I would like to stress that this design is not yet in commercial production, but a prototype is currently being tested off the coast of Scotland.

OK. Are there any questions so far? Does anyone have any comments? 99

\*   wind turbine: tall structure with parts that are turned by the wind, used for making electricity
\*\*  airfoil: curved part on an aircraft's wing that helps it to rise in the air

## The phrases you need ☞

### Signposts
*OK. Let's move on to … / turn our attention to … / take a look at …*
*This leads me to my next point, which is …*
*Earlier I mentioned …*
*I'll say more about this later. / I'll come back to this in a moment.*
*Just to digress for a moment, …*

### Develop a topic
*It might be useful to give a little background here.*
*Let's examine this in more detail.*
*Let me explain with a concrete example.*
*My own view on this is …*

### Focus
*Basically, … / To put it simply, …*
*So, for me, the main issue here is …*
*I think there are three questions to focus on.*
*I would like to stress / emphasize that …*

### Question–answer
*What is the reason for this? The reason is …*
*How much is this going to cost? Well, the figures show …*
*So what can we do about all this? I'll tell you. We plan to …*

### Refer to visuals
*As you can see on this next slide, …*
*I'd like to highlight two things on this table / chart / diagram …*
*What is interesting on this slide is …*
*I'd like to draw your attention to …*

### Ask for contributions
*Are there any questions so far?*
*Does anyone have any comments?*
*How does this relate to your own particular context?*

# Exercises

**52.1 Cover the opposite page with a piece of paper. Now try to remember the words below. Some letters have been given.**

1 This l_ _ _s me to my next point, which is …
2 Earlier I men_ _ _ned …
3 I'll c_ _ _ b_ _ _ to this point in a moment.
4 Just to di_ _ _ss (= sidetrack) for a moment, …
5 Let's examine this i_ m_ _ _ de_ _ _l.
6 Let me explain with a con_ _ _te ex_ _ _le.
7 I think there are three questions to f_ _ _ _ _n.
8 I would like to st_ _ _ _ (= emphasize) that …
9 _ _ you c_ _ s_ _ on this next slide, …
10 I'd like to high_ _ _ _t two things on this chart.
11 W_ _ _ i_ interesting in this slide is …
12 How does this re_ _te to your own particular cont_ _t?

**52.2 Complete the presentation extract with the words in the box. It is an alternative version of the presentation opposite.**

| at this point | emphasize | have a look | highlight two things |
| let's go on | my own view | notice | you can see how |

❝ OK, let's ¹ _____ at this next
slide. It shows the design for an offshore turbine that sits on
the surface of the sea.
I'd like to ² _____ on this diagram.
Firstly, ³ _____ the V-shaped
structure with 'sails' mounted along its length. Secondly,
⁴ _____ this whole structure can
turn on its base, powered by the action of the wind on the
sails. This is how electricity is generated.
⁵ _____ on this is that the design
is a big improvement on earlier versions – it's more efficient in
terms of energy production, and it's also more stable with its
solid base.
By the way, I must just ⁶ _____ that
this design is not in commercial production.
OK, are there any questions ⁷ _____ ?
No? Then ⁸ _____ to the next slide,
which is a graph showing the projected demand for offshore
wind energy over the next twenty years. ❞

The extract you just looked at shows several points about referring to visuals:
- The speaker introduces the slide clearly. A long pause at the end of the first paragraph would be good – giving the audience a chance to study the slide silently.
- The speaker uses 'firstly' and 'secondly' to list points. Again, pauses after each separate point would allow the listeners time to absorb the information.
- The speaker makes a personal comment. This creates interest and is one way to avoid the danger of just reading the text on the slide.
- The speaker gives a chance for questions about this slide.

**52.3 Read aloud these two versions of the same sentence. In the second, put a strong pause where you see the // symbol and a strong emphasis on the underlined syllables.**

**Version A** *The market for wind turbines is shifting from onshore to offshore.*
**Version B** *The market for wind turbines is shifting // from <u>on</u>shore // to <u>off</u>shore.*

Can you hear a difference? The second version has more clarity and more impact.

**Mark with a // symbol <u>three</u> places in this sentence where you can pause for clarity.**

1 As the wind passes over these they act like airfoils and this generates lift and turns the structure as a whole.

**Underline <u>two</u> syllables in this sentence that you can emphasize to create impact.**

2 It's more efficient in terms of energy production, and it's also more stable with its solid base.

**52.4 'I'd now like to discuss …' The words below can all replace 'discuss'. Fill in the missing vowels.**

1 m_v_ _n t_
2 t_lk _b_ _t
3 d_ _l w_th
4 t_rn my _tt_nt__n t_
5 t_k_ a l_ _k _t
6 _xpl_ _n
7 c_v_r
8 c_ns_d_r
9 m_nt__n
10 f_c_s _n

**52.5** ⊕ 7 **Speaking practice: listen and repeat. Repeat each phrase you hear and then listen to check.**

## 53 Presentations – closing and questions

The following sequence provides a guide for how to end a presentation effectively.

1 Signal the end: this means using a 'signpost' phrase to tell the audience explicitly that you're going to finish. (See unit 52 for the meaning of 'signpost phrase'.)

2 Summarize: summarize the main points, and add a few observations or details for interest. Perhaps have bullet points on a final slide, and then give a lively comment about what really matters for each one (a 'take-home message').

3 Conclude: you can conclude with a friendly comment, a final slide (with a strong image or message), by mentioning the benefits your talk has given the audience, or by looking forward to the future – with a call to action or an inspirational message. Finally, a strong 'Thank you all for coming' will hopefully produce some applause!

4 Invite questions: 'Do you have any questions?' is usually fine.

5 Deal with questions: the basic range of techniques are:
1 Respond positively, then answer.
2 Clarify / Ask for repetition.
3 Redirect to the questioner.
4 Redirect to the group.
5 Delay an answer.
6 Control the timing.

Read the presentation extract in the next column, which shows some of these techniques and phrases in context. It is the closing part of a 'welcoming visitors' presentation.

> " Right, that brings me to the end of my presentation.
> Just to summarize the main points again: I began by telling you a little about the history of our company, and you saw our growth from a small family firm to the international operation that we are today.
>
> Then I talked about our market, and how new technologies are opening up exciting possibilities for the future.
>
> After that I explained how customization is at the heart of our business model – our clients all get tailor-made solutions based on their individual needs.
>
> Finally I gave you some information about our manufacturing process, and you saw how we achieve our exceptional levels of quality and performance.
>
> OK, I'd like to finish by saying that it's a great pleasure for us to welcome you here today, and I hope that you enjoy the factory tour which we've planned for you. We'll start on the tour after a short break for refreshments. Thank you all for coming. *(applause)*
>
> I've got some handouts here – I'll pass them round. They show all the slides I used in my talk and my contact details are at the back.
>
> Do you have any quick questions before we break? Yes, the gentleman at the back with the red tie. "

● Compare the opening in unit 51 with the closing extract to the same presentation above. The presenter told the audience what she was going to say at the opening, and now here at the close she repeats the main points again. This reinforces the key ideas and makes them easier to remember.

## *The phrases you need* ☞

### Signal the end
*Right, that brings me nearly to the end of my presentation.*

### Summarize
*Just to summarize the main points again, …*
*So, to summarize, we looked at four main points. I began by telling you a little about … Then I talked about … After that I explained how … Finally I …*

### Conclude
*I'd like to finish by saying …*
*So, in conclusion, I hope that this talk has given you …*
*Now we have to … / I'm asking all of you to … / Our job is to …*
*Thank you all for coming. I hope it's been useful.*

### Practical matters
*I've got some handouts here.*
*Here's my email in case you want to get in touch.*

### Invite questions
*Do you have any questions? Yes, the gentleman / lady over there with the red tie / the black jacket.*
*Now, if you have any questions, I'll do my best to answer them.*

### Deal with questions
*That's a very good point. / I'm glad you asked me that.*
*Sorry, can you explain that again?*
*So, if I understand you correctly, you're asking …*
*That's an interesting question. What's your own opinion?*
*Has anyone else experienced the same thing?*
*I think that's outside the scope of this presentation, but I'm happy to discuss it with you afterwards.*
*OK, I think there's time for one last question.*

# Exercises

**53.1 Complete this extract from the close of a presentation with the words in the box. It is an internal presentation about departmental reorganization.**

> generated a lot of discussion    give the floor
> look at some options    may be forced    our job is to consider
> that covers everything    there is the option to
> the next steps    some difficult decisions    would lead to

❝ Right, I think [1] _____ I have to say. Before I finish I'll just briefly summarize the key points, and then we can try to come to a decision and focus on [2] _____ .

So, right at the beginning I said that the aim of my presentation was to [3] _____ for reorganizing our sales and marketing operations. And I explained the reasons why.

We explored three alternatives. Firstly, we looked at keeping both a sales department and a marketing department in every country as now, but reducing all budgets and looking for cost savings wherever possible. Spending on advertising will be cut back considerably, and when people leave the company they will not automatically be replaced. We can expect that everyone's workload will increase.

Secondly, [4] _____ break up the national marketing teams, while keeping the sales teams. All marketing campaigns would be run centrally from head office, leaving just a skeleton staff in other countries. This option [5] _____ , and I sense that many of you feel it's too drastic. However it's the option that offers the greatest cost savings, and we [6] _____ to consider it.

The final option is the possibility of merging sales and marketing into one large department in every market. This [7] _____ greater coordination, some cost savings, but also a loss of focus. I would like to hear more discussion about whether this option is viable.

So, in conclusion, now is the time to take [8] _____ . I'm asking all of you to leave departmental loyalties to one side – [9] _____ the future survival and profitability of the company as a whole.

Thank you all for your attention. Now I'll [10] _____ to you for your questions and comments. ❞

**53.2 Study the phrases for dealing with questions below. Try to guess the <u>single</u> missing word in each gap. Write your answers lightly at the side. Several answers may be possible.**

1  That's a very good _____ .
   (Think of something else besides 'question'.)
2  Sorry, can you _____ that again?
3  Has anyone else _____ the same thing?
4  OK, I think there's time _____ one last question.
5  That's an interesting question. What's your own _____ ?
6  Sorry, I didn't _____ that.
   (Think of something else besides 'understand'.)
7  I think that's outside the _____ of this presentation, but I'm happy to discuss it with you _____ .
8  I'm _____ you asked me that.
9  I promised to finish _____ time, and I see that it's nearly ten o'clock.
10  You _____ have thought quite a lot about this. What conclusion have you _____ to?
11  Could you be a little more _____ ?
12  Anyone like to _____ on that?
13  I don't have that information to _____ . Can I get _____ to you? Is that all right?
14  So, if I understand you _____ , you're asking …

**Now fill in the gaps above with the suggested words in the box below.**

> afterwards    back    catch    come    comment
> correctly    experienced    explain    for    glad    hand
> must    on    opinion    point    scope    specific

**53.3 Match phrases 1–14 from the previous exercise to the techniques below.**

a  Respond positively ☐ ☐
b  Clarify / Ask for repetition ☐ ☐ ☐ ☐
c  Redirect to the questioner ☐ ☐
d  Redirect to the group ☐ ☐
e  Delay an answer ☐ ☐
f  Control the timing ☐ ☐

**53.4 🌐 8 Speaking practice: listen and repeat. Repeat each phrase you hear and then listen to check.**

**Presentations – trends I**

The language of trends is important not just for presentations, but also for business reports. You may want to describe movements in financial indicators (eg profits, costs), sales and marketing indicators (eg sales, market share), or economic indicators (eg interest rates, unemployment). Often this language will be used to explain a graph or chart.

Many verbs describe the direction of movement:

| | |
|---|---|
| **Movement up and down**<br>go up / increase / rise<br>go down / decrease / fall<br> | **Stability and instability**<br>stay the same / be flat<br>fluctuate / vary /<br>move within a range<br> |
| **Smaller movement up and down**<br>edge up<br>edge down / dip<br> | **Larger movement up and down**<br>double / take off / boom /<br>increase tenfold<br>halve / plunge / crash<br> |

Alternatively, you may want to refer to turning points or individual points:

| | |
|---|---|
| **High points and low points**<br>peak / reach a peak<br>hit a low<br> | **Individual points on a graph**<br>stand at<br>be above / be below<br> |

Some verbs describe a change in size, and others say whether things are good or bad:

| | |
|---|---|
| **Change in size**<br>grow / expand<br>shrink / contract<br> | **Good / bad**<br>improve / get better / recover<br>deteriorate / get worse<br>Sales improved    Inflation improved |

To make your description more accurate you can then talk about the speed and amount of change:

| | |
|---|---|
| **Speed**<br>quickly / rapidly<br>gradually / steadily<br>slowly<br>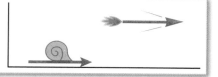 | **Amount**<br>considerably / significantly<br>moderately / to some extent<br>slightly / marginally<br> |

Try also to get the preposition right:

Sales stood **at** €1.2m          Sales increased **by** €0.2m / 15%
Sales rose **from** €1.2 **to** €1.4m          There was an increase **in** sales **of** €0.2m

And finally think about the verb form:

| Time period complete (past simple)<br>Sales **rose** by 2% **last quarter**. | Action / situation in progress in the past (past continuous)<br>Things were easier in the company a few years ago, while profits **were rising**. |
|---|---|
| Time period not complete (present perfect)<br>Profits **have risen** significantly **this year**. | Showing that one past event happened before another (past perfect)<br>Before the CEO resigned profits **had** already **fallen** by 20% in a year. |
| Present result of a past action (present perfect)<br>Prices **have risen** because of higher materials costs. | 'will' future for general beliefs, predictions and facts<br>Our competitors **will** face the same problems as us. |
| Action / situation in progress now (present continuous)<br>Inflation **is rising at the moment**. | 'going to' future when there is strong present evidence for a prediction<br>Everybody likes our new product line – I'm sure it's **going to be** a success. |

All the language above refers to describing trends. In unit 55 you'll see some language for analyzing trends.

# Exercises

**54.1 Match a verb on the left with a verb on the right so that they have the <u>same</u> meaning. Not all the words appear opposite.**

| | | |
|---|---|---|
| 1 | grow | recover |
| 2 | fall | rise |
| 3 | improve | contract |
| 4 | stay the same | drop |
| 5 | move higher | be stable |
| 6 | level off | expand |
| 7 | shrink | dip |
| 8 | edge down | stabilize |

If there are any verbs above or opposite that you aren't sure about, check their meaning carefully in a dictionary. For example, the word 'decline' – not mentioned in this unit – means both 'decrease' and 'get worse'. Also check to see if the verb can be used with an object – for example you cannot say *We rose our profits last year*.

**54.2 Match a verb on the left with a verb on the right so that they have the <u>opposite</u> meaning.**

| | | |
|---|---|---|
| 1 | boom | shrink |
| 2 | double | crash |
| 3 | edge up | vary |
| 4 | grow | dip |
| 5 | improve | deteriorate |
| 6 | peak | halve |
| 7 | stay the same | fall |
| 8 | rise | hit a low |

**54.3 Complete the table with the correct form of the words. You may need to use a dictionary.**

| | Verb | Past simple | Past participle |
|---|---|---|---|
| 1 | go up | *went up* | *gone up* |
| 2 | grow | | |
| 3 | rise | | |
| 4 | fall | | |

| | Verb | Noun |
|---|---|---|
| 5 | grow | *growth* |
| 6 | expand | |
| 7 | contract | |
| 8 | improve | |
| 9 | recover | |
| 10 | vary | |
| 11 | halve | |
| 12 | deteriorate | |

**54.4 Write the adjectives in the box in the correct space below. Not all the words appear opposite. Check any unknown words in a dictionary.**

> *disappointing    encouraging    enormous    excellent*
> *gradual    moderate    rapid    slight    sluggish*

| ↑ | | ↑ | | ↑ |
|---|---|---|---|---|
| FAST | | BIG | | GOOD NEWS |
| 1 _____ | 4 | _____ | 7 | _____ |
| 2 _____ | 5 | _____ | 8 | _____ |
| 3 _____ | 6 | _____ | 9 | _____ |
| SLOW | | SMALL | | BAD NEWS |
| ↓ | | ↓ | | ↓ |

**54.5 Rewrite the verb + adverb sentences as adjective + noun sentences.**

1 Sales grew slowly.
   There was _____ *slow growth* _____ in sales.
2 Costs rose significantly.
   There was a _____ in costs.
3 Profits deteriorated rapidly.
   We saw a _____ in profits.
4 Market share improved slightly.
   We had a _____ in market share.
5 Our sales forecasts varied considerably.
   There was a _____ in our sales forecasts.

**54.6 Fill in the missing prepositions in the presentation extract below.**

❝ After the marketing campaign at the start of March sales rose [1] _____ an initial figure [2] _____ €4.5m [3] _____ €5.2m by June. That means they went up [4] _____ 15%, the biggest increase [5] _____ sales of any recent campaign. They currently stand [6] _____ €4.9m. ❞

*Note: the preposition in #4 is often missed out in speech.*

**54.7 Underline the correct forms in italics. Each verb form is used once.**

❝ So far this year we [1]*saw / have seen* a lot of volatility in the financial markets. The current situation in the world economy [2]*is causing / had caused* a great deal of uncertainty in the minds of investors. No-one knows what the future [3]*will bring / is bringing*. Last year things were very different: everyone [4]*has been / was* optimistic and the markets [5]*were rising / have risen*. Of course we know now that our current problems [6]*have already begun / had already begun* well before last year. ❞

**See page 151 for some writing tasks.**

Unit 54 gave some language for describing trends. But in a presentation or report you will probably also have to give some analysis. You may want to give reasons for the trends, to show their results, or to give additional information.

Read this extract from an internal presentation, analyzing recent sales figures.

> 66 [1]Sales for the first half of the year were disappointing, mainly because of the lack of new product lines. [2]However, we launched two new lines in June and promoted them with a strong marketing campaign over the summer. [3]As a result of this campaign, sales began to improve. [4]By the end of August they were 10% higher on a year-on-year basis, although they fell back again over September and October. 99

- Sentence 1 has the structure 'result' (disappointing sales) ← 'reason' (lack of new product lines). Sentence 3 has the structure 'reason' (this campaign) → 'result' (sales began to improve). The words *because of, as a result of* and *due to* can all be used in sentence 1 and sentence 3 in a similar way.
- Sentence 2 begins with *however,* and this word adds an idea that is surprising or unexpected after the previous sentence. The words *however, nevertheless* and *even so* can all be used in a similar way. They're all followed by a comma.
- Sentence 4 has *although* in the middle of the sentence. This word introduces an idea that is surprising after a previous idea in the same sentence. Compare with *However* which refers back to a different sentence.
- *Although* can also be used at the beginning of a sentence, but the two contrasting ideas are still in the same sentence: *Although sales were higher at the end of August, they fell back again in September.* The words *although* and *even though* can be used in a similar way.

Now read this next extract from the same presentation.

> 66 [5]This drop in sales over September and October led to a series of meetings where we examined our whole strategy in depth. [6]Christmas was approaching, and the Christmas season produces a large part of our annual sales. [7]Moreover, we were losing market share to our main competitor. [8]As a result, we increased our advertising budget for November and December, and changed our use of different media. [9]Outdoor advertising on billboards, buses and bus stops increased, while our advertising in magazines and newspapers decreased. 99

- Sentence 5 has the structure 'reason' (drop in sales) → 'result' (series of meetings). The sentence uses the verb 'lead to' to express this. The verbs *lead to* and *result in* can be used in a similar way.

- Sentence 7 uses *Moreover* to give additional information that supports the previous sentence. The words *Moreover, Furthermore* and *In addition* can all be used in a similar way. They're all followed by a comma.
- Sentence 8 uses *As a result* to give the result of the previous sentence. The words *As a result, Because of this* and *Therefore* can all be used in a similar way. They're all followed by a comma.
- Sentence 9 has *while* in the middle of the sentence. This makes a simple contrast between two facts. (Compare with *although* where there is a sense of surprise.) The words *while* and *whereas* can be used in a similar way.

The table below presents all this language together. Note that some words like *Because of* and *In spite of* are followed immediately by a noun phrase, while other words like *Because* and *In spite of the fact that* are followed by a subject + verb:

*Because of **the marketing campaign** in June, sales increased.*
*Because **we had** a marketing campaign in June, sales increased.*
*In spite of **the poor weather in July**, sales …*
*In spite of the fact that **there was** poor weather in July, sales …*

## The phrases you need 👉

**Reason → result (ie cause → consequence)**
*Because of / Due to / As a result of + noun phrase, …*
*Because / Due to the fact that + subject + verb, …*
referring to the previous sentence:
*Because of this, / As a result, / Therefore, …*
using a verb:
*lead to / result in …*

**Result ← reason (ie consequence ← cause)**
*… because of / as a result of / due to …*
using a verb:
*result from …*

**Making a simple contrast**
*…, while / whereas …*

**Adding a surprising or unexpected idea**
*However, / Nevertheless, / Even so, …*
*In spite of / Despite + noun phrase, …*
*In spite of the fact that / Despite the fact that + subject + verb, …*
*… , although / even though …*
*Although / Even though … , …*

**Giving additional information**
*Moreover, / Furthermore, / In addition, …*

See unit 69 for other words like *As a result, However* and *Moreover* that begin a sentence by making a link to the previous sentence.

# Exercises

**55.1 Find and correct the one mistake in each sentence below. It could be a missing word, an extra word, or a wrong word.**

1 Because our considerable cost-cutting measures last quarter, profits rose slightly.

2 Because of we cut costs considerably last quarter, profits rose slightly.

3 Earnings fell by 8% last year due our increased materials costs.

4 Earnings fell by 8% last year as a result from our increased materials costs.

5 Difficult market conditions resulted a significant decline in market share.

6 The significant decline in market share resulted of difficult market conditions.

7 This chart shows that brand awareness increased in South-East Asia, where it fell in Latin America.

8 Our competitors are gaining market share. More, they have a whole new product line coming out next month.

9 In spite the fact that we delayed the launch of our new product range, we still had reasonable results last year.

10 Despite we delaying the launch of our new product range, we still had reasonable results last year.

**55.2 Complete the presentation extract with these words: *as a result, due to, even though, however, in spite of* and *moreover*. Use a capital letter where necessary.**

**Be careful! Read the whole text before you begin, and write your answers lightly at the side until you're sure.**

66 We are operating in a very difficult business environment, and this is largely ¹ _____ the high price of oil. Energy costs are one of the biggest costs in our business, ² _____ we've introduced a lot of energy-efficient machines in our factories over recent years. ³ _____ this investment in technology, energy still accounts for 38% of our direct costs – and ⁴ _____ it's very difficult to increase profit margins. ⁵ _____ , it's not all bad news. Market share is growing slowly and we've signed some important new contracts. ⁶ _____ , our recent acquisition of a company in Brazil gives us access to the Latin American market for the first time. 99

> Notice how a phrase like 'as a result' does not always have to come at the beginning of a sentence followed by a comma. In #4 it comes in the middle, after 'and'. Making a new sentence in #4 would mean that the presentation does not flow so well.

**55.3 In unit 54 you saw two simple forms for the future: *will* and *going to*. However the future is not certain, and to make forecasts for trends you need other language that shows different degrees of probability.**

**Match a sentence 1–5 with a sentence a–e with a similar meaning.**

1 It's highly likely that we'll meet our targets. ☐
2 We're likely to meet our targets. ☐
3 It might be that we meet our targets. ☐
4 We're unlikely to meet our targets. ☐
5 It's highly unlikely that we'll meet our targets. ☐

a There's a good chance we'll meet our targets.
b There's almost no way we'll meet our targets.
c There's not much chance we'll meet our targets.
d We're almost certain to meet our targets.
e There's a 50/50 chance we'll meet our targets.

**55.4 Complete the presentation extract with the words in the box. This exercise includes some new language as well as language from units 54 and 55.**

| | | | | |
|---|---|---|---|---|
| axis | a slight increase | although | have been flat | |
| highlight | highly likely | implications | in line with | lead to |
| notice | more rapidly | reached a peak | roughly | while |

66 OK, have a look at this next graph. There are two lines. The green line, with values on the left vertical ¹ _____ , shows sales. The red line, with values on the right vertical axis, shows profits.

I'd like to ² _____ two things here. The first is the sales graph. As you can see, sales rose steadily for many years, but they ³ _____ around two years ago. Since then, sales ⁴ _____ – with just ⁵ _____ in this last quarter.

Now look at profits. ⁶ _____ how profits increased ⁷ _____ sales for several years, but then they started to deteriorate, slowly at first and then ⁸ _____ . In the last year this drop in profits has been significant – ⁹ _____ 5%.

So, profits are down ¹⁰ _____ sales are flat.

The ¹¹ _____ of this are clear: we are not doing enough to control costs. ¹² _____ the sales figures taken alone don't look too bad, profits tell the real story.

It is a difficult market environment and we must act now, or it's ¹³ _____ that we will lose our competitiveness. In the long term this will ¹⁴ _____ a situation where the future of the company, and our jobs, are at risk. 99

**See page 152 for some writing tasks.**

## 56.1 Match the beginning of each phrase 1–10 with its correct ending a–j.

1  OK, let's … [b]
2  If you have any questions, … ☐
3  I'll come back … ☐
4  I've divided my talk … ☐
5  Just to digress for … ☐
6  Let's examine this … ☐
7  Let's move … ☐
8  My own view … ☐
9  OK, that's all I want … ☐
10  Right, let's begin …☐

a  a moment …
b  get started. Can everybody see?
c  in more detail.
d  into three main parts.
e  on this is …
f  on to the second point.
g  please feel free to interrupt.
h  to this in a moment.
i  with the first slide.
j  to say about the first point.

### Continue as before.

11  As you can see … ☐
12  I began by telling you … ☐
13  I'd like us to … ☐
14  Just to summarize … ☐
15  Let me explain … ☐
16  Now, do you have … ☐
17  Right, that brings me to … ☐
18  Thank you all … ☐
19  This leads me … ☐
20  What is the reason … ☐

k  a little about … Then I explained how … After that I talked about …
l  any questions?
m  focus our attention on two things on this chart …
n  for coming and I hope it's been useful.
o  for this? The reason is …
p  on this next slide, …
q  the end of my presentation.
r  the main points again before I finish.
s  to my third point, which is …
t  with a concrete example.

## 56.2 Complete the diagram below so that it includes all the twenty phrases from 56.1. You will see that eight phrases have already been used. Find and write the other twelve phrases by matching them with a picture clue.

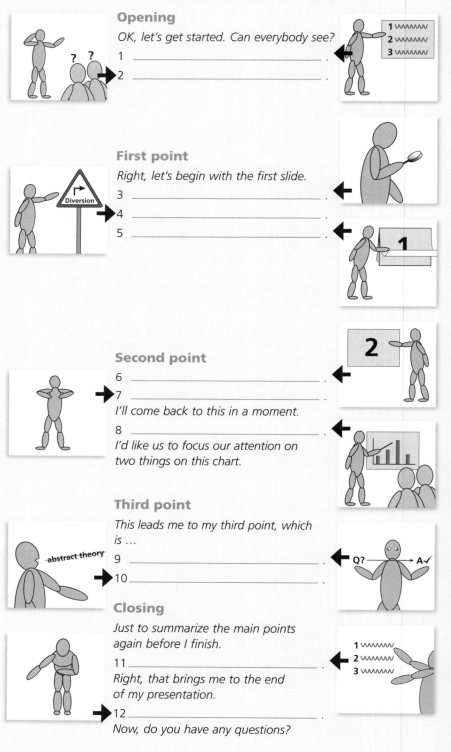

**Opening**

OK, let's get started. Can everybody see?

1  _____ .
2  _____ .

**First point**

Right, let's begin with the first slide.

3  _____ .
4  _____ .
5  _____ .

**Second point**

6  _____ .
7  _____ .
I'll come back to this in a moment.
8  _____ .
I'd like us to focus our attention on two things on this chart.

**Third point**

This leads me to my third point, which is …

9  _____ .
10  _____ .

**Closing**

Just to summarize the main points again before I finish.

11 _____ .
Right, that brings me to the end of my presentation.
12 _____ .
Now, do you have any questions?

When you finish, look back at the whole sequence and read the phrases aloud. Can you see how these 'signpost phrases' help the audience to follow the presentation?

**56.3 Fill in the gaps with the words in the box.**

| about | at | back | in | in | in | into | for |
|---|---|---|---|---|---|---|---|
| of | on | on | on | on | to | to | to | with |

1 Take a look _____ this picture. What does it tell you _____ our company?
2 I've divided my talk _____ four main parts.
3 Right, let's begin _____ the first slide.
4 Let's move _____ _____ the second point.
5 This leads me _____ my third main point.
6 I'll come _____ _____ this in a moment.
   *('on' is possible in #6, but isn't the answer here.)*
7 My own view _____ this is simple.
   *('of' is possible in #7, but isn't the answer here)*
8 I think there are three questions to focus _____ .
9 As you can see _____ this next slide, …
   *('in' is possible in #9, but isn't the answer here.)*
10 So, _____ conclusion, I hope that my talk has given you a good overview _____ our company.
11 Thank you all _____ coming.
12 Here's my email address _____ case you want to get _____ touch.

**56.4 Complete the sentences with the pairs of words in the box.**

| anyone / comments | brings / end | digress / moment |
|---|---|---|
| examine / detail | explain / again | explain / concrete |
| highlight / diagram | question / opinion | scope / afterwards |
| time / question | useful / background | start / introducing |

1 Let me _____ by _____ myself.
2 Just to _____ for a _____ .
3 It might be _____ to give a little _____ here.
4 Let's _____ this in more _____ .
5 Let me _____ with a _____ example.
6 I'd like to _____ two things on this _____ .
7 Does _____ have any _____ ?
8 Right, that _____ me nearly to the _____ of my presentation.
9 Sorry, can you _____ that _____ ?
10 That's an interesting _____ . What's your own _____ ?
11 I think that's outside the _____ of this presentation, but I'm happy to discuss it with you _____ .
12 OK, I think there's _____ for one last _____ .

**56.5 Underline the correct words in italics in this extract from an internal presentation.**

66 This next chart shows sales for our two main product lines, the Micro range and the Neka range. [1]*Mark / Notice* the scale on the vertical [2]*axis / axle* – it shows the number of [3]*units / unities* sold in thousands per month.

I'd like to [4]*draw / make* your attention firstly to the black line, which shows sales of the Micro range. You can see how last year sales [5]*rose / have risen* [6]*steady / steadily* all through the year. Since the beginning of this year they [7]*continued / have continued* to rise, [8]*although / in spite of* at a slower pace.

On balance, these results are good – [9]*steady / steadily* [10]*grow / growth* is what we like to see. This generally positive picture is [11]*due to / due from* the performance and reliability of the Micro range, and the fact that our competitors have been slow to respond. [12]*Even so / Even though*, we cannot be complacent. We have to build on this success going forward, and I want our sales teams to really focus [13]*about / on* the Micro range [14]*over / from* the next few months.

I'm going to set an ambitious target – to take sales of Micro products from their current level of 30,000 per month [15]*to / until* a [16]*figure / number* of 35,000 by the end of the year.

OK, now let's [17]*look at / look to* the purple line on the chart, which shows sales of the Neka range. As you know, we launched this range in December of last year, and sales [18]*took off / were taking off* immediately. For the first few months things [19]*were really looking good / had really looked good*. We were expecting this because we [20]*were doing / had done* a lot of market research before the launch. [21]*However / Whereas*, for no obvious reason, there [22]*was / has been* a [23]*sudden / suddenly* [24]*drop / reduce* in sales in recent weeks. The question is this: can we find out the [25]*motives / reasons* and what can we do [26]*about / for* it?

In a moment I'm going to open up the discussion and ask for your [27]*comments / commentaries*. But the implications are clear: it's [28]*high / highly* [29]*chance / likely* that we won't meet our target of 25,000 [30]*by / for* the end of the year. 99

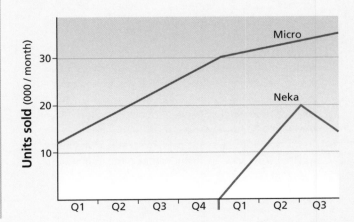

# 57 Meetings – opinions

Read the extract from a meeting in a household products company. Antoine (A), Brigitte (B) and Chris (C) are discussing their company's marketing strategy.

A: We need to do something radical to develop our brands. The retailers are becoming more and more powerful – they buy from us for whatever price they want, and sell to the public for whatever price they want.

B: Absolutely. Our profit margins are getting thinner and thinner.

C: I totally agree with you about the power of the retailers. And it's not just their pricing power – it's also their own-label products. Why should people pay more for branded items like ours?

A: Basically, we have to look at branding in a whole new way. In my opinion, we have to go beyond market research, beyond talking about quality, and beyond clever advertising slogans. What I'm trying to say is we need to make an emotional connection with consumers. We need consumers to love us, not just to need us.

B: I'm not so sure about that. We sell detergents and things for the home. How emotional are cleaning products? We're not a company like Apple or Nike who make exciting, lifestyle products. What do you think, Chris?

C: It seems to me that we have to do something – we can't just carry on as we are. It may be true that our products aren't very exciting, but we also have to consider that household products are an important part of family life, and families are near the centre of our emotions. Actually, I do think our advertising could appeal more to people's emotions.

B: OK, OK. You're probably right. But what did you have in mind, Antoine?

A: We need a new 'face' for our brands. A celebrity. Someone who the public loves. To put it simply, we need the most famous football player in the world to appear on screen, using our products.

B: Really? Do you think so? You think that if a famous footballer cleans their teeth and washes the floor, using our products, the public will love us? I think they will laugh at us, and at the footballer.

C: Obviously it would have to be done carefully, and a footballer may not be the best choice. Perhaps a film star from romantic comedy movies would be better. But in general I like Antoine's idea.

B: OK, I can see what you mean, but don't you think this is all going to be very expensive?

A: That's true. It will be. But from my point of view it's worth it. An emotional connection is the only way to justify a premium price.

## The phrases you need ☞

**Asking for opinions**
*What do you think, Chris?*
*Chris, what's your opinion?*
*What did you have in mind?*

**Giving an opinion**
*What I'm trying to say is … / The point is …*
*In my opinion … / The way I see it …*
*Basically … / Essentially …*
*Actually … / As a matter of fact …*
*Obviously … / Clearly …*
*In general … / Overall …*
*To put it simply … / In short …*

**Giving an opinion (more carefully)**
*It seems to me that …*
*I tend to feel that …*
*From my point of view …*

**Agreeing**
*That's true.*
*I totally agree with you. / Absolutely.*
*It's not just … , it's also …*
*You're probably right.*

**Agreeing partially**
*I agree up to a point, but …*
*OK, I can see what you mean, but don't you think … ?*
*It may be true that … , but we also have to consider …*

**Disagreeing**
*Really? Do you think so?*
*I'm not so sure about that.*
*I'm sorry, that's not how I see it.*
*I really can't agree with you there.*

● Notice the different ways to give an opinion in the box above. Many of these phrases appear in the extract.
● Notice the different ways to agree and disagree above. Many of these phrases appear in the extract.

# Exercises

**57.1 Underline the correct words in italics.**

1 Chris, *what / how* is your opinion?

2 What did you have *in mind / in your mind*?

3 It *seems me / seems to me* that we have to do something – we can't just carry on as we are.

4 From *my view / my point of view*, it's worth it.

5 *I am agree / I agree* with you.

6 *You're right / You have reason*.

7 I agree *to a point / up to a point*, but …

8 I can see what *you mean / you're meaning*, but don't you think this is going to be very expensive?

9 It *may / can* be true that our products aren't very exciting, but we also have to consider …

10 I'm not so sure *with / about* that.

**57.2 Look at the extracts from meetings below. Write a phrase from the box next to a phrase in italics with the same meaning. Be careful!**

| | | | | |
|---|---|---|---|---|
| *Actually* | *Basically* | *By the way* | *However* | *In general* |
| *In my opinion* | *Luckily* | *Obviously* | *The point is* | *In short* |

1 *On the other hand / _____* , there are some serious issues that we still haven't discussed.

2 *As a matter of fact / _____* , the project is three weeks behind schedule, not two.

3 *Fortunately / _____* , we have enough time.

4 *Clearly / _____* , they're not as cheap as other suppliers, but their quality and reliability is much better.

5 *Overall / _____* , it's a very positive proposal, but there are some important details that still need clarifying.

6 *What I'm trying to say is / _____* , June is a much better time to launch this product than April.

7 *Essentially / _____* , it's a good idea as long as it's not too expensive.

8 *While we're on the subject / _____* , did you get a chance to read that report I sent you?

9 *The way I see it / _____* , the whole thing is a complete waste of time.

10 *To put it simply / _____* , profits are falling and costs are rising and we have to do something – fast.

**57.3 Write one of these next to each sentence below: *Polite disagreement, Strong disagreement, Not gramatically possible*.**

1 I really can't agree with you. _____

2 I can't really agree with you. _____

3 I can't agree really with you. _____

**57.4 Put the phrases below into order: 1 is the most polite disagreement, and 4 is the strongest disagreement.**

☐ I'm sorry, that's not how I see it.

☐ Really? Do you think so?

☐ I'm not so sure about that.

☐ I really can't agree with you there.

**57.5 *'I think we need to make an emotional connection with consumers.'* Study the different replies a–g and then do the exercise below.**

→ a Yes, just like Apple or Nike.

→ b Yes, you're right.

→ c Yes, they should love our products, not just need them.

→ d Maybe, but how can a household products company do that?

→ e Isn't that idea too abstract? Wouldn't it be better to focus on something more practical?

→ f Do you think so?

→ g I'm sorry, I don't agree with you.

**Now match each reply with a technique for agreeing and disagreeing below.**

**Agreeing**

1 Using a standard phrase ☐

2 Saying the same thing again using different words ☐

3 Giving an example ☐

**Disagreeing**

4 Using a standard phrase ☐

5 *Yes, but …* ☐

6 Asking an open question to show doubt ☐

7 Asking a negative question (where your own answer is clearly 'yes') ☐

**57.6 🌐 9 Speaking practice: listen and repeat. Repeat each phrase you hear and then listen to check.**

# 58 Meetings – making things clear

Read the extract from a meeting between three senior managers from different departments in an investment bank. Agustin (A) has some bad news to announce to his colleagues Brian (B) and Cecilia (C). Brian and Cecilia cannot believe what they're hearing!

A: Well, good morning, everyone.
B: Good morning.
C: Good morning.
5 A: You're probably wondering why I called this urgent meeting at such short notice. I have some bad news for you. We have a rogue trader.
B: Sorry, I missed that. Could you say it again?
A: I said we have a rogue trader. Like Nick Leeson at Barings and Jerome Kerviel at Société Générale. We
10 have someone who has been trading beyond his authority.
C: Can I get this clear? You're saying that there has been fraud?
A: Yes, it appears so. On a massive scale. Two billion euros.
15 C: Sorry, how much did you say?
A: I said two billion euros.
B: How did you arrive at the figure of two billion?
A: It's just a guess.
B: What exactly do you mean by 'guess'? Don't you
20 know?
A: The person involved was trading complex financial instruments. Derivatives. It's very difficult to estimate the losses.
C: Correct me if I'm wrong, but you seem to be saying
25 that you have no clue what this person was trading and no clue how much money he has lost.
A: Please allow me to explain. I cannot know every detail of every transaction of every trader. I have spoken to the individual's line manager this morning, and the
30 figure of two billion looks like a reasonable guess.
B: You mentioned that the person was trading complex derivatives. Could you be a little more specific?
A: At this stage, no.
B: So, in other words, you don't understand the trades. And
35 probably the line manager doesn't understand either.
A: Perhaps I haven't explained myself clearly. What I meant was that we're investigating the matter. There are certain aspects of the trades that seem to have escaped our internal controls.
40 C: Could I just say something? I don't believe what I'm hearing! Does anyone in this place know what they're doing?
A: Can I just finish my point? What I was trying to say was that this is a very serious matter and I cannot blame
45 individuals or go into details until we have proof.
B: I just hope that the media haven't found out about this yet.
A: There are three journalists waiting in my office.

● Notice the different ways to make things clear. At line 7 Brian asks for repetition. At line 12 Cecilia uses her own words to check (paraphrasing). At line 15 Cecilia clarifies an individual point.

## The phrases you need ☞

### Ask for repetition
*Sorry, I missed that. Could you say it again?*
*Sorry, I don't understand, can you explain that again?*
*Can you run through / go over that again, please?*

### Use your own words to check
*So, in other words, …*
*If I understand you correctly, … . Is that right?*
*Can I get this clear? You're saying that …*
*Correct me if I'm wrong, but you seem to be saying that …*

### Clarify individual points
*Sorry, how much did you say?*
*Sorry, the project will start when?*
*What exactly do you mean by …?*
*How did you arrive at the figure of …?*
*You mentioned … . Could you be a little more specific?*

### Correct a misunderstanding
*I'm sorry, that's not what I meant.*
*No, sorry, there's been a slight misunderstanding.*
*Perhaps I haven't explained myself clearly.*

### Reformulate
*Please allow me to explain.*
*Let me put it another way, …*
*What I meant was …*
*What I was trying to say was …*

### Get your turn to speak
*Sorry, but …*
*Can I come in here?*
*Could I just say something?*
*Can I just finish my point?*

# Exercises

**58.1 Read the dialogue opposite aloud several times, then cover it with a piece of paper.**
**Now try to remember some of the missing words below. Write your answers lightly at the side.**

1 Sorry, I _____ that. Could you _____ it again?

2 Can I get this _____ ? You're _____ that there has been fraud?

3 Sorry, _____ did you _____ ?

4 How did you _____ at the _____ of two billion?

5 What _____ do you _____ by 'guess'?

6 _____ me if I'm _____ , but you seem to be saying that you have no clue what this person was trading.

7 Please _____ me to _____ . I cannot know every detail of every transaction.

8 You mentioned that the person was trading complex derivatives. Could you be a _____ more _____ ?

9 Perhaps I haven't _____ myself _____ . What I meant was …

10 Can I just _____ my _____ ? What I was trying to say was …

**After you have remembered whatever you can, use the pairs of words in the box below to complete the sentences.**

| | | | |
|---|---|---|---|
| allow / explain | arrive / figure | clear / saying | correct / wrong |
| exactly / mean | explained / clearly | finish / point | |
| how much / say | little / specific | missed / say | |

## 58.2 Fill in the missing letters.

1 Sorry, I don't und_ _ _ _ _ _d. Can you e_ _ _ _ _n that again?

2 Can you run _ _ _ _ _gh that again? (= explain quickly)

3 Can you go _ _ _r that again? (= repeat it in order that I can understand it)

4 No, sorry, there's been a sl_ _ _t misund_ _ _ _ _ _ing.

5 Let me _ _ _ it another _ _y.

6 Can I c_ _ _ _ _ here? (= enter the discussion / interrupt)

**58.3 A team leader is speaking in a conference call, but a colleague (Bob) doesn't understand very well. Complete Bob's questions with the words in the box.**

| | | | | |
|---|---|---|---|---|
| what | when | where | which | who |
| how long | how much | how often | | |

Team leader: This meeting today is just a quick briefing so that everyone understands their zxhkqf before the project starts.

Bob: Sorry, understands their [1] _____ ?

Team leader: Their roles. Yes, as I was saying, it's just a quick briefing – it'll only last around kfxhzq minutes.

Bob: Sorry, [2] _____ did you say?

Team leader: Around thirty minutes. OK, so the project will start at the beginning of qxkfzh.

Bob: Sorry, the project will start [3] _____ ?

Team leader: At the beginning of March. And once it's running, we'll have to meet regularly, xhkzqf a month.

Bob: Sorry, [4] _____ did you say?

Team leader: Once a month. OK, fzxhqk will be in overall charge of the budget.

Bob: Sorry, [5] _____ will be in charge of the budget?

Team leader: Martha. If you have any travel expenses, please fill in form qzfxkh and give it to her.

Bob: Sorry, [6] _____ form?

Team leader: Form TE30. If you think you will spend more than fzxhqk, you should get my authorization first.

Bob: Sorry, [7] _____ did you say?

Team leader: 400 euros. Copies of the form can be found on hxfkzq.

Bob: Sorry, we can find them [8] _____ ?

Team leader: On the company intranet.

Notice how Bob asks for clarification in two ways. Sometimes he simply says 'Sorry, (question word) did you say?' Other times he includes in his question some words that he did understand.

**58.5 🕐 10 Speaking practice: listen and repeat. Repeat each phrase you hear and then listen to check.**

## 59 Meetings – problem-solving

Read the extract from a meeting in a mining company. Annette (A), Ben (B) and Claude (C) are discussing an issue of social responsibility.

A: Our geological studies have shown that there's a lot of gold in this area, but the local population is against us – they say our mining operations will destroy the environment. There are several ways we could deal with this. I'd like to open up the discussion and hear your views.

B: I think we should offer some money to the local mayor, under the table. It's worked before.

A: I'm sorry, I don't think that's a good idea. What would be the consequences? This mayor seems honest and he could go straight to the newspapers. It would be a disaster.

B: Yes, I suppose you're right.

A: Claude? Any suggestions?

C: Well, it's just an idea, but what about offering to use some of our profits to support environmental charities? We could give money to organizations that protect the rainforest, that sort of thing.

A: That sounds like a good idea, but I don't think it would work in practice. Let's look at the pros and cons. On the one hand, it would improve our public image, that's true. But on the other hand, people would see it as a very cynical gesture. And it does nothing for the local population in that area.

B: Can I make a suggestion? Instead of being defensive, why don't we go on the attack with a big PR campaign in the media?

A: What do you mean?

B: Well – look at the benefits that our operations will bring. We'll bring jobs to the local community, and our employees will pay taxes to the government. We're on the side of progress.

A: Let's think carefully about the implications of that. We would have to spend a huge amount of money on press and TV advertisements, and we're only a small company. What do you think Claude?

C: In general it sounds like a good idea, although I agree that the cost may be too high. I think the best way forward is to get a more detailed estimate of how much gold the mine can produce, and then we'll be in a better position to decide about the PR campaign.

A: OK, let's do that. After all, we have a number of options. For example, we could run a local PR campaign instead of a national one, just emphasizing the jobs.

B: OK. The next thing to do is carry out a more detailed geological survey. I agree.

● Notice the process of exploring options, making suggestions, reacting, and accepting or rejecting the suggestions.

### The phrases you need ☞

**Present options**
*We have a number of options.*
*There are several ways we could deal with this.*

**Balance an argument**
*Let's look at the pros and cons.*
*On the one hand, … . But on the other hand, …*
*In general … , although …*
*On the whole … , but …*

**Make a suggestion**
*I think we should / could …*
*Can I make a suggestion? Instead of … , why don't we … ?*
*It's just an idea, but what about … (+ -ing)?*

**React**
*What would be the consequences?*
*Let's think carefully about the implications of that.*

**Accept a suggestion**
*OK, let's do that.*
*Yes, I think that would work really well.*

**Reject a suggestion**
*I can see one or two problems with that.*
*That sounds like a good idea, but I don't think it would work in practice.*
*I'm sorry, I don't think that's a good idea.*

**Next steps**
*I think the best way forward is …*
*What we've got to do now is …*
*The next thing to do is …*

# Exercises

**59.1 Cover the opposite page with a piece of paper. Now try to remember the words below. (Some letters have been given.)**

1 There are sev_ _ _l ways we could d_ _ _  w_ _ _  this.
2 I'd like to o_ _ _  u_ the discussion and hear your v_ _ _s.
3 Yes, I su_ _ _se you're r_ _t.
4 That s_ _ _ _s like a good idea, but I don't think it would w_ _ _ i_ pr_ _ _ _ _ _.
5 Let's look at the p_ _ _  and co_ _  (= advantages and disadvantages).
6 _ _  the _ _e _ _ _d, it would improve our public image, that's true. But _ _  the _ _ _ _r _ _ _d, people would see it as a very cynical gesture.
7 Can I _ _ _e a s_ _ _ _ _ _ion? I_ _ _ _ _d of being defensive, w_ _ _ _ _'t we go on the attack with a big PR campaign in the media?
8 Let's think carefully about the impl_ _ _ _ _ _ _s (= possible future results) of that.
9 In g_ _ _ _ _ _  it sounds like a good idea, a_ _ _ _ _gh I agree that the cost may be too high.
10 I think the b_ _t  w_y  f_ _ _ _ _d is to get a more detailed estimate.

**59.2 Make phrases by matching an item from each column.**

1 OK, let's — waste of time.
2 What — work really well.
3 That's a complete — about …?
4 Why — we …?
5 Yes, that would — don't we …?
6 Shall — do that.

7 That sounds — make a suggestion?
8 Can I — worth trying.
9 I can see — like a good idea.
10 I'm not really — would work in practice.
11 That might be — sure about that.
12 I don't think it — one or two problems with that.

**59.3 Write the phrase numbers from the previous exercise in the correct category below.**

a Make a suggestion ☐ ☐ ☐ ☐
b Accept a suggestion ☐ ☐ ☐ ☐
c Reject a suggestion ☐ ☐ ☐ ☐

**59.4 Complete the table by writing these nouns next to the verbs they go with: *a suggestion*, *a decision*, *a problem*, *a solution*. Check any unknown words in a dictionary.**

| | |
|---|---|
| analyze, approach, avoid, be faced with, cause, consider, explore, find a way round, get round, identify, look into, overcome, present (somebody with), resolve, run into, solve, tackle | 1 _____ |
| agree (on), arrive at, come up with, figure out, find, look for, offer, produce, propose, put forward, reach, work towards | 2 _____ |
| accept, act on, agree with, come up with, consider, make, follow up, go along with, lend weight to, put forward, reject, respond to, rule out, take up, welcome | 3 _____ |
| alter, arrive at, be faced with, come to, confirm, go back on, hesitate over, ignore, implement, justify, lie behind, make, postpone, reach, reconsider, reverse, take | 4 _____ |

**59.5 Fill each gap with a verb from the previous exercise in the correct form.**

1 If you _____ a problem, you're in a situation where you have to deal with it.
2 If you _____ a problem, you make an effort to deal with it *(metaphor from football)*
3 If you _____ a solution, you think about a problem until you find the answer or understand what has happened. *(= 'work out')*
4 If you _____ a solution, you do things that help you to make progress.
5 If you _____ a suggestion, you think of it.
6 If something _____ a suggestion, it provides evidence to make the suggestion seem like a good one.
7 If you _____ a decision, you take action to put it into practice.
8 If something _____ a decision, it is the true reason for the decision.

**59.6 🌐 11 Speaking practice: listen and repeat. Repeat each phrase you hear and then listen to check.**

## Meetings – leading a meeting

The person who leads the meeting is often called 'the chair', but other common terms are 'moderator', 'facilitator' and 'presiding officer'. Below you will find some typical extracts spoken by this person.

### Opening the meeting

Right, is everybody here? Good, I think we can start.
Well, good morning everyone, and thanks for coming.
Unfortunately Anneke is ill and sends her apologies.
Just a couple of housekeeping things before we begin
5  – we'll have a short break around ten thirty, and I aim
to finish the meeting on time, at twelve o'clock. The
bathroom is down the hall on the left.
OK. Do you all have a copy of the agenda? Good. Can
someone take the minutes? Thank you, Vikram.
10  Just before we begin, I'd like to introduce Agnieszka
from our Warsaw office. Would you like to say a few
words about yourself Agnieszka? … OK, thanks.
Right. Our objective today is to plan the launch of the
new range of large-screen televisions across all our European
15  markets. I've prepared some background information that I
hope will be useful, and I'll distribute it round the table now.
You can see from the agenda that we have a lot to get
through, so I would ask that you keep all contributions
brief and to the point.
20  OK, let's move straight to the first item. Henk, would
you like to kick off?

### Closing the meeting

OK, everyone, I think we can stop there – it's nearly twelve
o'clock.
I'd like to sum up. There are three main conclusions
from the meeting. First, … . Secondly, … . And finally … .
5  In terms of action points, we've decided to … – Jennifer
you're going to deal with that – and we've also agreed
that Miguel should prepare a report on … .
Are there any other points that anyone wants to make?
Have I missed anything?
10  Well, thanks for your input, everyone. We've had lots
of good ideas and I think it was a very useful meeting. I'll
circulate the minutes as soon as I get them from Vikram.
What about another meeting? Can we fix a date now?
Right, we'll close the meeting here. Enjoy your lunch.
15  Caitriona, can I just have a quick word with you before
you disappear?

### Managing the meeting

Between the open and the close there is the whole middle
section of the meeting where the chair manages and controls
the discussion. The table below contains phrases for this.
Unit 58 (Making things clear) is also very relevant here.

## The phrases you need ☞

### Ask for reactions

*What's your view on this, Nadine?*
*How do you feel about this, Klaus?*
*Antonio, this is your field. In a few words, can you tell us what you think?*
*Mike, after we've heard from Rosa can we have your views? I know you have some experience of this problem.*

### Deal with interruptions

*Could you just hang on a moment please?*
*One at a time, please. First Mirella, then Claude.*
*Pavol, could you just let Nikola finish? I'll come back to you in a moment.*

### Keep moving

*Perhaps we could get back to the main point?*
*I'm not sure that's relevant.*
*Let's leave that aside for the moment.*
*Can we come back to this later?*
*I think we should move on now.*

### Focus the discussion

*I think we need to look at this in more detail.*
*We need to analyze this in a little more depth.*

### Widen the discussion

*Is there anything else we should consider?*
*What other ways are there to approach this?*

### Check agreement

*Can we go round the table to see if everyone agrees?*
*Do we all agree on that? Good, that's settled.*

### Summarize

*So, basically, what you're saying is …*
*OK, let's go over what we've discussed so far.*

# Exercises

**60.1 Cover the opposite page with a piece of paper. Complete the sentences from the opening of a meeting with the pairs of words in the box.**

agenda / get through    background / useful    bathroom / hall
brief / point    copy / agenda    housekeeping / begin
ill / apologies    kick / off    right / start    say / words
straight / item    take / minutes

1   _____ , is everybody here? Good, I think we can _____ .

2   Unfortunately Anneke is _____ and sends her _____ .

3   Just a couple of _____ things before we _____ .

4   The _____ is down the _____ on the left.

5   Do you all have a _____ of the _____ ?

6   Can someone _____ the _____ ?

7   Would you like to _____ a few _____ about yourself Agnieszka?

8   I've prepared some _____ information that I hope will be _____ .

9   You can see from the _____ that we have a lot to _____ .

10  I would ask that you keep all contributions _____ and to the _____ .

11  OK, let's move _____ to the first _____ .

12  Henk, would you like to _____ ?

**60.2 Find a word or phrase from the previous exercise that matches the definitions below.**

1   a list of the subjects to be discussed at a meeting
_____

2   a written record of the decisions that people make at a formal meeting _____

3   (phrasal verb) do; finish dealing with _____

4   one of several things on a list _____

5   (phrasal verb) begin _____

**60.3 Write BrE (British English) or AmE (American English) on the right line.**

1   bathroom / restroom / washroom _____

2   loo (informal) / toilets / gents / ladies / WC _____

**60.4 Make phrases to close a meeting by matching an item from each column.**

1   I think we                main conclusions.
2   I'd like to sum           the minutes.
3   There are three           can stop there.
4   In terms                  fix a date now?
5   Are there                 missed anything?
6   Have I                    a quick word with you?
7   I think it was a          of action points, …
8   I'll circulate            any other points?
9   Can we                    up.
10  Can I just have           very useful meeting.

**60.5 Cover the opposite page with a piece of paper. Put the words into order. Write the answers under the correct heading below.**

I think in more detail look at this we need to.
Let's for the moment leave aside that.
Could you a moment hang on just please?
Is anything there we should consider else?
One at time, a please.
Can we if everyone agrees go round to see the table?
What ways are there to approach other this?
Let's so far what we've discussed go over.
Can we later to this come back?
We need to depth this in a little more analyze.

**Deal with interruptions**
1   _____
2   _____

**Keep moving**
3   _____
4   _____

**Focus the discussion**
5   *I think we need to look at this in more detail.*
6   _____

**Widen the discussion**
7   _____
8   _____

**Check agreement**
9   _____

**Summarize**
10  _____

**60.6 ⊙ 12 Speaking practice: listen and repeat. Repeat each phrase you hear and then listen to check.**

What do you think of when you hear the word 'negotiating'? You probably think of this process: two sides each have a starting position, then they make a series of concessions (= things they give in order to reach an agreement) until they find a compromise (= an agreement where both sides accept that they cannot have everything).

But this process is more accurately called 'bargaining', and it's just one of the phases of a negotiation. The phases are:

1 Relationship building: getting to know the other person, exchanging information about the two companies, discussing the market, and generally building trust.

2 Stating needs, exploring initial positions and asking questions. In a commercial negotiation, the supplier explains the product in depth and shows how it brings value to the customer's business.

3 Bargaining – not just on price, but on a range of linked issues such as quantity, minimum order, discounts, delivery time, service plans and warranties (guarantees), terms of payment, exclusivity in a particular market, the length of the contract, transport costs, arrangements for sharing advertising costs, penalties if clauses in the contract are not respected.

4 Closing the deal.

Read the dialogue below, which is an extract from phase 2 of a typical sales negotiation. For phases 3 and 4, see unit 62.

Supplier: OK, let's get down to business. What exactly do you need?
Customer: For us, the priorities are quality and reliability.
Supplier: When you say 'reliability', what do you mean?
5 Customer: I mean delivery. On time, every time. Can you do that?
Supplier: Yes, we can. Our customers are well-known firms who trust us and come back to us.
Customer: OK.
10 Supplier: What sort of quantity are you thinking of?
Customer: Around 1,000 pieces initially. But that may change. How flexible can you be on quantity?
Supplier: You can change the quantity up to five working days before the agreed delivery date, and we need a
15 minimum order of 500 pieces. But quantity is not a problem. Our main concern is that you don't change the basic specifications of your order.
Customer: Right, I understand. And in terms of delivery, what kind of timescale are we looking at?
20 Supplier: Two weeks from your firm order.
Customer: OK. Another question. We've been quoted a price of €950 per piece for a very similar product. Can you match that?
Supplier: We offer quality at a reasonable price, not at the
25 cheapest price. We don't try to compete on price. It's about a relationship between quality and price.
Customer: Of course. I see that. But what kind of guarantee can you give us in relation to your quality?

● Notice in this early part of the negotiation how there are a lot of questions, and how the speakers move freely from one topic to another.

## The phrases you need ☞

### State your needs
*For us, the priorities are …*
*Our main concern is …*
*We think the best option would be …*
*We'd prefer to see / have …*
*We need … . Can you do that?*

### Explore positions
*What exactly do you need?*
*What do you have in mind?*
*How would you feel about … ?*
*How flexible can you be on … ?*
*When you say … , what do you mean?*
*Can you be more specific?*
*Let me just check I understand you correctly.*

### Ask specific questions
*What sort of quantity are you thinking of?*
*What kind of timescale are we looking at?*
*What sort of figure are we talking about?*
*What kind of guarantee can you give us?*
*We've been quoted a price of … . Can you match that?*

### Suggest alternatives
*Alternatively, …*
*Can I suggest another way of moving forward?*
*There are a couple of alternatives we'd like to put forward.*
*Perhaps you would like to try the product on a trial basis?*

# Exercises

**61.1 Read the dialogue opposite aloud several times, then cover it with a piece of paper. Now try to remember some of the missing words below. Write your answers lightly at the side.**

1  OK, let's get down to _____ .
2  What _____ do you need?
3  For us, the _____ are quality and reliability.
4  When you say 'reliability', what do you _____ ?
5  Our customers are well-known firms who _____ us and come back to us.
6  How _____ can you be on quantity?
7  You can change the quantity up to five working days before the agreed _____ date.
8  We need a _____ order of 500 pieces.
9  Our main _____ (= feeling of worry) is that you don't change the basic specifications of your order.
10  In terms of delivery, what kind of _____ are we looking at?
11  We've been _____ (= told) a price of €950 per piece for a very similar product.
12  Can you _____ that (= provide something that is equal)?
13  We offer quality at a _____ price, not at the cheapest price.
14  But what kind of _____ can you give us in relation to your quality?

**After you have remembered whatever you can, use the words in the box below to complete the sentences.**

| | | | | |
|---|---|---|---|---|
| business | concern | delivery | exactly | flexible |
| guarantee | match | mean | minimum | priorities |
| | quoted | reasonable | timescale | trust |

**61.2 Fill in the missing letters in the phrases below.**

What k _ _ _ of | quantity | are you thinking _ _ ?
s _ _ _ of | disc_ _ _ _ | are we talking _ _ _ _ _ ?
| times_ _ _ _ | are we looking _ _ ?

**61.3 Complete the four mini-dialogues with the words and phrases in the box.**

| | | |
|---|---|---|
| a little low | have in mind | pre-payment |
| production schedule | quite high | regular customers |
| so long | something around | standard for this market |
| such large discounts | terms of payment | were you expecting |

**Price**
Supplier: The price per item is €140.
Customer: That seems [1] _____ .
Supplier: What sort of price [2] _____ ?
Customer: [3] _____ €120.
Supplier: I think you'll find our prices are [4] _____ .

**Discount**
Supplier: We give a discount of 3% on orders over €5,000 and 5% on orders over €10,000.
Customer: Isn't that [5] _____ ?
Supplier: What kind of discount were you looking for?
Customer: 5% on our order of €6,000.
Supplier: Well, we don't normally give [6] _____ .

**Delivery**
Supplier: Our delivery time is six weeks.
Customer: I didn't expect it to be [7] _____ .
Supplier: What exactly did you [8] _____ ?
Customer: We need delivery in four weeks. Can you do that?
Supplier: That doesn't give us very much time – our [9] _____ is very busy at the moment.

**Terms of payment**
Supplier: Our [10] _____ are 50% in advance, and 50% 30 days after delivery.
Customer: Couldn't you be a little more flexible?
Supplier: What do you mean?
Customer: We'd prefer, say, one third [11] _____ , one third after 30 days, and the final third after 60 days.
Supplier: I'm sorry, but we only offer conditions like that to [12] _____ .

**61.4 🔊 13 Speaking practice: listen and repeat. Repeat each phrase you hear and then listen to check.**

**Meetings – negotiating II**

The dialogue on page 126 in unit 61 showed some phrases for the early part of a negotiation: stating needs, exploring positions and asking questions. The dialogue below comes from a later part of the same negotiation. It shows phrases for bargaining and closing the deal.

Bargaining is a process of making offers ('proposals' are more formal and more final than offers), with the other side accepting them, refusing them, or coming back with a counter-offer. Inexperienced negotiators tend to work through issues (eg price, terms, delivery) one by one, while more experienced negotiators link issues, with all the pieces of the puzzle only fitting together right at the end. This allows much greater flexibility.

Experienced negotiators also tend to make frequent use of summarizing. Summarizing can be used to check understanding, give yourself time to think, keep a positive atmosphere by reviewing progress, break a deadlock, and close the negotiation.

Now read the dialogue.

---

Supplier: … Yes, our minimum order is 500 pieces.

Customer: That's a big risk for us – we'd prefer an initial order of, say, 300 pieces. We can look at further orders later.

5 Supplier: That's not really a viable option for us. It's not cost-effective for us to do a production run of just 300 pieces.

Customer: I see. And earlier you said that you need 50% pre-payment for first time customers.

10 Supplier: That's right.

Customer: 50% is a lot of money to pay upfront. I'm sorry, we can't accept that.

Supplier: We'd be prepared to offer better terms of payment, but only if you increased your order.

15 Customer: When you say 'better terms', what do you have in mind?

Supplier: Well, if you order 500 pieces, we'll accept 25% payment in advance, with the balance 60 days after delivery. That should help with your cash flow.

20 Customer: OK, we could accept that, but only on one condition.

Supplier: Yes?

Customer: That you can make the small customization that we talked about earlier at no extra cost.

25 Supplier: I'm not sure about that. I don't have the authority to make that decision by myself.

Customer: Well, if you can agree to that, we can close the deal today.

Supplier: OK. Can you give me a moment to make a call?

30 Customer: Sure.

Supplier: … Yes, we can make that customization. No problem. Now, let's just take a moment to review what we've discussed. So, …

---

- At line 5 the Supplier refuses an offer about the initial order, and gives a reason. At line 8 the Customer responds with a simple 'I see' and moves to another issue. Neither side feels it is necessary to finalize the initial order issue at this point.

- At line 11 the Customer refuses an offer about the % pre-payment. At line 13 the Supplier responds by linking a concession on this issue to a concession by the Customer on another issue.

- The bargaining and linking of issues continues at lines 17–24.

- The pieces of the puzzle only finally fit together at line 31. The Supplier closes the negotiation by summarizing.

## The phrases you need

**Bargain**
*If you (do that), we'll / we can (do this).*
*OK, we'd be prepared to (do that), but only if you (did this).*
*We could accept that, but only on one condition.*
*Would you be willing to accept a compromise?*

**Accept an offer**
*OK, we can agree to that.*
*That sounds reasonable.*
*I think that should be possible.*

**Refuse an offer**
*I'm not sure about that.*
*That's not really a viable option for us.*
*That would be very difficult for us because …*
*I'm sorry, we can't accept that.*

**Summarize**
*Let's just take a moment to review what we've discussed.*
*Can we just go through / go over what we've agreed so far?*
*So, …*

**Play for time**
*I'd like some time to think about it.*
*I think that's as far as we can go at this stage.*
*I don't have the authority to make that decision by myself.*

**Close the deal**
*If you can … , we can close the deal today.*
*I'm ready to sign today if you can …*
*If we agree to … , are you happy with the other points?*
*That's it, then. I think we have a deal.*
*So, if you'd just like to sign here.*

# Exercises

**62.1 Cover the opposite page with a piece of paper. Fill in the missing letters.**

1 Our mi_ _ _um  o_ _ _ _r is 500 pieces.
2 That's not really a via_ _ _  option for us. It's not c_ _t-eff_ _ _ _ _e for us to do a production r_ _  of just 300 pieces.
3 Earlier you said that you need 50% p_ _-pa_ _ _ _t for fi_ _t ti_ _ customers.
4 50% is a lot of money to pay up_ _ _ _t.
5 If you order 500 pieces, we'_ _  accept 25% payment in ad_ _ _ _ _, with the bal_ _ _ _ 60 days after d_ _ _ _ry. That should help with your c_ _ _  fl_ _ .
6 I don't have the au_ _ _ _ _ty to make that decision b_  my_ _ _ _.

**62.2 Find a word from the previous exercise that means:**

1 able to be done _____
2 *(informal)* in advance _____
3 remaining amount of money _____

**62.3 Complete the sentences with the pairs of words in the box.**

> accept / condition   close / deal   go / stage   have / mind
> just / sign   moment / review   prefer / order
> prepared / terms   should / possible   sounds / reasonable
> through / far   willing / compromise

1 We'd _____ an initial _____ of, say, 300 pieces.
2 We'd be _____ to offer better _____ of payment, but only if you increased your order.
3 When you say 'better terms', what do you _____ in _____ ?
4 We could _____ that, but only on one _____ .
5 Would you be _____ to _____ ?
6 Yes, that _____ be _____ .
7 That _____ _____ .
8 Let's just take a _____ to _____ what we've discussed.
9 Can we just go _____ what we've agreed so _____ ?
10 I think that's as far as we can _____ at this _____ .
11 If you can agree to that, we can _____ the _____ today.
12 If you'd _____ like to _____ here.

**62.4 Match a group of verbs 1–4 and a group of adjectives a–d to the nouns below. Check any unknown words in a dictionary.**

1 accept, agree on, close, do, make, offer somebody, reach, reject, sign
2 authorize, cancel, chase, delay, fax through, meet, place, process, put in, receive, ship
3 accept, clarify, come up with, consider, drop, explore, outline, make, put forward, reject, revise, study, withdraw
4 allow somebody, ask for, be available at, be entitled to, get, negotiate, offer somebody, qualify for

a alternative, compromise, concrete, detailed, helpful, interesting, sensible, tentative, vague
b cash, generous, good, huge, large, low, five percent, special, substantial, usual
c back, firm, initial, outstanding, regular, repeat, rush, special, urgent
d compromise, exclusive, fair, good, lucrative, major, package, two-year

| 2 | c | order |
| | | discount |
| | | proposal |
| | | deal |

**62.5 Continue as before.**

1 extend, fix, have, impose, (fail to) meet, miss, pass, set, work to
2 accept, agree on / to, arrive at, come to, find, look for, make, offer, reach, seek, suggest
3 discuss, figure out, finalize, go into, go over, itemize, sort out, work out
4 extract, get, grant, make, offer, win

a brief, complete, complex, concrete, final, full, minor, practical, precise, rough, technical
b generous, important, key, limited, major, minor, significant, sizeable, substantial
c acceptable, fair, necessary, potential, reasonable, (un)satisfactory, sensible
d flexible, strict, tight

| | | details |
| | | deadline |
| | | concession |
| | | compromise |

**62.6 ⏱ 14 Speaking practice: listen and repeat. Repeat each phrase you hear and then listen to check.**

Many learners of Business English think that it isn't necessary to know about indirect (diplomatic) language. They argue that directness is the best choice in business because then people can understand each other. Usually this is true. But stop to think about your own language. Compare how you talk to your friends and colleagues with:

- Talking to your boss.
- Talking to new customers.
- Participating in a large meeting where you're 'on show'.
- Negotiating a difficult issue while trying to keep a good atmosphere.

Diplomatic language is about showing respect and allowing the other person to 'save face'. Even if you come from a culture where directness is valued, there will be situations in your future business career where you will need to modify your natural directness. Diplomatic/indirect language shows other people that you're polite, educated and respectful of their opinions and feelings.

Compare the 'direct' conversation extract below with its 'softer' version underneath. Of course, the example is exaggerated to make a point.

---

### Version 1: direct

Customer: This product is very expensive.

Supplier: It's more expensive than the old model. But the quality is much, much better.

Customer: If we buy this product, will you give us a good discount?

5 Supplier: What do you mean?

Customer: We want 5%.

Supplier: That will be difficult. You owe us money on your account.

Customer: We have a problem with our cash flow.

Supplier: You must pay the money you owe us now. Otherwise a
10 discount on the new product is impossible.

---

### Version 2: softer, more indirect

Customer: To be honest, this product seems quite expensive.

Supplier: It's a little more expensive than the old model, that's true. But the quality is significantly better.

Customer: If we bought this product, would you give us a good
5 discount?

Supplier: What did you have in mind?

Customer: We were thinking of, say, something around 5%.

Supplier: That won't be easy. I'm just looking at my records here. Actually, you owe us money on your account.

10 Customer: Yes, I know. We have a bit of a problem with our cash flow right now.

Supplier: Why don't you pay some of the money you owe us? Then perhaps we could look again at the discount on the new product.

---

Study Version 2:

- Notice at line 1 how the Customer uses a warning phrase 'To be honest' and then changes 'is' to 'seems'.
- Notice at line 3 how the Supplier changes 'much better' to 'significantly better'. This is more business-like language.
- At line 4 the Customer uses a grammatical form called 'the second conditional'. The past forms *bought* and *would* make the language more hypothetical and indirect.
- At line 8 the Supplier says 'That won't be easy' instead of 'That will be difficult'. Using *not* + a positive word instead of a negative word is typical of indirect language.
- At line 12 the Supplier uses a negative question. This is also typical of indirect language.

---

## The phrases you need ☞

**'perhaps', 'maybe'**
*Perhaps we should …*
*Maybe we could …*

**'would', 'could', 'might'**
*We would need a quality guarantee.*
*Here's an idea we could look at.*
*That might be quite expensive.*

**'just'**
*Could I just go back to the point about …*
*There's just one thing I'd like to add.*

**'seems'**
*It seems to me that …*
*There seems to be a problem with …*

**Rephrase with 'not'**
*Our competitors aren't very cheap.*
*That doesn't give us very much time.*
*That won't be easy.*

**Warning phrase**
*Actually, …*
*To be honest, …*
*Unfortunately, …*

**Negative question**
*Why don't you …?*
*Wouldn't it be better / easier to …?*
*Isn't it the case that …?*

**Past forms**
*We were thinking of something around 5%.*
*What did you have in mind?*
*If we bought this product, …?*

# Exercises

**63.1 Write the line numbers from Version 2 opposite in the boxes below.**

a *perhaps, maybe* ☐
b *would, could, might* ☐ ☐
c *just* ☐
d *seems* [1]
e rephrase with *not* ☐
f warning phrase [1] ☐
g negative question ☐
h past tense ☐ ☐ ☐
i *quite / a little / a bit* (+ adjective) [1] ☐
j *a bit of a / a slight* (+ noun) ☐

---

- In Version 2, notice how the speakers are polite and respectful, yet at the same time firm and clear. In Version 1 the language is aggressive and creates a bad atmosphere.
- Other techniques in Version 2 include: acknowledging that the other person is right (eg 'that's true' in line 2, and 'yes I know' in line 10); avoidance of exaggeration (eg 'significantly' in line 3); the use of 'vague' language (eg 'say', 'something around 5%' in line 7); and suggesting that a problem is temporary (eg 'right now' in line 11).

---

**63.2 Match what you think 1–10 with what you say a–j.**

*You think …*

1 Stop speaking and let me say something for a change. ☐
2 Why are you always mixing up issues? ☐
3 I'm selling your product in my stores, and yet you want me to pay all the advertising costs myself. You're crazy. ☐
4 I have a really great idea! You're going to love this. ☐
5 You said that you could deliver these items by the end of the week. Now you've changed your story. Typical. ☐
6 The cost of that option is going to be way too high. ☐
7 I have no idea when we can deliver the items – there's a problem at the factory and no-one can solve it. ☐
8 You want it when!?! No way. ☐
9 If you want quality, go somewhere else. I'm offering you a cheap price. ☐
10 That's completely wrong. ☐

---

*You say …*

a I think it might be better to consider that issue separately.
b Here's an idea we could look at.
c I understood that you had these products in stock for immediate delivery.
d Our products are very good value for money in relation to our competitors.
e Could I just interrupt for a moment?
f That doesn't give us very much time.
g That might be quite expensive.
h There seems to be a bit of a problem with our production facility at the moment.
i With respect, that's not quite right.
j Wouldn't you agree that it's fairer if we share some of the promotional expenses?

**63.3 Make the comments more diplomatic using the words in brackets.**

1 There's one thing I want to add. (just / like)
_____

2 That is impossible. (honest / would / very difficult)
_____

3 You're being too optimistic. (seems / me / that / little)
_____

4 It would be better to use rail transport. (wouldn't)
_____

5 This line is unprofitable. (actually / not very)
_____

6 We should leave that point until later. (think / might / better)
_____

**63.4 Look at line 4 of Version 2 opposite.**

*If we bought this product, would you give us a good discount?*
In grammar this is called a 'second conditional':
*If we* + past simple, *would / could you …?*
With the past form the *if* sentence is more hypothetical and indirect – you're just exploring an idea in a tentative way.

**Change these sentences to second conditionals.**

1 If we order 5,000 pieces, what sort of discount can you give?
_____

2 If you pay 50% in advance, we will give you generous terms for the remaining 50%.
_____

**63.5 ⊕ 15 Speaking practice: listen and repeat. Repeat each phrase you hear and then listen to check.**

# 64 Meetings – review

**64.1 Fill in the missing letters in this extract from a meeting. Four people speak: the chair, Marek, Camille and Adriana.**

**The chair opens the meeting:**
R _ _ _ _ , I think we can start. Well, good morning everyone, and th_ _ _s f_ _ c_ _ _ _g. Unfortunately, Bruce is ill and s_ _ _s his apo_ _ _ _ _s.
Just a couple of hou_ _ _ _ _ping things before we begin – we'll have a sh_ _t b_ _ _k around ten thirty, and [...] .
Do you all have a c_ _y of the a_ _ _ _a? Good. Can someone t_ _e the mi_ _ _ _s? Thank you.
OK, let's move st_ _ _ _ _t to the first i_ _ _ . Marek, would you like to k_ _ _ o_ _ ?

**Marek presents some alternatives:**
There are several ways we could d_ _ _ w_ _ _ this iss_ _ . Let's look at the p_ _s and c_ _s of each opt_ _ _ [...] . So, in general I'm in fa_ _ _r of option one because of the cost advantages, al_ _ _ _gh [...] .

**The chair asks Camille for her reactions:**
Thank you, Marek. Camille, can you tell us what you think? This is your f_ _ld and I know you h_ _e s_ _e ex_ _ _ _ _ _nce of this problem.

**Camille speaks:**
I agree with Marek u_ t_ a p_ _ _t. It may be t_ _e that [...] , but we also have to consider [...] .
So what I'm tr_ _ _g to s_ _ is [...] . Or, to p_ _ it si_ _ly, [...] .

**Marek interrupts:**
Can I c_ _e i_ here?

**The chair blocks the interruption:**
Marek, could you j_ _ _ l_ _ Camille fi_ _ _ _? I'll c_ _e b_ _ _ to you in a moment.

**Camille continues:**
Co_ _ _ _t me if I'm wr_ _g, but Marek s_ _ _s to be saying that [...] .

**Marek corrects the misunderstanding:**
Perhaps I haven't exp_ _ _ned my_ _ _f cl_ _ _ly. That's not what I me_ _t. What I was t_ _ing to say was [...]. As a ma_ _ _r of f_ _ _ , [...] .

**Adriana makes a suggestion:**
Can I make a suggestion? It's j_ _ _ an id_ _ , but in_ _ _ _d of [...], why don't we [...] ?

**Marek rejects the suggestion:**
That s_ _ _ _s like a good idea, but I don't think it would w_ _ _ i_ pr_ _ _ _ _e. The p_ _nt is [...] .

**The chair widens the discussion:**
OK, what other ways are there to app_ _ _ch this? Is there any_ _ _ _g e_ _e we should con_ _ _er?

**Camille gives an opinion:**
From my p_ _ _t of v_ _w, I think that [...] .

**The chair reacts:**
Let's think car_ _ _lly about the im_ _ _ _ _ions of that. O_ the o_ _ h_ _ _ [...], but on the other hand [...] .

**Adriana focuses the discussion:**
I think we need to an_ _ _ze this in a l_ _le more d_ _th. [...] And so, because of that, I t_ _d to feel that [...] .

**Marek asks for clarification:**
You men_ _ _ned [...] . Could you be a little more sp_ _ _ _ic?

**Adriana reformulates:**
Yes, l_ _ me p_ _ it a_ _ _ _er way, [...] .

**The chair keeps the discussion moving:**
Let's le_ _e that as_ _e for the moment – I'm not sure it's rel_ _ _ _t.

**Camille suggests the next steps:**
I think the b_ _ _ way for_ _ _d is for us to [...] .

**The chair asks for repetition:**
Sorry, can you r_ _ thr_ _ _ _ that again? I want to be sure I understand.

**Camille repeats:**
Yes, _f c_ _ _ _e, [...] .

**The chair summarizes:**
I see now. OK, let's g_ o_ _ _ what we've discussed s_ f_ _ . [...]

**Camille speaks:**
Abs_ _ _ _ _ly. And it's not just [...], it's also [...] . So in terms of ac_ _on p_ _ _ts we need to [...] .

**The chair checks agreement:**
OK. Can we g_ r_ _ _ _ the t_ _ _e and see if everyone agrees? [...] Good, that's settled. I think we should m_ _e _n now.

**After some time, the chair closes the meeting:**
Well, thanks for your i_ _ut, everyone. I think it was a very u_ _ _ul discussion. Shall we f_ _ the t_ _ _ for the next meeting? [...] Oh, yes. Marek, can I just h_ _ _ a qu_ _ _ w_ _ _ with you before you disappear?

**64.2 Complete this negotiating dialogue with the words and phrases in the box.**

| | | |
|---|---|---|
| *a viable option* | *are we talking* | *are you happy* |
| *are you looking* | *be prepared* | *did you have* |
| *get down* | *have a deal* | *instead of* |
| *might be able* | *moving forward* | *really not sure* |
| *sounds reasonable* | *upfront* | |

Supplier: OK, let's ¹ _____ to business. So, you're interested in our greetings cards.

Customer: Yes, the Arts Cards range – the ones with the images of famous paintings.

Supplier: We sell a lot of those. What sort of quantities ² _____ for?

Customer: I run a chain of eight small retail outlets, and I'd like to put the cards on a display stand by the checkout at each one. What quantities do you suggest?

Supplier: We ³ _____ to help you with the stand. But let's get back to the quantity. Perhaps you should make an initial order of, say, 2,000 cards.

Customer: That seems like quite a large amount. I'd prefer to have 1,000 cards and see how they go.

Supplier: When you said 'display stand' earlier, what exactly ⁴ _____ in mind?

Customer: A stand for the counter.

Supplier: ⁵ _____ a counter stand, why don't you use a floor stand? The capacity is much bigger. A floor stand that turns round.

Customer: Yes, I think that would work well. Are they easy to find?

Supplier: We can give you one for each store, free of charge, but you would need to order a minimum number of cards.

Customer: What sort of figure ⁶ _____ about?

Supplier: 4,000 cards. If you sell 100 per week at each store, you'll get rid of them in five weeks.

Customer: No, I'm sorry; an order of 4,000 is not ⁷ _____ . I just don't have the cash flow to support that kind of purchase.

Supplier: Cash flow doesn't have to be a problem.

Customer: What do you mean?

Supplier: You don't need to pay everything in advance. If you order 4,000 cards, we'll give you very good terms of payment. Just 50% ⁸ _____ , and the balance after 30 days.

Customer: What is the cost per card?

Supplier: The suggested retail price to the public is €2.90. We sell them to stockists like yourselves for €1.20 each.

Customer: Well, to be honest, I'm ⁹ _____ . I'd like some time to think about it. It's a lot of money – unless we can negotiate the cost per card.

Supplier: I'm sorry, that's not negotiable.

Customer: Can I suggest another way of ¹⁰ _____ ? Would you be prepared to take back any unsold cards from our order? We don't know which ones people will buy.

Supplier: If we agree to that, ¹¹ _____ with the other points?

Customer: Well, an order of 4,000 cards is far more than I was thinking of initially, but I guess it's possible.

Supplier: OK, we'd ¹² _____ to take back any unsold cards, but only from the first order, and only if they were in perfect condition for us to resell.

Customer: That ¹³ _____ .

Supplier: That's it, then. I think we ¹⁴ _____ .

**64.3 Make the comments more diplomatic using the words in brackets.**

1 That will be expensive.
(might / quite)
_____

2 We will want a larger discount.
(would / significantly)
_____

3 There's one thing I want to clarify.
(just / like to)
_____

4 Splitting the order into two consignments would be a good idea.
(wouldn't / better)
_____

5 I'm unconvinced by this estimate.
(not totally)
_____

6 You said that we can have the products on a trial basis.
(understood / could)
_____

7 What quantity are you thinking of?
(sort of / were)
_____

8 It may be difficult to arrange that.
(unfortunately / may / very easy)
_____

9 We're having a lot of problems at our factory.
(one or two / issues / right now)
_____

10 We expected a two-year warranty.
(honest / expecting)
_____

11 I think that your new range is the same as your old range.
(seems / me / more or less)
_____

12 It would be easier to pay more and ship the goods by Air Express.
(wouldn't / little more)
_____

There are many different types of business report:

- A **sales report** gives sales figures for different products in different regions in different time periods.
- **Market research** analyzes a company's competitive position in the industry, identifying new markets and product areas, etc.
- A **financial report** might discuss budgets, or might be the text that accompanies company accounts such as the quarterly or annual income statement (unit 26).
- A **progress report** reports on the progress of an ongoing project.
- A **cost-benefit analysis (CBA)** looks at the resources needed and potential benefits of a future investment (eg an IT system).

- An **appraisal report** is written by a manager about an employee's performance, training needs, etc.
- A **feasibility study** is an investigation into whether a particular system, project, product line, etc is practical, desirable and financially viable.
- A **business plan** describes the medium to long-term strategy of the company. See unit 9.
- An **inquiry** is an investigation into an ongoing problem, identifying causes and recommending action.
- A **case study** is an analysis of one particular completed case (eg an engineering project) that allows professionals to learn lessons.
- A **quality report** is a regular report that monitors standards, identifies failings and suggests action.

All these types of report have certain features in common in terms of style, layout and structure. See the table below.

| Style | Layout | Structure | | |
|-------|--------|-----------|---|---|
| <ul><li>clear</li><li>concise</li><li>factual</li><li>careful</li><li>balanced</li><li>measured</li><li>high level of grammatical accuracy</li></ul> | <ul><li>systematic numbering of sections and sub-sections</li><li>bullet points and lists</li><li>visuals such as tables, charts, diagrams</li><li>areas of blank space at the margins for the reader to make notes</li></ul> | *(longer reports)*<ul><li>Cover page</li><li>Acknowledgements</li><li>(Table of) Contents</li><li>(Executive) Summary</li><li>Terms of Reference</li><li>Procedure</li><li>Findings</li><li>Conclusions</li><li>Recommendations</li><li>Appendix</li></ul> | *(shorter reports)*<ul><li>To / From / Date / Subject</li><li>Introduction</li><li>Findings</li><li>Conclusions</li><li>Recommendations</li></ul> | Note: in a business report the 'Findings' section will probably be replaced with sections related to the content of the report. For example: Advantages / Disadvantages Option A / Option B Market A / Market B |

## The phrases you need ☞

### Introduction

*The aim / purpose of this report is to …*

*As requested in your email of 16 November, here is my report summarizing / analyzing … together with my recommendations.*

*I'm writing this report at the request of … / This report was commissioned by …*

*It includes / consists of / is divided into / contains …*

*It is based on interviews with … / information obtained from …*

*Information was gathered from the following sources: face-to-face interviews, a questionnaire sent to … , internal company documents and market research carried out …*

### Findings

*We found that …*

*Our research shows that …*

*We identified the following key areas.*

*45% of those who replied to the questionnaire thought that …*

*The survey showed the following areas of concern.*

*This will inevitably have an impact on …*

*One of the big advantages of this proposal is …*

### Conclusion

*A key challenge facing us is …*

*In the light of the above findings, we reached the following conclusions.*

*On the basis of the figures presented above, … would be very profitable.*

*There is clearly a gap in the market, however serious obstacles still remain …*

*It is clear that there are significant levels of … . Unless these issues are addressed as a matter of urgency, …*

*This has the potential to be a successful project provided …*

### Recommendations

*There are three main recommendations to make.*

*We (strongly) recommend that …*

*The Marketing / Operations department should …*

*Further research should be carried out to find out …*

*A meeting should be set up between … and …*

*I recommend that we provide the funds for … and move to the next stage of development.*

*The next stage is …*

# Exercises

**65.1 Match some possible sections of a report in the box with their descriptions 1–10 below.**

> *acknowledgements    appendix    conclusions    contents*
> *cover page    executive summary    findings    procedure*
> *recommendations    terms of reference*

1   a short, overall view of the report together with the conclusions and recommendations (it helps others to decide whether they want to read the whole report)

_____

2   the main body of the report: it contains all the information that has been collected, presented in a logical order, and arranged under headings and subheadings

_____

3   includes some or all of these: the title; the name of the person who commissioned the report; the name of the report writer and his / her job title; the organization; the date the report was issued; a reference number; the degree of confidentiality; the distribution list

_____

4   the writer makes a personal judgement about specific actions that should be taken – these should be based directly on the results of the investigation

_____

5   a list of all the headings and subheadings that are included in the report, with the appropriate page numbers

_____

6   the methods of investigation used to find the information (eg meetings and visits, interviews, published reference sources, personal observation, questionnaires and surveys)

_____

7   supporting material that is too long, too detailed or too technical to be included in the main report (or material that is useful as background but isn't essential); it may include tables, diagrams, graphs, drawings, extracts from other publications, etc

_____

8   the exact subject of the report, its scope (= what it deals with; its range) and limitations, why it was written, who asked for it, who wrote it, when it was completed

_____

9   the significant results of the 'Findings' – this section flows logically from the facts and points discussed earlier

_____

10  a paragraph or two where you thank all the people and organizations who helped you during the preparation of the report

_____

**65.2 Match definitions 1–18 with the words associated with reports a–r below. Check any unknown words in a dictionary.**

1   the way in which text and illustrations are arranged on the page ☐
2   when a block of text is further to the right than the block above it ☐
3   an early version of a report that may have changes made to it before it's finished ☐
4   pictures and designs that can be digitally inserted into a report ☐
5   another word for 'summary' – used especially in scientific / technical reports ☐
6   the method of holding together the loose sheets of paper (often also the cover of the report) ☐
7   someone who answers questions (eg questions in a questionnaire) ☐
8   an item in a list with a small symbol in front of it ☐
9   a method of directing the reader to another part of the report ☐
10  letters of a particular style ☐
11  a note placed at the bottom of a page, or at the end of the report ☐
12  information that appears at the top / bottom of every page (eg the page number, some words or letters identifying the report) ☐
13  the target audience of the report ☐
14  an alphabetical list of unfamiliar, difficult or specialized words and phrases, with their explanations ☐
15  a consistent style of writing (and layout) used by everyone inside an organization ☐
16  checking and making corrections to a document (particularly in relation to spelling and inconsistencies in layout) ☐
17  a short piece of writing that introduces the report, written by someone other than the main author ☐
18  words printed near an illustration or diagram that explain what it is ☐

| | | |
|---|---|---|
| a  glossary | g  header / footer | m  respondent |
| b  draft | h  footnote | n  indentation |
| c  font | i  cross-reference | o  proofreading |
| d  caption | j  abstract | p  readership |
| e  binding | k  house style | q  clip art |
| f  layout | l  bullet point | r  foreword |

Unit 65 described the structure of a typical report and the table there gave some phrases for the main sections. In order to write a report, it's helpful to study the language areas given below, although note that they're very diverse.

## Topic sentences

Look at this paragraph.

*Next year the economy is likely to slow down significantly, but without going into recession. Consumer demand will decrease as people use a greater proportion of their income to save or to pay off debts. However the weaker euro will help exporters, and overseas demand in Brazil, India and China remains strong.*

The first sentence is called a 'topic sentence'. It introduces and summarizes the paragraph. Most paragraphs in formal writing begin with a topic sentence, and they give a solid structure to your writing.

## Signposts

Look at these phrases.

*The survey showed the following three areas of concern: …*
*Section 2.2 of the report will discuss this in more detail.*

These are 'signposts' – phrases that help the reader see where you're going, or where they need to go. They are aids to navigation.

## Balanced, careful style

In a report you don't want to sound too certain, or too inflexible, in your thinking. Issues in the real world are rarely black and white. So writers tend to use words and phrases that produce a balanced, careful, measured style (like *tend to* in this sentence). Other examples are:

> *In general, … however, …*
> *On the whole, … / but …*
>
> *Many / Some / Several / A majority of*
> *usually / typically / often*
>
> *would / could / may / might*
>
> *It is possible that …*
> *It seems that …*
>
> *The project is expected to …*
> *Inflation is likely to …*
>
> *substantially / considerably*
> *significantly / relatively*
> *marginally / slightly*

## Linking words

This is a major language area covered in more detail in unit 69. Examples are:

*in addition, however, therefore, alternatively, in general, clearly, in fact, in particular, on the other hand, in conclusion etc*

## Formal, impersonal language

The language of reports is more formal than speech, but not so formal that it is difficult to understand. Informal language should be avoided. The following sentence has *I* (too personal) and a contraction (too informal):

*I've divided this report into …*

Instead, you might write:

*This report is divided into …*

Ways to make your writing a little more formal include:

| | |
|---|---|
| The passive: | *a decision **is expected** soon* |
| | *the final payment **will be made** in December* |
| It + passive: | ***It should be emphasized** that …* |
| | ***It is recommended** that …* |
| Noun phrases: | *staff motivation / sales conference / transport insurance documents / company pension plan* |
| Vocabulary: | *get > receive, bad > negative, big > large, a lot of > considerable, money > financial resources* |

## Repetition of words / structures

Repeating words in a report can be boring and show a lack of imagination and poor style. But there are occasions when the repetition of a key word or structure adds clarity and impact:

*Sales in Italy dropped a little last year, while sales in Spain remained steady. However, sales in France actually increased by 2%.*

In this example, repetition of *sales in* [+ country] highlights the name of the countries and adds impact.

Here are two further examples of repetition to add impact:

*Our goal is to … . To achieve this goal we have to …*

*We've tried to develop flexibility with our … . However, this flexibility has come with a cost.*

## Language of trends

See units 54 and 55.

# Exercises

**66.1 Read the following paragraph from a report about IT spending carefully. The first sentence ('the topic sentence') is missing. Choose the best first sentence from the three options below.**

> [1] ... [2]This solution should be an integrated workspace that is both an intranet and a central resource for our organization. [3]We need to:
> - Access documents and information securely from anywhere.
> - Organize calendars and schedules in a centralized resource.
> - Meet live, online – anytime, anywhere.
> - Share presentations and demonstrations.
> - Collaborate with co-workers, partners and clients – anywhere.
> [4]Achieving these goals will result in increased creativity and increased efficiency.

a We need to invest in an IT solution that allows us to reduce costs in every department.

b We need to invest in an IT solution that allows us to become the market leader in our industry.

c We need to invest in an IT solution that allows us to share information and collaborate with colleagues more effectively.

**66.2 The extract above shows some examples of 'repetition of words and structures'. Find:**

1 two words in sentence 2 that refer back to 'IT solution' in the topic sentence _____

2 two verbs in the topic sentence that are repeated later in the bullet points _____

3 a two-word phrase in the second half of sentence 2 that is repeated in one of the bullets, with a slight change to the form of one of the words _____

4 a word that is repeated three times in the bullet points

_____

Notice also some repeating structures:
- a verb in the infinitive after each bullet
- 'increased' + abstract noun in sentence 4

> All these repetitions – combined with the clear, concise style – help to persuade the reader and give the paragraph impact.

**66.3 Underline the alternative in italics that you think is more typical of a business report.**

1 We've made *considerable / fantastic* progress, and quality levels *will / are expected to* return to normal within a few weeks.

2 Sales *tend to / nearly always* drop a little over the summer period, although this *probably won't be / might not be* the case this year if we continue the marketing campaign.

3 *Very soon / At the earliest possible opportunity* we will need to have *a meeting to plan the production / a production planning meeting*.

4 His performance over recent months has been *bad / quite poor*, and it *may be / will be* necessary to review his employment with us.

5 There is a *really / relatively* high risk of failure with this project unless we invest more *money / financial resources* at this early stage.

6 *It is possible that / Maybe* the survey is not very accurate as we only *got / obtained* a response rate of 25% to our questionnaire.

7 A loss of jobs *is / is likely to be* one of the *consequences / things that will happen* if the process is automated.

8 Today *everyone is / many people are* looking at teleworking as an option, but it *leads to / typically leads to* a sense of isolation.

9 Some suggestions *arising from / that come to my mind from* these results are *given in a list / presented* below.

10 We carried out *lots of / numerous* tests in our technical department and the results have been *pretty good / encouraging*.

**66.4 Rewrite these sentences using a passive form to avoid 'I', 'you' and 'we'.**

1 We can use the same strategy for other products in the range.
   _____*The same strategy can be used*_____ for other products in the range.

2 In section 2.4 I will consider the environmental impact of these changes.
   In section 2.4 the _____
   _____

3 You can only do this after the machines have been serviced.
   This _____ after the machines have been serviced.

4 I should emphasize that these results are only provisional.
   It _____ that these results are only provisional.

## 67 Business reports and proposals – proposals I

### What is a business proposal?

Business proposals are written when a supplier (AmE vendor) is trying to win a contract with a client company, in competition with other similar suppliers. The writer is trying to persuade – it's a sales document – and there will be stronger, more 'commercial' language than in a business report. The writer will use techniques from sales and marketing such as targeting the client's needs and offering clear benefits. Typical contexts are:

- Trying to get the contract for a small, independently produced piece of work. Example: some market research for a client company.
- Trying to win a contract for one part of a large integrated project, done in close co-operation with the client company. Example: a subcontractor who offers a specialized service and will work under the client company's project manager.
- Making a proposal to form a continuing relationship with the client. Example: a proposal from an advertising agency.
- Outlining the case for a more formalized partnership between two separate companies. Example: where two equal parties co-operate to develop a new product or enter a new market.

### Structure of a business proposal

A typical structure for a large-scale proposal is shown below. Shorter proposals will obviously be simpler.

1 Executive summary
2 Introduction (analysis of the current situation, the approach selected and why)
3 Goals (list of goals taken directly from what the client has told you, with measurable targets that your work will achieve)
4 Project scope and action plan (key components and actions that you will provide; defining your role in relation to the client's role)
5 Implementation (how you will work with the client; a timetable/Gantt chart; deliverables; resources needed such as office space or access to information)
6 Areas of special expertise (your specialized, and preferably unique, skills and know-how that show why you're the ideal supplier)
7 Project team members (a paragraph on each person to establish credibility with the client)
8 Pricing (your fee, other costs for you or the client, and possibly a short paragraph at the end, emphasizing how the proposal is cost-effective and how the client will benefit)
9 Conclusion (a cost-benefit analysis showing why the price is worth paying)
10 Appendix (a list of your past projects; full details of your team/the pricing/the Action Plan etc)

The table gives some example phrases taken from six different sections of six different proposals (ABC, JKL, MNO, etc are the names of the various client companies).

### *The phrases you need* ☞

#### Introduction
*ABC is looking for assistance in choosing and implementing … […] Upgrading to a new system will allow ABC to … and will cut inventory costs and shorten production run times. […] An upgraded, state-of-the-art system will position ABC as a leading player in the field of … with the ability to support the largest-sized customers.*

#### Goals
*JKL's main goal is to outsource … in order to reduce the number of in-house employees. These employees are fully occupied for only about 60% of the year. […] A secondary goal is to minimize the time that JKL managers spend on problems associated with … […] These goals are achievable, and our proposal offers an ideal solution. We are able to deal with … and our customer service team can handle any problems that might occur.*

#### Implementation
*We will deliver to MNO immediate stock of … and make a commitment to supply an additional … […] In addition, we will provide MNO with sales flyers and store displays for … […] We will also conduct a marketing survey of 250 end users, which can be used by MNO to … .*

#### Areas of special expertise
*STU needs a company with an in-depth understanding of …, and we have extensive knowledge of this field. […] Our personnel include a former … manager and two … engineers. The engineers have considerable experience of … […] We've worked on similar systems in 28 locations in … […] Included in the Appendix is a list of projects we've done … and testimonials from … .*

#### Pricing
*The total cost of the joint project with PQR will be €40,000. Of this total, our fee will be €30,000. The remaining €10,000 of expenses will be absorbed by PQR. […] PQR's goal is to convert one-time customers into regular customers by demonstrating the long-lasting benefits of … Our proposal shows how that can be achieved in a cost-effective manner. […] The resources that PQR commits to the project will also allow it to take advantage of opportunities in … markets.*

**See next column**

# Exercises

**67.1 Find a word from 'Structure of a business proposal' opposite that matches each definition below.**

1 the range of things that a particular activity deals with

_____

2 *(two words)* a diagram used in project management that shows when each task/phase should start and end

_____

3 tangible items that are produced as a result of a project such as physical items, design specifications, research reports

_____

**Now do the same for words in 'The phrases you need'.**

4 very new and modern _____
5 formal statements, written by previous clients, that describe the abilities of a person or company _____
6 an amount of money that you pay for professional services

_____

**67.2 Cover 'The phrases you need' opposite and below with a piece of paper. Fill in the missing letters.**

1 _ut inventory costs and sh_ _ten production run times
2 pos_ _ _ _n ABC as a lea_ _ _g pl_ _er in the field
3 a sec_ _ _ary goal
4 we will con_ _ _t (= do/carry out) a marketing su_ _ _y of 250 end users
5 a company with an i_-de_ _ _ understanding of …
6 we have exte_ _ _ve knowledge of this f_ _ _d
7 the rem_ _ _ _ _g €10,000 of expenses will be ab_ _ _ _ed by PQR
8 this can be achieved in a c_ _ _-eff_ _ _ _ _e ma_ _er
9 l_ _g-las_ _ng benefits
10 the estab_ _ _ _ed market leader with a 40% market sh_ _ _

**Conclusion**

*We recommend our solution as being the best option available to reduce costs over the medium to long term and reinforce XYZ's brand's image. […] The market is relatively new, and to date no significant competitors to XYZ have emerged. An improved image should help delay competition. […] When competition does emerge, XYZ will be seen as the established market leader and should be able to hold at least a 40% market share.*

**67.3 Look carefully at the example phrases in 'The phrases you need' opposite. Decide whether a or b is correct each time.**

1 In the Introduction section, the proposal:
   a is written from the supplier's point of view, showing a company history and a bulleted list of product features.
   b is written from the client's point of view, outlining a specific need and a specific solution justified on business grounds.
2 In the Goals section, the proposal:
   a presents some project goals that the supplier has analyzed and thinks are necessary.
   b presents some project goals that the client has explained to the supplier.
3 In the Pricing section, the proposal:
   a presents an itemized list of all the components of the project and their price.
   b states the total cost in a simple way, then moves on to match the client's goals to this cost and also state an extra benefit. (A detailed breakdown of costs is probably included as part of the Appendix.)
4 In the Conclusion section, the proposal:
   a summarizes the main points in a careful, balanced way, explaining again the different options for the project and why this particular one was chosen.
   b makes a strong recommendation that links to the client's goals, then moves on to identify additional value beyond the immediate goals and explains the benefit of this added value.

**67.4 If you understand the personality type of the decision-maker in the client company, you can use words in your proposal that are likely to produce a positive response. Match the personality types 1–4 with the words and phrases a–d.**

1 Analytical: values accurate facts and figures, wants detailed analysis ☐
2 Pragmatic: values action and results ☐
3 Consensus-seeking: wants a decision that everyone accepts ☐
4 Visionary: entrepreneurial, likes concepts and big ideas ☐

a easy to use, flexible, personal commitment, reliable, support, widely accepted, working relationship
b criteria, evidence, logical, methodology, objective, principles, procedures, proof, proven, tested
c breakthrough, cutting edge, creative, exciting opportunity, innovative, long-term view, original, winning
d bottom line, efficiency, performance, productive, profitability, return on investment, speed of delivery

In every successful proposal the supplier sends three main messages to the client:

### 1 We can match your needs as defined by you (= compliance)

The client wonders, 'Are they proposing what I need, or are they proposing what they have?' You won't win a contract by simply describing your products and services and saying how good they are. You have to recommend a specific solution that will solve a specific problem and produce positive business results.

This first theme needs to appear all the way through your proposal, but in terms of the structure outlined in unit 67, it needs to be especially strong in sections 1, 2, 3, 4 and 9.

### 2 We have the competence to deliver (= capabilities)

The client wonders, 'Can they do the job on time and on budget? Have they handled similar projects before? Is there a risk that they won't do the job properly?' To reassure the client you can include references, testimonials, a list of clients, a case study of a previous project, awards, published reviews, reports by independent analysts in the field, CVs of key team members, project plans, a brief company history that emphasizes growth through success, etc. But less is more in this area – one good case study from the same industry, showing the same kind of results that your client is seeking, may be enough to win the contract.

In terms of the structure in unit 67, this theme is especially relevant in sections 1, 5, 6, 7, 9 and 10.

### 3 We will give you what you want, plus maybe a little more, at a fair price (= value)

Clients want a fair price, with no hidden costs, and no underestimating of the effort and resources needed. They want to see what kind of return on investment they can expect, and they want to know if you're offering any added-value factors that go beyond the initial analysis. Your proposal must contain a clear, explicit value proposition – an argument that shows the client that they get more by buying from you than they can get from choosing another supplier.

The table opposite shows how 'value' can mean a variety of things, not just financial value.

In terms of the structure in unit 67, this theme is especially relevant in sections 1, 8, 9 and 10.

During the decision-making process, the client will probably use the three criteria above in the order shown, ie first they will check compliance, then capabilities, and finally value.

## Value: what matters to the client

**Financial**

get the lowest price, reduce operating expenses, increase revenue, improve cash flow, reduce bad debt, outsource to remove fixed costs from the payroll, increase the absolute value of each transaction, get a larger portion of each customer's total business

**Social**

Internal: increase employee job satisfaction, enhance job performance, reduce turnover among key staff members, reduce absenteeism, accelerate employee training
External: increase customer loyalty, improve brand recognition, create a positive image in the community, address a community / environmental concern

**Quality**

improve reliability, enhance maintainability, increase ease of use, comply with regulatory standards, conform to a specific quality methodology, reduce defect rates, reduce customer complaints

**Technology**

get all the different pieces of hardware and software to work together properly, improve system flexibility, implement the most advanced technology, preserve the value of legacy systems, reduce downtime, add new features or capabilities, automate a labour-intensive process

**Risk minimization**

avoid the risk of failure, implement the most proven approach, address health and safety issues, avoid liability concerns

**Competitive advantage**

overtake a competitor, become the market leader, enter new markets quickly, update products to keep them competitive, focus on core competencies

# Exercises

**68.1 Check any unknown words in 'Value: what matters to the client' in a dictionary. Then find a phrase that matches the meanings below. Write your answers in full.**

1 decrease the amount of money owed to you that you can not collect
   *reduce bad debt*

2 fire your own staff and have their work done by an outside company instead

3 get orders for larger amounts of money instead of smaller amounts of money

4 improve the standard of people's work

5 stop so many important people leaving the company

6 make it easier to service equipment

7 make sure that your products have the level of quality that the law requires

8 follow an established set of tools and standards such as the EFQM Excellence Model, the ISO 9000 series, Six Sigma

9 be able to still use your old technology alongside your new technology

10 decrease the time during which the machines in the factory are not working

11 put into practice something that has worked many times before (and so has limited risk)

12 make the workplace less dangerous

13 reduce the worry that people might sue you (= take you to court) because of damage or injury that you have caused

14 just do what your company does best

**68.2 Read the extract in the next column from a short business proposal. Tick (✓) the boxes at the end to show whether the extract contains examples of Compliance, Capabilities and/or Value.**

---

## PROPOSAL

From: *Custom Computing*
To: *Big Fridge Manufacturing Corporation*

### Key goals

Big Fridge is considering an upgrade of its ERP (Enterprise Resource Planning) software to allow it to expand its manufacturing base in Eastern Europe. Big Fridge wants to know what options are available, and in particular how it is possible to customize a standard ERP package.

### Custom Computing: special expertise

Custom Computing has extensive experience of installing, upgrading and customizing ERP software – a list of recent projects is included in the Appendix.

   We have particular expertise in the domestic appliances sector, and recently carried out a similar project for Quality Cookers. A follow-up survey at Quality Cookers indicated that the average manager saved 1.5 hours per week as a result of the new ERP system, and that the system paid for itself within six months as a result of improved productivity.

### Action plan and deliverables

We propose that Custom Computing works closely with the IT department and senior management of Big Fridge for a two-week period, to analyze the options and costs of any upgrade process.

   We will assign to this project our Senior Systems Analyst, Dr Klaus Mueller, one of the leading professionals in his field. His CV is included in the Appendix.

   At the end of the two-week period we will deliver a report to Big Fridge with our recommendations and full costings.

### Conclusion

Big Fridge is in a position where it can make significant advances in both productivity and profitability as a result of investments in ERP software. These investments will position Big Fridge as a leading player in the white goods industry.

   We recommend that Big Fridge choose Customer Computing to carry out the initial evaluation of the options available. Our track record shows that we are ideally placed to provide Big Fridge with this analysis.

   Should Big Fridge decide to go ahead with any upgrade solution, Custom Computing will be delighted to put in a further proposal to carry out the work.

Compliance ☐   Capabilities ☐   Value ☐

**See the Answer key for the specific references.**

**69** **Business reports and proposals – linking words**

Compare the two texts below.

### Version 1

66 Talking about the States, the problem is that we only have sales guys on the coasts. And do you know what? There's some tough competition out there. A couple of our competitors merged recently – their new company is walking all over us. Our next quarter's sales figures are going to be a disaster. But you have to look on the sunny side – maybe our head office will find a local company for us to buy. Then we have a chance. Anyway, head office has spent a lot of money over there – I guess they know what they're doing. 99

### Version 2

**In relation to** the US market, our sales force there is concentrated on the two coasts. **Moreover**, we face very strong competition from local players. **In fact**, two of our competitors have recently merged and the new company is taking some market share away from us. **Therefore** it is likely that the year-on-year revenue figures for next quarter will be flat, or even slightly down. **Nevertheless**, the long term outlook for the US is still very positive – particularly if we can make a local acquisition to increase our market penetration. **On the whole** we are confident that our investments in the US market will prove worthwhile.

Version 1 is speech. Sentences are short. Sometimes there is no linking of one sentence to the next, other times it is done with simple words like *And, But, Then, Anyway*, etc.

Version 2 has very similar content, but is clearly from a more formal context. This could be a written report, or it could be a spoken presentation or a contribution at a large meeting. Obviously the vocabulary and general tone is more formal, but pay particular attention to the linking words and phrases in bold. They're used to make the structure of the argument clear. The reader/listener is warned about what is coming next: a change of topic (*in relation to*), a second point that adds to the first one and reinforces the argument (*moreover*), a real situation that the writer wants to highlight (*in fact*), etc.

When using linking words, think about their position in the sentence:

● Most of the examples in 'The phrases you need' can be used at the beginning of a sentence, and where appropriate are followed by a comma (ie where you would pause in speech). Version 2 above shows this.

● Many of these words can also be used in the middle of a sentence after *and*:
…, and in fact …
…, and therefore …

● A few are used immediately after a comma. These include: *especially, such as* and *whereas*.

## The phrases you need ☞

**Introduce a new topic**
*regarding, with reference to, in relation to*

**Add a related point**
*moreover, furthermore, in addition*

**Show a consequence**
*so, therefore, as a result, for this reason*

**Give an example**
*eg, such as, for example, for instance*
*in particular, especially, above all*

**Explain by rephrasing**
*ie, in other words*

**Say the real situation**
*in fact, actually, as a matter of fact*

**Sequence**
*first(ly), second(ly), third(ly), finally*
*the first stage / step is …, then …, and after that …*

**Talk generally**
*in general, on the whole, in most cases*

**Add a surprising or unexpected idea**
*however, even so, nevertheless*

**Make a contrast**
*in contrast, on the other hand*
*whereas, while*

**State known information**
*of course, obviously, clearly*

**Conclude**
*in conclusion, on balance, overall, taking everything into consideration*

**actually** /ˈæktʃuəli/ adv ★★★
**1** used for emphasizing what is really true or what really happened: *We've spoken on the phone but we've never actually met.*
**2** used for emphasizing that something is surprising: *I think she actually agreed to go out with him.*
**3** *spoken* used when correcting a statement: *It was yesterday, no actually it was Monday morning.*
**4** *spoken* used for admitting something: *'Did you spend much money?' 'Well, yes. Quite a lot, actually.'*

**nevertheless** /ˌnevəðəˈles/ adv ★★ despite a fact or idea that you have just mentioned: *It's a difficult race. Nevertheless, about 1,000 runners participate every year.*

# Exercises

**69.1 Cover the opposite page with a piece of paper. Now match an item on the left with an item on the right with the same meaning.**

| | | | |
|---|---|---|---|
| 1 | regarding | a | as a result |
| 2 | moreover | b | on the whole |
| 3 | therefore | c | actually |
| 4 | in particular | d | in relation to |
| 5 | in fact | e | overall |
| 6 | in general | f | nevertheless |
| 7 | however | g | above all |
| 8 | clearly | h | furthermore |
| 9 | on balance | i | in other words |
| 10 | ie | j | of course |

**69.2 Complete the sentences below with either 'eg' or 'ie'.**

1 Fossil fuels, _____ oil, gas and coal, are likely to play a smaller role in the overall energy mix.

2 Fossil fuels, _____ oil and gas, are likely to play a smaller role in the overall energy mix.

> The words *eg* and *ie* have Latin origins (*exempli gratia* and *id est*). They can be used in speech as well as writing.

**69.3 Underline the correct words in italics.**

1 Sales rose in Germany and France. *Moreover / Therefore*, they rose in Poland, Hungary and the Czech Republic as well.

2 Sales increased in Germany and France. *Above all / In contrast*, they were flat in Poland and Hungary.

3 Sales rose in Germany and France. *For example / In fact*, they rose by over 10%.

4 *In general / Furthermore*, sales were strong in Western and Central Europe. However, they fell slightly in Spain and Portugal.

5 Sales rose strongly in Germany and France. *On the whole / Therefore* we will open new offices in Frankfurt and Marseille next year.

6 Sales were up in Western Europe. *In particular / For this reason*, France and the Benelux countries showed strong growth.

7 *Overall / For instance* it was a good year. Sales were up in all major markets.

8 Sales were strong in Brazil. *Even so / Clearly* this was due to rapid growth in the economy.

> **whereas** /weər'æz/ conjunction used for showing that there is an important difference between two things, people, situations etc: *Doctors' salaries have risen substantially, whereas nurses' pay has actually fallen.*

**69.4 Complete these four paragraphs taken from a report by a Chief Information Officer. Read carefully to see how each sentence and each paragraph links to the one before. Write a capital letter where necessary.**

| *clearly* | *in particular* | *regarding* |
|---|---|---|

1 _____ the longer term, there have been several requests by employees to change our office computers from Microsoft to Apple. 2 _____ this is something that we have to consider, as Apple has some significant advantages. 3 _____ , Apple offers a better operating system and is less vulnerable to hackers and viruses.

| *in fact* | *moreover* | *on the whole* |
|---|---|---|

4 _____ , Apple computers are already in use in our organization – the two graphic designers in the Communications department use them.
5 _____ , we've noticed that many other people bring to work the Mac laptops that they use at home. 6 _____ , this does not seem to create any serious problems – the Office suite runs perfectly well on a Mac.

| *for example* | *however* | *secondly* |
|---|---|---|

7 _____ , there are some serious obstacles to adopting Apple as the standard platform throughout the organization. Firstly, there is the question of price. Apples are significantly more expensive – they're targeted at the consumer market where fashion and design bring a premium price. 8 _____ , there are some serious technical issues. SAP, 9 _____ , doesn't run on Macs, and our IT support staff are unfamiliar with the Mac operating system.

| *on balance* | *so* | *whereas* |
|---|---|---|

10 _____ , to sum up, Microsoft offers familiarity and ease of technical support at a reasonable price, 11 _____ Apple offers design and greater security at a higher price. What conclusions can be drawn? 12 _____ , it seems that the best option is to continue using Microsoft PCs for the majority of staff. We will of course continue to monitor the situation, particularly as the Internet replaces Windows as a day-to-day software platform.

**70.1 Complete the report extract by underlining the correct words in italics.
Sometimes the choice is based simply on style or usage.**

**To:** CEO, Auto Corporation
**From:** Chief Economist, Auto Corporation
**Subject:** Outlook for the oil market and its implications for the Auto Corporation

### Introduction

[1]*Hans Oberlander, CEO of the Auto Corporation, asked me to write this report / This report was commissioned by Hans Oberlander, CEO of the Auto Corporation*. The [2]*aim / scope* of the report is to make a long-term forecast of trends in the [3]*market for oil / oil market*, and to analyze how the future price of oil will impact the automobile industry. [4]*In particular / Especially*, the report will look at our own company, the Auto Corporation, and whether we are positioned to meet future challenges in the marketplace.

### Oil market

The price of oil has been increasing [5]*steady / steadily* since around 1999. This has been driven by factors on both the supply side and the demand side. On the supply side, total world oil production has now peaked, with no [6]*significant / significantly* new discoveries on the horizon. [7]*Talking about demand / On the demand side*, the growth of economies such as China and India has meant a huge increase in the consumption of oil.

Our [8]*research shows / researches show* that these trends [9]*will / are likely to* continue, and that oil prices will remain high for the foreseeable future. This will inevitably have [10]*a force / an impact* on the auto industry, with high fuel prices causing customers to turn to models with lower running costs, [11]*such like / such as* electric cars.

### Fuel efficient engines

At Auto Corporation we currently manufacture two hybrid electric vehicles that combine a conventional gasoline engine with an on-board rechargeable electric battery.

Sales of these models have been [12]*disappointing / terrible*, and for this report we asked an independent [13]*company that does market research / market research company* to [14]*carry on / carry out* a survey to discover the reasons why. The survey showed the following areas of [15]*anxiety / concern* on the part of potential customers:

- The relatively high initial price of hybrid cars – [16]*typically / typical* a hybrid car pays for itself in terms of lower fuel costs after about three years.
- The fact that hybrid cars [17]*are unable to go very fast / go slowly*. The additional size and weight of the battery pack means that the conventional engine has to be smaller.
- The added risk in an accident that the driver, passengers and rescue workers will get electrocuted by the high voltage in the car.

### Conclusions

In the light of the above [18]*foundings / findings*, we reached the [19]*next / following* conclusions:

- Customers will [20]*increasingly / more and more* want fuel-efficient models, including electric cars, due to continuing high oil prices.
- Government legislation on reducing the emission of greenhouse gases by automobiles will also drive the [21]*trend / tendency* away from conventional engines.
- Auto Corporation has been slow to respond to the challenges ahead, [22]*because / due to* customer resistance to the current generation of electric vehicles.

### Recommendations

There are two [23]*main / most important* recommendations we would like to make:

- The Board of Auto Corporation needs to take a longer-term view of the market, [24]*paying more attention to / thinking about* the price of oil in its strategic decisions.
- Auto Corporation needs to invest considerably more [25]*money / financial resources* in R&D to develop a new generation of safe, inexpensive and reliable electric batteries.

**70.2  Read this extract from a business proposal then do the exercise below.**

## Understanding your stock losses

Thank you for meeting with us and helping us understand the stock loss situation at Fashion Superstore in more depth. We propose to conduct a review of your store to see how Closed Circuit Television (CCTV) cameras could be used most effectively, and then complete the installation of the system. Our approach is based on our twenty years' experience of providing security solutions in the retail sector.

## Key goals

Your goal is to reduce shoplifting by installing wall-mounted cameras inside your store, and to have these linked to monitors at a central security desk. You want to do this in a cost-effective way.

## Project scope

The project will include the following activities:

- Identify the best locations for CCTV cameras and install the cameras.
- Identify the best location for a central security desk, with the monitors and a visible presence of security personnel.
- Run a training program for the security personnel involved.

## Implementation and deliverables

A timetable for the different phases of the project is included as an appendix. We estimate that the total time required for this project is two weeks.

Deliverables for this project will include:

- Approximately 30 CCTV cameras, with two associated monitors at the central desk, all fully installed and checked.
- All additional materials such as cables.
- A three-day training program for security personnel, including how to work the cameras and monitors, and full simulations of shoplifting events and how to deal with them. We have run this program successfully in over sixty locations.

- A special report on how to manage security personnel, particularly with regard to always keeping their attention on the job.

## Staffing

We will assign to this project the following team:

- An in-store security expert, Mr Bob Parker, who has over ten years' experience in this field and previously worked for the police.
- Four qualified electricians.
- A trainer, Ms Beatrice Sterne, member of the Institute of Training.

## Fees

We will charge a total fee of €254,000 for this project. This includes all the items referred to above, with no hidden extras.

Based on the figures you provided us and on information obtained from previous assignments we have carried out, we estimate that this system will pay for itself within eighteen months. See the figures in the attached case study, which describes a very similar project that we carried out last year.

## Conclusion

We recommend that you contract our company to install a CCTV system inside Fashion Superstore. This system will dramatically reduce your losses due to shoplifting.

In addition, the system will help provide a safer environment for shoppers. When they see the cameras they will feel less worried about dangers such as leaving their bags unattended on the floor while they look at clothes. This safer environment is likely to lead to shoppers spending more time inside Fashion Superstore and therefore spending more money.

I will call you on Wednesday 6 June to discuss the next steps. We look forward to working with you to create a more secure and more profitable Fashion Superstore.

**Put a tick (✓) to show which sections of the proposal mention which of the three themes. See unit 68 for the themes.**

|  | Compliance | Capabilities | Value |
|---|---|---|---|
| **Understanding your stock losses** |  |  |  |
| **Key goals** |  |  |  |
| **Project scope** |  |  |  |
| **Implementation and deliverables** |  |  |  |
| **Staffing** |  |  |  |
| **Fees** |  |  |  |
| **Conclusion** |  |  |  |

**See the Answer key for the specific references.**

# Discussion topics

## Unit 1 Page 6

1  In your country, what do people think about the issue of free trade vs protectionism? What is your own view?
2  Free trade creates jobs in some industries and unemployment in others. Which? Why?
3  Should certain industries be protected? Which? Why?
4  Work in small groups:
   - Make your own list of arguments in favour of globalization, and arguments against.
   - Put your list on the table in front of you so that everyone can see it. Walk round the room and look at all the lists. Write down one or two questions that come into your head as you look.
   - Return to your seats. Ask your questions. Everybody can answer.

## Unit 2 Page 8

1  'The cycle of boom and bust is one of the wonders of capitalism – it's what Schumpeter called "creative destruction". It's the process by which inefficient industries get replaced by innovative new ones. Attempts by policy makers to prevent this cycle just support old-fashioned industries and make the economy less dynamic over the long term. Usually these attempts to control the markets fail anyway.'
   ○ Agree     ○ Disagree
2  Are you bullish or bearish on the general stock market in your country right now? Why? Is there a particular sector or industry where you hold the opposite view? Why?
3  If the business cycle exists, where are we on the clock on page 8 right now? (Think about the following questions. Was the last interest rate move up or down? Is the stock market rising or falling? Which sectors are doing well at the moment?)

## Unit 3 Page 10

1  What areas of conflict are there likely to be between an exporter and their foreign agent/distributor?
2  Work in small groups:
   - First, choose <u>one</u> of these products: small plastic children's toys, herbal medicines, high definition TV screens to hang on the wall.
   - A Vietnamese exporter wants to sell these goods into your market, and you're interested in being their agent. They need your local knowledge. Prepare a short presentation for them on the opportunities and challenges they face.
   - Use your own ideas and structure, although the seven bullet points on page 10 may give you a few ideas to get started.
   - When you finish, give your presentation.

## Unit 4 Page 12

1  Starting your own business vs working for a large company: what are the differences?
2  Think of an example of a small business that failed (perhaps from personal experience, or the experience of friends/family/colleagues, etc). Tell the group about the business, and why it failed. Could it have succeeded?
3  Work with a colleague:
   - You have each inherited €0.5m from rich aunts (€1m total) and now want to start a business together. Decide what your business will be.

- Use the contents page of the business plan on page 22 to prepare a short presentation to the rest of the group. You will explain your business plan to them. You don't have to cover every issue in the mind map.
- Give your presentation and ask for questions at the end.

## Unit 5 Page 14

1  'The Anglo-American model of putting the shareholder first is bad for the employees, bad for the community and bad for business.'
   ○ Agree     ○ Disagree
2  In your country, is there a tradition of having a strong and independent Board that represents the interests of the shareholders and can hire and fire the CEO?
3  What are the advantages and disadvantages of working for a medium-sized family-owned business, as compared to a large public company?
4  Has there been a story in the news recently about weak corporate governance at a particular company? Perhaps it led to a financial disaster, or a corruption scandal, or something else. What do you know about it?

## Unit 6 Page 16

1  Choose one of the six issues listed under 'Geopolitics and the world economy' on page 16. Discuss it with some colleagues. When you finish, choose another.
2  Choose one of the six replies given in the 'Management and business' section. Discuss it with some colleagues. When you finish, choose another.
3  'We cannot reduce energy consumption. No-one is going to voluntarily accept a decline in their living standards. Fighting global warming is useless. We're all going to fry. Let the cockroaches and rats take over – they were here before us anyway.'
   ○ Agree     ○ Disagree
4  'Globalization has gone too far.'
   ○ Agree     ○ Disagree

## Unit 7 Page 18

1  Looking at the three basic management styles mentioned on page 18, I would say that my own style is (or would be) … because …
2  'Good managers are born, not made.'
   ○ Agree     ○ Disagree
3  Look at the five main headings under 'Personal qualities' in the person specification. Can you add another few items under each heading?
4  Draw a mind map of your own personal management qualities. Put yourself in the middle, then have an inner ring of headings like the five in the person specification, and finally outer branches that show your qualities.
   Use your own ideas, but feel free to use the ideas in the unit as a starting point.
   When you finish, show your mind map to a colleague and discuss it.

## Unit 8 Page 20

1  Look at the list of six time management tips in the text on page 20. Can you add any other tips? Which ones do you personally do?
2  What is the one thing that you could do – starting tomorrow – to manage your time more efficiently?

3 Look at what managers manage. Can you add another item or two under each main heading?

4 Draw your own personalized mind map of 'How I spend my time'. If possible, focus on time at work. Otherwise, just think about your time in general.

When you finish, show your mind map to a colleague and discuss it.

## Unit 9 Page 22

1 'Planning is the basis of spontaneity.'
○ Agree ○ Disagree

2 Harold Macmillan, a British Prime Minister, was asked what was the greatest difficulty he faced. He replied 'Events, dear boy, events'. Give an example from your own life of how events changed (or destroyed) your plans.

3 Brainstorming. Close this book (everybody except one person or the teacher).

On the board, write section headings 1–8 from the contents page of the business plan on page 22. Everybody brainstorm sub-sections for each section. It isn't a memory test.

## Unit 10 Page 24

1 'Leaders and managers are different.'
○ Agree ○ Disagree

2 A leader I admire is … because …

3 'Leaders have to take difficult decisions. You'll never be a leader if you need to be liked by other people.'
○ Agree ○ Disagree

4 Look again at the bar chart showing the results of the survey on page 24. Do you think that people in their thirties responded in the same way as people in their fifties? Do you think that men responded in the same way as women?

5 Talk about a recent occasion when you successfully influenced someone (or a group). Describe how you did it.

## Unit 11 Page 26

1 If you're working, explain the two or three biggest risks that your company currently faces. If you aren't working, talk to a friend or family member who has a job and knows their business well. Ask them about the risks their company faces, and then explain them to the class in the next lesson.

2 Do you know:
● anyone who made a work-related insurance claim?
● anyone who failed to check the small print on a legal document?
● anyone who worked in a company where there was a case of embezzlement?
If your answer is 'yes' to any of these questions, tell the story.

3 'In America people are too quick to sue each other.'
○ Agree ○ Disagree

4 What is your own attitude to risk? Give an example of something in your life that you nearly did, but decided against because it was too risky. Do you have any regrets about that decision now?

## Unit 12 Page 28

1 Did your country go through the same cycle described in the text: manufacturing boom in the middle of the last century, then decline, then rebirth? If not, how and why was it different?

2 Does your country have a 'Rust Belt'? What is life like in that area now? Is there a strategy to redevelop the area?

3 Many Western countries have lost large parts of their manufacturing base over recent years. Is that necessarily a bad thing?

4 Do you know the character Dilbert from the American comic strip of the same name? Dilbert is an engineer. What kind of personality and behaviour does Dilbert have? Are engineers generally like this?

## Unit 13 Page 30

1 'Factories that make real things are the heart of an economy. The service and financial sectors are just people smiling at customers and playing with computers.'
○ Agree ○ Disagree

2 Do you work in a factory? If so, draw a diagram on the board to show the layout. Then explain what happens in the different areas of the factory.
If not, have you ever been inside a factory? Describe what you saw and your general impressions.

3 Would you be prepared to do shiftwork in a modern factory if it was an interesting, well-paid job requiring some skill? Why? / Why not?

## Unit 14 Page 32

1 How do you think the day-to-day work of a purchasing manager is different to the work of other managers in the field of production and operations?

2 Managers involved in the procurement process will spend a lot of their time negotiating. What do you know about negotiation strategies and tactics?

3 Do you know any news stories about companies using bribery? Or maybe you yourself have been in a situation where someone expected you to give them a small 'gift' to obtain a service? Tell the story.

4 If you're working, talk about how global sourcing has affected your own company. If you're a student, summarize what you have learnt about this topic on your course.

## Unit 15 Page 34

1 SCM means that the manufacturer has to share a lot of commercial information with suppliers and customers, treating them like partners. Are there any risks to this?

2 Compare air, sea, road and rail from a logistics point of view.

3 Work with a colleague. Draw a mind map of 'logistics' showing what the term means to you. Close this book before you start and use your own ideas. At the end, compare with another pair.

4 Make notes to prepare a presentation on 'Logistics in my company'. Use the headings and ideas from exercise 15.4 to help you. When you finish, give your presentation.

## Unit 16 Page 36

1 Do you know anything else about TPS, JIT, lean production or kaizen that is not mentioned in the text?

2 How could you change the organization of your own workplace to eliminate waste (of time, money and materials) and improve productivity? Draw a mind map to show your ideas. When you finish, explain your ideas to a colleague using your mind map.
If you're a student, you can do this activity for any part-time job that you've had.

# DISCUSSION TOPICS

## Unit 17 Page 38

1 What does the word 'quality' mean to you? Brainstorm as many ideas as possible and write them on the board.

2 What else do you know about TQM – beyond what is mentioned in the text?

3 Does your own organization have procedures to check quality? If so, describe them.

4 'You get what you pay for': is this always true? Think of some examples for both sides of the argument.
Here is an idea to get you started:
A packet of high-price, brand-name cereals is sitting on a supermarket shelf. Next to it on the shelf is a packet of the supermarket's own-label brand, selling at a lower price. The contents are identical – the supermarket bought the cereals from the manufacturer and repackaged them.

## Unit 18 Page 40

1 The first paragraph of the text on page 40 suggests in a humorous way that sales people and marketing people sometimes don't value each other's work. In your experience, is this true?

2 Brainstorm either 'What qualities does a salesperson need?' or 'Modern sales techniques'. Close your book before you start. (It isn't a memory exercise.)

3 Can you think of any situations where a 'hard sell' might be appropriate?

4 Think carefully about the last time that a salesperson sold you something. How did they discover your needs? How did they present their case? How did they handle your objections? Are there any special techniques that they used but that you were unaware of at the time?

## Unit 19 Page 42

1 A well-known slogan for customer service is: 'Under-promise and over-deliver'. What does it mean? Do you agree with it?

2 Have you ever heard of a 'Chief Customer Service Officer'? Why does 'customer service' have such a low priority inside companies?

3 Tell a story from your own experience about an example of particularly good or particularly bad customer service. What are the lessons?

4 Work in small groups. Brainstorm ideas for customer service under the headings: 'Little things that make a big difference' and 'Don't forget your existing customers'.
Close the book while you do the brainstorming. (It isn't a memory exercise.)
When you finish, discuss your ideas with the class.

## Unit 20 Page 44

1 Each person choose a product that you have with you today (eg in a bag or an object in the room). For each product, discuss the target market.

2 Do the following:
● On the board, write the four headings: Product, Place, Promotion and Price.
● Each student choose one item of vocabulary (a single word or a phrase) for each heading that you think your colleagues won't know. You can use a bilingual dictionary to help you.

● Go up to the board and write your vocabulary items under the correct headings.
● When everyone has finished, go round the group and explain all the words.

3 'Marketing is just there to make us buy things we don't need.'
○ Agree   ○ Disagree

4 Discuss how marketing is different to sales.

## Unit 21 Page 46

1 Look again at the thirty adjectives describing features in exercise 21.5. How many others can you think of? Brainstorm ideas on the board. Ignore easy, obvious words such as 'expensive', 'fast', 'modern'.

2 Think of an example of a product with poorly designed packaging. How would you improve it?

3 Each member of the group choose one personal item that you have with you today. Choose something that has a strong marketing campaign behind it. Take a few minutes to prepare, then describe to the group:
● the product's functional benefits
● the product's psychological benefits
● the brand image
● why you chose this particular model (if the product is part of a line of products)
● whether you think the marketing campaign influenced your purchase

## Unit 22 Page 48

1 What are the key elements of merchandising (how products are arranged and displayed inside a store)?

2 How is technology changing the face of retailing? Give some examples from your personal experience.

3 Choose two or three retailers that all sell in a similar market. Discuss the differences between them.

4 Direct marketing (catalogues, mailshots, TV shopping channels, ads in the press with a toll-free number) is often ignored in discussions about marketing. How does the distribution channel affect product, promotion and price?

## Unit 23 Page 50

1 It's increasingly difficult to reach customers through advertising. Media channels are becoming ever more diverse and fragmented. What is the advertising industry doing to meet this challenge?

2 'The better an advertisement is, the more people remember the advertisement and the less they remember the product.' Can you think of an example of this? What are the implications a) for the advertising agency, and b) for the client company?

3 Work with a colleague. Make a mind map with the word 'Promotion' in the middle. Close this book before you start. (It isn't a memory exercise.) When you finish, walk around and look at other people's mind maps.

4 Do you agree with what is written in every box in exercise 23.5?

## Unit 24 Page 52

1 Is it true that marketers talk less about price than about product, distribution or promotion? If so, why do you think it happens?

2 If you work in the marketing/sales area, describe how prices are set in your own company.

3   Each person choose an item that you have with you now (eg in your bag). It has to be one where you remember the exact price you paid. Then:
    ● Show it to your colleagues. First let them try to guess the price.
    ● Say what the price was.
    ● Say whether at the time you thought this was expensive, reasonable or cheap.
    ● Say the absolute maximum that you would have paid for this product.
    ● Discuss, from a marketing point of view, whether this item was priced correctly.

## Unit 25 Page 54

1   Have you ever taken part in market research – either as a potential customer or as a researcher? Describe your experiences.

2   Work with a colleague. Produce a mind map:
    ● If you're working, use ideas from your company and write 'Our marketing strategy' in the centre.
    ● If you're a student, use ideas you've studied on your course and write 'Elements of a marketing strategy' in the centre.
    ● When you finish, walk around and look at other people's mind maps. Discuss them.

3   Presentation. 'New Product Development'. Work with a colleague:
    ● Think of an idea for a completely new product. You're going to present the concept to your colleagues – make some notes first.
    ● Before giving the presentation, decide which person will talk about which points. It will be a team presentation – you can change the presenter once or several times.
    ● When you're ready, give your presentation. Your colleagues should listen carefully, take notes, then ask practical questions at the end.

## Unit 26 Page 56

1   Follow these instructions:
    Study the text on page 56 one more time. In a moment you're going to try to write down the elements of an income statement on a separate piece of paper. No figures are needed – just the headings. You'll do this with the help of a partner. Close this book now, and start.

2   You run a chain of small coffee/snack bars in your country. (Your nearest competitor is Starbucks.) Last quarter, both revenue and costs were above budget. This balanced out, so that the operating profit was in line with the budgeted figure. Brainstorm as many reasons for this variance as possible.

## Unit 27 Page 58

1   Follow these instructions:
    ● Study the box 'What can a balance sheet show?' at the bottom of page 58 one more time.
    ● Write down on a separate piece of paper these words: *liquidity*, *leverage*, *book value* and *profitability*.
    ● Working with a partner, write a short paragraph that explains each of these concepts. Close your book before you begin!

2   Is there anyone in the group who knows about accounts or investing? Ask them this: 'You're thinking about investing in a company, but can only look at one financial document, either the income statement or the balance sheet; which one would you choose, and why?'

## Unit 28 Page 60

1   Is there anyone in the group who knows about accounting or investing? Ask them to explain why the study of a company's cash flow is important, and in particular how it shows things that cannot be seen just from the P&L (income statement) and balance sheet.

2   How do you manage your own personal cash flow? Do you always have a negative bank balance at the end of the month? How could you manage your cash better?

## Unit 29 Page 62

1   Look again at the story of Manuela in exercise 29.5. What could she (and the other players) have done differently?

2   Work in pairs (A and B):
    ● Background. Student A and Student B work in the accounts departments of two different companies. A received a large invoice from B last month, but still hasn't paid it (due to A's own internal cash flow problems).
    ● Personalize. A and B now prepare a few more details together. What is the business activity of the two companies? What was the invoice for? How much was it for?
    ● Role play. Sit back to back. Student B make a telephone call to Student A about the unpaid invoice. Try to negotiate a settlement that is good for both sides.

## Unit 30 Page 64

1   Follow these instructions:
    ● Study the text, graphs and exercises on page 64–65 one more time.
    ● Write on the board the words 'breakeven analysis', 'operating leverage' and 'contribution margin'.
    ● Work in pairs, A and B. Close your books. As explain to Bs the three concepts written on the board. Bs should listen, ask occasional questions, and help if necessary.
    ● Keep the same roles, but work with a new partner. Now Bs have your turn to explain while As listen.

2   If you're working, explain how you analyze profitability in your company. If you're a student, describe any other areas of management accounting that you've studied.

## Unit 31 Page 66

1   'Financial markets have little to do with the real world. It's just overpaid yuppies in front of computer screens chasing the latest financial bubble.'
    ◯ Agree    ◯ Disagree

2   Look again at the table of players in the market on page 66. Can you add any extra information about any of these players?

3   Do you work in the financial markets? Describe your job.

4   The bond market and foreign exchange market are much less well-known than the stock market – but the amount of money traded on them is far larger. Can you explain why they get so little public and media attention?

## Unit 32 Page 68

1   Do you follow the stock market? What is happening at the moment? Can you explain this?

2   Do you personally own any stocks or funds? Why did you choose them? How often do you check their price? When will you sell them?

3   If you had €10,000 to invest in just one stock, which one would you choose? Why?

### Unit 33 Page 70

1  Describe your company's recruitment procedure. Is it successful? How could it be improved?

2  Work on your CV (resume) for homework – if you need to. In the next class:
   ● Put the CVs on the wall round the room. (Alternatively, lay them out on the desks.)
   ● Go round and look at other people's CVs. You may be able to get some new ideas.
   ● Go back to your desk and work with a partner. Read each other's CVs carefully. Discuss them together.
   ● If necessary, make any changes to your CV.

   If you don't want to work on your own CV or you think it is too personal, then simply help other people by reading their CVs and asking questions.

### Unit 34 Page 72

1  How important is pay? Would you work in a creative, satisfying job if the pay wasn't very good?

2  What do you think about performance-related pay?

3  Are you paid what you're worth? Imagine that you're talking to your boss, trying to persuade them to pay you more. (You've been invited to join another company so you are speaking from a position of strength.) Explain why they should pay you more.

### Unit 35 Page 74

1  Look through all the workplace issues on page 74. Are any of these the subject of discussion in your workplace?

2  Look at the following list of workplace issues. Which ones are more serious and could lead to dismissal?
   ● arriving late and leaving early
   ● being drunk at work
   ● bullying and harassment
   ● damage to property
   ● discrimination
   ● failing to follow health and safety procedures
   ● fraud
   ● personal appearance
   ● personal use of the Internet outside of rest periods
   ● theft
   ● work standards

   Choose one of the issues. Write a short, imaginary dialogue between line manager and employee where the issue is discussed for the first time.

3  Do you work in HR, or do you know anyone who does? Which parts of the job, besides recruitment, take up the most time?

### Unit 36 Page 76

1  Practise speaking about your background and career:
   ● Write a short script – the text on page 76 will give you some ideas. When you're ready, read it aloud to your colleagues. Your colleagues should listen, make a few notes, and ask questions at the end.
   ● In the next class, look at your script again briefly, then put it away. Now work with a colleague, and explain your background and career as a free speaking exercise. Your partner should ask clarification questions and encourage you to give more details.

### Unit 37 Page 78

1  Produce a SWOT analysis for a company that you know. It could be your own, or one that you've studied as a student. You can use the table on page 78 for ideas, but feel free to include other areas.

   When you finish, present your SWOT analysis to the group and then ask for questions.

2  Write a company presentation for a company that you know. It could be your own, or one that you've studied as a student. You can use the text on page 78 and exercise 37.3 for ideas, but feel free to include other areas.

   When you finish, read your text to the group and then ask for questions.

### Unit 38 Page 80

1  Practise speaking about your job:
   ● Write a short script – the text on page 80 will give you some ideas. When you're ready, read it aloud to your colleagues. Your colleagues should listen, make a few notes, and ask questions at the end.
   ● In the next class, look at your script again briefly, then put it away. Now work with a colleague, and explain your job as a free speaking exercise. Your colleague should ask clarification questions and encourage you to give more details.

2  If you don't have a job, or as an additional activity, do one of the following:
   ● Interview a friend or family member and ask them about their job. Tell your colleagues in the next class.
   ● Think of someone you know and role play them, describing their job. Remember to say 'I' – not 'he' or 'she'.

# Writing tasks

## Unit 45 Page 94

1 You work for an international pharmaceutical company with a best-selling heart drug. You're part of an international team, preparing a report on competitors' products worldwide.
- Write an email to a colleague in Japan, Akiko Yamada (a woman). Write 40–50 words.
- Give the reason for writing.
- Request information about the competitors in Japan (market share, advertising).
- Offer to provide information about your own market.

2 Personalization. Write two emails similar to ones that you have to write in your own real-life job. Use the table on page 94 to help you.

## Unit 46 Page 96

1 You're the finance director of an international company. You've just finished the company accounts for last year and the results were very good. However the outlook for next year looks more challenging. Write an email to your colleagues, telling them the news. Write 40–50 words.
- Give the reason for writing.
- Give the good news about last year. Thank everyone.
- Give the bad news about next year.

2 Personalization. Write two emails similar to ones that you have to write in your own real-life job. Use the table on page 96 to help you.

## Unit 47 Page 98

1 Follow these instructions:
- Look one more time at emails 1 and 2 on page 98, and at the two emails in exercise 47.4. Then work with a colleague to create a similar business situation:
  *What product / service is the customer interested in?*
  *How did the customer find out about it?*
  *What information does the customer want?*
  *What information will the supplier give?*
- Now, working individually, write an enquiry based on the situation you created. Note that you and your colleague will be in the same role writing a similar email.
- When you finish, exchange emails and write a reply to your colleague's enquiry. Again you will both be in the same role.
- When you finish, compare your emails.

2 Personalization. Write a similar pair of emails based on ones that you have to write in your own real-life job. Use the table on page 98 to help you.

## Unit 48 Page 100

1 Follow these instructions:
- Look one more time at emails 2 and 3 on page 100, and at the emails in exercise 48.3 and 48.4. Then work with a colleague to create a similar business situation:
  *What product / service is the customer complaining about?*
  *Why is the customer complaining?*
  *What reply is the supplier going to give?*
- Now, working individually, write a complaint based on the situation you created. Note that you and your colleague will be in the same role, writing a similar email.
- When you finish, exchange emails and write a reply to your colleague's complaint. Again you will both be in the same role.
- When you finish, compare your emails.

2 Personalization. Write a similar pair of emails based on ones that you have to write in your real-life job. Use the table on page 100 to help you.

## Unit 49 Page 102

1 Work with a colleague. You will exchange emails, inviting each other to visit. For simplicity, keep the two situations separate when you write.
- Before you begin, look one more time at the emails on page 102.
- Now write the following short emails:
  a) As host, invite your colleague to visit you. Give the finished email to your colleague.
  b) As guest, reply to the email you just received. Accept the invitation. Give the finished email to your colleague.
  c) As host, suggest an itinerary. (This could include some local sightseeing.) Give the finished email to your colleague.
  d) As guest, reply to the email you just received. Include details of your flight, hotel, etc. Give the finished email to your colleague.
  e) As host, confirm everything. Give the finished email to your colleague.
- When you finish, compare your emails.

2 Personalization. Write one or two similar emails based on ones that you have to write in your real-life job. You can be the host, the guest, or take both roles for different emails. Use the table on page 102 to help you.

## Unit 54 Page 112

1 Find an article about business (in a magazine, newspaper or online) written in your own language. It has to be one that describes a development or trend, and that contains at least one graph.
Write four or five sentences in English describing the trend. Try to use a good variety of language from the unit. You can invent additional information, for example what happened in previous years.

2 Choose a real-life, general-interest topic that shows a trend over several years. You may choose something like house prices in your country, or something personal like time spent doing sports / learning English. Draw an approximate graph – the exact details don't matter. Label the X and Y axes.
Write a few sentences describing movements in the graph. Try to use a good variety of language from the unit.

## Unit 55 Page 114

1 Study the graphs below. You may wish to invent more context, for example the industry sector and the name of the company.

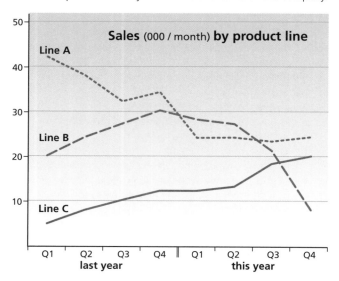

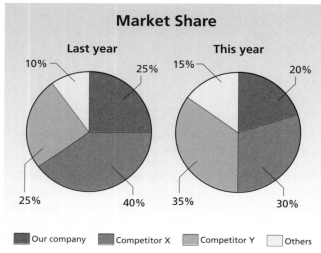

Write a short presentation extract where you describe and analyze the trends. Try to use a good variety of language from units 54 and 55.

If you're working in class, read your presentation to your colleagues when you finish. Ask for questions at the end.

2 Personalization. Repeat the exercise, but this time draw a few graphs from your real life. These could be:

● Business trends. Perhaps sales or profits or production volumes for various product lines, or market share of your company and its competitors, or any KPIs (key performance indicators) that you deal with.

● Ways that you use your time. Choose either a work context (perhaps pie charts comparing time spent on various activities last year and this year), or a domestic context (perhaps a line graph showing time spent with children on different days of the week, or time spent doing sports over several months).

Draw the graphs and label the X and Y axes. Then write a few paragraphs, describing and analyzing the trends.

# Interviews

## 1 Interview with a private equity investor

### Exercises

**1 Guess the missing words (some letters have been given to help you).**

1 When a private equity firm buys a target company, it uses a newly-formed company called an 'SPV' (Special Purpose Vehicle). As an example, half the money the SPV needs might come from eq_ _ _ _ (capital provided by the new owners and the existing shareholders) and half might come from d_ _ _ (a bank loan that has to be repaid).

2 After buying the target company, the private equity firm restructures it. This can involve a 'b_ _ _d up' (making the company larger) or a 'b_ _ _k down' (making it smaller).

3 After restructuring, the private equity firm needs an e_ _t strategy.

4 There are many other pl_ _ _ _s involved in the buy-out process, including la_ _ _rs, t_ _ consultants and business consulting companies.

**2 ⊛ 16 Now listen to the interview and check your answers.**

**3 Listen again with your eyes closed. Then listen a third time while you follow the script (page 157).**

**4 Discuss any interesting issues with some colleagues.**

### Glossary

**due diligence** investigation into the details of a potential investment
**from scratch** from the beginning
**IPO** initial public offering (selling shares on the stock market for the first time)
**leveraged buy-out** buying a company with a small amount of your own money and a large bank loan

## 2 Interview with an entrepreneur

### Exercises

**1 Underline the words in italics that you think describe the profile of a typical entrepreneur.**

1 They come from *poor / rich* families.
2 They are *risk-takers / careful*.
3 They *only trust themselves / have good instincts about other people*.
4 They *go / don't go* to university.
5 They like to *lead from the top / work alongside employees*.
6 They *get bored quickly / are perfectionists who enjoy finishing projects properly*.
7 They *function well working on their own / need a good team behind them*.
8 They often have *difficult / stable* family backgrounds.

**2 ⊛ 17 Now listen to the interview and see whether this particular entrepreneur matches your ideas.**

**3 Listen again with your eyes closed. Then listen a third time while you follow the script (page 158).**

**4 Discuss any interesting issues with some colleagues.**

### Glossary

**capital gain** a profit from money you have invested
**collateral** property or other goods that you promise to give to the bank if you cannot repay a loan
**refurbish** repair and improve a building by cleaning and painting it etc.

## 3 Interview with a management trainee

### Exercises

**1 You are going to hear a management trainee talk about their experiences of an assessment centre. During one full day there are a variety of tests. Predict the sequence of tests, from 1 to 6.**

☐ an interview with an HR manager with normal job-related questions
☐ lunch, where social skills are observed
☐ a test for numerical and problem-solving skills
☐ a teamwork test where a group of people discuss a scenario and choose the best idea
☐ a report writing exercise
☐ a roleplay exercise to test management skills

**2 ⊛ 18 Now listen to the interview and find out the sequence of tests done by this particular trainee.**

**3 Listen again with your eyes closed. Then listen a third time while you follow the script (page 159).**

**4 Discuss any interesting issues with some colleagues.**

### Glossary

**assessment** a process in which you make a judgement about a person or situation
**assessor** someone who decides how well someone has done in an activity
**pitch** try to sell something by saying how good it is
**scenario** a written description of a particular situation – with a place, some characters, some background information, some things that may happen etc.

## 4 Interview with a supply chain manager
### Exercises

**1 Decide whether these statements are true (T) or false (F).**

1 The supply chain is: raw materials supplier ➡ first tier supplier ➡ second tier supplier ➡ manufacturing company. **T / F**
2 Many modern manufacturers are really just assemblers. **T / F**
3 It is important for the manufacturer to keep commercial information (such as demand forecasts) confidential, and not to share too much information with suppliers. **T / F**
4 In modern manufacturing production is 'pulled' by real customer orders, rather than being 'pushed' by forecasts. **T / F**

**2** 🕐 **19 Now listen to the interview and check your answers.**

**3 Listen again with your eyes closed. Then listen a third time while you follow the script (page 160).**

**4 Discuss any interesting issues with some colleagues.**

## Glossary

*cluster* a small group of things that are very close to each other
*economies of scale* a reduction in the cost of producing an individual unit, resulting from an increase in the overall production volume
*Just-In-Time* a strategy for inventory management in which raw materials, parts and components are delivered from the supplier immediately before they are needed
*tracking* following the progress of

## 5   Interview with a sales manager

### Exercises

**1 Make short notes in answer to the following questions.**

1   What is a 'key account manager'?
2   We all have an idea of the typical work of a sales consultant – but how is this work different if it is in the B2B (business-to-business) sector?
3   With a 'cold call', how do you stop the other person putting down the phone within five seconds?
4   All sales people face the standard objection that the client already works with another company, or that another company is offering a better price. How can you deal with those objections?
5   Inside a company, what other department might come into conflict with Sales?

**2** 🕐 **20 Now listen to the interview and find out how the sales manager discusses the same issues.**

**3 Listen again with your eyes closed. Then listen a third time while you follow the script (page 160).**

**4 Discuss any interesting issues with some colleagues.**

## Glossary

*cold call* an unexpected telephone call by someone trying to sell something
*'play it by ear'* decide what to do as a situation develops, rather than planning what to do
*prospects* potential clients
*testimonial* a written statement about how well a person or organization has done, provided by someone who has had previous contact with them

## 6   Interview with a marketing director

### Exercises

**1 You are going to hear an interview with the marketing director of an agrochemical company. Which idea do you think he will discuss under each heading below, a or b?**

*Product*
a   genetically modified crops that respond well to chemicals
b   running a focus group of farmers

*Price*
a   generous discounts for long-term customers
b   paying for the chemicals not with money, but with crops

*Place (Distribution)*
a   working closely with third-party logistics providers
b   different distribution channels for big, medium and small growers

*Promotion*
a   using billboards at the side of roads in rural areas
b   making a 3D movie with flying saucers and aliens

**2** 🕐 **21 Now listen to the interview and check your answers.**

**3 Listen again with your eyes closed. Then listen a third time while you follow the script (page 161).**

**4 Discuss any interesting issues with some colleagues.**

## Glossary

*crop* a plant grown for food, usually on a farm

## 7   Interview with a finance director

### Exercises

**1 The table below shows how the finance function can be divided up in a large company. Complete the table with the words in the box.**

| auditors | cash flow | governance | invoices | overdraft |
| receivable | sheet | variance | | |

| Treasurer | accounts payable<br>accounts [1]_____<br>contact with banks (eg [2]_____ facility) |
|---|---|
| Chief Accounting Officer | preparing accounts (income statement, [3]_____ statement, balance [4]_____ )<br>preparing [5]_____<br>tax planning |
| Financial Controller | internal auditing<br>budgeting ([6]_____ between planned and actual budget)<br>financial planning |
| Finance Director | supervising the three people above<br>taking issues to the senior management team<br>corporate [7]_____<br>working with external [8]_____<br>financing of large projects |

**2** 🔘 **22 Now listen to the interview and check your answers.**

**3 Listen again with your eyes closed. Then listen a third time while you follow the script (page 162).**

**4 Discuss any interesting issues with some colleagues.**

## Glossary

> ***corporate governance*** the rules and practices that control a company, especially the relationship between management and shareholders
> ***outstanding*** still not paid
> ***overdraft*** an agreement with the bank that allows you to operate with a negative balance

## 8 Interview with a human resources director

### Exercises

**1 You are going to hear an interview with an HR director who works in a European office of an American multinational. Predict the answers to the questions below.**

1  In the European context there is some difficulty in implementing the HR policy from head office in the US. Which **two** areas below need to be adapted for local conditions?
   a  training and coaching     c  equal opportunities
   b  dealing with poor          d  health and safety
       performance

2  Which of these two options do mothers employed by the company prefer?
   a  a free kindergarten
   b  more flexible hours

3  Which **one** area of training is very popular at the moment?
   a  teambuilding               c  influencing skills
   b  English language           d  conflict management

**2** 🔘 **23 Now listen to the interview and check your answers.**

**3 Listen again with your eyes closed. Then listen a third time while you follow the script (page 163).**

**4 Discuss any interesting issues with some colleagues.**

## Glossary

> ***appraisal*** an interview (often annual) between a manager and an employee where they discuss the employee's performance, training needs and future career path
> ***compensation*** salary and benefits
> ***equal opportunities*** where everyone has the same work opportunities and no-one is treated unfairly because of their race, gender, age etc.
> ***gender*** the fact of being either male or female

# Listening scripts

## Listen and repeat exercises

 **Track 1**

### Exercise 39.7

Good morning, ICT. Teresa speaking. How can I help you?
Please hold while I try to connect you.
I'd like to speak to someone in your accounts department.
The reason I'm calling is because of the sales figures.
How nice to hear from you!
Thanks for calling – did you get my email?
Is this a good time to talk?
Are you in the middle of something?
Is there anything else I can help you with today?
OK, leave it with me – I'll call you tomorrow afternoon.

 **Track 2**

### Exercise 40.5

Just bear with me for a moment.
Right, sorry to keep you waiting.
Sorry, she's out of the office this afternoon.
What's it in connection with?
Can you ask him to call me back?
Would you like to leave a message?
Let me just get a pen. OK. Go ahead.
Is that 'i' as in Italy, or 'e' as in Egypt?
Let me read that back to you.
I'll make sure he gets the message.

 **Track 3**

### Exercise 41.6

Can you speak more slowly, please?
Sorry, I didn't catch that.
Did you say fifty, five-zero?
What exactly do you mean by 'short term'?
Let me just check that I understand.
Can I just go over that again?
Can you speak up a bit?
It's a really bad line. You keep breaking up.
My battery is very low.
We got cut off. Sorry about that.

 **Track 4**

### Exercise 42.4

What time would be good for you?
What time are you thinking of?
How about February the ninth?
Could we make it the following day instead?
Would eleven-thirty suit you?
I'd prefer a bit later if you don't mind.
I'll send an email to confirm the details.
Unfortunately I can't make next Tuesday.
Something urgent has come up. Can we reschedule?
I hope it's not a problem for you.

**Track 5**

### Exercise 43.6

We received the order this morning but you only shipped 80 pieces.
There seems to be a problem with the invoice.
I do apologize. I'm sure we can sort it out.
What exactly is the problem?
I need to ask you a few quick questions.
Can you leave it with me?
I'll look into it and get back to you this afternoon.

I need to check at this end and see what's going on.
I'll send a replacement immediately by special delivery.
I'm sorry again for any inconvenience this has caused.

 **Track 6**

### Exercise 51.5

OK, let's get started.
Before I begin, I'd like to thank Françoise for inviting me here today.
On behalf of BCC International I'd like to welcome you here to our offices.
Let me start by introducing myself.
The aim of this presentation is to give you an overview of our company.
I'll speak for about thirty minutes.
I've divided my talk into four main sections.
If you have any questions, please feel free to interrupt.
If you have any questions, I'll be happy to answer them at the end.
OK, let's begin with this first slide.

 **Track 7**

### Exercise 52.5

OK. Let's move on to the next point.
I'll come back to this in a moment.
It might be useful to give a little background here.
Let me explain with a concrete example.
I think there are three questions to focus on.
What is the reason for this? The reason is the design.
As you can see on this next slide, the trend is up.
I'd like to highlight two things on this chart.
Are there any questions so far?
Does anyone have any comments?

 **Track 8**

### Exercise 53.4

Right, that brings me to the end of my presentation.
Just to summarize the main points again …
Thank you all for coming. I hope it's been useful.
I've got some handouts here. I'll pass them round.
Here's my email in case you want to get in touch.
Do you have any questions? Yes, the gentleman at the back.
That's a very good point.
That's an interesting question. What's your own opinion?
I think that's outside the scope of this presentation.
OK, I think there's time for one last question.

 **Track 9**

### Exercise 57.6

What do you think, Chris?
What I'm trying to say is we have no other option.
It seems to me that we have no other option.
Basically, we have to look at branding in a new way.
From my point of view it's worth it.
I totally agree with you.
I agree up to a point, but I can see one or two problems.
Don't you think this is going to be very expensive?
Really? Do you think so?
I'm not so sure about that.

 **Track 10**

### Exercise 58.5

Sorry, I don't understand – can you explain that again?
Can you go over that again, please?
If I understand you correctly, you're in favour of option B. Is that right?
How did you arrive at the figure of 1.5 million euros?

Could you be a little more specific?

Sorry, there's been a slight misunderstanding.

Perhaps I haven't explained myself clearly.

Let me put it another way: it's a good idea but it's too expensive.

Could I just say something?

Can I just finish my point?

 **Track 11**

## Exercise 59.6

There are several ways we could deal with this.

Let's look at the pros and cons.

On the one hand, it would save time. But on the other hand, it would cost money.

In general I agree, although the cost may be too high.

Can I make a suggestion? Instead of waiting, why don't we do something?

Let's think carefully about the implications of that.

Yes, I think that would work really well.

I can see one or two problems with that.

That sounds like a good idea, but I don't think it would work in practice.

I think the best way forward is to carry out a survey.

 **Track 12**

## Exercise 60.6

Antonio, this is your field. What do you think?

Mike, after we've heard from Rosa can we have your views?

One at a time, please. First Mirella, then Claude.

I'll come back to you in a moment, Nikola.

Perhaps we could get back to the main point?

I think we should move on now.

We need to look at this in more detail.

What other ways are there to approach this?

Can we go round the table to see if everyone agrees?

OK, let's go over what we've discussed so far.

 **Track 13**

## Exercise 61.4

OK, let's get down to business. What exactly do you need?

For us, the priorities are quality and reliability.

When you say 'reliability', what do you mean?

How flexible can you be on price?

What do you have in mind?

What sort of quantity are you thinking of?

What kind of timescale are we looking at?

What sort of figure are we talking about?

What kind of guarantee can you give us?

Can I suggest another way of moving forward?

 **Track 14**

## Exercise 62.6

We'd be prepared to offer better terms of payment.

But only if you increased your order.

Would you be willing to accept a compromise?

OK, we can agree to that.

That would be very difficult for us.

Let's just take a moment to review what we've discussed.

I think that's as far as we can go at this stage.

I don't have the authority to make that decision by myself.

If you can agree to that, we can close the deal today.

So, if you'd just like to sign here.

 **Track 15**

## Exercise 63.5

That might be quite expensive.

Could I just interrupt for a moment?

There seems to be a problem with the invoice.

It seems to me that you are being a little optimistic.

Actually, this line is not very profitable.

That doesn't give us very much time.

To be honest, that would be very difficult.

Wouldn't it be easier to ship via Hamburg?

We were thinking of something around 5%.

I understood you had these products in stock.

## Interviews

 **Track 16**

### 1 Interview with a private equity investor

PEI = Private equity investor

**INTERVIEWER** *I'd like you to explain a little about private equity. I read about it in the financial press, but I've never really understood it.*

**PEI** Sure. The business of a private equity company is to invest money in two very specific ways. The first way is as venture capital – that means looking for a small start-up company that needs capital, funding the company to allow it to grow, and then later selling the company to make a profit. That's a separate branch of private equity, and it's not what I do.

**INTERVIEWER** *OK. What's the second way that private equity invests money?*

**PEI** The other side of private equity is buy-outs, which is what I'm involved in.

**INTERVIEWER** *So tell me a little more about that.*

**PEI** The first stage in a buy-out is to look for a target company to buy. We call that 'scouting'. A typical target might be a medium-sized company with a strong cash flow where the owners are prepared to sell a stake in the company. For example, it might be a company that an entrepreneur has built up from scratch, but now he or she's approaching retirement or has other plans.

**INTERVIEWER** *OK. So how do you actually buy the company?*

**PEI** Let's imagine that the value of the target is 40 million euros, so we need 40 million to buy it. We will buy the target company with a newly-formed company called a 'Special Purpose Vehicle'. Half the money that the SPV needs, 20 million, might come from equity. The original shareholders sell us their shares – they keep some of the money for themselves, but reinvest the rest in the SPV. Perhaps they contribute 8 million of the 20 million the SPV needs. We provide the remaining 12 million. In this example we own more equity than them, so we have a controlling stake in the SPV. If we own less than them, we call it a minority interest.

**INTERVIEWER** *OK, so half of the money to buy the target comes as equity, from yourselves and from the original shareholders. What about the other half?*

**PEI** The other half, the other 20 million, comes as debt. It's a loan from the bank. That's why it's called a leveraged buy-out – we use a small amount of our own money to raise a large amount of funds.

**INTERVIEWER** *Right, and as I understand it, you repay this bank loan with the cash flow of the target company.*

**PEI** That's right. The loan might be for a period of three to seven years, and over that period the business just keeps running normally and we repay the loan from the cash flow. At the end, the SPV owns the company with no debt.

**INTERVIEWER** *You say 'running normally', but of course private equity is controversial because sometimes there are big changes during this period.*

**PEI** Sometimes there are, sometimes not. The cases where there are big changes are when we buy a public company listed on a stock market, then de-list it and restructure it, and then re-list it after we've made it more profitable.

**INTERVIEWER** *What happens during the restructuring?*

**PEI** Sometimes we do a 'build up'. That means buying other smaller companies and merging them with the original target company to make a new, larger, more profitable company. Other times we do a 'break down'. That means selling non-core assets, cutting costs, making the business more efficient, and generally refocusing the business.

**INTERVIEWER** *Cutting costs and looking for efficiency means that some people will lose their jobs.*

**PEI** Our argument is that we make the whole business more viable in the long term. People would have lost their jobs anyway if we hadn't made the necessary changes sooner rather than later. We make the company profitable.

**INTERVIEWER** *OK. You mentioned re-listing on the stock market as an option after the restructuring. What other exit strategies do you have?*

**PEI** Well, often the company was never listed in the first place, it was always in private hands, and so then we do an IPO – a listing for the first time. But the other exit strategies open to us are firstly to sell to a much larger company that is looking to diversify or expand – for them it's just a normal acquisition – or secondly to sell to another private equity company. There is a second buy-out. That's quite common.

**INTERVIEWER** *OK, I think it's much clearer now what is involved. It's all happening at the level of the ownership of the company – buying it, restructuring it, then selling it. The people at the bottom might just carry on their jobs as normal, unaware of what's happening, or might suddenly find that their offices are closed, or that they are transferred to another job, or that they've lost their job completely – all for reasons outside of their control or understanding.*

**PEI** That's right. It's capitalism. Just speeded up a little.

**INTERVIEWER** *And a final question. What other players are involved in the process?*

**PEI** First there are the lawyers. The whole process is very complex from a legal point of view. Then there is a financial advisor who evaluates the value of the target company – in fact that's my own job. There are accounting firms to do the due diligence and check the books of the target company to make sure that everything is OK. There are tax consultants to make sure that there is no outstanding tax. Then there are the investment banks. They arrange the debt to buy the target company. For example, they go to commercial banks and present the figures of the target company, the structure of the repayment and so on. The commercial banks actually provide the loan. Finally there are business consulting companies. They are the ones who analyze how the business is going to be restructured or developed.

**INTERVIEWER** *And all these people get a slice of the pie?*

**PEI** Oh yes. If the value of the target is 40 million euros, we might actually need to raise another four or five million on top to pay all these different people.

 Track 17

**2 Interview with an entrepreneur**

EPNR = Entrepreneur

**INTERVIEWER** *Can you tell me a little about yourself?*

**EPNR** Yes, I'm 37 years old, married, and I have three kids. I've always worked in the property field. I was an employee in various

real estate companies in the past, but as soon as I felt that I'd learned enough, I left. I launched my own business. That was about two years ago. It's always been my dream.

**INTERVIEWER** *And now you are a property developer in the residential sector.*

**EPNR** Yes, that's right. I buy houses or apartments, refurbish them, and then rent them to tenants. Sometimes I sell the property immediately after refurbishment, but usually it's more profitable to hold the property and collect the rent.

**INTERVIEWER** *So that you get a capital gain as well as the rent, at least while house prices are going up.*

**EPNR** Exactly.

**INTERVIEWER** *How much money did you have when you started up by yourself? You need a lot of money to start this kind of business – to buy a property, spend money on it, and then wait for the rent to come in month by month.*

**EPNR** I didn't have a lot. I come from a poor family and everything I have, I've earned. I saved money from earlier jobs, and then to start my business I got a bank loan and used my own house as collateral on the loan.

**INTERVIEWER** *So you are a risk-taker.*

**EPNR** Yes. I needed to borrow a lot of money from the bank, and it was a little frightening because my own future and the future of my family were at stake. But I enjoy taking risks, and I'm confident that I have enough determination and energy to succeed. I suppose I'm a typical entrepreneur in that respect.

**INTERVIEWER** *I'd like to explore this theme of the profile of a typical entrepreneur. You've touched on two areas: being comfortable with risk, and having self-confidence and determination. What would you add to that list?*

**EPNR** For me, the most important thing for an entrepreneur is to have very good instincts about people. It's a feeling thing. You don't really need a good education. I didn't go to university because I thought it would be boring – I wanted to start working and earning money. No, I would say that what you need is very good intuition to decide immediately if the person in front of you is honest or not.

**INTERVIEWER** *And an instinct for a deal as well as for a person?*

**EPNR** Yes. You can smell a good deal. Of course the figures must add up, but you need that special gift of spotting straight away how to make money – without doing too much analysis.

**INTERVIEWER** *OK. What else?*

**EPNR** You have to be very direct with people, without being rude. I think other people like it when you're honest and don't fool around.

**INTERVIEWER** *What about your attitude to employees?*

**EPNR** With employees I think you have to be informal, allow them to dress casually and so on. Of course I do draw certain lines between me and my employees, but it's very important to me that staff feel at home in the office. It makes them more productive. I don't like the bureaucratic atmosphere in a large company. The best way to manage people is to be there working alongside them, not have all sorts of reporting procedures and meetings. I hate all that.

**INTERVIEWER** *So your management style is to work closely with staff as a team leader, to be a motivator by example, and with a big emphasis on personal relationships.*

**EPNR** Yes.

**INTERVIEWER** *What happens when things go wrong?*

**EPNR** I can give you an example. I had an employee who was having a bad influence on the other staff. I won't go into details. But I took him to a restaurant. We had a good heart-to-heart discussion over lunch. I was very direct with him, and very honest. I told him that I was going to change the way I paid him – with a lower fixed salary but a higher commission for each deal that he closed. That solved everything – his performance really improved and everything was OK.

**INTERVIEWER**  *Let's go back again to this topic of the personality of an entrepreneur. We know that he or she is creative, dynamic, and a fast decision maker. But maybe an entrepreneur is also someone who gets bored quickly – so they are very good at starting projects but less good at consolidating and building. They want to move on and start something else.*

**EPNR**  Yes, I think you are absolutely right. That's why every entrepreneur needs a good team behind them. An entrepreneur is different to a self-employed person – if you really want the freedom to work entirely on your own, you become self-employed.

**INTERVIEWER**  *OK, one final thing. I hope it's not too personal. I've read that entrepreneurs often have a difficult family background, with divorced parents and so on. This gives them the drive to succeed and make money, because they want the security which they never had as children.*

**EPNR**  Well, if we take my own family, yes, my parents got divorced when I was young. You know I've never thought about it like that before – I mean as a positive influence, in a way. Very interesting!

**INTERVIEWER**  *Great. Thanks very much. Let's finish here.*

🌐 Track 18

## 3 Interview with a management trainee

MT = Management trainee

**INTERVIEWER**  *So, Agata, you're going to tell us a little about your experiences of an assessment centre.*

**MT**  Yes. Many large companies use assessment centres to select and recruit new employees. They are mainly used for people in their twenties, because recent graduates all have very similar CVs and so it's not easy to choose the best candidates. In an assessment centre the company really sees how you operate at a personal level, and they can spot people with future management potential.

**INTERVIEWER**  *OK, so first tell us about your own particular case.*

**MT**  I'm 27, and I applied for a position within a graduate management trainee scheme for a large, international company in the hospitality sector. The process started online: first with an application form, and then with a series of tests – numerical tests, problem-solving tests and so on. After that there was a personality test, again online. After passing all the tests and waiting a few days between each one, they did a short telephone interview. Finally, they asked me to come to the assessment centre.

**INTERVIEWER**  *Where was the assessment centre?*

**MT**  It was in a hotel abroad and it lasted for two days. They told us that the first day was just to meet the other people and to understand what was going to happen, but of course I guessed that the assessment would begin from the moment I arrived.

**INTERVIEWER**  *How many people were chosen to go to the assessment?*

**MT**  They told us that there were 3,800 candidates who had filled in the initial application form, and of these 38 were invited to the assessment centre.

**INTERVIEWER**  *So exactly one in a hundred. And how many of those 38 were they going to offer a job to?*

**MT**  Between ten and fifteen people.

**INTERVIEWER**  *OK. So talk me through the second day, the assessment day.*

**MT**  Yes. First we were retested for our numerical and problem-solving skills, and they also gave us some logic tests and use-of-language tests. They wanted to check that it was really us who

had done the online tests, and not a maths genius brother or something like that! Then we all went upstairs for an interview.

**INTERVIEWER**  *What kind of interview?*

**MT**  It was a fairly conventional one-on-one interview, with an HR manager from the company. She asked me what I liked about my last job, what the worst thing about it was, why you would like to work for my company in particular – normal questions. Then we had to give a Powerpoint presentation. I forgot to tell you – one week before they had given us a topic and we had to prepare a whole Powerpoint presentation, making up the slides and so on. The whole interview including the presentation lasted about an hour. Then it was time for lunch.

**INTERVIEWER**  *OK.*

**MT**  Yes, it was a standing-up lunch in the foyer with canapés, and we all moved around and chatted. I'm sure they were observing our social skills during the lunch as well!

**INTERVIEWER**  *I'm sure they were! What happened after lunch?*

**MT**  After lunch there was a roleplay exercise. They gave you a background situation, and you had half an hour to read it and think about it. Then you did the roleplay with one other person who also had a role. In the room there was a silent assessor who took notes.

**INTERVIEWER**  *What kind of roleplay was it?*

**MT**  I had to play the role of an assistant manager – like the job I would really have if I was successful – and the other person was a problem employee. They were doing their job badly, they were challenging our authority, they had been rude to some customers, and so on. But the team was short of members and it was difficult to find staff in the local labour market – and so I couldn't fire them. Also, I was only the assistant manager and I didn't have the authority to do that – in the scenario the main manager was away on holiday, and so I had to talk to the employee and try to control the situation.

**INTERVIEWER**  *Very challenging! How did you handle it?*

**MT**  I can't tell you. It's confidential – it would be too much help to other people if they were in the same situation.

**INTERVIEWER**  *OK, so what happened after the roleplay?*

**MT**  Next we had a teamwork test. There were eight people around a table – again we were given a background scenario with a problem to solve, and we had to discuss together and come up with a solution. In the room there were three silent assessors this time.

**INTERVIEWER**  *Can you give me an idea of the scenario?*

**MT**  Yes. We were supposed to be the Board members of a company, discussing ideas for how to improve the business. Each person had to pitch their own idea, which they gave you. For example, rewarding the employees in a different way, bringing a new product onto the market, a loyalty scheme for customers, etc. At the end you could only choose one idea.

**INTERVIEWER**  *The silent assessors interest me. What do you think it was that they were looking for?*

**MT**  Well, communication skills obviously – to see if you can explain your ideas clearly and directly and also listen to other people and ask them good questions. Also to see if you can influence other people and convince them that your ideas are right.

**INTERVIEWER**  *Was there anything else after that?*

**MT**  There was one last exercise – a report writing exercise. Again we were given a background situation, and they gave us half an hour to read it – it was quite lengthy. Then we had two hours to write a report based on the situation.

**INTERVIEWER**  *What was the situation this time?*

**MT**  We worked for a company that wanted to move its offices, and we had to choose between two options. One location was very expensive, but it had good infrastructure, and the other location was cheap, but it was old and lacked some basic facilities. You had to choose a location, justify it, and also give some financial analysis. The idea was to write something that a top manager could read at a glance and make the final decision.

**INTERVIEWER**   *So the whole day was very comprehensive. As well as the conventional interview they looked at your numerical and logical skills, your interpersonal skills, your management skills with the awkward employee, your teamworking ability, your writing ability – everything.*

**MT**   Oh yes.

**INTERVIEWER**   *And were you successful?*

**MT**   Yes I was! I got the job. Now I have one year's training – six months in two different countries – and then I will be an assistant manager and I can choose where to work.

 Track 19

### 4 Interview with a supply chain manager

SCM = Supply chain manager

**INTERVIEWER**   *OK, Andrea, you're going to explain to me about supply chain management.*

**SCM**   Yes, supply chain management is a revolution in the way that we see logistics. Instead of a company just having an internal focus, it has to have a direct connection with its suppliers and customers.

**INTERVIEWER**   *So give me an example of the different companies involved in a supply chain.*

**SCM**   Let's take an automobile company as an example. They'll buy a whole module like the dashboard or the door from a first tier supplier, and this first tier supplier will buy small parts and components from a second tier supplier. This company will in turn buy from a raw materials supplier.

**INTERVIEWER**   *It sounds like a complex system.*

**SCM**   In fact, supply chain management has developed because it reduces complexity. In the past a car manufacturer used to buy a huge number of components and then put them together itself to make all the modules needed in the car. It was very difficult to manage all the processes and to maintain quality. Now they just buy in the finished modules and assemble them.

**INTERVIEWER**   *How does it all work in terms of logistics? Everyone has to deliver to everyone else.*

**SCM**   Normally the assembly plant is located in a low-cost country, and the suppliers to this plant need to be very close – in order to put into practice 'Just-In-Time' delivery. So a little cluster of suppliers grows up around the plant. It provides employment and also some skills transfer to the low-cost country.

**INTERVIEWER**   *You've mentioned the manufacturer (who is really just an assembler), and its suppliers. Who else is involved?*

**SCM**   There are all the logistics partners. You've got the companies responsible for transporting and warehousing, and these companies could be involved at any point between first tier, second tier, manufacturer and distributor. If we stick with our example of the automobile industry, then you can also include the financial services providers. If a customer buys a car they might want credit to help them to do that, or they might want to lease rather than buy. These financial services are provided by partner companies, and in a way they are part of the supply chain.

**INTERVIEWER**   *It must be very difficult to integrate the business operations of all the companies involved.*

**SCM**   Yes, you're right. We use IT to do that. We integrate the information systems of all the companies involved. I'm talking about tracking the location of items in transit, about sharing production forecasts, about providing information regarding

technical specifications, and many other things. Over recent years there have been big advances in this field of integrating IT systems.

**INTERVIEWER**   *I guess that in the past some of this business information would have been considered confidential.*

**SCM**   Yes. But it's important. For example, the more information that a supplier has about future demand, the less stock they need to carry.

**INTERVIEWER**   *This means that you need a long-term relationship with your suppliers, and they become more like partners.*

**SCM**   Exactly. And it's not just in terms of needing them to make just-in-time deliveries, it's more than that. For example, we work with them on developing new products according to our requirements.

**INTERVIEWER**   *So far we've talked about the upstream end of the supply chain. What about the downstream end, from the manufacturer to the distributor?*

**SCM**   Yes. Here it depends a lot on the relative power of the two sides. Big distributors are very powerful, and they can force the manufacturer to adopt just-in-time methods just as the manufacturer forces the suppliers to do the same.

**INTERVIEWER**   *So everybody wants just-in-time, all the way down the chain.*

**SCM**   You're right. We call it a 'pull' system. In modern manufacturing all the business activity right down the chain is pulled by customer orders. You only make what you need to. The opposite, the old way, is called a 'push' system. With a push system you work on forecasts – you manufacture and distribute on the basis of your forecasts. The products are just there, ready-made, waiting for someone to buy them.

**INTERVIEWER**   *But surely some parts of the supply chain still work like that?*

**SCM**   Yes. To be exact, the parts of the chain that work on a push system are those where you can achieve economies of scale. If you can save money by making a lot of something all at one time, then you go ahead and make it, according to your forecasts. You don't wait until it's needed. But you must have accurate forecasts, otherwise you make too much product and you waste money.

**INTERVIEWER**   *Earlier you used the automobile industry as your example on several occasions – how widespread are these ideas in other industrial sectors?*

**SCM**   Supply chain management was developed initially in bigger companies, especially those producing cars and white goods. But now it's used for all manufactured consumer goods – cell phones, laptops, everything. Dell, for example, is very well-known for its just-in-time systems.

 Track 20

### 5 Interview with a sales manager

KAM = Key account manager

**INTERVIEWER**   *OK, can you tell me your job title and the industry you work in?*

**KAM**   Yes, I am a key account manager, and I work in a lighting company. Our clients are large companies in the hotel and retail sectors who are looking to either construct a new building, or renovate an old one.

**INTERVIEWER**   *What is a key account manager?*

**KAM**   It's a job on the sales side, but dealing with large clients only. The important clients want one specific person as their point of contact inside a supplier company.

**INTERVIEWER**   *OK, so what do you do during a typical day?*

**KAM**   First of all I build our database of prospects. I use the Internet, newspapers, magazines, etc to see which companies might have plans for new buildings. Then I contact them, by telephone or email, and try to get an appointment to visit them and make a sales presentation.

**INTERVIEWER**   *And if the client is interested?*

**KAM**   Then I get into a more detailed conversation with them about the specific project. But the architect who is working for the client is the real decision maker – the architect has to be involved at an early stage. The building contractor is also important, but they usually follow what the architect says. So we have a series of meetings with all the parties involved, and if everything goes well, then we can begin to talk about the time schedule for the installation, the price, the warranty, and so on.

**INTERVIEWER**   *How is your job different to the typical idea that we have of a sales consultant?*

**KAM**   Well, your idea of a sales consultant is probably based on B2C, not B2B. In B2B the discussions are more complex and more technical. With the architect we have to talk about our manufacturing process, quality, reliability, and so on. With the contractor we have to talk about ease of installation, delivery and timing. With the final client we have to talk about how lighting creates an identity for their hotel, or their retail space, or their offices – how it helps to create an image.

**INTERVIEWER**   *OK. Can I go back to one or two things you said earlier?*

**KAM**   Yes.

**INTERVIEWER**   *First, about the initial call to the client. That's a 'cold call', in other words the client hasn't asked for it, and most people put down the phone within five seconds. How do you stop that happening?*

**KAM**   The first person you speak to is probably a secretary. Here, there are three things. First, you have to immediately give the impression that this call is about something important. You want the secretary to feel that if she doesn't deal with your call, then she might get into trouble. Then, you have to try to create some kind of feeling or empathy with the person very quickly. And finally you have to get the name of the person inside the company who you really want. Sometimes the secretary will put you through, other times take a message. But you need a name.

**INTERVIEWER**   *And when you finally get through to the right person?*

**KAM**   Our brand name opens doors. Right at the start of the conversation I say the brand name, with some pride in my voice. They are usually prepared to listen because at the end of the day they do need us or one of our competitors – all buildings have to have lighting. Then you have to get right to the point. In B2B people are really busy and they don't like it if you waste their time.

**INTERVIEWER**   *OK, let's get to the stage where you arrive at their offices and meet them in person for the first time. What is important?*

**KAM**   You have to create an immediate sensation of being business-like, but also friendly and positive. Being friendly is important because you're selling to a person, not a company. I bring a nice brochure as well as a promotional DVD to play on my laptop, and I put the brochure on the desk to have something to refer to. Then I play it by ear. Sometimes people want a little more social conversation and relationship building, other times less. I feel it intuitively. But I would say that I nearly always begin by asking them questions, for example about how their business is going. You want to give a message that you are interested in them, and their business, and you want to be a part of their business.

**INTERVIEWER**   *So not so much in the role of a salesman, more as a partner.*

**KAM**   Yes, more as a partner. A good sales person doesn't give the impression they are selling. They are there to listen and then to give their knowledge and to give a service.

**INTERVIEWER**   *And how do you deal with the standard objection that they already work with another lighting company, or another company is offering a better price or whatever?*

**KAM**   You have to believe in your products and talk about them with a passion and commitment. The client will feel this immediately. But you don't get into a conversation about price. If you are saying that your products are the best, then it's a mistake to try to compete on price. The best is never the cheapest. You talk about quality, about innovation, about delivery guarantees, about service levels, and also about other satisfied customers. It's good to have some testimonials – we have them in the brochure.

**INTERVIEWER**   *OK, one final question. Can you tell me if there is any tension inside your company between Sales and Production? For example, you promise the client delivery at a certain time, but then Production says that they can't make the lamps by that time.*

**KAM**   Yes, you call Production and say 'I have this big order and the client needs it in ten days' and Production says it's impossible. So then I go and speak to Production in person and try to persuade them that my order is more important than all the others. In the end you have to use your influencing and persuading skills not just with the client, but inside your own organization as well!

🔘 **Track 21**

## 6 Interview with a marketing director

MD = Marketing director

**INTERVIEWER**   *Today we're going to be talking about the classic marketing mix of the 'four Ps': product, price, place and promotion, but in your case some of the details are very unusual.*

**MD**   That's right.

**INTERVIEWER**   *You'd better begin by explaining the first 'P', the product that you sell.*

**MD**   Sure. I manage the marketing of one particular agricultural chemical used for one particular crop in one particular developing country. Before we formulated this chemical, we first ran a focus group of farmers. We asked them what would be their ideal product in an ideal world.

**INTERVIEWER**   *What did they say?*

**MD**   They said that they wanted a combined product which was both an insecticide and a fungicide. The idea of a combined product was a new concept in the market, and it came directly from the farmers.

**INTERVIEWER**   *OK, good. Now tell us a little bit about your pricing strategy, because I believe it's quite unusual.*

**MD**   Yes. Again, we asked the farmers how they would like to pay in an ideal world. And they said that in an ideal world they would like to pay not with money, but by giving us some of their crops in exchange.

**INTERVIEWER**   *That's like the old days – exchanging one product directly for another, without going through the medium of cash.*

**MD**   Exactly. For the farmers it's a very attractive solution. They are good at producing the crops, but not so good at commercializing them.

**INTERVIEWER**   *OK, but some risk passes to you because you then have to sell the crops. You are a chemical company – selling agricultural products is not your business.*

**MD**   We use commodity traders who sell on the open market – we don't sell ourselves. Here's how it works. We go to the traders and say that we have a forecast of 'X' bags of crops from the farmers for the next season – how much can you pay? The traders give us a price. Notice that it's already better for the farmers because we can use our large volumes to get a better price than they could if they sold individually. Then, after that, we create a price list for the farmers: for example one kilogram of our product for one bag of crops. The farmers decide how much of our product they want, and they sign a contract with us. When the crop is ready, they deliver it to the trader, not to us, and the trader pays us. We never get involved in selling the crops on the market. That risk passes to the trader – but they know their business.

**INTERVIEWER**   *OK. So we've covered product, we've covered price, now please tell us a little bit about place, in other words the distribution channel.*

**MD**   Yes. We have segmentation in the market, according to the size of the farm. We have big, medium and small growers, and we take a different approach with each segment. With the big farmers we use a B2B approach. We have a key account manager inside our company so that the farmer can pick up the phone and talk to one person. The negotiation is just about price. With the medium-size farmers it's different. We send a sales rep to visit their farms, but in fact this kind of sales rep is also an agricultural consultant. The reps have a science background – they are agronomists. The farmers really appreciate this technical support, and our competitors don't offer it. The large-size farmers don't need this technical support because they have their own agronomists working for them.

**INTERVIEWER**   *And the small farmers?*

**MD**   The small farmers don't get technical support. They just order their chemicals directly from a distributor who delivers the product to them. We supply the distributor, and pay them to go round the farms doing the deliveries. The distributor can also go to the medium and large farms, or sometimes we do that directly – for example the sales rep can take the product.

**INTERVIEWER**   *So no money changes hands between the farmers and the distributors.*

**MD**   Exactly. If you remember from before, the farmers pay for their chemicals with bags of crops delivered to the commodity traders. The distributors are paid by us, out of the money that we get from the commodity traders. It's a win-win partnership between us, distributor, farmer and trader.

**INTERVIEWER**   *OK, there's one final 'P' left: promotion. I think that's the most interesting of all.*

**MD**   Yes, in our market the mass media is less important, because farmers don't watch so much TV and anyway there's a lot of competition for TV spots. So we decided to be really innovative. We've made a movie – exactly the same as in the cinema with some big-name stars – and we invite the farmers to come to the cinema to see it. It's a 3D movie. We organize buses to take the farmers to the cinema, and then when they arrive, we give them some popcorn and a beer. You have to remember that these farmers rarely go to the cinema.

**INTERVIEWER**   *And what is the film about? What's the story?*

**MD**   It starts with a flying saucer. It lands in our country and some aliens appear. The local farmers start asking the aliens questions, and the aliens take the farmers to their planet. When they get to the planet, they find that the aliens used to have the same problems with their crops as the farmers are having right now here on Earth.

**INTERVIEWER**   *And of course the aliens have solved their problems by using your products!*

**MD**   Of course! How did you guess? But you should see the aliens' eyes in 3D – it's really amazing!

---

🔘 **Track 22**

## 7 Interview with a finance director

FD = Finance director

**INTERVIEWER**   *I think it would be interesting to know how the finance function is divided up inside a large company. To a non-business person, finance is somehow more mysterious than Sales or Marketing or Production or HR.*

**FD**   Well, I'll do my best. I think my company is quite typical and I can describe how it works. I'm the Finance Director and I have three managers reporting to me, each with a different area of responsibility. The first area is the treasury, the second is accounting, and the third is budgeting and planning.

**INTERVIEWER**   *OK, let's take those one by one.*

**FD**   The Treasurer is responsible for cash and cash flow. He has a small team that are responsible for accounts payable and accounts receivable, so they make payments to suppliers and collect from customers. The Treasurer is also the point of contact inside the company for our banks, and they talk together about our overdraft facility, or alternatively how to get the best interest rate on any spare cash that's available. These days there is also quite a lot of discussion about special financial instruments that the bank can offer.

**INTERVIEWER**   *What kind of instruments?*

**FD**   For example, derivatives to swap variable interest rates into fixed interest rates – that minimizes our risk if we take out a long-term loan.

**INTERVIEWER**   *OK. Next is accounting.*

**FD**   We have a Chief Accounting Officer who's responsible for preparing the accounts, so that's the income statement and cash flow statement on a quarterly and annual basis, and the balance sheet just annually. The most important thing for her is to prepare everything for the annual report, which we have a statutory duty to provide because we're a public company. The accounting team also prepares the invoices to send to customers, and processes the invoices that we receive from suppliers.

**INTERVIEWER**   *Right. And the third area?*

**FD**   Finally we have a Financial Controller who's responsible for internal auditing, budgeting and financial planning. This person receives all the key indicators relating to costs, income, profitability, efficiency, etc from Production, Purchasing and Sales – and using these figures he prepares a weekly report for other managers throughout the company.

**INTERVIEWER**   *By 'budgeting' do you mean setting the budget, or looking at how the budget is used?*

**FD**   I mean the latter – the control aspect of budgeting. So, looking at the variance between the planned budget and the actual budget for all the costs of the company. The first type of budgeting – deciding how much money each department needs and can spend in the future – is done by all the managers together as part of the wider business plan. That's an annual process and it has to relate to the overall strategy of the company.

**INTERVIEWER**   *So the Financial Controller is the person who really understands what is happening in the company day by day.*

**FD**   Yes, if an activity is going over budget we need to know immediately. We have to take action to rectify the situation.

**INTERVIEWER**   *Right. Can I just go back to something? You said that the treasury was responsible for accounts payable and accounts receivable, but the accounts department was responsible for invoicing. That seems strange because in my mind I associate accounts receivable with invoicing.*

**FD**   Well, invoicing is a purely administrative process – invoices are generated automatically by our IT system. Invoicing is important for keeping the books, just like purchases and orders, and so these things come under the control of the accounts office. But accounts receivable is a more human and managerial process – a credit controller might need to telephone a customer about an outstanding bill, send them a reminder, deal with bad debts, and so on. It's the flow of cash into the company, and so it comes under the treasury. It's not just an administrative thing.

**INTERVIEWER** *OK, so that's the three areas. Now what about you – the Finance Director. Do you have any specific responsibilities that are not covered by the three people under you?*

**FD** Yes, good question. Besides managing these three people and taking any important financial issues to the senior management team, I also have responsibility for corporate governance. So I'm the one who calls the shareholders' meetings and takes the minutes of those meetings, and I'm the one who works closely with the external auditors. And if there's a very big project to be financed, then I'll speak to the banks rather than the Treasurer.

**INTERVIEWER** *Great. I think the only thing you haven't mentioned so far is tax and tax planning.*

**FD** The Chief Accounting Officer has to prepare the tax returns, and so naturally that person is very involved in tax planning. But this is a complex area and we often use external consultants to help us, and in that case I would get involved as well.

**INTERVIEWER** *And my final question is this: what is the one thing that would make your life easier and allow you to be more effective in your job?*

**FD** That's easy. All financial directors suffer from information overload. Every day and every week we see columns and columns of figures, with lots of indicators, and buried deep within those columns there are some small pieces of information that are important. But this information can be very difficult to spot. The challenge is to reduce the amount of information coming in to us, to filter out the background noise, so that we see just a summary and we can focus on the real problems and the bigger picture.

🌐 **Track 23**

## 8 Interview with a human resources director

HRD = Human resources director

**INTERVIEWER** *I know that you work in Human Resources in a local office of a large American food company.*

**HRD** That's right.

**INTERVIEWER** *Can you tell me a little about the HR function in your company?*

**HRD** Yes. There are about 200 people in our office in total, and of those, there are four of us in HR. Each person has their own responsibilities. So there is one person for compensation and benefits, one person in charge of training, one junior person for administration, and then me – I'm the HR director. I focus especially on recruitment – I have to develop and implement all the procedures, policies and initiatives.

**INTERVIEWER** *Do those policies come from head office in the US?*

**HRD** Yes, most of them. We have to introduce them locally, sometimes adapting them, according to our laws.

**INTERVIEWER** *Can you give me an example of one policy or procedure which came from head office and which was difficult to adapt to your local situation?*

**HRD** For instance in our country it's very difficult to dismiss someone. Now my company is very fair, but it's also very strict with poor performers. In the US there are targets to meet and objectives to achieve for all employees, and if you are a poor performer you can stay in the company for maybe two years, but no more. In my country things don't work like that. Our laws don't allow us to dismiss someone for poor performance alone.

**INTERVIEWER** *Are there any other examples?*

**HRD** Another example is equal opportunities. Head office has asked me to develop a diversity strategy – that's very important in the States – and we are focusing first on gender, and then on age. We don't traditionally think about investing in older people – it even sounds like a strange phrase. But Europe has an aging population and we will need more older people inside companies.

**INTERVIEWER** *What are you doing in relation to gender? How are you trying to attract and retain women in your organization?*

**HRD** We offer flexible hours, part-time working for mothers returning to work, a free kindergarten – that kind of thing.

**INTERVIEWER** *A kindergarten is an important decision. With childcare there's a financial cost – you have to set up a special room, organize food every day, find and pay a qualified person to run it …*

**HRD** We tried to set up a kindergarten last year, with the backing of head office. The first problem was that we only have a few women here with babies of the right age to use it, and then there is the problem of our location. We're half an hour's drive outside the city centre and the mothers had to bring the babies here and take them back again, with the babies crying in the back seat of the car in the rush hour. It was very difficult.

**INTERVIEWER** *Practical problems.*

**HRD** Yes, so I have to be honest and say that the women preferred to leave their children at home – in our culture the grandmother often looks after the child during the day. But what the mothers are much more interested in is work-life balance – having more time working out of the office.

**INTERVIEWER** *And what is your policy there?*

**HRD** We encourage mothers to work from home one day a week, and we also have a contract where they can work slightly fewer hours for slightly less money, but they can go home early and pick up the children from school. That's very popular. In fact we find that these women manage their time very well, and do more or less the same amount of work as everyone else.

**INTERVIEWER** *OK, before we finish, can we come back to that issue of performance culture you mentioned earlier? You said that people can't be dismissed for poor performance, so how do you manage performance?*

**HRD** Two ways. First, compensation is based on a three-way formula. There's a fixed part to the salary, the biggest part, but then there is also a part that depends on company performance, and a part that depends on individual performance. So we motivate people through pay. The other way to manage performance is through our appraisal process. Every year the line manager meets with the employee to review their performance, and the outcome of that meeting is an individual development plan.

**INTERVIEWER** *Involving coaching and training?*

**HRD** Yes, the big thing right now is influencing skills. The aim is to help people in their everyday working relationships. You know we have to work in a high-pressure, modern business environment, to have contact with people in other departments, to work in cross-functional teams, and much more. In order to do all this we have to influence other people all the time, to obtain their help and their agreement.

**INTERVIEWER** *But can this be trained? I'm very dubious. Surely it just comes from inside the person, or it's something that develops with life experience. Can you actually increase someone's influencing skills by sending them on a course?*

**HRD** In my opinion, yes. Particularly through roleplay, and also analyzing case studies of what someone did in a particular situation in terms of their behaviour, and why they got or didn't get the result they wanted. You have to invite people to reflect on these things. I think it can make a difference.

# Answer key

## 1 The economy

### Exercise 1.1
1 drives    2 deregulation    3 subsidies    4 quotas    5 tariffs
6 constrained    7 liquidity    8 bubbles    9 underlying
10 differentials    11 prosperity    12 literacy

### Exercise 1.2
1 consumer spending    2 free movement of capital
3 growth and contraction    4 life expectancy    5 open borders
6 standard of living    7 environmental damage
8 goods and services    9 interest rates    10 cheap credit
11 social mobility    12 underlying strength

### Exercise 1.3
1 consumer spending    2 cheap credit    3 standard of living
4 growth and contraction    5 interest rates    6 underlying strength

### Exercise 1.4
1 on the verge of stalling    2 slump    3 boosting    4 the Fed
5 roughly

## 2 The business cycle

### Exercise 2.1
a 1 an upturn    2 expansion    3 a downturn    4 contraction
b 1 recovers    2 peaks    3 turns down    4 bottoms

### Exercise 2.2
1 b    2 d    3 c    4 a    5 e    6 h    7 f    8 g    9 j    10 i

### Exercise 2.3
1 low / picks up    2 end / turning down    3 bond / fixed
4 more expensive / cools    5 contract / recession    6 anticipate
7 before    8 bull / bullish

### Exercise 2.4
1 policy makers    2 new borrowing    3 side-effects    4 tax cuts
5 government debt    6 labour market

## 3 International trade

### Exercise 3.1
1 economies of scale    2 on your behalf    3 warranty
4 warehouse    5 expertise    6 trademark    7 fee    8 royalty
9 invoice    10 bill of lading

### Exercise 3.2
1 take advantage of any under-used capacity
2 rely on just your domestic market
3 spread the risk
4 act on somebody's behalf
5 establish a presence in a foreign market
6 keep your own legal identity
7 handle the exchange of documents
8 pay according to the terms of the contract

### Exercise 3.3
1 Cash-in-advance    2 Letter of credit    3 Documentary collection
4 Open account    5 Consignment purchase

### Exercise 3.4
1 customs    2 handling    3 premises    4 truck    5 loading
6 freight    7 documentation    8 transit    9 terminal
10 clearance

## 4 Setting up and growing a business

### Exercise 4.1
1 edge    2 backers    3 collateral    4 legal entity    5 invoices
6 piling up    7 turnover    8 a going concern    9 acquisitions
10 thoroughly    11 sticking with    12 false economy
13 neighbourhood    14 seed money    15 loyalty    16 complacency

### Exercise 4.2
1 achieve a critical mass    2 wait for invoices to be paid
3 grow or shrink year by year    4 employ more staff
5 spot a gap in the market    6 take on the risk of the business failing
7 bring in a huge amount of money    8 enter a growth phase
9 extend a line of credit    10 go public
11 grow organically or by acquisitions
12 sell the business as a going concern

### Exercise 4.3
1 overexpand    2 undercut    3 underperform    4 overtake
5 overspend    6 undercharge    7 override    8 underestimate

### Exercise 4.4
1 outlet    2 fee    3 fulfill    4 standards    5 running

## 5 Company types and corporate governance

### Exercise 5.1
1 debt / liabilities    2 owner / proprietor    3 share / divide
4 shareholder / stockholder / stakeholder    5 a dividend / profits

### Exercise 5.2
entity

### Exercise 5.3
1 fully    2 legally    3 personally    4 potentially    5 hold
6 trade

### Exercise 5.4
1 oversee    2 auditors    3 dividend    4 stake    5 integrity
6 transparency

### Exercise 5.5
1 limited liability    2 detailed legislation    3 legal entity
4 non-profit organization

### Exercise 5.6
1 Chief Executive Officer    2 Annual General Meeting
3 Public Limited Company    4 Limited Liability Company

## 6 Global issues for the 21st century

### Exercise 6.1
1 geopolitical influence    2 climate change    3 global warming
4 sustainable growth    5 peak oil    6 green activists
7 major battlefield    8 living standards    9 pricing power
10 declining birthrate    11 knowledge worker
12 environmental impact

### Exercise 6.2
1 be short of resources    2 be hungry for resources
3 be in short supply    4 have a common Asian currency
5 price oil in dollars    6 accuse someone of hypocrisy
7 in the coming decades    8 for the foreseeable future
9 hold a virtual meeting    10 have access to world markets

### Exercise 6.3
1 value-for-money    2 loyalty    3 creatives    4 retain    5 gender
6 sustainable    7 backlash    8 sourcing

### Exercise 6.4
1 warming / destruction / threatening
2 activists / influential / environmental
3 engineering / controversial / growth / production
4 economic / industrialization / strengths / weaknesses

### Exercise 6.5
1 standards    2 principles    3 poverty    4 access    5 gender
6 premium    7 subsidy    8 overproduction

## 7 Management styles and qualities

**Exercise 7.1**
1 authoritarian   2 demanding   3 consensual   4 coaching
5 mentoring   6 liaison   7 hierarchical   8 proactive
9 conscientious   10 thorough   11 determined   12 setback

**Exercise 7.2**
1 bureaucratic   2 decentralized   3 unco-operative / unhelpful
4 uncoordinated   5 indirect   6 inflexible / rigid   7 hands-on
8 dishonest   9 rational   10 careless   11 disorganized / messy
12 relaxed / calm   13 unsupportive   14 bottom-up   15 unclear

**Exercise 7.3**
1 stressed   2 inflexible   3 hands-on   4 messy   5 bureaucratic
6 transparent

**Exercise 7.4**
1 lack vision and fail to show leadership   2 know where you stand
3 work on your own and be self-motivated   4 take the initiative
5 keep up to date with developments in the field   6 give feedback in
an appropriate way   7 recover quickly after a setback   8 translate
general strategy into specific objectives

**Exercise 7.5**
1 issuing   2 guiding   3 progress   4 running   5 carry out
6 breathing   7 report back   8 feedback

## 8 Organizing time and work

**Exercise 8.1**
1 ahead / workflow / chart / stickers / guidelines / prioritize /
challenges / face / meet / stimulating / rewarding / sense / achievement
2 workload / paperwork / time-consuming / behind / deadline /
stressed out / short-cuts / circumstances beyond / frame / quick / dirty

**Exercise 8.2**
1 spend   2 find   3 run out of   4 allow   5 put in   6 waste
7 save   8 make up

**Exercise 8.3**
1 budget   2 competencies

**Exercise 8.4**
1 constraints   2 tackle   3 brief   4 be in the loop   5 snag
6 figuring out

**Exercise 8.5**
It should be 'the person responsible'

## 9 Planning and setting objectives

**Exercise 9.1**
1 stakeholders   2 contingency plan   3 assumptions
4 trends   5 legislation   6 highlights   7 plant   8 targets
9 going forward   10 forecast

**Exercise 9.2**
1 implement   2 achieve   3 meet   4 make   5 reach
6 set up

**Exercise 9.3**
target: 1b   plan: 3a   issue: 2c

**Exercise 9.4**
1 exceed / initial   2 fall short of / annual   3 implement / three-year
4 shelve / long-term   5 raised / complex

**Exercise 9.5**
objective: 2a   schedule: 1c   budget: 3b

**Exercise 9.6**
1 set / overall   2 stick to / tight   3 submit / draft

## 10 Leading and motivating

**Exercise 10.1**
1 from scratch   2 the big picture   3 role   4 empathy
5 intuition   6 empowering   7 trustworthy   8 outcomes

**Exercise 10.2**
praise

**Exercise 10.3**
2 ✓

**Exercise 10.4**
1 positive feedback from your boss   2 negative experiences with
colleagues   3 sense of achievement   4 lack of recognition
5 company politics   6 physical environment   7 task-oriented
business world   8 financial reward

**Exercise 10.5**
1 a) leading b) leader c) leadership
2 a) motivating b) demotivated
3 a) managing b) unmanageable
4 a) satisfaction b) unsatisfactory
5 a) analytical b) analysis

**Exercise 10.6**
1 achieve   2 assertiveness   3 acknowledged   4 buzz   5 moan

## 11 Insurance and risk management

**Exercise 11.1**
1 prudent   2 liability   3 sue   4 indemnity   5 vandalism
6 awards damages   7 exclusion clauses   8 renewal notice
9 pay out   10 compensation   11 bad debt   12 compliance

**Exercise 11.2**
1 be legally obliged to do something.   2 try to prove negligence
3 award damages   4 be liable for the difference
5 take out an insurance policy   6 take on too much risk
7 be sent a renewal notice   8 check the small print

**Exercise 11.3**
1 dispute   2 reject   3 potential   4 avoid   5 minimize

**Exercise 11.4**
1 on   2 for   3 take out   4 against / up to   5 for
6 on   7 made / for   8 to / from   9 at / of being
10 court / rightful

**Exercise 11.5**
1 exposure to risk   2 risk assessments   3 contingency plan
4 escalation procedure   5 remedial action   6 damage limitation

## 12 Manufacturing and engineering

**Exercise 12.1**
1 raw materials   2 rust   3 blue-collar   4 unions   5 outdated
6 inventory   7 scope   8 breakdown   9 dams   10 devices
11 disposal   12 embedded

**Exercise 12.2**
1 mass production   2 well-paid job   3 heavy industry
4 core concepts   5 continuous improvement   6 wide scope
7 residential buildings   8 consistent quality

**Exercise 12.3**
1 machinery / equipment   2 process / procedure
3 waste / pollution

**Exercise 12.4**
analyze / examine / go over
construct / assemble / put together
determine / establish / find out
implement / put into operation / carry out
monitor / supervise / keep an eye on
eliminate / remove / get rid of
evaluate / assess / weigh up
manage / run / be in charge of
repair / fix / put back into working order
simulate / replicate / model
*The verbs in the third column are more informal.*

**Exercise 12.5**
1 mould   2 reliability   3 sum   4 upgrade   5 workforce
6 up and running   7 economies of scale   8 risk

## 13 Inside a factory

### Exercise 13.1
1 plant   2 fitters   3 -wise   4 shift   5 discrepancies   6 facility
7 tailored   8 throughput   9 rolling off   10 idle   11 wear and tear   12 downtime

### Exercise 13.2
1 long   2 wide   3 high   4 length   5 width   6 height
7 cross-section   8 square   9 weighs   10 rounded up

### Exercise 13.3
1 run out   2 snap off   3 burst   4 work loose   5 be jammed
6 seize up

## 14 Procurement and purchasing

### Exercise 14.1
1 quotation   2 track record   3 trials   4 delivery   5 backhander
6 collusion   7 tendering   8 invoices   9 back-office
10 undertake   11 synergy   12 drawbacks

### Exercise 14.2
1 quotation / quote   2 estimate   3 proposal   4 tender

### Exercise 14.3
procurement = sourcing + purchasing

### Exercise 14.4
1 offshore   2 onshore   3 nearshore

### Exercise 14.5
1 1st group (supplier) give / prepare / provide / submit
   2nd group (customer) ask for / get / accept
2 1st group (supplier) draw up / make / put forward / outline / submit
   2nd group (customer) accept / consider / reject
3 1st group (supplier) bid for / submit / put in / win
   2nd group (customer) invite / put something out to / announce / award
4 1st group key / large / leading / major / principal
   2nd group external / foreign / outside / overseas / offshore
5 1st group lengthy / protracted / prolonged
   2nd group unsuccessful / fruitless / unproductive

## 15 Supply chain management and logistics

### Exercise 15.1
1 upstream   2 downstream   3 batches   4 warehouses
5 distribution centres   6 third party logistics providers   7 flag up
8 bottlenecks   9 inbound   10 merchandise   11 unloading
12 hub and spoke   13 pallets   14 fork-lift trucks   15 track
16 stacked up   17 trailers   18 pick-and-pack

### Exercise 15.2
1 cargo   2 freight

### Exercise 15.3
1 supply chain   2 finished goods   3 final customer
4 logistics provider   5 distribution channel   6 forwarding agent

### Exercise 15.4
1 Ensuring   2 forecasting   3 handling   4 balancing   5 Linking
6 Selecting   7 Negotiating   8 Warehousing

## 16 Lean production

### Exercise 16.1
1 idle time   2 flow   3 defects   4 rework   5 error-proofing
6 delivered   7 lead time   8 manpower   9 incremental
10 shine   11 tools   12 storage boxes

### Exercise 16.2
1 add value   2 be willing to pay for something   3 deliver parts
4 eliminate waste   5 make sure something doesn't happen again
6 perform a task   7 attach a kanban card to an item
8 clean up the equipment so that it shines   9 error-proof a system
10 handle materials   11 minimize inventory
12 optimize the flow of materials

### Exercise 16.3
1 industrial / economy / productive   2 analysis / improvements
3 wasteful / exceeded   4 delivery / assembly

### Exercise 16.4
1 bottleneck   2 shape   3 straight   4 sub-assemblies
5 synchronization   6 branch   7 customized

## 17 Quality

### Exercise 17.1
1 features   2 durability   3 conformance to requirements
4 sampling   5 spot checks   6 waste   7 framework
8 results orientation   9 fad   10 cycle times
11 design-for-manufacture   12 supplier capability surveys
13 scrap   14 product recalls

### Exercise 17.2
1 outstanding   2 variable   3 inferior   4 poor   5 ensure
6 enhance   7 specify   8 monitor

### Exercise 17.3
1 random sampling   2 spot checks   3 zero defects
4 right first time   5 results orientation   6 continuous improvement
7 employee involvement   8 cycle time   9 warranty claims
10 product recalls

### Exercise 17.4
1 performance / best in class   2 parameter / vary from the norm
3 compliance / certified   4 mark / spoils the appearance
5 methodology / eliminating defects   6 measures / throughout business   7 predict / fewer mistakes   8 warranty claims / improve quality

## 18 Sales

### Exercise 18.1
1 fancy   2 tailor-made   3 rapport   4 competitive advantage
5 script   6 jargon   7 knocking   8 acknowledge

### Exercise 18.2
1 a   2 f   3 c   4 g   5 e   6 d   7 h   8 b

### Exercise 18.3
1 d   2 c   3 a   4 b   5 e   6 g   7 f

### Exercise 18.4
1 go ahead   2 up and running   3 knock   4 latest   5 on sale
6 for sale   7 volumes   8 accounts for

## 19 Customer service

### Exercise 19.1
1 logged   2 refer upwards   3 commitments
4 bulk purchase   5 flyer

### Exercise 19.2
1 follow up a purchase with a quick call   2 provide a flyer inside every package   3 be passed from person to person
4 make specific commitments   5 include a life-time guarantee
6 log details on a CRM system   7 resist the urge to argue
8 acknowledge any inconvenience caused

### Exercise 19.3
1 an initial enquiry   2 information   3 a quotation
4 the quotation   5 an order   6 the order   7 an invoice (with the goods)   8 the payment   9 a complaint   10 the problem

### Exercise 19.4
1 body posture   2 channel of communication   3 common ground
4 on-screen information   5 preferred customers
6 pre-sales enquiry   7 bulk purchase discount
8 money-back guarantee   9 satisfaction survey   10 warranty claim

### Exercise 19.5
1 warranty / guarantee   2 Frequently Asked Questions
3 run-around

### Exercise 19.6
1 satisfaction   2 loyalty   3 feedback   4 survey   5 experience
6 expectations   7 profile   8 requirements

## 20 Markets and marketing

**Exercise 20.1**
1 segments   2 gender   3 peers   4 purchasing
5 patterns of demand   6 reps   7 target   8 feasible
9 price points   10 niche market   11 catalyst   12 features
13 label   14 elasticity of demand

**Exercise 20.2**
1 marketing   2 promotion   3 advertising   4 publicity

**Exercise 20.3**
*market* forces / leader / price / sector / share
*marketing* agency / campaign / mix / strategy / tool

**Exercise 20.4**
1 market forces   2 marketing mix   3 market share
4 marketing tool

**Exercise 20.5**
1 e   2 b   3 c   4 h   5 g   6 a   7 d   8 f

**Exercise 20.6**
*break into*: enter / open up / penetrate
*take over*: capture / corner / dominate
*be forced out of*: be driven out of / withdraw from

## 21 Product

**Exercise 21.1**
1 complimentary   2 enhanced   3 catchy   4 switch

**Exercise 21.2**
1 image   2 manager   3 leader   4 loyalty   5 equity
6 stretching   7 association   8 awareness

**Exercise 21.3**
1 brand awareness   2 brand stretching

**Exercise 21.4**
1 exclusive / luxury / upmarket / upscale
2 economy / value-for-money   3 traditional
4 best-selling / favourite / leading   5 well-known

**Exercise 21.5**
1 innovative   2 fully automatic   3 built-in   4 portable
5 compact   6 rechargeable   7 well-made   8 state-of-the-art
9 integrated   10 adjustable   11 easy to clean   12 optional
13 energy-efficient   14 economical   15 recycled
16 environmentally friendly   17 reliable   18 available in a range
19 high-performance   20 waterproof   21 high-tech
22 shock-absorbent   23 hard-wearing   24 standard   25 stylish
26 limited   27 user-friendly   28 long-lasting
29 expandable   30 one-touch

**Exercise 21.6**
1 d   2 c   3 b   4 a

## 22 Distribution (place)

**Exercise 22.1**
1 fee   2 retail outlets   3 mass coverage   4 settle for   5 layout
6 decor   7 keeping pace with   8 drives down

**Exercise 22.2**
1 convenience store   2 corner shop   3 E-tailer   4 speciality store
5 supermarket   6 department store   7 cash and carry
8 franchise

**Exercise 22.3**
1 mark-up   2 margin

**Exercise 22.4**
1 signage   2 tag   3 merchandise   4 garment   5 device
6 checkout   7 furnishings   8 mix and match

## 23 Promotion

**Exercise 23.1**
1 billboards   2 sponsorship   3 coverage   4 press kit   5 stunts
6 goodwill   7 philanthropy   8 convergence   9 tracking
10 GPS

**Exercise 23.2**
1 build awareness of a new product   2 stimulate demand by
offering a free trial   3 take an initial concept through to the final
advertisement   4 place an ad in the media   5 issue a news release
6 keep in contact with customers   7 monitor how consumers
respond to advertisements   8 push targeted ads to a mobile device

**Exercise 23.3**
1 placed / published / put / ran / took out   2 carried / published / ran

**Exercise 23.4**
1 contest   2 coupon   3 discount   4 free sample   5 free trial
6 free product   7 loyalty program   8 personal appearance
9 trade-in

**Exercise 23.5**
1 advertising   2 sales promotions   3 PR   4 personal selling

## 24 Price

**Exercise 24.1**
1 adjustable   2 revenue   3 miss out on   4 covers
5 gain a hold   6 consistency   7 trick   8 charge a premium
9 markup   10 round number   11 bundle   12 incentives

**Exercise 24.2**
1 lose sales and market share   2 take several factors into
consideration   3 require a minimum return on your investment
4 cover the costs with sales revenue   5 gain a hold in a new market
6 position yourself at the high end of the market   7 set the final
price that the end user pays   8 sell below cost to attract customer
traffic

**Exercise 24.3**
1 prompt   2 scale / passed on   3 channel   4 slack / sales

**Exercise 24.4**
increase / raise / put up
lower / cut / bring down
set / establish / determine
negotiate / arrive at / settle on
calculate / figure out / work out

**Exercise 24.5**
1 high / excessive / exorbitant / inflated   2 low / bargain / budget
/ reduced   3 good / attractive / fair / reasonable   4 retail / list /
recommended / selling

**Exercise 24.6**
1 set   2 held down   3 were forced to raise
4 received complaints about   5 matched   6 undercut
7 re-thought   8 drop   9 freeze   10 agreed to

## 25 Marketing management

**Exercise 25.1**
1 core competencies   2 threats   3 survey   4 questionnaire
5 qualitative   6 focus groups   7 competitive advantages
8 screening   9 breakeven point   10 beta testing   11 prototype
12 allocate

**Exercise 25.2**
1 cost structure   2 product line   3 core competencies
4 bargaining power   5 quantitative research   6 focus group
7 customer base   8 competitive advantage
9 concept development   10 breakeven point   11 beta test
12 technical implementation

**Exercise 25.3**
1 competitive advantage   2 bargaining power
3 core competencies   4 concept development
5 focus group   6 technical implementation

**Exercise 25.4**

1 look towards    2 gain    3 treat with    4 carry out
5 particular    6 large

**Exercise 25.5**

1 design    2 manufacture    3 launch    4 sell    5 upgrade
6 discontinue

**Exercise 25.6**

1 suggest the need for    2 put money into    3 carry out
4 see the limitations of    5 cut back on    6 abandon

## 26 Income statement

**Exercise 26.1**

1 revenue    2 profit    3 the indirect costs of selling a product and
running the office    4 in different places    5 amortization    6 gross

**Exercise 26.2**

1 Cost of goods sold    2 EBIT    3 Income taxes    4 Dividends

**Exercise 26.3**

1 fiscal    2 tangible assets    3 interplay

**Exercise 26.4**

1 invest    2 boost    3 guarantee    4 offset    5 satisfactory
6 interim

**Exercise 26.5**

1 record / legitimate    2 extraordinary / exceptional
3 red / bankrupt / liquidation    4 writes off    5 adverse    6 accrual

## 27 Balance sheet

**Exercise 27.1**

1 own    2 owe

**Exercise 27.2**

1 debt    2 bonds    3 goodwill    4 set aside    5 mortgage
6 pay off

**Exercise 27.3**

1 into    2 by    3 to    4 in    5 for    6 back    7 through
8 on    9 out of    10 Over

**Exercise 27.4**

accounts payable

**Exercise 27.5**

*have*: hold / own / possess
*buy*: accumulate / acquire / build up
*sell*: dispose of / realize

**Exercise 27.6**

*collect*: build up / incur / run up
*pay back*: clear / honour / pay off / repay / service / settle

**Exercise 27.7**

1 tied up    2 defaults

**Exercise 27.8**

1 patent    2 copyright    3 trademark

## 28 Cash flow statement

**Exercise 28.1**

1 plant    2 issuing    3 sums    4 deducted    5 outstanding
6 capital

**Exercise 28.2**

1 26,960    2 10,500    3 9,560    4 940    5 27,900

**Exercise 28.3**

1 F    2 T (labour and salaries)    3 T (it's paid in January at the
start of the business, and then again in February)    4 F (the first
utilities payment is in February, but the business was almost certainly
using utilities from the start)    5 T    6 F (the negative cash flow
is due to buying the inventory that the business needs to start
trading)    7 T    8 F (the entry is made for the month when the cash
is actually received, ie February)    9 F    10 T

**Exercise 28.4**

1 record something as an expense    2 pay off a credit account in full
3 apply the same logic    4 raise capital by issuing new shares
5 present information in a certain way    6 subtract one figure from
another    7 buy back shares from the market    8 borrow money
from the bank

**Exercise 28.5**

1 on    2 in    3 as    4 on    5 by

## 29 Managing cash flow

**Exercise 29.1**

1 reassured    2 overdraft    3 persistent
4 fixed costs    5 shortfall

**Exercise 29.2**

2

**Exercise 29.3**

1 have a healthy cash flow    2 be a well-established company
3 have daily operating expenses    4 be managed on a day-to-day
basis    5 take advantage of a line of credit    6 see something from
a strict accounting viewpoint    7 make an initial deposit
8 run credit checks    9 have heavily discounted offers
10 have persistent slow-paying customers    11 negotiate extended
credit terms    12 give an early payment discount

**Exercise 29.4**

be short of / run out of, in advance / up front, inflows / receipts,
infusion / injection, generate / raise, holdings / reserves, loose / spare,
needs / requirements, payment (in full) / settlement, shortage / shortfall

**Exercise 29.5**

1 turnover    2 delivery    3 overdraft    4 limit    5 outstanding
6 clear    7 squeeze    8 fulfil

## 30 Profitability

**Exercise 30.1**

1 120    2 €200,000    3 20% / 100%    4 operating leverage

**Exercise 30.2**

1 A (advertising is a fixed cost – see the text opposite)
2 B (materials is a variable cost)

**Exercise 30.3**

1 fewer    2 more

**Exercise 30.4**

1 B    2 C    3 A

## 31 Financial markets

**Exercise 31.1**

1 founders    2 bonds    3 exchange rate    4 speculators
5 volatility    6 underlying    7 on behalf of    8 policyholders
9 pool    10 venture capital    11 buy-outs    12 budgetary surplus

**Exercise 31.2**

bear / depressed / falling / weak
booming / bull / healthy / rising / strong
good / profitable / secure / sound / worthwhile
high-risk / risky / speculative

**Exercise 31.3**

1 go public with an IPO    2 list shares on a stock market
3 raise capital by issuing bonds    4 pay back a loan with interest
5 fund short-term debt with 'commercial paper'    6 manipulate
the exchange rate    7 chase short-term trends in the market
8 buy shares on behalf of a client    9 support a start-up with venture
capital    10 take over a company, then restructure it

**Exercise 31.4**

1 pegs    2 props up    3 floats    4 appreciates    5 depreciates

**Exercise 31.5**

1 crude oil, natural gas    2 cocoa, cotton    3 wheat, soybeans
4 cattle, hogs    5 copper, iron ore

**Exercise 31.6**

1 Leverage    2 downside risk    3 Hedging    4 commodity
contracts

## 32 Investing in stocks

**Exercise 32.1**
1 capital gain   2 index   3 benchmark   4 outperforming
5 diversified portfolio   6 picks   7 SWOT   8 pipeline
9 prospects   10 barriers to entry   11 support
12 trading channels   13 sentiment   14 seasonality

**Exercise 32.2**
1 make a dividend payment   2 quote a bid / offer spread
3 have a diversified portfolio   4 past performance   5 risk profile
6 growth prospects   7 chart patterns   8 investor sentiment

**Exercise 32.3**
1 metrics   2 earnings   3 bluff your way   4 profitability
5 overpriced   6 share price   7 assets   8 capital gain

## 33 Recruitment

**Exercise 33.1**
1 skillset   2 premises   3 allocate   4 qualifications
5 headhunting   6 new recruits   7 covers up (for)
8 looking through   9 template   10 rapport   11 rate
12 vacancy

**Exercise 33.2**
1 be on a permanent contract   2 recruit temps through an agency
3 work off the premises as a freelancer   4 allocate work in a
different way   5 start looking elsewhere for a job   6 ask
open-ended questions   7 focus on achievements rather than skills
8 keep an interview on track   9 do some background checks
10 draw up a shortlist of candidates

**Exercise 33.3**
employ / appoint / hire / recruit / take on
dismiss / fire / lay off / make redundant / terminate
hand in your notice / quit / resign / stand down

**Exercise 33.4**
dismiss / fire

**Exercise 33.5**
1 an applicant / a candidate   2 classified ad / display ad
3 highlight / outline

**Exercise 33.6**
1 submit   2 carry out   3 succeed in   4 be faced with
5 thankless   6 contract   7 policy   8 mindset

**Exercise 33.7**
considerable / extensive, direct / first-hand, relevant / appropriate,
practical / hands-on, previous / prior, limited / little

**Exercise 33.8**
boring / dead-end, challenging / demanding, decent / worthwhile,
ideal / dream, manual / blue-collar, regular / steady

## 34 Pay and benefits

**Exercise 34.1**
1 white-collar jobs   2 retain   3 increments   4 pros and cons
5 pulling their weight   6 resent   7 undermining   8 compliance
9 mandatory   10 discrimination   11 disability   12 fringe benefits

**Exercise 34.2**
1 compensation package   2 bargaining power
3 incentive scheme   4 life insurance   5 minimum wage
6 maternity leave   7 pension plan   8 end-of-year bonus

**Exercise 34.3**
1 retirement   2 life insurance   3 pension

**Exercise 34.4**
1 wage   2 salary   3 income   4 remuneration   5 overtime
6 commission   7 royalty   8 bonus   9 weighting   10 perk

**Exercise 34.5**
1 incentive   2 benefit   3 reward

**Exercise 34.6**
1 on / of   2 under   3 over   4 into   5 for

## 35 Issues in the workplace

**Exercise 35.1**
1 union   2 enforce   3 leave   4 norm   5 statutory
6 hygiene   7 cut corners   8 harrassment   9 bullying
10 compensation award   11 grievance   12 address   13 appeal
14 diversity   15 precedent   16 whistle-blowing

**Exercise 35.2**
1 become the norm   2 sort something out informally
3 involve a union representative   4 create a precedent
5 be clear in principle   6 appeal against a decision
7 give warnings to an employee   8 promote diversity
9 address and resolve a grievance   10 enforce the rules strictly

**Exercise 35.3**
1 grievance procedures   2 work-life balance   3 health and safety
4 legal requirements   5 equal opportunities   6 gross misconduct

**Exercise 35.4**
1 statutory   2 legislation   3 regulations   4 complaint / claim
5 incident / accident

**Exercise 35.5**
1 cause for concern   2 alleged breach of discipline
3 mitigating circumstances   4 redeployment   5 suspend
6 hearing

## 36 Your background and career

**Exercise 36.1**
1 grades   2 extracurricular activities   3 dropped out
4 grant   5 degree   6 intern   7 vocational   8 staying on
9 graduating   10 hectic   11 burnt out   12 gave in my notice
13 backpacked   14 settle down   15 vacancy

**Exercise 36.2**
1 get a place at university   2 drop out after a few months
3 work your way through college   4 spend a year as an intern
5 be short-listed for a job   6 be promoted to Senior Analyst
7 register with an online agency
8 find a vacancy almost immediately

**Exercise 36.3**
4 ✓

**Exercise 36.4**
1 make / concentrate on   2 break / take off   3 move / be over
4 promising / ladder   5 chosen / opportunities

**Exercise 36.5**
1 was working   2 had just finished   3 was writing   4 got
5 was   6 hadn't contacted   7 waited   8 was listening
9 called   10 were waiting   11 had already found out
12 wanted

## 37 Your company

**Exercise 37.1**
1 milestones   2 restructuring   3 market capitalization
4 subsidiaries   5 overview   6 competitive advantages   7 tailored
8 overall   9 shrinking   10 product pipeline   11 morale
12 commitment   13 market saturation   14 shortage

**Exercise 37.2**
1 market share   2 product range   3 a standard product
4 social trends   5 R&D   6 SWOT analysis   7 distribution network
8 cost advantages   9 substitute products   10 annual turnover

**Exercise 37.3**
1 business model   2 affordable   3 founder   4 industry standard
5 state-of-the-art   6 consumer tastes   7 prime locations
8 turnover   9 income   10 continued expansion

## 38 Your job

**Exercise 38.1**
1 track record   2 draws up   3 oversee   4 sign off   5 liaise
6 number crunching

**Exercise 38.2**
1 challenging / demanding   2 my boss / my line manager
3 colleague / coworker   4 opposite number / counterpart

**Exercise 38.3**
1 b   2 c   3 a

**Exercise 38.4**
1 make initial contact with a client   2 take a back seat for a while
3 oversee the whole process   4 handle incoming calls
5 keep on top of the filing   6 be on first-name terms

**Exercise 38.5**
1 for   2 in   3 in   4 for   5 to   6 at   7 with   8 to
9 in   10 with   11 of   12 on   13 on / from home
14 out of work / off work   15 work / get to / at   16 checking

**Exercise 38.6**
1 ✓   2 ✗   3 ✓   4 ✗   5 ✓

## 39 Telephoning – making and taking calls

**Exercise 39.1**
1 this / speaking   2 nice / hear   3 good / time / middle
4 close / down   5 reason / because   6 thought / might
7 get / back / to   8 leave / with   9 appreciate

**Exercise 39.2**
1 Do you have a second?   2 Do you want me to call back later?
3 Are you busy right now?

**Exercise 39.3**
1 I was just calling to see if everything's OK for Friday.
2 I wanted to ask you a question about Simon.
3 I thought you might be interested in this.

**Exercise 39.4**
1 How can I help you?   2 I'd like to speak
3 Can I have your name, please?   4 It's   5 hold
6 Gianfranco speaking   7 ask / about   8 can

**Exercise 39.5**
1 T (although in theory a and c are more polite, and b is more informal)   2 F   3 T

**Exercise 39.6**
1 a / c   2 b / d

## 40 Telephoning – messages

**Exercise 40.1**
1 speak / to   2 for   3 bear / with   4 must / in   5 need
6 call / back   7 make / of   8 in   9 out of   10 leave   11 let
12 for   13 on   14 ask   15 make   16 put / on   17 on
18 read / back

**Exercise 40.2**
1 as   2 that   3 anything   4 calling

**Exercise 40.3**
1 Hold on a moment. I'll just check.   2 Right, sorry to keep you
waiting.   3 I'm sorry but she's on maternity leave.   4 She's not
at her desk at the moment.   5 Do you know how long he'll be?
6 What's it in connection with?   7 Can you ask him to call me back?
8 I'll make sure she gets the message.

**Exercise 40.4**
1 c   2 h   3 a   4 j   5 b   6 l   7 f   8 i   9 d   10 k
11 e   12 g

## 41 Telephoning – checking, clarifying, active listening

**Exercise 41.1**
1 It's a really bad line.   2 You keep breaking up.   3 I didn't
catch that.   4 We got cut off.   5 Thanks for letting me know.
6 I have to go now.   7 Can you speak up a bit?   8 I'll just go
outside.   9 Can you hear me now?   10 What exactly do you mean
by …?   11 Let me just check that I understand.   12 Are you saying
that …?   13 My battery is very low.   14 We're going to get cut
off.   15 I'll give you a call tomorrow.   16 Thanks for calling.

**Exercise 41.2**
1 cut off   2 speak up   3 breaking up   4 go over   5 hold on
6 get through

**Exercise 41.3**
1 Right / I see / Sure.   2 Yuh / Mhm / Uh-huh.   3 Exactly.
4 That's right.   5 Great!   6 That's wonderful!   7 Did you?
8 Has she?   9 Half a million euros!   10 Vietnam!
11 And why was that?   12 So what did you do?

**Exercise 41.4**
1 Great!   2 Vietnam!   3 Has she?   4 Exactly. (or That's right.)
5 So what did you do?

**Exercise 41.5**
1 I'll have to stop there. I have someone waiting to see me.
2 It's been nice talking to you. And I'll send the details you wanted
by email. Bye.   3 Anyway I won't keep you any longer. I'm sure
you're busy.   4 Is there anything else I can help you with today?

## 42 Telephoning – arranging a meeting

**Exercise 42.1**
1 this is   2 meet up   3 a little more depth   4 thinking of
5 suit you   6 Shall we say   7 sounds fine   8 if you don't mind
9 instead   10 be my guest   11 by the way   12 two blocks away

**Exercise 42.2**
1 over there   2 for the time of year   3 Look   4 can't make it
5 come up   6 These things happen   7 reschedule   8 still open
9 would be good   10 sorry again   11 fits my plans   12 'll

**Exercise 42.3**
appointment

## 43 Telephoning – complaints

**Exercise 43.1**
1 b   2 f   3 l   4 h   5 k   6 g   7 a   8 d   9 j   10 c
11 e   12 i

**Exercise 43.2**
1 1b   2 5k   3 10c   4 3l   5 12i   6 7a

**Exercise 43.3**
1 Can you leave it with me?   2 I'll look into it.
3 I'll get back to you this afternoon.   4 I understand how you feel.
5 I need to check at this end.   6 I do apologize once more.
7 I'm sure we can sort it out.   8 What exactly is the problem?
9 Sorry again for any inconvenience this has caused.   10 I'll send
a replacement immediately.   11 I'll make sure the items are sent
to you.   12 I've had a word with the warehouse.

**Exercise 43.4**
1 I think there may be an issue with our suppliers.   2 It's not going
to be easy to send a technician today.   3 There might be a short
delay while we process the new order.   4 There seems to be a small
problem with the invoice.   5 I need to just have a quick word with
my level two supervisor about this.   6 Wouldn't it be easier for you if
we simply issued a new invoice?

**Exercise 43.5**
look into / sort out / get back to

## 44 Telephoning – review

**Exercise 44.1**
1 in / with   2 from   3 for   4 on   5 out of   6 on   7 back
8 in   9 back   10 over   11 with / for   12 up   13 up
14 off   15 for   16 of   17 with   18 into / back   19 on
20 by

**Exercise 44.2**
1 f   2 c   3 g   4 b   5 e   6 a   7 d   8 h

**Exercise 44.3**
1 Just bear with me.   2 Shall I put you through to   3 Speaking.
4 Would you like to leave a message?   5 Sorry, I didn't catch that.
6 Let me just read that back to you.   7 Exactly.   8 I'll ask her to
call you back.

**Exercise 44.4**
1 I'd like to speak   2 while I try to connect you   3 How nice to
hear from you   4 How are things in Athens   5 is this a good time
to talk   6 Just give me a moment   7 Go ahead   8 The reason
I'm calling is   9 I thought you might be   10 Of course
11 Let me just check (that) I understand   12 Can I just go over that
again   13 I'll get back to you   14 Is there anything else
15 thanks for calling   16 It's been nice talking to you, too.

**Exercise 44.5**
1 B   2 C   3 D   4 B   5 C   6 A   7 B   8 B   9 A
10 D   11 C   12 A

## 45 Emails – basics

**Exercise 45.1**
1 I'm writing with regard to   2 Please feel free to contact me if …
3 I look forward to hearing from you.   4 Thank you very much for
sending your CV.   5 If I can offer any further assistance, please…
6 I hope you're well.   7 This is just a quick note to …
8 I was wondering if you could help me.   9 I'd really appreciate it.
10 Great to hear from you again.   11 Shall I send you a copy of …?

**Exercise 45.2**
First email: Reason for writing / Body of email / Final comments
Friendly close
Second email: Previous contact / Body of email / Final comments / Offer help
Third email: Friendly open / Reason for writing / Request (or Body of
email) / Friendly close / Final comments
Fourth email: Friendly open / Body of email / Offer help / Friendly close

**Exercise 45.3**
1 great pleasure   2 very impressed   3 with regard
4 useful discussion   5 wondering if   6 grateful for
7 hearing from   8 As requested   9 an attachment
10 relation to   11 don't hesitate   12 further assistance
13 re   14 Please   15 get back   16 Do you want

## 46 Emails – internal communication

**Exercise 46.1**
1 say / 'll   2 quick note / remind / Please
3 let / know / advance / co-operation

**Exercise 46.2**
1 here's / attached   2 Unfortunately / significantly   3 want / to
4 Let / know / else   5 Shall   6 Get back

**Exercise 46.3**
1 I'm pleased to tell you that …   2 I'm sure you will be pleased to
hear that …   3 I would also like to take the opportunity to tell you
about …   4 Would all staff please note that …   5 I thought you'd
be interested to know that …   6 I would like to thank you all for
your valuable contribution.   7 Thanks again for all your help. I really
appreciate it.   8 I'm very grateful for everything you have done.

**Exercise 46.4**
1 c   2 d   3 b   4 a   5 h   6 g   7 f   8 e

**Exercise 46.5**
Email 1: 1c + 8e
Email 2: 2d + 6g
Email 3: 4a + 5h
Email 4: 3b + 7f

## 47 Emails – commercial

**Exercise 47.1**
1 stand   2 brochure / specifications / range   3 particular / suitable
4 draw / attention   5 meantime / hesitate / direct line
6 Following / attached   7 delivered / latest   8 conditions / terms
9 shipping / invoices   10 acknowledge

**Exercise 47.2**
1 PD   2 DT   3 PR   4 P   5 PD   6 PR   7 PD   8 PR
9 P   10 DT   11 PR   12 P   13 PD   14 P   15 P

**Exercise 47.3**
1 if you have any further questions   2 I'm confident that we can
supply   3 I also notice that you can personalize   4 I would be
happy to make a sample   5 we do offer quantity discounts
6 I have been looking at your website   7 I can find no mention
of discounts   8 you need to set up a trade account

**Exercise 47.4**
1 I have been looking at your website   2 I also notice that you can
personalize   3 I can find no mention of discounts   4 I'm confident
that we can supply   5 We do offer quantity discounts
6 you need to set up a trade account   7 I would be happy to
make a sample   8 If you have any further questions

## 48 Emails – customer issues

**Exercise 48.1**
1 I'm sorry to tell you that I have to postpone our meeting next week.
2 Once again, please accept my sincere apologies for any
inconvenience caused.   3 I'm pleased to tell you that the items you
ordered are now in stock. We will be shipping your order today.
4 I can assure you that we're doing everything possible to resolve this
issue as quickly as possible.   5 You will be pleased to hear that we're
extending our online sale for another week.   6 I've talked to the staff
involved and I'm confident that our procedures are robust and working
properly.   7 We regret to inform you that we cannot process your
order due to a large outstanding balance on your account.
8 Thank you very much for bringing this matter to my attention.

**Exercise 48.2**
a) 3 / 5   b) 1 / 7   c) 4 / 6   d) 2 / 8

**Exercise 48.3**
1 reference   2 still   3 delivery   4 assured   5 shipped
6 inconvenience   7 sales   8 insist   9 attention   10 satisfactory
11 forced   12 long-term

**Exercise 48.4**
I was very concerned to learn about the ~~so~~ late delivery of the parts
~~what~~ you ordered from us.
I have ~~been~~ spoken to our staff in the packing department and I'm ~~too~~
confident that the goods left here last week. I can only assume ~~it~~ that
there is an issue with the courier.
I will contact ~~with~~ them personally and make sure that they resolve ~~me~~
this matter today.
Once again, please accept ~~that~~ my sincere apologies for any
inconvenience caused ~~you~~.
Should you have any ~~some~~ questions, please do not hesitate to contact
me.

## 49 Emails – arranging a visit

**Exercise 49.1**
1 d   2 h   3 c   4 a   5 g   6 e   7 f   8 b

**Exercise 49.2**
1 in / in   2 off / for   3 on / from / to   4 at / on   5 in   6 at
7 at   8 for / at / with

**Exercise 49.3**
1 lose   2 be annulled

**Exercise 49.4**
dropped me off / check-in / excess baggage charge / through / queue /
gate / rush / board / turbulence / touched down / picked / rank / stuck /
rip me off / receipt / early night

**Exercise 49.5**

1 freeway   2 exit   3 signposted   4 on   5 for   6 miss
7 Turn   8 past   9 down   10 blocks   11 on   12 main
13 follow   14 for   15 on

## 50 Emails – review

**Exercise 50.1**

1 feel / contact   2 Shall   3 wonder   4 offer / hesitate
5 remind   6 know / do   7 would / take   8 appreciate   9 note
10 postpone   11 welcome / discuss   12 send   13 take / resolve
14 notice   15 assure   16 offer   17 insist   18 click
19 acknowledge   20 accept

**Exercise 50.2**

a) 5 / 7 / 9   b) 3 / 8   c) 2 / 10   d) 1 / 4 / 6   e) 14
f) 11 / 16 / 18   g) 12 / 19   h) 13 / 17   i) 15 / 20

**Exercise 50.3**

1 note   2 remind   3 finalized   4 attached   5 event
6 attend   7 get back   8 co-operation   9 re   10 put
11 circulate   12 make sure   13 tell   14 done

**Exercise 50.4**

1 e   2 h   3 g   4 n   5 i   6 d   7 a   8 c   9 j   10 l
11 f   12 b   13 m   14 k

**Exercise 50.5**

1 with / to   2 in / to   3 for   4 for   5 back / to   6 on / over
7 in   8 at / in   9 In / for   10 about / from   11 In
12 for / of   13 by / at   14 on   15 with

**Exercise 50.6**

1 going   2 wondering   3 requested   4 caused   5 Following
6 doing   7 made   8 hearing   9 using   10 concerned
11 getting   12 buying   13 attached   14 forwarded

## 51 Presentations – opening

**Exercise 51.1**

1 On behalf of BCC I'd like to …   2 Can everyone see at the back?
3 Just a few words about myself   4 I'm in charge of public relations
5 I'd like to show you …   6 I'll talk about our market and how …
7 I'll move on to discuss customization   8 We focus on tailoring our
products …   9 I'll give you a little technical background   10 Let's
begin with this first slide

**Exercise 51.2**

1 c   2 e   3 h   4 b   5 f   6 g   7 a   8 d

**Exercise 51.3**

1 h   2 e   3 i   4 g   5 c   6 j   7 a   8 d   9 k   10 b
11 f   12 l

**Exercise 51.4**

1 discuss   2 give   3 show   4 talk   5 report   6 look   7 fill
8 take   9 bring   10 make   11 outline   12 deal

## 52 Presentations – main body

**Exercise 52.1**

1 leads   2 mentioned   3 come back   4 digress
5 in more detail   6 concrete example   7 focus on   8 stress
9 As / can see   10 highlight   11 What is   12 relate / context

**Exercise 52.2**

1 have a look   2 highlight two things   3 notice
4 you can see how   5 My own view   6 emphasize
7 at this point   8 let's go on

**Exercise 52.3**

1 As the wind passes over these // they act like airfoils // and this
generates lift // and turns the structure as a whole.   2 It's more
efficient in terms of energy production, and it's also more stable with
its solid base.

**Exercise 52.4**

1 move on to   2 talk about   3 deal with   4 turn my attention to
5 take a look at   6 explain   7 cover   8 consider   9 mention
10 focus on

## 53 Presentations – closing and questions

**Exercise 53.1**

1 that covers everything   2 the next steps   3 look at some options
4 there is the option to   5 generated a lot of discussion
6 may be forced   7 would lead to   8 some difficult decisions
9 our job is to consider   10 give the floor

**Exercise 53.2**

1 point   2 explain   3 experienced   4 for   5 opinion
6 catch   7 scope / afterwards   8 glad   9 on   10 must / come
11 specific   12 comment   13 hand / back   14 correctly

**Exercise 53.3**

a) 1 / 8   b) 2 / 6 / 11 / 14   c) 5 / 10   d) 3 / 12   e) 7 / 13
f) 4 / 9

## 54 Presentations – trends I

**Exercise 54.1**

1 grow / expand   2 fall / drop   3 improve / recover
4 stay the same / be stable   5 move higher / rise
6 level off / stabilize   7 shrink / contract   8 edge down / dip

**Exercise 54.2**

1 boom / crash   2 double / halve   3 edge up / dip
4 grow / shrink   5 improve / deteriorate   6 peak / hit a low
7 stay the same / vary   8 rise / fall

**Exercise 54.3**

1 went up / gone up   2 grew / grown   3 rose / risen
4 fell / fallen   5 growth   6 expansion   7 contraction
8 improvement   9 recovery   10 variation   11 half
12 deterioration

**Exercise 54.4**

1 rapid   2 gradual   3 sluggish   4 enormous   5 moderate
6 slight   7 excellent   8 encouraging   9 disappointing

**Exercise 54.5**

1 slow growth   2 significant rise   3 rapid deterioration
4 slight improvement   5 considerable variation

**Exercise 54.6**

1 from   2 of   3 to   4 by   5 in   6 at

**Exercise 54.7**

1 have seen   2 is causing   3 will bring   4 was   5 were rising
6 had already begun

## 55 Presentations – trends II

**Exercise 55.1**

1 Because of our …   2 Because of we cut …   3 due to our
increased …   4 a result of our …   5 resulted in a significant …
6 resulted of from difficult …   7 whereas it fell …   8 Moreover,
they …   9 In spite of the fact that …   10 Despite we delaying …

**Exercise 55.2**

1 due to   2 even though   3 In spite of   4 as a result
5 However   6 Moreover

**Exercise 55.3**

1 d   2 a   3 e   4 c   5 b

**Exercise 55.4**

1 axis   2 highlight   3 reached a peak   4 have been flat
5 a slight increase   6 Notice   7 in line with   8 more rapidly
9 roughly   10 while   11 implications   12 Although
13 highly likely   14 lead to

## 56 Presentations – review

**Exercise 56.1**

1 b   2 g   3 h   4 d   5 a   6 c   7 f   8 e   9 j   10 i
11 p   12 k   13 m   14 r   15 t   16 l   17 q   18 n
19 s   20 o

**Exercise 56.2**

1 I've divided my talk into three main parts.    2 If you have any questions, please feel free to interrupt.    3 Let's examine this in more detail.    4 Just to digress for a moment, …    5 OK, that's all I want to say about the first point.    6 Let's move on to the second point.    7 My own view on this is …    8 As you can see on this next slide, …    9 What is the reason for this? The reason is …    10 Let me explain with a concrete example.    11 I began by telling you a little about … Then I explained how … After that I talked about …    12 Thank you all for coming and I hope it's been useful.

**Exercise 56.3**

1 at / about    2 into    3 with    4 on to    5 to    6 back to    7 on    8 on    9 on    10 in / of    11 for    12 in / in

**Exercise 56.4**

1 start / introducing    2 digress / moment    3 useful / background    4 examine / detail    5 explain / concrete    6 highlight / diagram    7 anyone / comments    8 brings / end    9 explain / again    10 question / opinion    11 scope / afterwards    12 time / question

**Exercise 56.5**

1 Notice    2 axis    3 units    4 draw    5 rose    6 steadily    7 have continued    8 although    9 steady    10 growth    11 due to    12 Even so    13 on    14 over    15 to    16 figure    17 look at    18 took off    19 were really looking good    20 had done    21 However    22 has been    23 sudden    24 drop    25 reasons    26 about    27 comments    28 highly    29 likely    30 by

## 57 Meetings – opinions

**Exercise 57.1**

1 what    2 in mind    3 seems to me    4 my point of view    5 I agree    6 You're right    7 up to a point    8 you mean    9 may    10 about

**Exercise 57.2**

1 However    2 Actually    3 Luckily    4 Obviously    5 In general    6 The point is    7 Basically    8 By the way    9 In my opinion    10 In short

**Exercise 57.3**

1 Strong disagreement    2 Polite disagreement    3 Not grammatically possible

**Exercise 57.4**

1 Really? Do you think so?    2 I'm not so sure about that.    3 I'm sorry, that's not how I see it.    4 I really can't agree with you there.

**Exercise 57.5**

1 b    2 c    3 a    4 g    5 d    6 f    7 e

## 58 Meetings – making things clear

**Exercise 58.1**

1 missed / say    2 clear / saying    3 how much / say    4 arrive / figure    5 exactly / mean    6 Correct / wrong    7 allow / explain    8 little / specific    9 explained / clearly    10 finish / point

**Exercise 58.2**

1 understand / explain    2 through    3 over    4 slight misunderstanding    5 put / way    6 come in

**Exercise 58.3**

1 what    2 how long    3 when    4 how often    5 who    6 which    7 how much    8 where

## 59 Meetings – problem-solving

**Exercise 59.1**

1 several / deal with    2 open up / views    3 suppose / right    4 sounds / work in practice    5 pros / cons    6 On the one hand / on the other hand    7 make a suggestion / Instead / why don't    8 implications    9 general / although    10 best way forward

**Exercise 59.2**

1 OK, let's do that.    2 What about …?    3 That's a complete waste of time.    4 Why don't we …?    5 Yes, that would work really well.    6 Shall we …?    7 That sounds like a good idea.    8 Can I make a suggestion?    9 I can see one or two problems with that.    10 I'm not really sure about that.    11 That might be worth trying.    12 I don't think it would work in practice.

**Exercise 59.3**

a) 2 / 4 / 6 / 8    b) 1 / 5 / 7 / 11    c) 3 / 9 / 10 / 12

**Exercise 59.4**

1 a problem    2 a solution    3 a suggestion    4 a decision

**Exercise 59.5**

1 are faced with    2 tackle    3 figure out    4 work towards    5 come up with    6 lends weight to    7 implement    8 lies behind

## 60 Meetings – leading a meeting

**Exercise 60.1**

1 Right / start    2 ill / apologies    3 housekeeping / begin    4 bathroom / hall    5 copy / agenda    6 take / minutes    7 say / words    8 background / useful    9 agenda / get through    10 brief / point    11 straight / item    12 kick / off

**Exercise 60.2**

1 agenda    2 minutes    3 get through    4 item    5 kick off

**Exercise 60.3**

1 AmE    2 BrE

**Exercise 60.4**

1 I think we can stop there.    2 I'd like to sum up.    3 There are three main conclusions.    4 In terms of action points, …    5 Are there any other points?    6 Have I missed anything?    7 I think it was a very useful meeting.    8 I'll circulate the minutes.    9 Can we fix a date now?    10 Can I just have a quick word with you?

**Exercise 60.5**

1 Could you just hang on a moment please?    2 One at a time, please.    3 Let's leave that aside for the moment.    4 Can we come back to this later?    5 I think we need to look at this in more detail.    6 We need to analyze this in a little more depth.    7 Is there anything else we should consider?    8 What other ways are there to approach this?    9 Can we go round the table to see if everyone agrees?    10 Let's go over what we've discussed so far.

## 61 Meetings – negotiating I

**Exercise 61.1**

1 business    2 exactly    3 priorities    4 mean    5 trust    6 flexible    7 delivery    8 minimum    9 concern    10 timescale    11 quoted    12 match    13 reasonable    14 guarantee

**Exercise 61.2**

kind of / sort of / discount / timescale / thinking of / talking about / looking at

**Exercise 61.3**

1 quite high    2 were you expecting    3 Something around    4 standard for this market    5 a little low    6 such large discounts    7 so long    8 have in mind    9 production schedule    10 terms of payment    11 pre-payment    12 regular customers

ANSWER KEY

## 62 Meetings – negotiating II

### Exercise 62.1
1 minimum order   2 viable / cost-effective / run   3 pre-payment / first time   4 upfront   5 'll / advance / balance / delivery / cash flow   6 authority / by myself

### Exercise 62.2
1 viable   2 upfront   3 balance

### Exercise 62.3
1 prefer / order   2 prepared / terms   3 have / mind   4 accept / condition   5 willing / compromise   6 should / possible   7 sounds / reasonable   8 moment / review   9 through / far   10 go / stage   11 close / deal   12 just / sign

### Exercise 62.4
2c order / 4b discount / 3a proposal / 1d deal

### Exercise 62.5
3a details / 1d deadline / 4b concession / 2c compromise

## 63 Meetings – diplomatic language

### Exercise 63.1
a) 13   b) 4 / 13   c) 8   d) 1   e) 8   f) 1 / 9   g) 12   h) 4 / 6 / 7   i) 1 / 2   j) 10

### Exercise 63.2
1 e   2 a   3 j   4 b   5 c   6 g   7 h   8 f   9 d   10 i

### Exercise 63.3
1 There's just one thing I'd like to add.   2 To be honest, that would be very difficult.   3 It seems to me that you're being a little optimistic.   4 Wouldn't it be better to use rail transport?   5 Actually, this line is not very profitable.   6 I think it might be better to leave that point until later.

### Exercise 63.4
1 If we ordered 5,000 pieces, what sort of discount could you give?   2 If you paid 50% in advance, we would give you generous terms for the remaining 50%.

## 64 Meetings – review

### Exercise 64.1
*The chair opens the meeting*
Right / thanks for coming / sends his apologies / housekeeping / short break / copy of the agenda / take the minutes / straight / item / kick off
*Marek presents some alternatives*
deal with this issue / pros and cons / option / favour / although
*The chair asks Camille for her reactions*
field / have some experience
*Camille speaks*
up to a point / true / trying to say / put it simply
*Marek interrupts*
come in
*The chair blocks the interruption*
Just let / finish / come back
*Camille continues*
Correct / wrong / seems
*Marek corrects the misunderstanding*
explained myself clearly / meant / trying / matter of fact
*Adriana makes a suggestion*
just an idea / instead
*Marek rejects the suggestion*
sounds / work in practice / point
*The chair widens the discussion*
approach / anything else / consider
*Camille gives an opinion*
point of view
*The chair reacts*
carefully / implications / On the one hand
*Adriana focuses the discussion*
analyze / little / depth / tend
*Marek asks for clarification*
mentioned / specific
*Adriana reformulates*
let me put it another way
*The chair keeps the discussion moving*
leave that aside / relevant
*Camille suggests the next steps*
best way forward
*The chair asks for repetition*
run through
*Camille repeats*
of course
*The chair summarizes*
go over / so far
*Camille speaks*
Absolutely / action points
*The chair checks agreement*
go round the table / move on
*After some time, the chair closes the meeting*
input / useful / fix the time / have a quick word

### Exercise 64.2
1 get down   2 are you looking   3 might be able   4 did you have   5 Instead of   6 are we talking   7 a viable option   8 upfront   9 really not sure   10 moving forward   11 are you happy   12 be prepared   13 sounds reasonable   14 have a deal

### Exercise 64.3
1 That might be quite expensive.   2 We would want a significantly larger discount.   3 There's just one thing I'd like to clarify.   4 Wouldn't it be better to split the order into two consignments?   5 I'm not totally convinced by this estimate.   6 I understood we could have the products on a trial basis.   7 What sort of quantity were you thinking of?   8 Unfortunately, it may not be very easy to arrange that.   9 We're having one or two issues at our factory right now.   10 To be honest we were expecting a two-year warranty.   11 It seems to me that your new range is more or less the same as your old range.   12 Wouldn't it be easier to pay a little more and ship the goods by Air Express?

## 65 Business reports and proposals – reports I

### Exercise 65.1
1 executive summary   2 findings   3 cover page   4 recommendations   5 contents   6 procedure   7 appendix   8 terms of reference   9 conclusions   10 acknowledgements

### Exercise 65.2
1 f   2 n   3 b   4 q   5 j   6 e   7 m   8 l   9 i   10 c   11 h   12 g   13 p   14 a   15 k   16 o   17 r   18 d

## 66 Business reports and proposals – reports II

### Exercise 66.1
c

### Exercise 66.2
1 this solution   2 share / collaborate   3 central resource   4 anywhere

### Exercise 66.3
1 considerable / are expected to   2 tend to / might not be   3 At the earliest possible opportunity / a production planning meeting   4 quite poor / may be   5 relatively / financial resources   6 It is possible that / obtained   7 is likely to be / consequences   8 many people are / typically leads to   9 arising from / presented   10 numerous / encouraging

### Exercise 66.4
1 The same strategy can be used   2 the environmental impact of these changes will be considered.   3 can only be done   4 should be emphasized

## 67 Business reports and proposals – proposals I

### Exercise 67.1
1 scope   2 Gantt chart   3 deliverables   4 state-of-the-art   5 testimonials   6 fee

**Exercise 67.2**

1 cut / shorten    2 position / leading player    3 secondary
4 conduct / survey    5 in-depth    6 extensive / field
7 remaining / absorbed    8 cost-effective manner    9 long-lasting
10 established / share

**Exercise 67.3**

1 b    2 b    3 b    4 b

**Exercise 67.4**

1 b    2 d    3 a    4 c

## 68 Business reports and proposals – proposals II

**Exercise 68.1**

1 reduce bad debt    2 outsource to remove fixed costs from the
payroll    3 increase the absolute value of each transaction
4 enhance job performance    5 reduce turnover among key staff
members    6 enhance maintainability    7 comply with regulatory
standards    8 conform to a specific quality methodology
9 preserve the value of legacy systems    10 reduce downtime
11 implement the most proven approach    12 address health
and safety issues    13 avoid liability concerns    14 focus on core
competencies

**Exercise 68.2**

Compliance ✓ (first and third sentences of 'Action Plan and
Deliverables')
Capabilities ✓ (first two sentences of 'Custom Computing: special
expertise'; second sentence of 'Action Plan and Deliverables'; fourth
sentence of 'Conclusion')
Value ✓ (third sentence of 'Custom Computing: special expertise')

## 69 Business reports and proposals – linking words

**Exercise 69.1**

1 d    2 h    3 a    4 g    5 c    6 b    7 f    8 j    9 e    10 i

**Exercise 69.2**

1 ie    2 eg

**Exercise 69.3**

1 Moreover    2 In contrast    3 In fact    4 In general    5 Therefore
6 In particular    7 Overall    8 Clearly

**Exercise 69.4**

1 Regarding    2 Clearly    3 In particular    4 In fact    5 Moreover
6 On the whole    7 However    8 Secondly    9 for example
10 So    11 whereas    12 On balance

## 70 Business reports and proposals – review

**Exercise 70.1**

1 This report was commissioned by Hans Oberlander, CEO of the Auto
Corporation.    2 aim    3 oil market    4 In particular    5 steadily
6 significant    7 On the demand side    8 research shows
9 are likely to    10 an impact    11 such as    12 disappointing
13 market research company    14 carry out    15 concern
16 typically    17 are unable to go very fast    18 findings
19 following    20 increasingly    21 trend    22 due to    23 main
24 paying more attention to    25 financial resources

**Exercise 70.2**

|  | Compliance | Capabilities | Value |
|---|---|---|---|
| Understanding your stock losses | ✓ | ✓ | ~ |
| Key goals | ✓ | ~ | ✓ |
| Project scope | ✓ | ~ | ~ |
| Implementation and deliverables | ✓ | ✓ | ✓ |
| Staffing | ~ | ✓ | ~ |
| Fees | ~ | ✓ | ✓ |
| Conclusion | ✓ | ~ | ✓ |

*Compliance*:

We propose to conduct a review of your store to see how Closed
Circuit Television (CCTV) cameras could be used most effectively, and
then complete the installation of the system.

Your goal is to reduce shoplifting by installing wall-mounted cameras
inside your store, and to have these linked to monitors at a central
security desk.

The project will include the following activities:
● Identify the best locations for CCTV cameras and install the cameras.
● Identify the best location for a central security desk, with the
   monitors and a visible presence of security personnel.

A timetable for the different phases of the project is included as an
appendix. We estimate that the total time required for this project is
two weeks.

Deliverables for this project will include:
● Approximately 30 CCTV cameras, with two associated monitors at
   the central desk, all fully installed and checked.
● All additional materials such as cables etc.

We recommend that you contract our company to install a CCTV
system inside Fashion Superstore. This system will dramatically reduce
your losses due to shoplifting.

*Capabilities*:

Our approach is based on our twenty years' experience of providing
security solutions in the retail sector.

We have run this program successfully in over sixty locations.

We will assign to this project the following team:
● An in-store security expert, Mr Bob Parker, who has over ten years'
   experience in this field and previously worked for the police.
● Four qualified electricians.
● A trainer, Ms Beatrice Sterne, member of the Institute of Training.

See the figures in the attached case study, which describes a very
similar project that we carried out last year.

*Value*:

You want to do this in a cost-effective way.

A special report on how to manage security personnel, particularly with
regard to always keeping their attention on the job.

We will charge a total fee of €254,000 for this project. This includes all
the items referred to above, with no hidden extras.

Based on the figures you provided us and on information obtained
from previous assignments we have carried out, we estimate that this
system will pay for itself within eighteen months.

In addition, the system will help provide a safer environment for
shoppers. When they see the cameras they will feel less worried about
dangers such as leaving their bags unattended on the floor while they
look at clothes. This safer environment is likely to lead to shoppers
spending more time inside Fashion Superstore and therefore spending
more money.

## Interviews

### 1 Interview with a private equity investor

1 equity / debt    2 build up / break down    3 exit
4 players / lawyers / tax

### 2 Interview with an entrepreneur

1 poor    2 risk-takers
3 have good instincts about other people
4 don't go to    5 work alongside employees
6 get bored quickly    7 need a good team behind them
8 difficult

### 3 Interview with a management trainee

1  a test for numerical and problem-solving skills
2  an interview with an HR manager with normal job-related questions
3  lunch, where social skills are observed
4  a roleplay exercise to test management skills
5  a teamwork test where a group of people discuss a scenario and choose the best idea
6  a report writing exercise

### 4 Interview with a supply chain manager

1  F (first tier supplier and second tier supplier are reversed)
2 T    3 F    4 T

### 5 Interview with a sales manager

See script

### 6 Interview with a marketing director

Product b    Price b    Place b    Promotion b

### 7 Interview with a finance director

1 receivable    2 overdraft    3 cash flow    4 sheet
5 invoices    6 variance    7 governance    8 auditors

### 8 Interview with a human resources director

1 b / c    2 b    3 c